# *MEN in BLACK,UFOs,NAZI BELL AND THE MYSTERIOUS VON KÁRMÁN: THE CLOSE ENCOUNTER MAN*

**Kenneth Arnold**

SAUCERIAN PUBLISHER

ISBN:**978-1-955087-19-3**

# Prologue

In popular culture and UFO conspiracy theories, Men in Black (MIB) are supposed men dressed in black suits who claim to be government agents who harass or threaten UFO witnesses to keep them quiet about what they have seen. It is sometimes implied that they may be aliens themselves. The term is also frequently used to describe mysterious men working for unknown organizations, as well as various branches of government allegedly designed to protect secrets or perform other strange activities. The term is generic, used for any unusual, threatening or strangely behaved individual whose appearance on the scene can be linked in some fashion with a UFO sighting. Several alleged encounters with the men in black have been reported by UFO researchers and enthusiasts.

MIBs are popularly described as:

- Appearing in threes
- Travelling in large, black, old-model cars (usually Cadillacs in the USA), which appear to be brand new and have untraceable registrations
- Having 'dark' complexions
- Appearing only rarely outside the USA
- Possessing knowledge known only to the witness.

In general, the Men in Black (MIB) usually have one main purpose: to muzzle witnesses of strange, paranormal phenomena. They almost always wear black suits and hats with dark sunglasses, drive black cars and arrive in groups of two or three. Some describe them as would an FBI agent, while others recall the MIB as having strange appearances, sometimes with supernatural features like glowing eyes and strange complexions.

Who are these Men in Black (MIB)? The answer to this question could be found in the FBI portal. Among the many functions for this agency found in the FBI portal, the best that match the Men in Black descriptions mentioned above are: The FBI has law enforcement capabilities, and mostly works inside the U.S. and its territories. However, On foreign soil, FBI agents generally do not have authority to make arrests except in certain cases with the consent of the host country. , Congress has granted the FBI extraterritorial jurisdiction. Unlike the FBI, the CIA is prohibited from collecting information regarding "U.S. Persons," a term that includes U.S. citizens, resident aliens inside the U.S. and its territories. As a result, these MIB are from the FBI, the CIA is ruled out.

Theodore von Kármán was a Hungarian-born research engineer best known for his pioneering work in the use of mathematics and the basic sciences in aeronautics and astronautics. His laboratory at the California Institute of Technology later became the National Aeronautics and Space Administration (NASA) Jet Propulsion Laboratory.

During the closing months of WWII, the U.S. Army Air Forces took advantage of the victories of the Allies and created a task force headed by von Kármán to evaluate captured German aeronautical data and laboratories for the US. Air Force. Von Kármán team followed the steps of the advancing American, and British forces searching German laboratories, and airfileds. The group was ordered to travel to many european countries as possible. Operation LUSTY (Luftwaffe Science and Technology), has begun. A model airplane with triangular, arrow-shaped wings was found in the Luftfahrforschungsanstalt.

The most exciting discovery during this mission was a secret aerodinamical laboratory in a pine forest near Volkenrode, a village outside the city of Braunschweig. It was the Luftfahrforschungsanstalt Herman Goering or the Herman Goering Aerodynamical Institute These facilities included an eight meter wind tunnel, a high speed wind tunnel, two supersonic wind tunnels, an armament laboratory. Many of the buildings were looted, but the equipment were intact. Americans used metal detectors to recover thousands of metal boxes buried with top secret documents. This facility was a treasure trove of documents, yielded the greatest return in the field of research.

Where did all those technological advances come from? In 1936 a 'flying saucer' allegedly crashes in the Schwarzwald (Black Forest) near Freiburg, opening the door for advanced German technology in aeronautics and space (reverse engineering). The ship and its occupants were spirited away to the dark heart of Nazi Germany, where all was dismantled and diligently studied. A resulting program was called Haunebu. Von Kármán was the master mind in the captured of all this technology from the Third Reich.

Von Kármán took the atention of the Men in Black (FBI) in 1941 because some confidential information received by Bureau agents mentioned his communist sympathies. Also, his sister was considered by the FBI to be a Nazi sympathizer. Most of the information in von Kármán's FBI File deals with Soviet Agents, Nazi and Communist sympathizer, and the Von Karman's post under the Bela Kun socialist regime in Hungary during 1919. The File did not mention his whereabouts in Operation Lusty. The reason could be that this mission was so secret that even an official agency in charge of the national security of the United States, like the FBI, was forbidden to investigate. However, this File has been included in this publication. Some pages in this file were not included as a result of the Security Act of 1947 & the CIA Act of 1949 by the FBI censors. FBI censors focused their attention on Part.2b of von Kármán FBI's File. Seems that this part it is the most sensitive, and several pages can not be made public.

Saucerian Publisher was founded with the mission of promoting books in Ufology, Paranormal, and the Occult. Our vision is to preserve the legacy of literary history by reprint editions of books which have already been exhausted or are difficult to obtain. Our goal is to help readers, educators and researchers by bringing back original publications that are difficult to find at reasonable price, while preserving the legacy of universal knowledge. This book is an authentic reproduction of the original printed text in shades of gray. This book is an authentic reproduction of the original Von Kármán's FBI File printed text in shades of gray. **IMPORTANT**, despite the fact that we have attempted to accurately maintain the integrity of the original work, the present reproduction has missing and blurred pages, poor pictures and FBI censorship's pencil markings from the original scanned copy. **Many of the original FBI documents pages are shadowy, and faint.** Withhold information are generally marked with white boxes where something should have been in the file that is considered by the Bureau censor "sensitive". In other cases, the information has been blacking out. **ILLEGIBLE PAGES HAVE A NOTE.** Because this material is culturally important, we have made available as part of our commitment to protect, preserve and promote knowledge in the world.

This edition is a collection of documents regarding von Kármán's life, and has the following parts : 1.Wonder Weapons of the Third Reich, 2. Theodore von Kármán: The Close Encounter Man, 3. Operation Lusty', 4. Von Kármán's FBI File.

Kenneth Arnold
2021

INDEX

# *The Wonder Weapons of the Third Reich*

It's not a mystery that the Nazi's searched even the most remote places on Earth for devices, ancient manuscripts describing paranormal energies, and places that would help them in their ultimate goal: World domination. Some declassified documents exist claiming that the Germans created airplanes shaped like a flying saucer and even incandescent flying spheres to disconcert allied pilots during the war. Ever since the conclusion of the Second World War, an increasing number of revelations have surfaced regarding various outlandish and even occult-based scientific and technological experiments being conducted by the Nazis throughout the duration of the Third Reich.

From the beginning, but especially towards the last years of World War II, the Allied secret services received a large amount of fragmentary reports, mostly rumors, of new and fantastic weapons being developed by the Germans. Some of them referred to the development of the V-1 and V-2 or other weapon systems, but many others spoke of fantastic weapons: giant missiles, destructive bombs of various types and effects, deadly gases, death rays, etc , and the like.

In World War II, the so-called "foo fighters", a variety of unusual and anomalous aerial phenomena, were witnessed by both Axis and Allied personnel. Some UFO sightings duringWorld War II were thought by the Allies to be prototype enemy aircraft designed to harass Allied aircraft through electromagnetic disruption; a technology similar to telectromagnetic pulse (EMP) weapons.

The term "foo fighter" was used by Allied aircraft pilots during World War II to describe various UFOs or mysterious aerial phenomena seen in the skies over both the European and Pacific theaters of operations. Though "foo fighter" initially described a type of UFO reported and named by the U.S. 415th Night Fighter Squadron, the term was also commonly used to mean any UFO sighting from that period. Formally reported from November 1944 onwards, witnesses often assumed that the foo fighters were secret weapons employed by the enemy. The Robertson Panel explored possible explanations, for instance that they were electrostatic phenomena similar to St. Elmo's fire, electromagnetic phenomena, or simply reflections of light from ice crystals. The word "foo" emerged in popular culture during the early 1930s, first being used by cartoonist Bill Holman, who peppered his Smokey Stover fireman cartoon strips with "foo" signs and puns. This term was borrowed from Smokey Stover by a radar operator in the 415th Night Fighter Squadron, Donald J. Meiers, who (it is agreed by most 415th members) gave the foo fighters their name. Meiers was from Chicago and was an avid reader of Holman's strip, which was run daily in the *Chicago Tribune*. Smokey Stover's catch-phrase was "where there's foo, there's fire". In a mission debriefing on the evening of November 27, 1944, Fritz Ringwald, the unit's S-2 Intelligence Officer, stated that: *Meiers and Ed Schleuter had sighted*

**The author of Smokey Stover comic from the 1930s claimed that he originally got the word from a figurine that said "foo" on the bottom. "Foo" in this case comes from the mandarin chinese 福 /fú which means good fortune, happiness, luck. That's why it'd be on a random chinese figurine.**

*a red ball of fire that appeared to chase them through a variety of high-speed maneuvers.* Fritz said that: *Meiers was extremely agitated and had a copy of the comic strip tucked in his back pocket.* He pulled it out and slammed it down on Fritz's desk and said: *I]t was another one of those fuckin' foo fighters!" and stormed out of the debriefing room.*

According to Ringwald, because of the lack of a better name, it stuck. And this was originally what the men of the 415th started calling these incidents: "fuckin' foo fighters". In December 1944, a press correspondent from the Associated Press in Paris, Bob Wilson, was sent to the 415th at their base outside of Dijon, France, to investigate this story. It was at this time that the term was cleaned up to just "foo fighters". The squadron commander, Capt. Harold Augsperger, also decided to sanitize the term to "foo fighters" in the historical data of the squadron.

It is overwhelmingly accepted that the first "foo fighter" sightings occurred in November 1944, when pilots flying over Western Europe by night reported seeing fast-moving round glowing objects following their aircraft. However, the first  sightings happened, two years before, on late 24 February to early 25 February 1942, over Los Angeles, California. The incident later called Battle of Los Angeles, also known as the Great Los Angeles Air Raid, occurred less than three months after the United States entered World War II in response to the Imperial Japanese Navy's surprise attack on Pearl Harbor, and one day after the bombardment of Ellwood near Santa Barbara on 23 February. The official version of this incident published in 1949 blamed a meteorological balloon sent aloft at 1:00 am as the culprit to  "started all the shooting", and concluded that "once the firing started, imagination created all kinds of targets in the sky and everyone joined in". In 1983, the U.S. Office of Air Force History attributed the event to a case of "war nerves" triggered by a lost weather balloon and exacerbated by stray flares and shell bursts from adjoining batteries. No detail description of these orbs that flew over Los Angeles could be made at this time.

However, pilots of the U.S. 415th Night Fighter Squadron  provided detail descriptions of these orbs. According to them, these objects were variously described as fiery, and glowing red, white, or orange. Some pilots described them as resembling Christmas-tree lights and reported that they seemed to toy with the aircraft, making wild turns before simply vanishing. Pilots and aircrew reported that the objects flew formation with their aircraft and behaved as if they were under intelligent control, but never displayed hostile behavior. However, they could not be outmaneuvered or shot down. The phenomenon was so widespread that the lights earned a name – in the European Theater of Operations they were often called "Kraut fireballs", but for the most part called "foo fighters". The military took the sightings seriously, suspecting that the mysterious sightings might be secret German weapons, but further investigation revealed that German and Japanese pilots had reported similar sightings.

On 13 December 1944, the Supreme Headquarters Allied Expeditionary Force in Paris issued a press release, which was featured in the New York Times the next day, officially describing the phenomenon as a "new German weapon". Follow-up stories, using the term "Foo Fighters", appeared in the New York Herald Tribune and the British Daily Telegraph.

In its 15 January 1945 edition, *Time Magazine* carried a story entitled "Foo-Fighter", in which it reported that the "balls of fire" had been following USAAF nightfighters for over a month, and that the pilots had named it the "foo-fighter". According to Time, descriptions of the phenomena varied, but the pilots agreed that the mysterious lights followed their aircraft closely at high speed.

The "balls of fire" phenomenon reported from the Pacific Theater of Operations differed somewhat from the foo fighters reported from Europe; the "ball of fire" resembled a large burning sphere which "just hung in the sky", though it was reported to sometimes follow aircraft. There was speculation that the phenomena could be related to the Japanese fire balloon campaign. As with the European foo fighters, no aircraft were reported as having been attacked by a "ball of fire".

The postwar Robertson Panel cited foo fighter reports, noting that their behavior did not appear to be threatening, and mentioned possible explanations, for instance that they were electrostatic phenomena similar to St. Elmo's fire, electromagnetic phenomena, or simply reflections of light from ice crystals. The Panel's report suggested that if the term 'flying saucers' had been popular in 1943–1945, these objects would have been so labeled.

Foo fighters were reported on many occasions from around the world; a few examples are noted below.

•Sighting from September 1941 in the Indian Ocean was similar to some later foo fighter reports. From the deck of the S.S. Pułaski (a Polish merchant vessel transporting British troops), two sailors reported a "strange globe glowing with greenish light, about half the size of the full moon as it appears to us." They alerted a British officer, who watched the movements of the object with them for over an hour.

•Charles R. Bastien of the US Eighth Air Force reported one of the first encounters with foo fighters over the Belgium/Netherlands area; he described them as "two fog lights flying at high rates of speed that could change direction rapidly". During debriefing, his intelligence officer told him that two RAF nightfighters had reported the same thing, and it was later reported in British newspapers.

•Career U.S. Air Force pilot Duane Adams often related that he had witnessed two occurrences of a bright light which paced his aircraft for about half an hour and then rapidly ascended into the sky. Both incidents occurred at night, both over the South Pacific, and both were witnessed by the entire aircraft crew. The first sighting occurred shortly after the end of World War II while Adams piloted a B-25 bomber. The second sighting occurred in the early 1960s when Adams was piloting a KC-135 tanker.

At that time, blaming Nazi Germany responsible for the flying glowing orbs wasn't too far-fetched. For one thing, the sightings took place over Nazi-occupied Europe, at a time when Germany's Luftwaffe was making tremendous strides. However, the sightings stopped once the German army was defeated....at least momentarily.

According to Italian turbine expert, Giuseppe Belluzzo, in an article entitled: *The flying saucers was created in 1942 in Italy and Germany* that was published on March 24-25, 1950 claimed to have personally participated in the design of a flying saucer in 1942.

Belluzzo was the Ministry of Industry during the WWII and declared that on September 8, 1943, the German Air Force took possession of the plans and models of a disk-shaped telearma. In order for the improvement of the Italian weapon to proceed with due secrecy, an experimental center was built in the forests of north-western Norway, where four basic types of

NE - LIRE 20 **ULTIMISSIMA**

# D'ITALIA

25 — Prezzo della copia L. 15 (4 pagine), L. 20 (6 pagine). Arretr. il doppio — PUBBLICITA': concess. esclus.
mmerciali e spettacoli L. 500 - Cronaca L. 400 . Finanziari e legali L. 400 - Necrologie L. 200 per mil.
— Il Giornale si riserva il diritto di accettare o non gli ordini — *Spedizione in abbonamento postale*

SABATO 25 MARZO 1950
ANNO XLIX NUM. 72

# I DISCHI VOLANTI furono ideati nel 1942 IN ITALIA E IN GERMANIA

## *Mussolini e Hitler se ne interessarono - Oggi qualche grande potenza sta utilizzando l'arma a scopo di studio*

*Il mondo è oggi posto a rumore dalla notizia della, secondo alcuni presunta e secondo altri constatata, esistenza dei cosidetti dischi volanti che hanno fatto lavorare la fantasia di coloro i quali, non conoscendo i progressi e le nuove possibilità della tecnica, hanno sollevato dei dubbi sulla possibile esistenza di questi nuovi istrumenti di distruzione.*

*La verità vera è che questi istrumenti di distruzione si possono costruire e fare funzionare, e che di essi già nel 1942 si erano studiati e disegnati in Germania ed in Italia alcuni prototipi nell'intento di fornire alla Patria in guerra uno strumento formidabile per la vittoria. Vittoria che si sarebbe realizzata se la moralità e la competenza di alcuni uomini che oggi vanno per la maggiore, fossero state diverse.*

*Ma ritorniamo, è il caso di scriverlo, a bomba, giacchè i nuovi istrumenti di guerra potevano allora trasportare, senza pericolo per guidatori che non erano necessarii, cariche di esplosivo di ogni specie e peso, ed oggi bombe atomiche in grado di distruggere intere città anche con dieci chilometri di diametro.*

*Il principio del disco volante è semplice, e ne è molto*

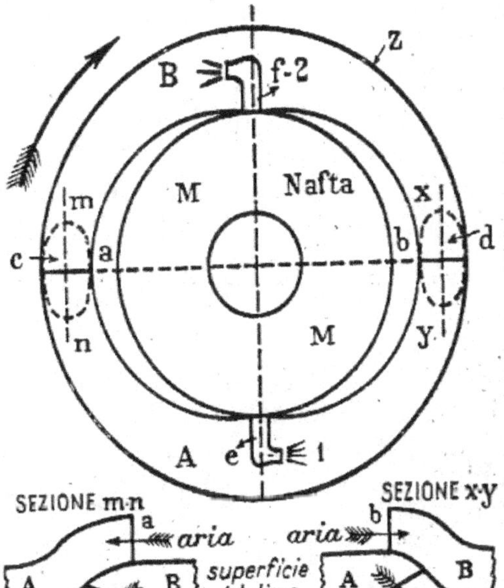


**Lo schema del disco progettato in Italia**

*to simmetricamente disposti rispetto all'asse del disco, hanno una sezione variabile da un minimo ad un massimo. Con*

*zione della velocità in pressione nel funzionamento a terra si arriva alla pressione di 2,4 chilogrammi per centimetro*

*400 metri al secondo alla periferia, il disco volante e nello stesso tempo grazie ad una studiata inclinazione delle bocche c e d di efflusso dai condotti A e B genera una spinta verso l'alto in modo da provocare il moto ascensionale del disco ruotante, il quale percorre pertanto un'elica cilindrica, spostandosi nello spazio a grandissima velocità.*

*L'iniezione della nafta nella sezione massima dei condotti A e B ha luogo per effetto della forza centrifuga cui il combustibile è assoggettato, per effetto della rotazione del disco, nel condotto anulare collegato al disco stesso che lo contiene. Questo condotto anulare nella figura annessa è indicato con M e con e ed f sono indicati schematicamente gli iniettori che comunicano con il serbatoio della nafta.*

*La partenza da terra del disco volante avviene con la accensione e combustione rapida di una cartuccia analoga, salvo le maggiori dimensioni, a quella che provoca l'avviamento dei siluri nella marina, cartuccia posta nelle sezioni di scarico dei due condotti A e B. La combustione della cartuccia provoca il moto rotatorio e l'innalzamento iniziale del di-*

devices were tested:

a) flying bombs for long range bombardment (discoidal telearms);
b) air defense projectiles (discoidal air mines);
c) "aircraft shear" flying saucers (sickle bombs or flying rams);
d) manpiloted aircraft (discoid fighters).

The special type of anti-aircraft discoid bullet was in an advanced experimental stage in the last months of the war. It had an armored and sharp edge and whirling in the midst of flying bombers in formation in tight ranks to resist the attack of the hunters, it would literally mow them down, then explode with spent fuel by means of a special chemical composition contained in it, which would produce for a few seconds a huge sphere of fire in the sky, psychologically affecting the raiders. Foo Fighters?

These experimental devices fell into British hands because on June, 16, 1945 an official news from London communicated; " The military secrets of Hitler Germany were discovered by a British special corps known under the name of "Unit T".

Less than a week following Belluzzo's claim, on March 30, 1950, Germany's Der Spiegel published an article about the allegation of German work on flying saucers, by way of an interview with a German named Rudolf Schriever, who claimed to have designed a flying spinning disc more than 40 feet in diameter. Schriever declared that he had worked on the disc from a base in Czechoslovakia in 1942, and that the design reached completion in 1945, just before the Russians marched in.

About the same time, another German by the name of Dr. Heinrich Richard Miethe, jumped into the scene and declared that he was the lead designer of a German team tasked with developing a flying disc. Miethe was the designer and builder of the wartime German saucer project, the V-7. Dr Miethe worked during the war at a German facility in Breslau, now part of modem Poland. After the war, he was recruited by the Americans and Canadians to recapitulate his earlier work for Germany in America.

All these claims seem to be real, and it was reported in a CIA memorandum by 1954. The document reported sightings in Sweden Denmark and West Germany. In Germany, a glowing object, like a Foo Fighter, were reporting flying between Frankfurt and Duesseldorf. The object was not tracked by the US. Radar. However, the CIA has reports like this since the first "foo fighter" sightings in 1940's.

After the WWII, the CIA kept a close eyes, as far as South America, for posible clues on UFOs developments by former Nazi scientists. At the time, the Agency took seriously the possibility that former Nazis could develop this kind of weapons. Dr. Eduard Ludwig, who lived at the time in Chile, published an article entitled: The Mystery of The Flyind Disc in Condor, a German language magazine. CIA prepared a report of the article, and translated it to the English language.

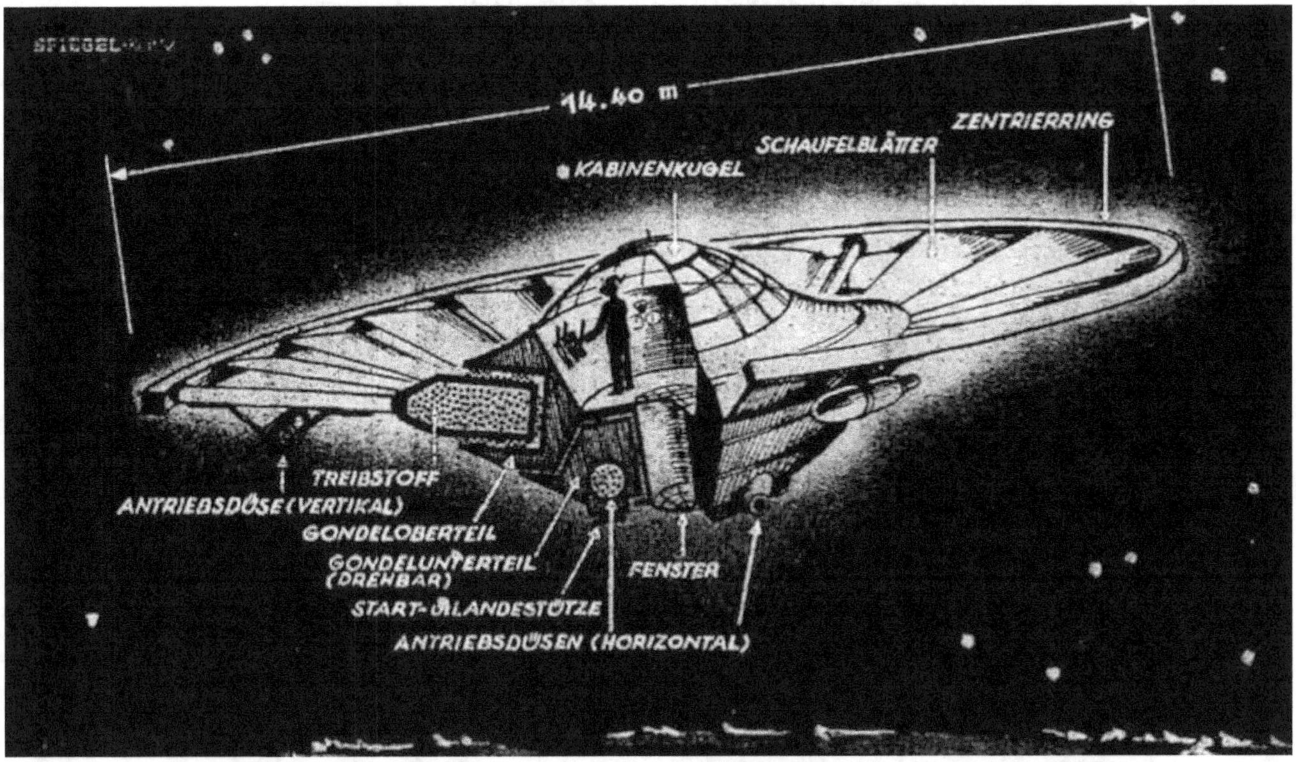


**Rudolf Schrievers'jet driven flying saucer *Die Deutsche illustrierte (*1953)**

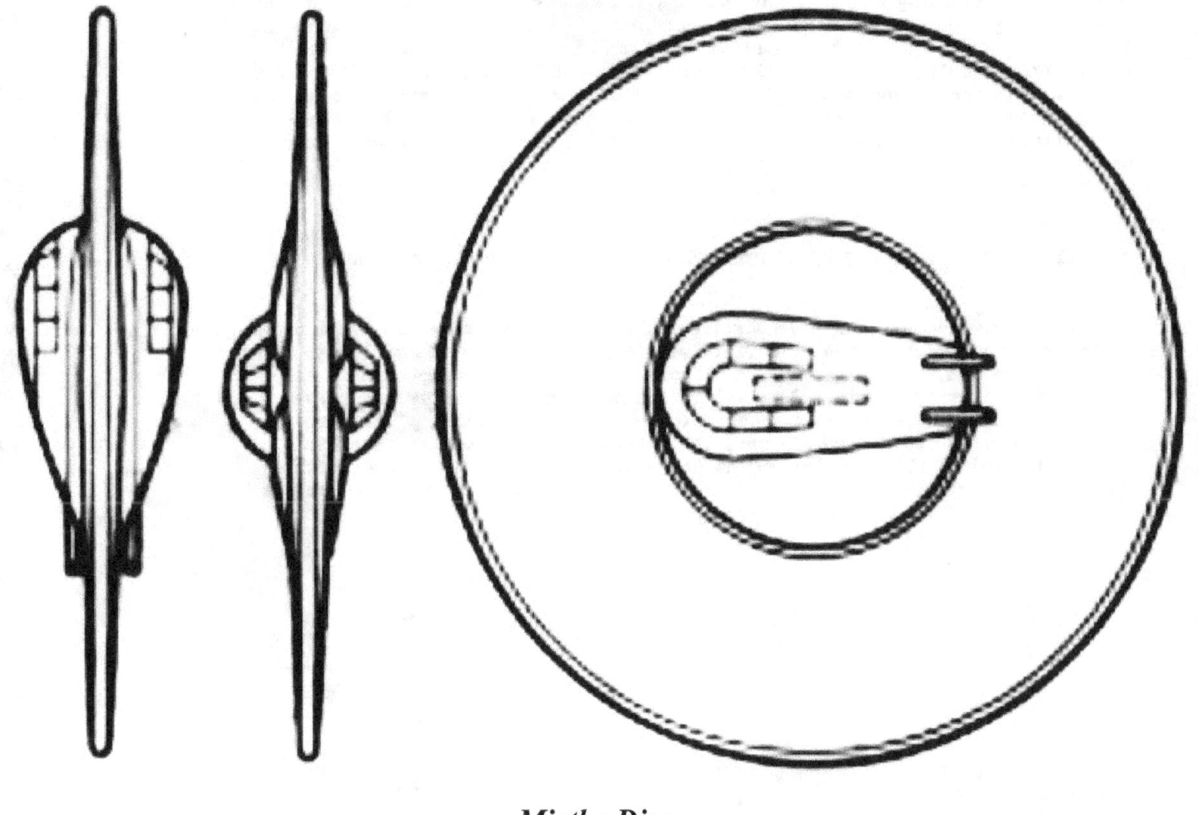

*Miethe Disc*

79

CLASSIFICATION [redacted]

CENTRAL INTELLIGENCE AGENCY
INFORMATION FROM
FOREIGN DOCUMENTS OR RADIO BROADCASTS

REPORT NO. 00-W-30883

CD NO. --

| | | | |
|---|---|---|---|
| COUNTRY | Non-Orbit | DATE OF INFORMATION | 1954 |
| SUBJECT | Military - Unidentified flying objects | | |
| HOW PUBLISHED | Newspapers | DATE DIST. | 25 Aug 1954 |
| WHERE PUBLISHED | As indicated | NO. OF PAGES | 2 |
| DATE PUBLISHED | 7 May-20 Jun 1954 | | |
| LANGUAGE | Swedish, Turkish, French, German | SUPPLEMENT TO REPORT NO. | |

[redacted]

THIS IS UNEVALUATED INFORMATION

SOURCE As indicated.

## SIGHTINGS OF UNIDENTIFIED FLYING OBJECTS

ADDITIONAL WITNESSES TO PREVIOUS SIGHTINGS IN SWEDEN -- Stockholm, Svenska Dagbladet, 18 May 54

Lulea -- A snowstorm on 17 May made it impossible for the Gaellivare police to investigate the celestial objects which were recently seen in various places in northern Norrbotten Province. The police do not think that the objects were meteorological balloons but do not have any theories to account for the sightings. The latest eyewitness account was given by Valdemar Ylinentalo from Kuusijaervi, who declared that he saw a silvery football-shaped object coming from the Finnish side of the boundary; it had a fiery tail 70-80 meters long and appeared to descend to earth about half a kilometer from where he was. Jenny Karlsson, another eyewitness, stated that she saw a sphere-shaped object attached to a meter-long rod pass her at a distance of 4-5 meters [sic] and come to earth in the forest, a short distance from her. No traces of this object have been found.

CELESTIAL OBJECT TO BE DUG UP IN DENMARK -- Stockholm, Svenska Dagbladet, 24 May 54

In the near future, an investigation will be made to determine whether a flying object which landed in a field near Spjellerup about 6 months ago is a meteor, a shell, or some part of a "flying saucer." The object made a hole in the field about 3.5 meters deep and 25 centimeters in diameter and passed through a thick stratum of flint. The owner of the land pushed a long iron rod into the hole and determined that the object at the bottom is metallic. It is said that at the time the object descended to earth, there were quite a number of unidentified flying objects over the area. Excavation of the object will be performed with assistance from the military.

APPROVED FOR RELEASE
DATE 6 Nov 75



ARCHIVAL RECORD
PLEASE RETURN TO
[redacted] AGENCY ARCHIVES, [redacted]

CLASSIFICATION [redacted]

| | | | | |
|---|---|---|---|---|
| STATE | NAVY | NSRB | DISTRIBUTION | |
| ARMY | AIR | FBI | | |

#15

SIGHT UNIDENTIFIED CRAFT OVER TAURUS MOUNTAINS OF TURKEY -- Istanbul, Yeni Sabah, 7 May 54

Mersin, 6 May 1954 -- Today, an unidentified aircraft was sighted by residents of the town of Mersin at approximately 1130 hours. The craft, which appeared over the Taurus Mountains, seemed to be about 10 meters in length and was traveling in a straight line. It was visible only for a few minutes and then disappeared.

UNIDENTIFIED FLYING OBJECTS SEEN OVER WEST GERMANY -- Douala, L'Eveil du Cameroun, 17 Jun 54

Two unidentified flying objects were reported to have been seen recently for about 10 seconds by a PTT (Postes, Telegraphes, et Telephones, Post, Telegraph, and Telephone Service) engineer and by another person between Frankfurt and Darmstadt, near the Rhein-Main Air Base. The objects were described as glowing disks, which descended almost vertically to a certain [unspecified] distance above the earth at high speed and then rose rapidly, describing a parabola. US radar did not pick up the objects.

New York, N. Y. Staats-Zeitung und Herold, 20 Jun 54

Employees of various air lines at the Duesseldorf airport recently observed a shiny, round object which approached from the south at high speed, then turned toward the west, and disappeared above the 6,000-meter overcast. An employee of the Condor aerial-advertising firm, who happened to be watching a skywriter of his firm at the time, called the object a "flying saucer" and stated that it could not possibly have been an airplane, balloon, or aerial measuring device. Several other airport employees confirmed his observation.

- E N D -

LIBRARY SUBJECT & AREA CODES

[redacted] 25 AUG 1954

[redacted]



[redacted]

# GERMAN SCIENTIST'S ARTICLE ON 'FLYING DISCS'

**Document Type:**
FOIA
**Collection:**
UFOs: Fact or Fiction?
**Document Number (FOIA) /ESDN (CREST):**
0000015283
**Release Decision:**
**Original Classification:**
U **Document Page Count:**
8
**Document Release Date:**
October 5, 1978
**Sequence Number:**
**Case Number:**
**Publication Date:**
June 1, 1950
**File:**
**Attachment Size**
DOC_0000015283.pdf
807.71

[redacted] ral 35

CLASSIFICATION [redacted]

CENTRAL INTELLIGENCE AGENCY

# INFORMATION REPORT

REPORT NO. SO DB-27123

CD NO.

COUNTRY Chile/Germany

SUBJECT German Scientist's Article on "Flying Discs"

PLACE ACQUIRED [redacted]



DATE OF INFO. Prior to mid-1950

DATE DISTR. 31 July 1950

NO. OF PAGES 1

NO. OF ENCLS. (LISTED BELOW) 1 [redacted]

SUPPLEMENT TO REPORT NO.

[redacted]

* Documentary

THIS IS UNEVALUATED INFORMATION

SOURCE

Attached for your information is a copy, in translation, of an article submitted by Dr. Eduard Ludwig for publication in Condor, a German language magazine published in Chile. The article is entitled "The Mystery of the 'Flying Discs,' a contribution to its possible explanation".

[redacted]

Good report but lousy translation

The significant conclusion drawn by the scientist in this report is that the old handicap of "boundary layer" on a moving object or

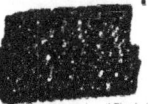

PLACE ACQUIRED [redacted]

Return to CIA Library

NO. OF ENCLS. (LISTED BELOW) 1 [redacted]

DATE OF INFO. Prior to mid-1950

TEXT ON THIS PAGE IS ILLEGIBLE
WE HAVE LEFT THE PAGE AS REFERENCE

SUPPLEMENT TO REPORT NO.

[redacted]

* Documentary

THIS IS UNEVALUATED INFORMATION

SOURCE

Attached for your information is a copy, in translation, of an article submitted by Dr. Eduard Ludwig for publication in Condor, a German language magazine published in Chile. The article is entitled "The Mystery of the 'Flying Discs,' a contribution to its possible explanation".

[redacted]

Good report but lousy translation

The significant conclusion drawn by the scientist in this report is that the old handicap of "boundary layer" on a moving object or airfoil has been exploited to produce an advantageous reaction and is the factor controlling the success of the "flying saucer" type of airfoil.

CLASSIFICATION [redacted]

| STATE | | NAVY | X | NSRB | | DISTRIBUTION | | | | | | |
|---|---|---|---|---|---|---|---|---|---|---|---|---|
| ARMY | X | AIR | X | FBI | | | | | | | | |



D-#1

6 Nov 78

# THE MYSTERY OF THE "FLYING DISCS"

A contribution to its possible explanation.

By Dr. Eduard Ludwig, Santiago, Chile.
Av. Cristobal Colon 1916

Though the continuously reappearing reports on the appearance of new, mysterious aircraft of unknown construction should be considered with severe skepticism as the result of a sort of mass-hypnosis, nevertheless some of the detailed and coinciding accounts of technically trained observers deserve attention and permit one to draw conclusions as to the probable classification of these new aircraft.

Since so far the observations have been made mainly in the dark, which means that only the luminous parts of the craft are visible, every report brings the description of shining discs or circles. If one should discard the absurd conjecture that these aircraft originate from beyond this earth, then it is easy to arrive at the conclusion that the shining circles bear a relation to the exhaust of a rotary gas-turbine. The possibility exists that the rotor of a turbine is used at the same time as a stabilizing top and is therefore fixed vertically to the level of the other turbine rings, which in the darkness produces the effect of the "rings of Saturn".

These observations remind me of a completely new type of aircraft which was developed during the years I worked in the research plant of Professor Junkers in Dessau, which was attached to the airplane factories known all over the world. I do not know how many of my co-workers are still alive today, but I do know that Dr. Bock, Professor at the Technical High School of Berlin, and who was at that time my chief and friend of many years, has been deported to the Soviet Union.

The name of Professor Bock was never widely known due to his modest character, but he may have been the greatest genius of German airplane theoretics, and later, in view of his extraordinary faculties, he was named head constructor of the Ministr of German Airways and Director of the German Institute of Airways Research in Berlin-Adlershof.

In order to explain to a wider circle of readers the basic idea of the new aircraft, I should like to submit first the following explanations:

[redacted]

The first [physician] and mathematician who considered the new Science of Aerodynamics after the commencement of purely experimental developments of aircraft construction was the Russian Professor Jukovski of Moscow. Before the first World War and together with my esteemed teacher, Dr. Kutta from the Technical High School of Stuttgart, Germany, he developed the theory of airplane-wingbeam. Professor Kutta succeeded in establishing the famous "Differential equation of the [boundary stratum]" which for the first time throws light on the processes in current particles and which in any case explains for the first time theoretically the reason why a planewing can bear a load while moving forward through the air. Since then the "Kutta-Jukowski Theory of Airplane-wingbeam" has been the foundation of all aerodynamics. As already mentioned, the core of this work is the so-called "boundary ~~stratum~~", which consists of the thin layer of air in which the transition of Velocity Zero to the Velocity of the Moving Object takes place. If the object is streamlined then the boundary stratum will endeavor not to sever, no whirlwinds will occur, and therefore no loss of energy will take place in that stratum. Since nature always functions most economically, it always tries to avoid loss of energy,

Though the continuously reappearing reports on the appearance of new, mysterious aircraft of unknown construction should be considered with severe skepticism as the result of a sort of mass-hypnosis, nevertheless some of the detailed and coinciding accounts of technically trained observers deserve attention and permit one to draw conclusions as to the probable classification of these new aircraft.

Since so far the observations have been made mainly in the dark, which means that only the luminous parts of the craft are visible, every report brings the description of shining discs or circles. If one should discard the absurd conjecture that these aircraft originate from beyond this earth, then it is easy to arrive at the conclusion that the shining circles bear a relation to the exhaust of a rotary gas-turbine. The possibility exists that the rotor of a turbine is used at the same time as a stabilizing top and is therefore fixed vertically to the level of the other turbine rings, which in the darkness produces the effect of the "rings of Saturn".

These observations remind me of a completely new type of aircraft which was developed during the years I worked in the research plant of Professor Junkers in Dessau, which was attached to the airplane factories known all over the world. I do not know how many of my co-workers are still alive today, but I do know that Dr. Bock, Professor at the Technical High School of Berlin, and who was at that time my chief and friend of many years, has been deported to the Soviet Union.

The name of Professor Bock was never widely known due to his modest character, but he may have been the greatest genius of German airplane theoretics, and later, in view of his extraordinary faculties, he was named head constructor of the Ministry of German Airways and Director of the German Institute of Airways Research in Berlin-Adlershof.

In order to explain to a wider circle of readers the basic idea of the new aircraft, I should like to submit first the following explanations:

should be translated as physicist - [redacted]

The first [physician] and mathematician who considered the new Science of Aerodynamics after the commencement of purely experimental developments of aircraft construction was the Russian Professor Jukovski of Moscow. Before the first World War and together with my esteemed teacher, Dr. Kutta from the Technical High School of Stuttgart, Germany, he developed the theory of airplane-wingbeam. Professor Kutta succeeded in establishing the famous "Differential equation of the [boundary stratum]" which for the first time throws light on the processes in current particles and which in any case explains for the first time theoretically the reason why a planewing can bear a load while moving forward through the air. Since then the "Kutta-Jukowski Theory of Airplane-wingbeam" has been the foundation of all aerodynamics. As already mentioned, the core of this work is the so-called "boundary ~~stratum~~" layer, which consists of the thin layer of air in which the transition of Velocity Zero to the Velocity of the Moving Object takes place. If the object is streamlined then the boundary stratum will endeavor not to sever, no whirlwinds will occur, and therefore no loss of energy will take place in that stratum. Since nature always functions most economically, it always tries to avoid loss of energy, and therefore a planewing would rather bear weight than cause a disruption of the course of the current and let the wing drop.

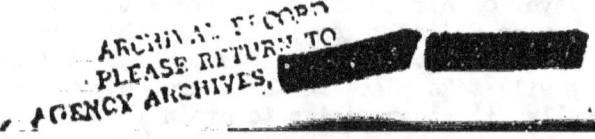

The logical conclusions based on these theoretic discoveries were obvious: already in the year 1915 Professor H. C. Bauman, also from the Technical High School of Stuttgart, received a patent on the "Splitwing" through which the artificial interruption of the course of the current, the tearing of the boundary stratum and the consequent braking and diminishing of the landing speed would be attained. This procedure was later applied to a great extent to the fighter plane Muster Ju. 88 under the name of "dive-brake". This patent had to be handed to the English factory Handley-Page after World War I, which explains that the name of "Handley-Page Splitwing" is more widely known.

However, developments proceeded. It was principally the Aerodynamic Experimental Institute of the Gottingen University, directed by the renowned Professors Prandtl and Betz, and Constructor Flettner, which drew its conclusions from the theory of the airplane-wing-beam. Flettner proved that the conditions of a rotating object are similar to those which appear in a "translatorischen" movement. Thus evolved the "Flettner-Rotor".

Professor Junkers, head of the well known airplane works in Dessau, who in the year 1915 received his pathbreaking patent on the one-piece metal wing without junctures, ordered a research group, which was headed by Professor Dr. Bock, and to which I had the honor to belong, to investigate to what extent the uplift of a wing could be increased through the attachment of a Flettner-Rotor in the shape of a cylinder turning at great speed. The cylinder was two-thirds of the length of the wing and was installed in the nose of the wing, where it could best be adapted to the wing's profile. To assist us with aerodynamic problems, the Gottingen University sent us Professor Prandtl. The experiments turned out to be extremely difficult and involved many casualties. The purely technical question of the speedy uplift of a long cylinder of light construction could not be solved at that time. Inexplicable vibrations and axle breakages occurred time after time which Professor Junkers ordered us to investigate, and with which we were occupied for months. Not less than four men, all experienced and tried pilots of the first World War and outstanding engineers, died in these experiments. It was clear to us that only a gas-turbine could produce the direct uplift of the cylinder. However, since meanwhile more pressing problems awaited solution, experiments with this type of aircraft were interrupted.

Meanwhile the Aerodynamic Experimental Institute of Gottingen made new and enlightening discoveries. Professor Betz found that supersonic speeds, such as are produced by quickly rotating propellers, created entirely new conditions. This investigation, however, needed the furnishing of a wind tunnel for supersonic speeds which could only be built many years later, and which after the war was forwarded to the United States where it greatly amazed all scientists.

Now light was shed on many things. It was found that the tearing of the boundary stratum at supersonic speeds involved much greater resistance, so that an object with full atmospheric pressure practically "hangs" from the upper layer of air, and theoretically experiences there the same uplift as an object of the same surface in the water. The converting of the revelations found in research into reality, however, needed the solution of the starting force through a gas-turbine or another equivalent machine or instrument.

Many heretofore unexplained phenomena now found an explanation. For example it had often been observed that the range of ~~quickly~~ rapidly rotating missiles ("Drallwirkung") was much greater than could be explained according to the laws of ballistics. Paradoxical explanations were sought for this such as that the air resistance decreases with growing speeds. Today we know that these quickly rotating missiles "swim" in the surrounding layers of air and therefore lose part of their weight. Full clarification was brought about only with supersonic speeds, which were obtained in the experiments with rockets (V-2) and were arrived at by flights of many hundreds and thousands of kilometers, and which can only be explained by the way in which these missiles literally "hang" in the air. The surprise of the specialized scientists the world over at the astounding results of the German V-2 was not less than that which is produced today by the appearance of the mysterious from the theory of the airplane-wing-beam. Flettner proved that the conditions of a rotating object are similar to those which appear in a "translatorischen" movement. Thus evolved the "Flettner-Rotor".

Professor Junkers, head of the well known airplane works in Dessau, who in the year 1915 received his pathbreaking patent on the one-piece metal wing without junctures, ordered a research group, which was headed by Professor Dr. Bock, and to which I had the honor to belong, to investigate to what extent the uplift of a wing could be increased through the attachment of a Flettner-Rotor in the shape of a cylinder turning at great speed. The cylinder was two-thirds of the length of the wing and was installed in the nose of the wing, where it could best be adapted to the wing's profile. To assist us with aerodynamic problems, the Gottingen University sent us Professor Prandtl. The experiments turned out to be extremely difficult and involved many casualties. The purely technical question of the speedy uplift of a long cylinder of light construction could not be solved at that time. Inexplicable vibrations and axle breakages occurred time after time which Professor Junkers ordered us to investigate, and with which we were occupied for months Not less than four men, all experienced and tried pilots of the first World War and outstanding engineers, died in these experiments. It was clear to us that only a gas-turbine could produce the direct uplift of the cylinder. However, since meanwhile more pressing problems awaited solution, experiments with this type of aircraft were interrupted.

Meanwhile the Aerodynamic Experimental Institute of Gottingen made new and enlightening discoveries. Professor Betz found that supersonic speeds, such as are produced by quickly rotating propellers, created entirely new conditions. This investigation, however, needed the furnishing of a wind tunnel for supersonic speeds which could only be built many years later, and which after the war was forwarded to the United States where it greatly amazed all scientists.

Now light was shed on many things. It was found that the tearing of the boundary stratum at supersonic speeds involved much greater resistance, so that an object with full atmospheric pressure practically "hangs" from the upper layer of air, and theoretically experiences there the same uplift as an object of the same surface in the water. The converting of the revelations found in research into reality, however, needed the solution of the starting force through a gas-turbine or another equivalent machine or instrument.

Many heretofore unexplained phenomena now found an explanation. For example it had often been observed that the range of quickly rotating missiles ("Drallwirkung") was much greater than could be explained according to the laws of ballistics. Paradoxical explanations were sought for this such as that the air resistance decreases with growing speeds. Today we know that these quickly rotating missiles "swim" in the surrounding layers of air and therefore lose part of their weight. Full clarification was brought about only with supersonic speeds, which were obtained in the experiments with rockets (V-2) and were arrived at by flights of many hundreds and thousands of kilometers, and which can only be explained by the way in which these missiles literally "hang" in the air. The surprise of the specialized scientists the world over at the astounding results of the German V-2 was not less than that which is produced today by the appearance of the mysterious "Flying Discs".

In the same way in which the ingenious discernment of Professor Junkers pointed the way for airplane construction for the whole world, thus also may his idea of attaching Flettner Rotors have a revolutionary effect. Airplanes of this type must have such an enormous carrying capacity as to be practically comparable to amphibious planes of the same size. The lack of uplift produced by the Flettner Rotors can easily be achieved through the oblique position of the entire airplane

[redacted]



with a positive starting angle in connection with the enormously high starting speed. The attaching of speedily rotating tops assures side stability. There is also the possibility of attaching horizontal auxiliary propellers of the helicopter type. And what about the question of the starting force? The safety of such an aircraft stands and falls on the starting force of the cylinders, and only too well do I remember the casualties inflicted by the lack of it. As I mentioned before, only the development of a gas-turbine can bring the solution, since it consists only of rotating parts and works with the dependability of a steam engine.

There is only one more question to be answered: could such an aircraft carry enough fuel for world-wide journeys? This question is easily answered in the affirmative. In the first place such an aircraft has a tremendous carrying capacity, as we have already seen; and in the second place chemical research has made astounding developments in this respect. We know today—quite apart from atomic energy—carriers of energy of unsuspected power and duration. [It should be remembered that the missiles of German anti-tank weapons were coated with chemical substances which melted up to 20 cmts. of steel plates within fractions of a second.] Energy carriers of this type, if applicable to a gas-turbine, should make an action-radius possible which far surpasses that of gasoline engines.

The future will show whether the "Flying Discs" are only the products of imagination or whether they are the results of a far-advanced German science which, possibly, as well as the nearly finished atomic bombs, may have fallen into the hands of the Russians.

only too well do I remember the casualties inflicted by [illegible] mentioned before, only the development of a gas-turbine can bring the solution, since it consists only of rotating parts and works with the dependability of a steam engine.

There is only one more question to be answered: could such an aircraft carry enough fuel for world-wide journeys? This question is easily answered in the affirmative. In the first place such an aircraft has a tremendous carrying capacity, as we have already seen; and in the second place chemical research has made astounding developments in this respect. We know today—quite apart from atomic energy—carriers of energy of unsuspected power and duration. It should be remembered that the missiles of German anti-tank weapons were coated with chemical substances which melted up to 20 cmts. of steel plates within fractions of a second. Energy carriers of this type, if applicable to a gas-turbine, should make an action-radius possible which far surpasses that of gasoline engines.

The future will show whether the "Flying Discs" are only the products of imagination or whether they are the results of a far-advanced German science which, possibly, as well as the nearly finished atomic bombs, may have fallen into the hands of the Russians.

**Unloading of captured Horten Ho 229 V3 in the U.S by Operation Lusty.**

**Horten H.IX**

The **Horten H.IX**, RLM designation Ho 229 (or Gotha Go 229for extensive re-design work done by Gotha to prepare the aircraft for mass production) was a German prototype fighter/bomber initially designed by Reimar and Walter Horten to be built by Gothaer Waggonfabrik late in World War II. It was the first flying wing to be powered by jet engines.

The design was a response to Hermann Göring's call for light bomber designs capable of meeting the "3×1000" requirement; namely to carry 1,000 kilograms (2,200 lb) of bombs a distance of 1,000 kilometres (620 mi) with a speed of 1,000 kilometres per hour (620 mph). Only jets could provide the speed, but these were extremely fuel-hungry, so considerable effort had to be made to meet the range requirement. Based on a flying wing, the Ho 229 lacked all extraneous control surfaces to lower drag. It was the only design to come even close to the requirements, and received Göring's approval. Its ceiling was 15,000 metres (49,000 ft)

The Horten H.IX, RLM designation Ho 229 (or Gotha Go 229 for extensive re-design work done by Gotha to prepare the aircraft for mass production) was a Germa prototype fighter/bomber initially designed by Reimar and Walter Horten to be built by Gothaer Waggonfabrik late in World War II. It was the first flying wing to be powered by jet engines.

The design was a response to Hermann Göring's call for light bomber designs capable of meeting the "3×1000" requirement; namely to carry 1,000 kilograms (2,200 lb) of bombs a distance of 1,000 kilometres (620 mi) with a speed of 1,000 kilometres per hour (620 mph). Only jets could provide the speed, but these were extremely fuel-hungry, so considerable effort had to be made to meet the range requirement. Based on a flying wing, the Ho 229 lacked all extraneous control surfaces to lower drag. It was the only design to come even close to the requirements, and received Göring's approval. Its ceiling was 15,000 metres (49,000 ft).

In the early 1930s, the Horten brothers had become interested in the flying wing design as a method of improving the performance of gliders. The German government was funding glider clubs at the time because production of military and even motorized aircraft was forbidden by the Treaty of Versailles after World War I. The flying wing layout removed the need for a tail and associated control surfaces and theoretically offered the lowest possible weight, using wings that were relatively short and sturdy, and without the added drag of the fuselage. The result was the Horten H.IV.

In 1943, Reichsmarschall Göring issued a request for design proposals to produce a bomber that was capable of carrying a 1,000 kilograms (2,200 lb) load over 1,000 kilometres (620 mi) at 1,000 kilometres per hour (620 mph); the so-called "3×1000 project". Conventional German bombers could reach Allied command centers in Great Britain, but were suffering devastating losses from Allied fighters. At the time, there was no way to meet these goals—the new Junkers Jumo 004B turbojets could provide the required speed, but had excessive fuel consumption.

The Hortens concluded that the low-drag flying wing design could meet all of the goals: by reducing the drag, cruise power could be lowered to the point where the range requirement could be met. They put forward their private project, the H.IX, as the basis for the bomber. The Government Air Ministry (Reichsluftfahrtministerium) approved the Horten proposal, but ordered the addition of two 30 mm cannons, as they felt the aircraft would also be useful as a fighter due to its estimated top speed being significantly higher than that of any Allied aircraft.

The H.IX was of mixed construction, with the center pod made from welded steel tubing and wing spars built from wood. The wings were made from two thin, carbon-impregnated plywood panels glued together with a charcoal and sawdust mixture. The wing had a single main spar, penetrated by the jet engine inlets, and a secondary spar used for attaching the elevons. It was designed with a 7g load factor and a 1.8× safety rating; therefore, the aircraft had a 12.6g ultimate load rating. The wing's chord/thickness ratio ranged from 15% at the root to 8% at the wingtips. The aircraft utilized retractable tricycle landing gear, with the nosegear on the first two prototypes sourced from a He 177's tailwheel system, with the third prototype using an He 177A main gear wheelrim and tire on its custom-designed nosegear strutwork and wheel fork. A drogue parachute slowed the aircraft upon landing. The pilot sat on a primitive ejection seat. A special pressure suit was developed by Dräger. The aircraft was originally designed for the BMW 003 jet engine, but that engine was not quite ready, and the Junkers Jumo 004 engine was substituted.

Control was achieved with elevons and spoilers. The control system included both long-span (inboard) and short-span (outboard) spoilers, with the smaller outboard spoilers activated first. This system gave a smoother and more graceful control of yaw than would a single-spoiler system.

Given the difficulties in design and development, Russell Lee, the chair of the Aeronautics Department at the National Air and Space Museum, suggests an important purpose of the project for the Horten Brothers was to prevent them and their workers from being assigned to more dangerous roles by the German military.

The first prototype H.IX V1, an unpowered glider with fixed tricycle landing gear, flew on 1 March 1944. Flight results were very favorable, but there was an accident when the pilot attempted to land without first retracting an instrument-carrying pole extending from the aircraft. The design was taken from the Horten brothers and given to Gothaer Waggonfabrik. The Gotha team made some changes: they added a simple ejection seat, dramatically changed the undercarriage to enable a higher gross weight, changed the jet engine inlets, and added ducting to air-cool the jet engine's outer casing to prevent damage to the wooden wing.

The H.IX V1 was followed in December 1944 by the Junkers Jumo 004-powered second prototype H.IX V2; the BMW 003 engine was preferred, but unavailable. Göring believed in the design and ordered a production series of 40 aircraft from Gothaer Waggonfabrik with the RLM designation Ho 229, even though it had not yet taken to the air under jet power. The first flight of the H.IX V2 was made in Oranienburg on 2 February 1945. All subsequent test flights and development were done by Gothaer Waggonfabrik. By this time, the Horten brothers were working on a turbojet-powered design for the Amerika Bomber contract competition and did not attend the first test flight. The test pilot was Leutnant Erwin Ziller. Two further test flights were made: on 2 February 1945 and on 18 February 1945. Another test pilot used in the evaluation was Heinz Scheidhauer.

The H.IX V2 reportedly displayed very good handling qualities, with only moderate lateral instability (a typical deficiency of tailless aircraft). While the second flight was equally successful, the undercarriage was damaged by a heavy landing caused by Ziller deploying the brake parachute too early during his landing approach. There are reports that during one of these test flights, the H.IX V2 undertook a simulated "dog-fight" with a Messerschmitt Me 262, the first operational jet fighter, and that the H.IX V2 outperformed the Me 262. However, the Me 262 was considered by many as unsuitable for fighter missions, being slow in turning. Additionally, pilots and aiming devices had not yet adapted to the speed of jet aircraft, forcing pilots to slow their airplanes to accurately fire at bombers, leaving them momentarily at the reach of Allied gunmen.

Two weeks later, on 18 February 1945, disaster struck during the third test flight. Ziller took off without any problems to perform a series of flight tests. After about 45 minutes, at an altitude of around 800 m, one of the Jumo 004 turbojet engines developed a problem, caught fire and stopped. Ziller was seen to put the aircraft into a dive and pull up several times in an attempt to restart the engine and save the precious prototype.Ziller undertook a series of four complete turns at 20° angle of bank. Ziller did not use his radio or eject from the aircraft. He may already have been unconscious as a result of the fumes from the burning engine. The aircraft crashed just outside the boundary of the airfield. Ziller was thrown from the aircraft on impact and died from his injuries two weeks later. The prototype aircraft was completely destroyed.

Despite this setback, the project continued with sustained energy. On 12 March 1945, nearly a week after the U.S. Army had launched Operation Lumberjack to cross the Rhine River, the Ho 229 was included in the Jäger-Notprogramm (Emergency Fighter Program) for accelerated production of inexpensive "wonder weapons". The prototype workshop was moved to the Gothaer Waggonfabrik (Gotha) in Friedrichroda, western Thuringia. In the same month, work commenced on the third prototype, the Ho 229 V3.

The V3 was larger than previous prototypes, the shape being modified in various areas, and it was meant to be a template for the pre-production series Ho 229 A-0 day fighters, of which 20 machines had been ordered. The V3 was meant to be powered by two Jumo 004C engines, with 10% greater thrust each than the earlier Jumo 004B production engine used for the Me 262A and Ar 234B, and could carry two MK 108 30 mm cannons in the wing roots. Work had also started on the two-seat Ho 229 V4 and Ho 229 V5 night-fighter prototypes, the Ho 229 V6 armament test prototype, and the Ho 229 V7 two-seat trainer.

During the final stages of the war, the U.S. Military initiated Operation Paperclip, an effort to capture advanced German weapons research, and keep it out of the hands of advancing Soviet troops. A Horten glider and the Ho 229 V3, which was undergoing final assembly, were transported by sea to the United States as part of Operation Seahorse for evaluation. On the way, the Ho 229 spent a brief time at RAE Farnborough in the UK, during which it was considered whether British jet engines could be fitted, but the mountings were found to be incompatible with the early British turbojets, which used larger-diameter centrifugal compressors as opposed to the slimmer axial-flow turbojets the Germans had developed. The Americans were just starting to create their own axial-compressor turbojets before the war's end, such as the Westinghouse J30, with a thrust level only approaching the BMW 003A's full output.

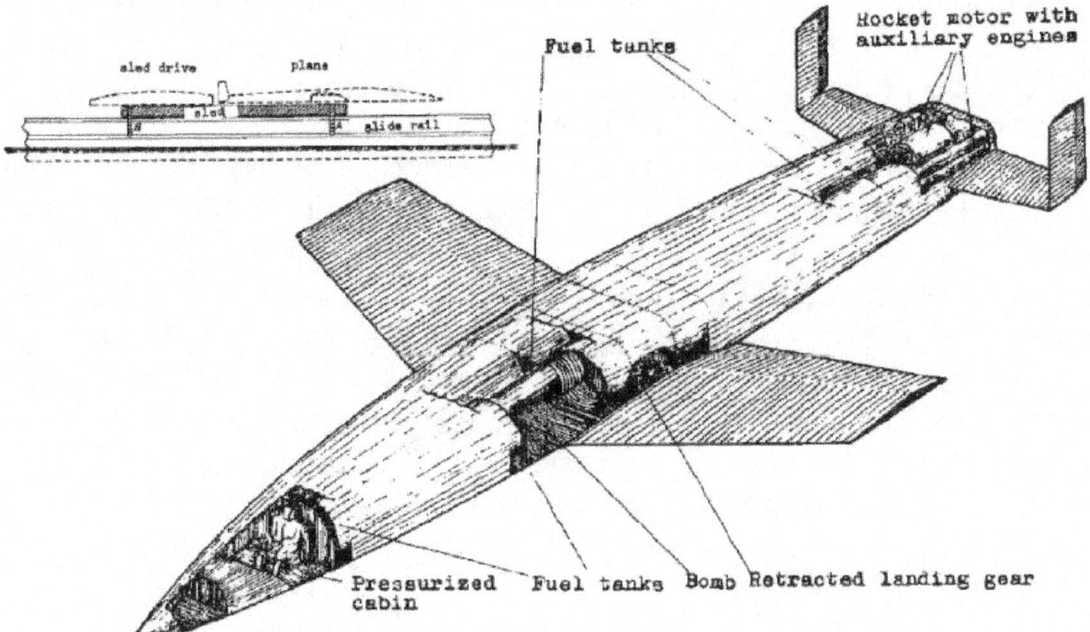


**Antipodal bomber Silbervogel, also known as the Silver Bird**

## Silbervogel

**Silbervogel** was the first design of a multi-use spacecraft that could fly from opposite side of the Earth. It was develop by Nazi Germany's scientists between 1932 and 1942, they developed an antipodal bomber Silbervogel. At the centre of this idea was the concept of undulant gliding. The craft would glide from space in a series of short hops, bouncing back from the drag-producing atmosphere layers. Such mechanism was needed to increase the distance the Silver Bird could overcome in one launch, simultaneously dropping bombs on different targets over the world.

The design was a significant one, as it incorporated new rocket technology and the principle of the lifting body, foreshadowing future development of winged spacecraft such as the X-20 Dyna-Soar of the 1960s and the Space Shuttle of the 1970s. In the end, it was considered too complex and expensive to produce. The design never went beyond mock-up test.

The Silbervogel was intended to fly long distances in a series of short hops. The aircraft was to have begun its mission propelled along a 3 km (2 mi) long rail track by a large rocket-powered sled to about 1,930 km/h (1,200 mph). Once airborne, it was to fire its own rocket engine and continue to climb to an altitude of 145 km (90 mi), at which point it would be travelling at about 21,800 km/h (13,500 mph). It would then gradually descend into the stratosphere, where the increasing air density would generate lift against the flat underside of the aircraft, eventually causing it to "bounce" and gain altitude again, where this pattern would be repeated. Because of aerodynamic drag, each bounce would be shallower than the preceding one, but it was still calculated that the Silbervogel would be able to cross the Atlantic, deliver a 4,000 kg (8,800 lb) bomb to the continental United States, and then continue its flight to a landing site somewhere in the Empire of Japan–held Pacific, a total journey of 19,000 to 24,000 km (12,000 to 15,000 mi).

Postwar analysis of the Silbervogel design involving a mathematical control analysis unearthed a computational error, and it turned out that the heat flow during the initial atmospheric re-entry would have been far higher than originally calculated by Sänger and Bredt; if the Silbervogel had been constructed according to their flawed calculations, the craft would have been destroyed during re-entry. The problem could have been solved by augmenting the heat shield, but this would have reduced the craft's already small payload capacity.

On 3 December 1941 Sänger sent his initial proposal for a suborbital glider to the *Reichsluftfahrtministerium* (RLM) as Geheime Kommandosache Nr. 4268/LXXX5. The 900-page proposal was regarded with disfavor at the RLM due to its size and complexity and was filed away. Then Sänger went to work on more modest projects such as the Skoda-Kauba Sk P.14 ramjet fighter.

Professor Walter Gregorii had Sänger rework his report, and a greatly reduced version was submitted to the RLM in September 1944, as UM 3538. It was the first serious proposal for a vehicle which could carry a pilot and payload to the lower edge of space.

Two manned and one unmanned version were proposed: the Antipodenferngleiter (antipodal long-range glider) and the Interglobalferngleiter (intercontinental long-range glider). Both were to be launched from a rocket-powered sled. The two manned versions were identical, except in payload. The Antipodenferngleiter was to be launched at a very steep angle (which would shorten the range) and after dropping its bomb load on New York City was to land at a Japanese base in the Pacific.

On 3 December 1941 Sänger sent his initial proposal for a suborbital glider to the *Reichsluftfahrtministerium* (RLM) as Geheime Kommandosache Nr. 4268/LXXX5. The 900-page proposal was regarded with disfavor at the RLM due to its size and complexity and was filed away. Then Sänger went to work on more modest projects such as the Skoda-Kauba Sk P.14 ramjet fighter.

Professor Walter Gregorii had Sänger rework his report, and a greatly reduced version was submitted to the RLM in September 1944, as UM 3538. It was the first serious proposal for a vehicle which could carry a pilot and payload to the lower edge of space.

Two manned and one unmanned version were proposed: the Antipodenferngleiter (antipodal long-range glider) and the Interglobalferngleiter (intercontinental long-range glider). Both were to be launched from a rocket-powered sled. The two manned versions were identical, except in payload. The Antipodenferngleiter was to be launched at a very steep angle (which would shorten the range) and after dropping its bomb load on New York City was to land at a Japanese base in the Pacific.

**The Messerschmitt Me 262 Schwalbe (jet engine) - The first jet-powered aircraft to ever fly in combat**

**Me 262 A-1a/U4 - A 'Bomber Destroyer' variant of the Me 262 with a 50mm anti-tank gun in the nose.**

**Messerschmitt Me 262**

The Messerschmitt Me 262, nicknamed Schwalbe (German: "Swallow") in fighter versions, or Sturmvogel (German: "Storm Bird") in fighter-bomber versions, was the world's first operational jet-powered fighter aircraft. Design work started before World War II began, but problems with engines, metallurgy and top-level interference kept the aircraft from operational status with the Luftwaffe until mid-1944. The Me 262 was faster and more heavily armed than any Allied fighter, including the British jet-powered Gloster Meteor. One of the most advanced aviation designs in operational use during World War II, the Me 262's roles included light bomber, reconnaissance and experimental night fighter versions.

Several years before World War II, the Germans foresaw the great potential for aircraft that used the jet engine constructed by Hans Joachim Pabst von Ohain in 1936. After the successful test flights of the world's first jet aircraft—the Heinkel He 178—within a week of the invasion of Poland to start the war, they adopted the jet engine for an advanced fighter aircraft. As a result, the Me 262 was already under development as Projekt 1065 (P.1065) before the start of World War II. The project originated with a request by the Reichsluftfahrtministerium (RLM, Ministry of Aviation) for a jet aircraft capable of one hour's endurance and a speed of at least 850 km/h (530 mph; 460 kn). Woldemar Voigt headed the design team, with Messerschmitt's chief of development, Robert Lusser, overseeing.

Plans were first drawn up in April 1939, and the original design was very different from the aircraft that eventually entered service, with wing root-mounted engines, rather than podded ones, when submitted in June 1939. The progression of the original design was delayed greatly by technical issues involving the new jet engine. Because the engines were slow to arrive, Messerschmitt moved the engines from the wing roots to underwing pods, allowing them to be changed more readily if needed; this would turn out to be important, both for availability and maintenance. Since the BMW 003 jets proved heavier than anticipated, the wing was swept slightly, by 18.5°, to accommodate a change in the center of gravity. Funding for the jet engine program was also initially lacking as many high-ranking officials thought the war could easily be won with conventional aircraft. Among those were Hermann Göring, head of the Luftwaffe, who cut the engine development program to just 35 engineers in February 1940 (the month before the first wooden mock-up was completed); Willy Messerschmitt, who desired to maintain mass production of the piston-powered, 1935-origin Bf 109 and the projected Me 209; and Major General Adolf Galland, who had initially supported Messerschmitt through the early development years, flying the Me 262 himself on 22 April 1943. By that time, problems with engine development had slowed production of the aircraft considerably. One particularly acute problem arose with the lack of an alloy with a melting point high enough to endure the high temperatures involved, a problem that by the end of the war had not been adequately resolved. The aircraft made its first successful flight entirely on jet power on 18 July 1942, powered by a pair of Jumo 004 engines, after a November 1941 flight (with BMW 003s) ended in a double flameout.

The project aerodynamicist on the design of the Me 262 was Ludwig Bölkow. He initially designed the wing using NACA airfoils modified with an elliptical nose section. Later in the design process, these were changed to AVL derivatives of NACA airfoils, the NACA 00011-0.825-35 being used at the root and the NACA 00009-1.1-40 at the tip. The elliptical nose derivatives of the NACA airfoils were used on the horizontal and vertical tail surfaces. Wings were of single-spar cantilever construction, with stressed skins, varying from 3 mm (0.12 in) skin thickness at the root to 1 mm (0.039 in) at the tip. To expedite construction, save weight and use less strategic materials, late in the war, wing interiors were not painted. The wings were fastened to the fuselage at four points, using a pair of 20 mm (0.79 in) and forty-two 8 mm (0.31in) bolts.

In mid-1943, Adolf Hitler envisioned the Me 262 as a ground-attack/bomber aircraft rather than a defensive interceptor. The configuration of a high-speed, light-payload Schnellbomber ("fast bomber") was intended to penetrate enemy airspace during the expected Allied invasion of France. His edict resulted in the development of (and concentration on) the Sturmvogel variant. It is debatable to what extent Hitler's interference extended the delay in bringing the Schwalbe into operation;it appears engine vibration issues were at least as costly, if not more so.Albert Speer, then Minister of Armaments and War Production, in his memoirs claimed Hitler originally had blocked mass production of the Me 262, before agreeing in early 1944. Hitler rejected arguments the aircraft would be more effective as a fighter against the Allied bombers destroying large parts of Germany, and wanted it as a bomber for revenge attacks. According to Speer, Hitler felt its superior speed compared to other fighters of the era meant it could not be attacked, and so preferred it for high altitude straight flying.

The Me 262 is often referred to as a "swept wing" design as the production aircraft had a small, but significant leading edge sweep of 18.5° which likely provided an advantage by increasing the critical Mach number. Sweep, uncommon at the time, was added after the initial design of the aircraft. The engines proved heavier than originally expected, and the sweep was added primarily to position the center of lift properly relative to the center of mass. (The original 35° sweep, proposed by Adolf Busemann, was not adopted.). On 1 March 1940, instead of moving the wing backward on its mount, the outer wing was re-positioned slightly aft; the trailing edge of the midsection of the wing remained unswept. Based on data from the AVA Göttinge and wind tunnel results, the inboard section's leading edge (between the nacelle and wing root) was later swept to the same angle as the outer panels, from the "V6" sixth prototype onward throughout volume production.

Testing showed that the ME262 handled much better than previous fighters such as the BF-109 or FW-190. Handling was so improved over previous aircraft that a report by Major Ernst Englander stated that any BF-109 pilot could convert to the ME262 with only an hour of instruction. According to his report, even bomber pilots who Converted to fly the ME262 only required three instruction flights, and less than 5% had any difficulty retraining. The ME-262 had a gentle stall and gentle landing characteristics compared to previous German fighters. Its handling improved with speed, and would lose much less speed during turning. It had a cruising speed of 465mph, which was faster than the top speed of most other fighters of the day. It also had far better visibility in every direction compared to previous German fighters. Due to lack of engine torque, if a single engine was lost the aircraft remained easily controlled and landed without issue. Its only major deficiency was that brakes could not be used until the nose wheel had touched down, because engaging them before would smash the nose wheel strongly into the runway, potentially destroying the nose wheel and the aircraft. Quality of the aircraft was high, with only 10% of aircraft returned for minor defects such as wings being out of alignment by under 1 degree. It could reach 515mph without issue, although because it could reach extreme speeds in dives, components such as bomb racks would sometimes tear off.

Test flights began on 18 April 1941, with the Me 262 V1 example, bearing its Stammkennzeichen radio code letters of PC+UA, but since its intended BMW 003 turbojets were not ready for fitting, a conventional Junkers Jumo 210 engine was mounted in the V1 prototype's nose, driving a propeller, to test the Me 262 V1 airframe. When the BMW 003 engines were installed, the Jumo was retained for safety, which proved wise as both 003s failed during the first flight and the pilot had to land using the nose-mounted engine alone. The V1 through V4 prototype airframes all possessed what would become an uncharacteristic feature for most later jet aircraft designs, a fully retracting conventional gear setup with a retracting tailwheel—indeed, the very first prospective German "jet fighter" airframe design ever flown, the Heinkel He 280, used a retractable tricycle landing gear from its beginnings, and flying on jet power alone as early as the end of March 1941.

The V3 third prototype airframe, with the code PC+UC, became a true jet when it flew on 18 July 1942 in Leipheim near Günzburg, Germany, piloted by test pilot Fritz Wendel. This was almost nine months ahead of the British Gloster Meteor's first flight on 5 March 1943. Its retracting conventional tail wheel gear (similar to other contemporary piston powered propeller aircraft), a feature shared with the first four Me 262 V-series airframes, caused its jet exhaust to deflect off the runway, with the wing's turbulence negating the effects of the elevators, and the first takeoff attempt was cut short.

On the second attempt, Wendel solved the problem by tapping the aircraft's brakes at takeoff speed, lifting the horizontal tail out of the wing's turbulence. The aforementioned initial four prototypes (V1-V4) were built with the conventional gear configuration. Changing to a tricycle arrangement—a permanently fixed undercarriage on the fifth prototype (V5, code PC+UE), with the definitive fully retractable nosewheel gear on the V6 (with Stammkennzeichen code VI+AA, from a new code block) and subsequent aircraft corrected this problem.

Test flights continued over the next year, but engine problems continued to plague the project, the Jumo 004 being only marginally more reliable than the lower-thrust (7.83 kN/1,760 lbf) BMW 003. Airframe modifications were complete by 1942 but, hampered by the lack of engines, serial production did not begin until 1944, and deliveries were low, with 28 Me 262s in June, 59 in July, but only 20 in August.

By Summer 1943, the Jumo 004A engine had passed several 100-hour tests, with a time between overhauls of 50 hours being achieved. However, the Jumo 004A engine proved unsuitable for full-scale production because of its considerable weight and its high utilization of strategic material (Ni, Co, Mo), which were in short supply. Consequently, the 004B engine was designed to use a minimum amount of strategic materials. All high heat-resistant metal parts, including the combustion chamber, were changed to mild steel (SAE 1010) and were protected only against oxidation by aluminum coating. The total engine represented a design compromise to minimize the use of strategic materials and to simplify manufacture. With the lower-quality steels used in the 004B, the engine required overhaul after just 25 hours for a metallurgical test on the turbine. If it passed the test, the engine was refitted for a further 10 hours of usage, but 35 hours marked the absolute limit for the turbine wheel. While BMW's and Junkers' axial compressor turbojet engines were characterised by a sophisticated design that could offer considerable advantage – also used in a generalized form for the contemporary American Westinghouse J30 turbojet – the lack of rare materials for the Jumo 004 design put it at a disadvantage compared to the "partly axial-flow" Power Jets W.2/700 turbojet engine which, despite its own largelycentrifugal compressor-influenced design, provided (between an operating overhaul interval of 60–65 hours an operational life span of 125 hours.

Operationally, carrying 2,000 litres (440 imperial gallons; 530 US gallons) of fuel in two 900-litre (200-imperial-gallon; 240-US-gallon) tanks, one each fore and aft of the cockpit; and a 200-litre (44-imperial-gallon; 53-US-gallon) ventral fuselage tank beneath, the Me 262 would have a total flight endurance of 60 to 90 minutes. Fuel was usually J2 (derived from brown coal), with the option of diesel or a mixture of oil and high octane B4 aviation petrol. Fuel consumption was double the rate of typical twin-engine fighter aircraft of the era, which led to the installation of a low-fuel warning indicator in the cockpit that notified pilots when remaining fuel fell below 250 l (55 imp gal; 66 US gal).

**Me-323 Gigant's landing gear**

**Flying Whale – The Messerschmitt 323 Gigant**

**Messerschmitt 323 Gigant**

The **Me 323** was built following a request by the German Luftwaffe for a large assault glider which would serve in Operation Sea Lion, the planned invasion of Great Britain. They needed an aircraft which could fly vehicles and other heavy equipment during the expedition. Operation Sea Lion was, however, annulled. But the Me 323 was still required–this time for Operation Barbossa, the invasion of the Soviet Union. There was nothing like in the Allied Arsenal.

Messerschmitt, along with Junkers, was given a 14 day ultimatum to submit a proposal detailing a large transport glider with emphasis on its assault role. The heavy transport glider was to have an 8mm anti-aircraft and anti-tank artillery gun along with a Panzer IV medium tank. Junkers' prototype was scrapped, and Messerschmitt's prototype was adopted.

Borrowing the designs of the long-range Messerschmitt Me 261, it was designated Me 261w. Its name evolved from Me 261w to Me 263 and eventually became Me 321. This Me 321 served as a transport in Russia but never played its intended role as an assault glider.

Feedback from Transports Command pilots in Russia, in early 1941, led to the decision to manufacture a motorized version of the Me 321, which was produced between 1942 and 1944. After about 198 were built, the Me 323 was introduced.

The key identifiable feature of the Me 323 was its six engines, three on each wing, for its propulsion. The Me 323s had a maximum speed of only 136 miles per hour at sea level, and its speed dropped with an increase in altitude. Its defensive armament consisted of 5 13 mm MG 131 machine guns firing from a dorsal position just behind the wings and from the fuselage. Each aircraft was manned by a crew of five comprising two pilots, two flight engineers, and a radio operator.

The first variants of the Me 323 included the V1 which was the first prototype, powered by Gnome-Rhone 14N-48/49 engines; and V2 which was the second prototype, which used six engines and became a standard for the D series. The production variants included the D series which ran from D1 to D3, the V13, V14, V16 and V17, and the E series which ran from E1 to E2.

In September 1942, M323s were deployed for the campaign in Tunisia. The M323s joined the Mediterranean stage in November 1942, supplying Rommel's Afrika Korps with equipment.

On April 22nd, 1943, a formation of 27 M323s was being escorted across Silica Straits when they were intercepted by seven squadrons of Spitfires and P-40s. In the aerial skirmish that ensued, 21 M323s were lost.

Despite being limited in numbers, the M323 aircraft was an invaluable asset to the Germans and was used extensively

**Arado Ar 234 Blitz was the world's first operational jet-power jet bomber**

**Arado Ar 234 Blitz**

The **Arado Ar 234 Blitz** (English: lightning) was the world's first operational jet-powered bomber, built by the German Arado company in the closing stages of World War II.

Produced in limited numbers it was used almost entirely in the reconnaissance role. In its few uses as a bomber it proved to be nearly impossible to intercept. It was the last Luftwaffe aircraft to fly over the UK during the war, in April 1945.

In late 1940, the Reich Air Ministry (German: Reichsluftfahrtministerium, abbreviated RLM) offered a tender for a jet-powered high-speed reconnaissance aircraft with a range of 2,156 km (1,340 mi). Arado was the only company to respond, offering their E.370 project, led by Professor Walter Blume. This was a high-wing conventional-looking design with a Junkers Jumo 004 engine under each wing.

Arado estimated a maximum speed of 780 km/h (480 mph) at 6,000 m (20,000 ft), an operating altitude of 11,000 m (36,000 ft) and a range of 1,995 km (1,240 mi). The range was short of the RLM request, but they liked the design and ordered two prototypes as the Ar 234. These were largely complete before the end of 1941, but the Jumo 004 engines were not ready, and would not be ready until February 1943. When they did arrive they were considered unreliable by Junkers for in-flight use and were cleared for static and taxi tests only. Flight-qualified engines were finally delivered, and the Ar 234 V1 made its first flight on 30 July 1943 at Rheine Airfield (presently Rheine-Bentlage Air Base).

By September, four prototypes were flying. The second prototype, Arado Ar 234 V2, crashed on 2 October 1943 at Rheine near Münster after suffering a fire in its port wing, failure of both engines and various instrumentation failures. The aircraft dived into the ground from 1,200 m (3,900 ft), killing pilot Flugkapitän Selle. The eight prototype aircraft were fitted with the original arrangement of trolley-and-skid landing gear, intended for the planned operational, but never-produced Ar 234A version.

The sixth and eighth of the series were powered with four BMW 003 jet engines instead of two Jumo 004s, the sixth having four engines housed in individual nacelles, and the eighth flown with two pairs of BMW 003s installed within "twinned" nacelles underneath each wing. These were the first four-engine jet aircraft to fly. The twin-Jumo 004 powered Ar 234 V7 prototype made history on 2 August 1944 as the first jet aircraft ever to fly a reconnaissance mission, flown by Erich Sommer.

The projected weight for the aircraft was approximately 8 tonnes (7.9 long tons; 8.8 short tons). To reduce the weight of the aircraft and maximize the internal fuel, Arado did not use the typical retractable landing gear. Instead, the aircraft was to take off from a jettisonable three-wheeled, tricycle gear-style trolley known as a Bugradstartwagen (nosewheel takeoff-carriage in English, as-described in an Ar 234A Typenblatt factory drawing for the Ar 234 V8 prototype) and land on three retractable skids, one under the central section of the fuselage, and one under each engine nacelle. This central main skid beneath the fuselage was originally intended to fully retract into the fuselage with skid-bay doors enclosing it, and was originally shown in a

1942-dated Arado engineering drawing, under its overall E 370 airframe factory development designation, as intended to be made from a three-sided channel-section component, featuring a set of nine triple-beaded wooden rollers within the channel-section mainskid, for ground contact purposes. However, as with the operational Messerschmitt Me 163B rocket fighter which used a landing skid, it was discovered that such a skid-format landing gear for the Ar 234A design's prototypes did not allow mobility after the end of the landing run, which would have left aircraft scattered widely over an airfield's acreage, unable to taxi off the runway without remounting every aircraft on a trolley for towing off the landing area. Erich Sommer himself once noted for late 20th-century television that the landing skid-equipped prototypes, when touching down on a wet-turf airstrip, had a landing run characteristic that "was like greased lightning" and "like soap", from the complete lack of braking capability of the landing skid system.

**The Landkreuzer P 1500 was one of the largest man-made vehicles ever proposed. With a proposed length of 150 feet, this mobile artillery barrage would have been able to reduce to a pile of rubbles.**

**Landkreuzer P 1500**

On 23 June 1942 the German Ministry of Armaments proposed a 1,000-tonne tank — the Landkreuzer P. 1000 Ratte. Adolf Hitler expressed interest in the project and the go-ahead was granted. In December, Krupp designed an even larger 1,500 tonne vehicle — the P. 1500 Monster. The P. 1500 was to be 25 m (82 ft) long, weighing 1800 tonnes, with a 250 mm hull front armor, four Daimler-Benz MB.501 diesel aero engines, and an operating crew of over 100 men. This "land cruiser" would have been a self-propelled platform for the 800mm Dora/Schwerer Gustav K (E) gun artillery piece also made by Krupp – the heaviest artillery weapon ever constructed by shell weight and total gun weight, and the largest rifled cannon by calibre.

The Schwerer Gustav fired a 7-tonne projectile up to 37 km (23 mi) and was designed for use against heavily fortified targets. The main armament could have been mounted without a rotating turret. Such a configuration would have allowed the P. 1500 to operate in a similar manner to the original 800mm railroad gun and Karl 600mm self-propelled mortars, launching shells without engaging the enemy with direct fire.

**The Kugelpanzer**

**Kugelpanzer**

The one wheel tank was a huge tank that was initially designed to destroy everything around it. It had to be operated by three people who would be placed inside the ball. The main issue with this was that the guys inside had no idea where the ball tank was going. The idea was the one wheel tank was finally laid to rest after the German built only the prototype.

**Messerschmitt Me-163**

## Messerschmitt Me-163

The Messerschmitt Me 163 Komet is a German interceptor aircraft designed for point-defence that is the only rocket-powered fighter aircraft ever to have been operational and the first piloted aircraft of any type to exceed 1000 km/h (621 mph) in level flight. Designed by Alexander Lippisch, its performance and aspects of its design were unprecedented. German test pilot Heini Dittmar in early July 1944 reached 1,130 km/h (700 mph), an unofficial flight airspeed record unmatched by turbojet-powered aircraft for almost a decade.

Over 300 Komets were built, but the aircraft proved lackluster in its dedicated role as an interceptor and destroyed between 9 and 18 Allied aircraft against 10 losses. Aside from combat losses, many pilots were killed during testing and training, at least in part due to the highly volatile and corrosive nature of the rocket propellant used in later models of the aircraft. This includes one pilot by the name of Oberleutnant Josef Pohs, who was dissolved by the rocket fuel following an incident that resulted in a ruptured fuel line.

Work on the design started around 1937 under the aegis of the Deutsche Forschungsanstalt für Segelflug (DFS)—the German Institute for the study of sailplane flight. Their first design was a conversion of the earlier Lippisch Delta IV known as the DFS 39 and used purely as a glider testbed of the airframe. A larger follow-on version with a small propeller engine started as the DFS 194. This version used wingtip-mounted rudders that Lippisch felt would cause problems at high speed. Lippisch changed the system of vertical stabilization for the DFS 194's airframe from the earlier DFS 39's wingtip rudders, to a conventional vertical stabilizer at the rear of the aircraft. The design included a number of features from its origins as a glider, notably a skid used for landings, which could be retracted into the aircraft's keel in flight. For takeoff, a pair of wheels, each mounted onto the ends of a specially designed cross-axle, were needed due to the weight of the fuel, but the wheels, forming a takeoff dolly under the landing skid, were released shortly after takeoff.

The initial test deployment of the Me 163A, to acquaint prospective pilots with the world's first rocket-powered fighter, occurred with Erprobungskommando 16 (Service Test Unit 16, EK 16), led by Major Wolfgang Späte and first established in late 1942, receiving their eight A-model service test aircraft by July 1943. Their initial base was as the Erprobungsstelle (test facility) at the Peenemünde-West field. They departed permanently the day after an RAF bombing raid on the area on 17 August 1943, moving southwards, to the base at Anklam, near the Baltic coast. Their stay was brief, as a few weeks later they were placed in northwest Germany, based at the military airfield at Bad Zwischenahn from August 1943 to August 1944. EK 16 received their first B-series armed Komets in January 1944, and was ready for action by May while at Bad Zwischenahn. Major Späte flew the first-ever Me 163B combat sortie on 13 May 1944 from the Bad Zwischenahn base, with the Me 163B armed prototype (V41), bearing the Stammkennzeichen PK+QL.

As EK 16 commenced small-scale combat operations with the Me 163B in May 1944, the Me 163B's unsurpassed velocity was something Allied fighter pilots were at a loss to counter. The Komets attacked singly or in pairs, often even faster than the intercepting fighters could dive. A typical Me 163 tactic was to fly vertically upward through the bombers at 9,000 m (30,000 ft), climb to 10,700–12,000 m (35,100–39,400 ft), then dive through the formation again, firing as they went. This approach afforded the pilot two brief chances to fire a few rounds from his cannons before gliding back to his airfield. The pilots reported it was possible to make four passes on a bomber, but only if it was flying alone.

Glider pilots were the preferred trainees, using the Stümmelhabicht, with a 6 metres (20 ft) wingspan, to mimic the ME 163 handling characteristics. Training included gunnery practice with a machine pistol mounted in the glider nose. As the cockpit was unpressurized, the operational ceiling was limited by what the pilot could endure for several minutes while breathing oxygen from a mask, without losing consciousness. Pilots underwent altitude chamber training to harden them against the rigors of operating in the thin air of the stratosphere without a pressure suit. Special low fiber diets were prepared for pilots, as gas in the gastrointestinal tract would expand rapidly during ascent.

Following the initial combat trial missions of the Me 163B with EK 16, during the winter and spring of 1944 Major Späte formed the Luftwaffe's first dedicated Me 163 fighter wing, Jagdgeschwader 400 (JG 400), in Brandis, near Leipzig. JG 400's purpose was to provide additional protection for the Leuna synthetic gasoline works which were raided frequently during almost all of 1944. A further group was stationed at Stargard near Stettin to protect the large synthetic fuel plant at Pölitz (today Police, Poland). Further defensive units of rocket fighters were planned for Berlin, the Ruhr and the German Bight.

The first actions involving the Me 163B in regular Luftwaffe active service occurred on 28 July 1944, from I./JG 400's base at Brandis, when two USAAF B-17 Flying Fortress were attacked without confirmed kills. Combat operations continued from May 1944 to spring 1945. During this time, there were nine confirmed kills with 10 Me 163s lost. Feldwebel Siegfried Schubert was the most successful pilot, with three bombers to his credit. Allied fighter pilots soon noted the short duration of the powered flight. They would wait and, when the engine exhausted its propellant, pounce on the unpowered Komet. However, the Komet was extremely manoeuvrable in gliding flight. Another Allied method was to attack the fields the Komets operated from and strafe them after the Me 163s landed. Due to the skid-based landing gear system, the Komet was immobile until the Scheuch-Schlepper tractor could back the trailer up to the nose of the aircraft, place its two rear arms under the wing panels, and jack up the trailer's arms to hoist the aircraft off the ground or place it back on its take-off dolly to tow it back to its maintenance area.

At the end of 1944, 91 aircraft had been delivered to JG 400 but lack of fuel had kept most of them grounded. It was clear that the original plan for a huge network of Me 163 bases would never be realized. Up to that point, JG 400 had lost only six aircraft due to enemy action. Nine were lost to other causes, remarkably few for such a revolutionary and technically advanced aircraft. In the last days of the Third Reich, the Me 163 was given up in favor of the more successful Me 262. At the beginning of May 1945, Me 163 operations were stopped, the JG 400 disbanded, and many of its pilots sent to fly Me 262s.

In any operational sense, the Komet was a failure. Although it shot down 16 aircraft, mainly four-engined bombers, it did not warrant the effort put into the project. Due to fuel shortages late in the war, few went into combat, and it took an experienced pilot with excellent shooting skills to achieve "kills". The Komet also spawned later weapons like the vertical-launch, similarly rocket-powered Bachem Ba 349 Natter, and the postwar, American turbojet-powered Convair XF-92 delta wing interceptor.

The Heinkel He-162 "Volksjaeger", propelled by a turbo-jet unit mounted above the fuselage

Underground facility located in Hinterbrühl, Austria and produced 40-50 He 162s per month.

**Heinkel He-162**

The turning point of the war for Germany was the defeat at Stalingrad in Russia and El Alamein in Egypt. From thereon, the Luftwaffe strained under the onslaught of the Allied air forces. No longer could Messerschmitt bf 109s and Focke-Wulf 190s strike with impunity at Allied bombers formations as they flew deep into Germany. As the war progressed, escort fighters such as the P-51 Mustang and P-47 Thunderbolt could now escort bombers all the way into Germany. By January 1943, the Luftwaffe's operational strength was down to less than 4,000 aircraft and these were scattered along the Western, Mediterranean and Russian fronts.

This limited the Luftwaffe's ability to stop the large Allied bombing raids on Germany which took its toll on armament, aircraft and particularly oil production facilities, bringing the once mighty Third Reich to its knees.

With the Third Reich crumbling from the barrage of Allied attacks, Albert Speer in a desperate effort, proposed building something new. The German Ministry of Aviation (Reichsluftfahrtministerium, or RLM) issued a proposal on September 8, 1944 to build a huge fleet of fast, agile, single-engine jet fighters. Scarce resources were already allocated to aircraft currently in production and aluminum and advanced alloys were in short supply. This required construction to be of nonstrategic materials, such as wood and steel, using semi-killed labor. Other requirements were:

- Endurance of not less than 30 minutes.
- Takeoff distance within 500 m (1,640 ft.)
- Armament to consist of two Mk 108 30 mm cannons.
- Wing loading of not more than 200 kg/m2 (40 lbs/ft2.)
- The gross weight could be not more than 2,000 kg (4,400 lbs.)
- The top speed required was 750 km/hr (466 mph) at sea level.
- The airplane had to be ready for flight testing by December 1, 1944.
- The airplane had to be ready for production by January 1, 1945.3

Seven top firms that included Arado, Blohm & Voss, Fieseler, Focke-Wulf, Junkers, Heinkel and Messerschmitt were asked to view the proposal. Messerschmitt declined as they were already concentrating their efforts on the Me 262. Blohm & Voss submitted a plan to build the P.211, a jet fighter with a nose air intake and engine buried in the fuselage. Heinkel, who had built the world's first jet aircraft, the He 178 and He 280, submitted a proposal to build the P.1073 which had already been envisioned by its special branch director, Siegfried Günter. The P.1073 had a tubular frame fuselage and wings, twin rudders and a retractable landing gear. It would be powered by the BMW 003 axial-flow turbojet engine placed in a nacelle on top of the fuselage or below the cockpit.

The Blohm & Voss P.211 was preferred, because its engine didn't block the pilot's view to the rear, however, it was not accepted because of the complexity and time required to construct it. Time was running out for the hard-pressed Luftwaffe and in the end, Heinkel's proposal was accepted. It required fewer man-hours to build and had the best chance of meeting the required delivery dates.

The BMW 003 was a very troublesome engine when it first appeared and was installed on a Messerschmitt Me 262 prototype. Both engines failed during the test hop, but the plane managed to make it back to the airport powered by a backup piston-engine. The 003 suffered from the same problems as the Jumo 004, but after further development, the engine was finally ready for production. (After the war, the Russians reversed engineered the BMW 003 and developed it as the RD-20. The RD-20 powered the MiG-9, but the engine remained unreliable due to persistent flameouts.)

Heinkel redesigned the P.1073 to fit the RLM's needs and the contract was awarded to Heinkel on October 19, 1944. Although Ernst Heinkel named the plane the Spatz for Sparrow, the He 162 was mostly known as the Salamander, because of the creature's mythical ability to live through fire. The prototype He-162 V1 emerged in 74 days and weighed 6,180 lbs., fully loaded. One third of the weight of the aircraft was wood for the airframe, wings, landing gear doors and nose cone. It had a high mounted wing straight wing with a forward swept trailing edge and a slight dihedral. Twin vertical stabilizers were installed with a high dihedral horizontal stabilizer placed to clear the jet exhaust.

The flap system and landing gear were powered hydraulically from an engine-driven pump. The tricycle landing gear retracted into the fuselage (using Bf-109 main landing gear to simplify production) and was then lowered by springs compressed during retraction.6. It was also the first aircraft equipped with an ejection-seat as standard equipment. It was powered by an explosive cartridge that allowed the pilot to get clear the engine intake that was just aft of the cockpit.

The first prototype was flown on December 6, 1944 and reached a top speed of 522 mph. The aircraft handled well except for some longitudinal stability problems. The flight ended when one of the wooden main gear doors separated from the aircraft, due to defective bonding of the plywood. Four days later, the aircraft crashed after the wooden leading edge of the right wing delaminated, killing Heinkel's chief test pilot, Flugkapitan Gotthard Peter. The wing failure was a result of defective bonding after the Goldschmitt Tego-Film factory was bombed and an alternative bonding agent was used. As it turned out the new bonding method was too acidic causing the wooden structure to deteriorate. Despite the crash, the He 162 program continued.
To correct longitudinal stability, Dr. Alexander Lippisch suggested adding small downward turning winglets on the wing tips. This corrected the problem and the winglets became known as Lippisch Ohren or Lippisch Ears. Other changes included:

- The wing root trailing edges were turned downward to prevent tip stalling.
- Lead ballast was added in the nose rather than lengthening the fuselage to move the center of gravity forward.
- Small stall strips on the inboard leading edges were installed to improve stability and slow-speed handling.

Production aircraft were the He-162A-1 armed with a Mk 108 30 mm cannon and the He-162A-2 armed with a MG 151 20 mm cannon. Only a few A-1s were built because the nose structure was to light to handle the recoil of the 30 mm cannons.

The plane was to be flown by new pilots of the Hitler Youth, but as it turned out the plane was difficult to fly, requiring experienced pilots. Adolf Galland was opposed the Volksjager (Peoples' Fighter) project, on the grounds that it would drain valuable resources for the Me-262 and would be a death trap in inexperienced hands. However, Galland was overruled by Goering and Speer.

Because of the extreme shortage of qualified pilots, only two fighter units, I./JG 1 and II./JG 1 managed to convert to the type before the end of hostilities. During February, 1945, 1st Gruppe of Jagdgeschwader 1 traded their Fw-190s for He-162s. By April, they had transferred to Leck, near the Danish border, where they continued to learn to operate the new fighter. The first claimed victory by an He-162 was on April 19, 1945. Feldwebel Kirchner was credited with shooting down a British aircraft, but he crashed before he could return to base. On April 20, Leutnant Rudolf Schmitt became the first and possibly only pilot to use the jet's ejection seat and survive. Ten days later, Unteroffizier Rechenbach was credited with a British aircraft and confirmed. In early May, Schmitt made the only confirmed kill by an He 162, shooting down a Hawker Tempest flown by Flight Officer M. Austin.

The He-162's small fuel load and the engine's high fuel consumption gave it an endurance of around 30 minutes at sea level. It was said that it had good handling qualities and an excellent roll rate, but was a difficult to handle at low airspeeds. Overenthusiastic use of the rudders to increase the jet's already excellent roll rate could cause the tail section to fail, which is what happened to an unfortunate RAF test pilot during a post-war demonstration.

In the traffic pattern, the throttle could not be reduced to idle until landing was assured. Once at idle, the engine took more than 20 seconds to spool up to full power (if it didn't flame out) when the throttle was pushed up to initiate a go-around. The also jet had a bad tendency to settle as the flaps came up.

Royal Navy test pilot Captain Eric Brown found the He-162 to be a very unforgiving airplane, but a very stable gun platform. The view from the cockpit was excellent, except for the critical six o'clock position, which was blocked by the engine. In Brown's opinion, had the Luftwaffe been able to take the time to fully develop the He 162 with fully-trained pilots in the cockpits, the world's first operational single-engine jet fighter would have become a very formidable opponent.

Like every other early jet aircraft, the He 162 was underpowered, but it had the worst safety record of all the early jet aircraft. This was in part to its being rushed into production, before the prototypes were completed. It's been said that the He 162 inflicted more casualties on German pilots than the enemy. Of the 65 factory pilots assigned to He 162s, only five were left at the end of the war. None were lost to combat—they died or crashed during ferry flights or learning to fly them.

The top speed of the He 162 A-2 was 553 mph at sea level, and 562 mph at 19,500 ft. making it the fastest jet aircraft of the war. Its loaded weight was 6,180 lbs. A total of 116 He 162s were completed, and an additional 800 were in various stages of completion,14 but the actual amount of aircraft produced varies depending on the source. Only seven He-162s survived the war.

**Kamikaze-style version of the V1 rocket which included a small cockpit so it could be flown accurately. Only 150 of them were made**

**The pilot has to bail out of the rocket at the last moment but it was ultimately a suicide mission as the airspeed would have been 550mph**

## Kamikaze-style version of the V1 rocket

**Kamikaze-style version of the V1 rocket** was the secret weapon which Hitler hoped would help destroy London during World War II. Although 5,000 V1 rockets were launched by the Germans from France and Holland to bomb London, this is a rare Kamikaze-style version.

Because the target of the V-1 was so random, the bombs dropped when they ran out of fuel, 150 of them were modified with a small cockpit so they could be flown accurately into targets.This was a high-risk move, the pilot was meant to bail out of the rocket at the last moment but it was ultimately a suicide mission as the airspeed would have been 550mph.

Due to the lack of airmen willing to volunteer with the exception of a few Hitler fanatics.The Germans dropped the idea in the end, largely because airmen realised it was a suicide mission. The rocket is 28ft long, has a wingspan of 22ft and is fitted with an Argus 109-014 pulse jet engine.

**The Natter ("Grass Snake")**

**Natter's Wooden Frame**

**Building Natter's Wooden Frame**

**Natter's Launching Pad**

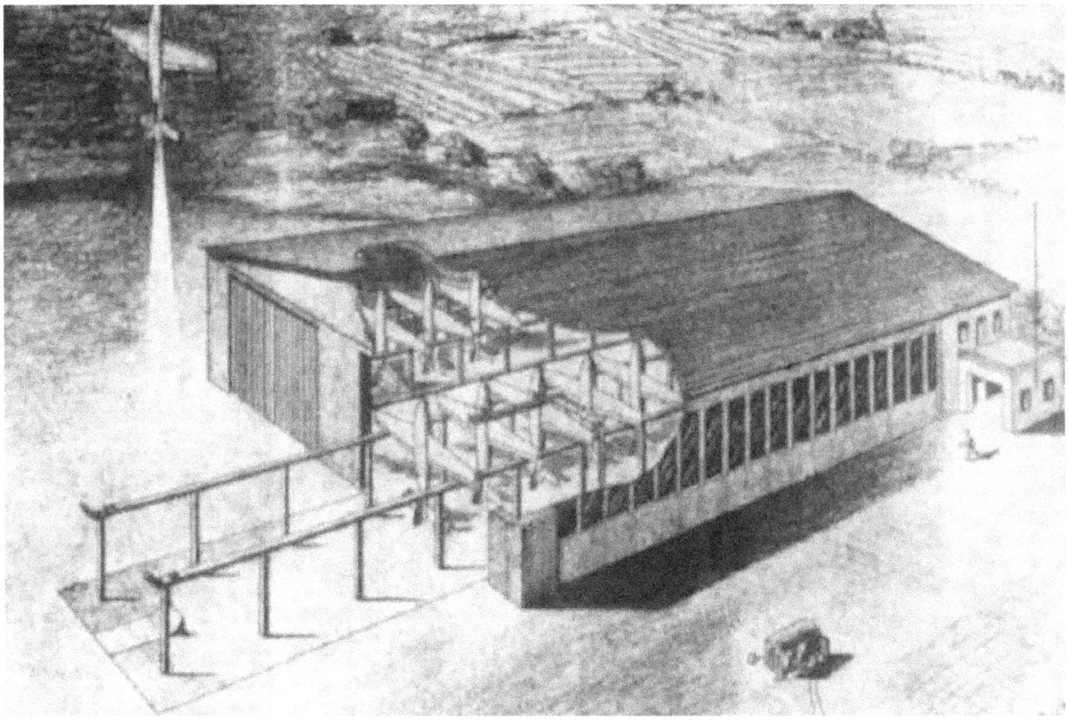

**Natter's Launching Bunker**

**The Natter Soaring Through the Sky**

**Natter is preparing for launching.**

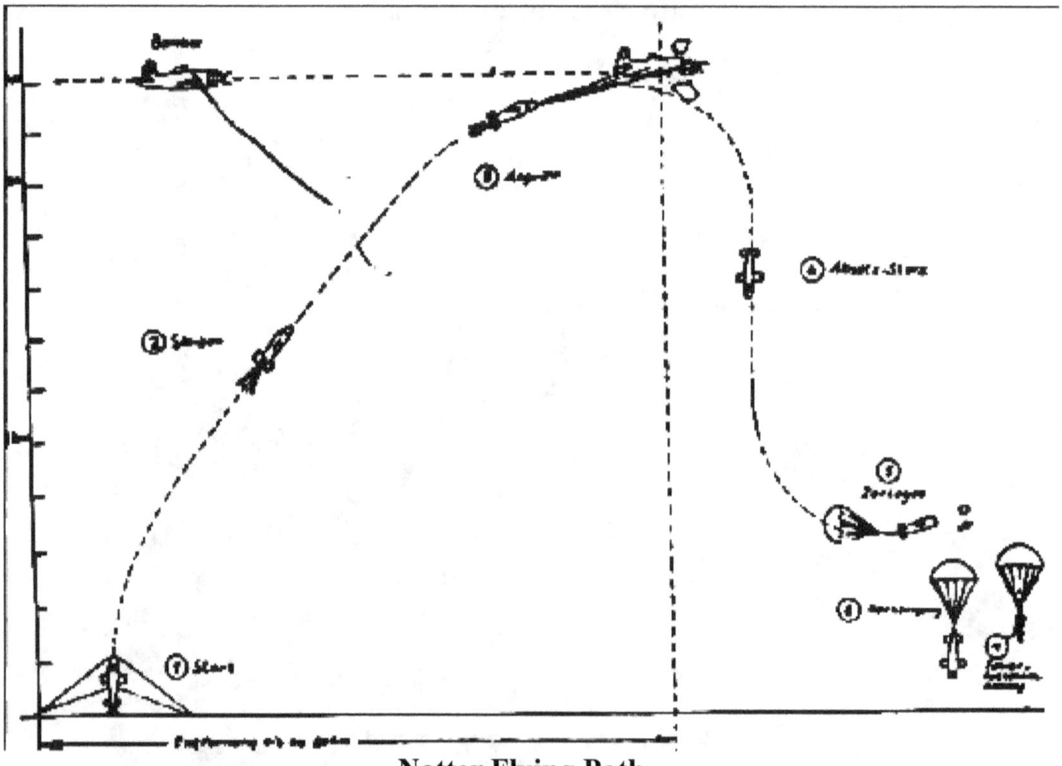

**Natter Flying Path**

## Bachem Ba 349 Natter

The **Bachem Ba 349 Natter** (English: Colubrid, grass-snake was a World War II German point-defence rocket-powered interceptor, which was to be used in a very similar way to a manned surface-to-air missile. After a vertical take-off, which eliminated the need for airfields, most of the flight to the Allied bombers was to be controlled by an autopilot. The primary role of the relatively untrained pilot was to aim the aircraft at its target bomber and fire its armament of rockets. The pilot and the fuselage containing the rocket motor would then land using separate parachutes, while the nose section was disposable.

In 1943 Luftwaffe air superiority was being challenged by the Allies over the Reich and radical innovations were required to overcome the crisis. Surface-to-air missiles appeared to be a promising approach to counter the Allied strategic bombing offensive; a variety of projects were started, but invariably problems with the guidance and homing systems prevented any of these from attaining operational status. Providing the missile with a pilot, who could operate a weapon during the brief terminal approach phase, offered a solution.

Submissions for a simple target defence interceptor were requested by the Luftwaffe in early 1944 under the umbrella of the German: Jägernotprogramm, literally "Fighter Emergency Program". A number of simple designs were proposed, including the Heinkel P.1077 Julia, in which the pilot lay prone (on his stomach), to reduce the frontal area.

The Julia was the front-runner for the contract. The initial plan was to launch the aircraft vertically, but this concept was later changed to a conventional horizontal take-off from a tricycle-wheeled trolley, similar to that used by the first eight prototypes of the Arado Ar 234 jet reconnaissance bomber.

Erich Bachem's BP-20 ("Natter") was a development from a design he had worked on at Fieseler, the Fi 166 concept, but considerably more radical than the other submissions. It was built using glued and nailed wooden parts with an armour-plated bulkhead and bulletproof glass windshield at the front of the cockpit. The initial plan was to power the machinc with a Walter HWK 109-509A-2 rocket motor; however, only the 109-509A-1, as used in the Me 163, was available.It had a sea level thrust variable between 100 kg (220 lb) at "idle" to 1,600 kg (3,500 lb) at full power, with the Natter's intended quartet of rear flank-mount Schmidding SG34 solid fuel rocket boosters used in its vertical launch to provide an additional 4,800 kg (10,600 lb) thrust for 10 seconds before they burned out and were jettisoned. The experimental prototypes slid up a 20 m (66 ft)-tall vertical steel launch tower for a maximum sliding length of 17 m (56 ft) in three guideways, one for each wing tip and one for the lower tip of the ventral tail fin. By the time the aircraft left the tower it was hoped that it would have achieved sufficient speed to allow its aerodynamic surfaces to provide stable flight.

Under operational conditions, once the Natter had left the launcher, it would be guided to the proximity of the Allied bombers by an autopilot with the possibility of an added beam guidance similar to that used in some V-2 rocket launches. Only then would the pilot take control, aim and fire the armament, which was originally proposed to be a salvo of nineteen 55mm R4M rockets.Later, 28 R4Ms or a number of the larger, 73mm Henschel Hs 297 Föhn rockets were suggested,with either variety of unguided rocket fired from the Natter's nose-mounted cellular launch tubes. The Natter was intended to fly up and over the bombers, by which time its Walter motor would probably be out of propellant. Following its one-time attack with its rockets, the pilot would dive his Natter, now effectively a glider, to an altitude of around 3,000 m (9,800 ft), flatten out, release the nose of the aircraft and a small braking parachute from the rear fuselage. The fuselage would decelerate and the pilot would be ejected forwards by his own inertia and land by means of a personal parachute.

In an early proposal in August 1944, the Natter design had a concrete nose; it was suggested that the machine might ram a bomber, but this proposal was subsequently withdrawn in later Project Natter outlines. Bachem stated clearly in the initial proposal that the Natter was not a suicide weapon and much effort went into designing safety features for the pilot. However, owing to the potential dangers for the pilot inherent in the operation of this precarious aircraft, the Natter is sometimes listed as a suicide craft. The design had one decisive advantage over its competitors – it eliminated the necessity to land an unpowered gliding machine at an airbase, which, as the history of the Me 163 rocket aircraft had clearly demonstrated, made an aircraft extremely vulnerable to attack by Allied fighters.

Heinrich Himmler became interested in Bachem's design. The Reichsführer-SS granted Bachem an interview and fully supported the project. In the middle of September 1944 the Technical Office of the Waffen-SS made an order for Bachem to develop and manufacture the Natter at his Waldsee factory. In December 1944 the project came largely under the control of the SS and Hans Kammler. This decision is said to have been the only time the SS significantly interfered with aircraft design and air fighting strategy. Early-on in the project, the Reichsluftfahrtministerium (RLM) undertook an engineering assessment of the Natter, which it reported on 28 October 1944.

The Natter was designed to be built by unskilled labor with poor-quality tools and inexpensive material. Various stringent economies were imposed on an already frugal design. The Natter had no landing gear, which saved weight, expense and construction time. Consequently, one of the most unusual features of the machine was the escape of the pilot and recovery of the machine.

The proposed sequence of these events was as follows: After the attack, the Natter might dive to a lower altitude and flatten out into level flight. The pilot would then proceed with a well-practised escape sequence. He would open the cockpit canopy latch, which would allow the canopy to flick backwards on its hinge in the airstream. Next, the pilot would undo his seat belt and remove his feet from the rudder pedal stirrups. By squeezing a lever mounted on the control column, he would release a lock at the base of the column, which would allow him to tilt the column forwards where it could engage in and undo a safety latch for the nose release mechanism. He would then lean a little further forward and pull a lever hinged near the floor at the front of the cockpit, freeing the nose section, which self-jettisoned as a result of the reduced aerodynamic pressure at the front of the fuselage.

As the nose section separated, it was intended to briefly pull on two cables that released a small ribbon parachute stored on the starboard side of the rear fuselage. The parachute subsequently opened and decelerated the Natter. The pilot would be ejected from the cockpit by his own inertia and as soon as he was clear of the fuselage, he would open his personal parachute and descend to the ground.

A parachute was to eject the valuable Walter rocket motor from the rear, which would decelerate the aircraft and eject the pilot with inertia, but associated problems were still not fully resolved prior to the war's end.

Professor Wilhelm Fuchs reportedly calculated the Natter's aerodynamics at the Technische Hochschule, Aachen using a large analog computer. Wind tunnel testing on a wooden model, scaled to 40% of full size, was performed at the Deutsche Versuchsanstalt für Luftfahrt (DVL), the Institute for Aerodynamics at Berlin-Adlershof in September 1944 at speeds up to 504 km/h. Results from these tests were reported in January 1945 to the Bachem-Werk. Further model tests were carried out at the Luftfahrtforschungsanstalt Hermann Göring (LFA) facility in Völkenrode-Braunschweig, at speeds close to Mach 1.In March the Bachem-Werk simply received a statement that satisfactory flying qualities should be expected with speeds up to 1,100 km/h.

Construction of the first experimental prototype Natter, Versuchsmuster 1, was completed on 4 October 1944. V1 was subsequently referred to as Baumuster1 BM1) and later still the "B" was dropped and the machine became known as the M1. Most subsequent prototypes were known by 'M' codes, as the later prototypes of the Heinkel He 162 were. Manned glider flights began on 3 November 1944. The first glider M1 was towed to around 3,000 m by a Heinkel He 111 bomber with a cable (Tragschlepp mode) at Neuburg an der Donau. The pilot was Erich Klöckner, who made all four documented Tragschlepp ("towed") flights.

After carrying out the test programme of the M1, he bailed out and the machine crashed into the ground. It was found that the towing cable, and in the case of the M3, the undercarriage interfered with the flight characteristics of the gliders and consequently the results were difficult to interpret. To clear any lingering doubts about the Natter in the glider mode, Hans Zübert made a daring free flight in the M8 on 14 February, and showed that the Natter was indeed a very good flying machine.

The vertical take-off trials were conducted on high ground called the Ochsenkopf at the Truppenübungsplatz (military training area) Heuberg near Stetten am kalten Markt, Württemberg. The first successful unmanned vertical take-off from the experimental launch tower occurred on 22 December 1944. The test machine, the M16, was powered only by the Schmidding solid boosters, as were all the early vertical launch trials. Up to and including 1 March 1945, 16 prototypes had been used, eight in glider trials and eight in VTO trials.

By January 1945 Bachem was under pressure from the authorities in Berlin to carry out a manned flight by the end of February. On 25 February, M22 was in the experimental launch tower. It was as complete an operational machine as possible with the Walter HWK 109-509 A1 motor installed for the first time. A dummy pilot was in the cockpit. Lift-off from the tower was perfect. The engineers and ground crew watched as the M22 ascended under the combined power of the four Schmidding boosters and the Walter motor, an estimated total thrust of 6,500 kg (14,300 lb). The nose separated as programmed and the dummy pilot descended safely under its personal parachute. The remainder of the fuselage came down under its two large salvage parachutes, but when it hit the ground the Walter liquid-propellant rocket motor's residual hypergolic propellants (T-Stoff oxidizer and C-Stoff fuel) exploded and the machine was destroyed.

Despite Bachem's concerns that the test programme had been significantly cut short, a young volunteer Luftwaffe test pilot, Lothar Sieber, climbed into the cockpit of the fully fuelled M23 on 1 March. The aircraft was equipped with an FM transmitter for the purpose of transmitting flight data from various monitoring sensors in the machine.

A hard wire intercom appears to have been provided between Sieber and the engineers in the launch bunker using a system similar to that used in the manned glider flights. Around 1100 am, the M23 was ready for take-off. Low stratus clouds lay over the Ocksenkopf. The Walter liquid-fueled rocket motor built up to full thrust and Sieber pushed the button to ignite the four solid boosters. Initially, it rose vertically. at an altitude of about 100 to 150 m (330 to 490 ft), the Natter suddenly pitched up into an inverted curve at about 30° to the vertical. At about 500 m (1,600 ft) the cockpit canopy was seen to fly off. The Natter continued to climb at high speed at an angle of 15° from the horizontal and disappeared into the clouds. The Walter motor stalled about 15 seconds after take-off. It is estimated the Natter reached 1,500 m (4,900 ft), at which point it nose-dived and hit the ground with great force about 32 seconds later, some kilometres from the launch site. Unknown at the time, one of the Schmidding boosters failed to jettison and its remains were dug up at the crash site in 1998.

The pilot was likely unconscious long before the crash. Bachem surmised Sieber had involuntarily pulled back on the control column under the effect of the 3 G acceleration. Examination of the canopy, which fell near the launch site, showed the tip of the latch was bent, suggesting it may not have been in the fully closed position at launch. The pilot's headrest had been attached to the underside of the canopy and as the canopy flew off the pilot's head would have snapped back suddenly about 25 cm (9.8 in), hitting the solid wooden rear upper cockpit bulkhead, and either knocking Sieber unconscious or breaking his neck.

The accident reinforced Bachem's long held belief that the take-off and flight in the vicinity of the target bombers should be fully automated. The canopy latch was strengthened and the headrest was attached to the backboard of the cockpit. Before the introduction of the autopilot in the test programme, the control column would have a temporary locking device on it, which would allow the machine to ascend vertically to at least 1,000 m (3,300 ft) and then be removed by the pilot. The Walter motor probably ceased operation because the Natter was virtually upside-down and air may have entered the intake pipes in the propellant tanks, starving the motor. Sieber had become the first man to take off vertically from the ground under pure rocket power, 16 years before Yuri Gagarin's Vostok 1 pioneering, peacetime orbital flight.

Following Sieber's death, several pilots offered to take his place, and three more manned launches were performed in quick succession. The RLM now decided that the Natter had displayed an acceptable standard of reliability to warrant operational evaluation, and preparations were made for 10 fully armed aircraft at Kirchheim, near Stuttgart.

The SS ordered 150 Natters, and the Luftwaffe ordered 50, but none were delivered by the end of the war. Much debate has surrounded the number of Natters built at the Bachem-Werk and their disposition. According to Bachem, 36 Natters were produced at the Bachem-Werk in Waldsee by the end of the war. Up to April 1945, 17 aircraft had been used in unmanned trials comprising five gliders, all slung under an He 111 in the Mistelschlepp configuration prior to launch, and 12 VTO examples. Five aircraft were prepared for manned trials, four gliders and one VTO version. The M3 was flown twice, and then rebuilt at which time it was given the new code BM3a but was never flown. The total number of launches to early April 1945 was 22, as was the total number of Natters constructed up to that time. Bachem reported further that there were 14 more finished or almost finished aircraft in April 1945. Four of these were prototype A1 operational Natters built for test launching from a wooden pole launcher, which had been designed for field deployment.[This new launcher was also constructed on the Heuberg, not far from the experimental steel tower. There is documentary evidence for two pole launches in April but not three as claimed by Bachem in his post-war presentation. The documentation for this third flight may have been destroyed by the SS at war's end. Ten A1 operational Natters, called K-Maschinen, were constructed for the Krokus-Einsatz ("Operation Crocus").

The fate of these 14 A1 Natters was as follows: Three were fired from the vertical launch tower according to Bachem, four were burnt at Waldsee, two were burnt at Lager Schlatt, Oetztal, Austria, four were captured by US troops at Sankt Leonhard im Pitztal, Austria, and one, which had been sent as a sample model to a new factory in Thuringia, was captured by the Red Army. Consequently, the total of 36 test and operational aircraft constructed at the Bachem-Werk can be accounted for. However, Natter carcasses were used for a variety of ground-based purposes; for example, as a static booster rocket, armament and strength testing and pilot seat position tests. Some fuselages were reused after flight testing; for example, the M5, 6 and 7.

Of the four Natters captured at Sankt Leonhard im Pitztal, two went to the United States. Only one original Natter built in Germany in the Second World War survives in storage at the Paul E. Garber Preservation, Restoration, and Storage Facility in Suitland, Maryland, under the auspices of the Smithsonian Institution. The fate of the other Natter brought to the US is unknown. There is no documentary evidence that a Natter was ever flown from Muroc Field. The tail section of one of the Natters at Sankt Leonhard im Pitztal was broken off while it still rested on its trailer.

In early February 1945 the positions of the centre of gravity for the A1 operational machine during its flight profile were giving the RLM and the SS cause for concern. They wanted these figures to be decided upon for the upcoming construction of the A1 aircraft for Krokus-Einsatz (Operation Crocus), the field deployment of the Natter. The position of the centre of gravity is expressed as a percentage of the chord (distance between the leading and trailing edges) of the main wing. Thus 0% is the leading edge and 100% is the trailing edge. In the manned glider trials the centre of gravity had been varied between 20 and 34%.

At a meeting of engineers held on 8 February, the variations in the centre of gravity expected in the A1 Krokus machine were discussed. At take-off with the weight of the four solid boosters, the centre of gravity would be brought back to 65%, but after releasing these rockets it would move forwards to 22%. The free flight by Zübert on 14 February had showed unequivocally that the little Natter had excellent flying characteristics as a glider. The centre of gravity problem was solved initially by the addition of one-metre-square auxiliary tailfins that were released simultaneously with the jettisoning of the boosters. The Krokus aircraft had vanes that would direct the Walter rocket exhaust gases so as to assist vehicle stabilisation at low speed similar to those used in the V-2 rocket.

French forces had captured Waldsee by 25 April 1945 and presumably took control of the Bachem-Werk. Shortly before the French troops arrived, a group of Bachem-Werk personnel set out for Austria with five A1 Natters on trailers. At Bad Wörishofen, the group waited for another squad retreating from Nabern unter Teck with one completed Natter. Both groups then set out for the Austrian Alps. One group with two Natters ended up at the junction of the river Inn and one of its tributaries, the Ötztaler Ache, at Camp Schlatt. The other group went to St. Leonhard im Pitztal with four aircraft. US troops captured the first group at Camp Schlatt around 4 May and the second group on the following day.

At some time during the project, the Bachem-Werk was ordered to give complete details of the BP-20 Natter to the Japanese, but there was doubt over whether they had received them. They were, however, known to have a general knowledge of the Natter and showed considerable interest in the project.

**DFS-346. An experimental rocket-powered Nazi parasite aircraft**

**The DFS 346**

(Samolyot 346) was a German rocket-powered swept-wing aircraft which began development during World War II in Germany. It was designed by Felix Kracht at the Deutsche Forschungsanstalt für Segelflug (DFS), the "German Institute for Sailplane Flight". A prototype was constructed but did not reach completion before the end of the war. It was taken to the Soviet Union where it was completed, tested and flown (with indifferent success).

The DFS 346 was a parallel project to the DFS 228 high-altitude reconnaissance aircraft, designed under the direction of Felix Kracht and his team at DFS. While the DFS 228 was essentially of conventional sailplane design, the DFS 346 had highly-swept wings and a highly streamlined fuselage that its designers hoped would enable it to break the sound barrier.

Like its stablemate, it also featured a self-contained escape module for the pilot, a feature originally designed for the DFS 54 prior to the war. The pilot was to fly the machine from a prone position, a feature decided from experience with the first DFS 228 prototype. This was mainly because of the smaller cross-sectional area and easier sealing of the pressurized cabin, but it was also known to help with g-force handling.

The 346 design was intended to be air-launched from the back of a large mother ship aircraft for air launch, the carrier aircraft being the Dornier Do 217. After launch, the pilot would fire the 346's Walter 509B/C twin-chamber "cruiser" engine to accelerate to a proposed speed of Mach 2.6 and altitude of 30,500 meters (100,000 ft). This engine had two chambers — the main combustion chamber as used on the earlier HWK 509A motor; but capable of just over two short tons (4,410 lbf) of thrust at full power (more at altitude), and the lower-thrust Marschofen throttleable chamber of either 300 kg (B-version) or 400 kg (C-version) top thrust levels mounted beneath the main chamber. After reaching altitude, the speed could be maintained by short bursts of the lower Marschofen cruise chamber. The question of what form of Walter 109 or 109s is not adequately addressed here.

In an operational use the plane would then glide over England for a photo-reconnaissance run, descending as it flew but still at a high speed. After the run was complete the engine would be briefly turned on again, to raise the altitude for a long low-speed glide back to a base in Germany or northern France.

Since the aircraft was to be of all-metal construction, the DFS lacked the facilities to build it and construction of the prototype was assigned to Siebel Werke located in Halle, where the first windtunnel models and partially built prototype were captured by the advancing Red Army.

On 22 October 1946, the Soviet OKB-2 (Design Bureau 2), under the direction of Hans Rössing and Alexandr Bereznyak, was tasked with continuing its development. The captured DFS 346, now simply called "Samolyot 346" ("Samolyot" - Aircraft) to distance it from its German origins, was completed and tested in TsAGI wind tunnel T-101. Tests revealed some aerodynamic deficiencies which would result in unrecoverable stalls at certain angles of attack. This phenomenon involved a loss of longitudinal stability of the airframe. After the wind tunnel tests, two wing fences were installed on a more advanced, longer version of the DFS-346, the purpose of fences was to interrupt the spanwise movement of airflow that would otherwise bring the boundary-layer breakdown and transition from attached to stalled airflow with loss of lift and increase of drag.

This solution was used on the majority of Soviet planes with swept wings of the 1950s and 1960s. In the meantime, the escape capsule system was tested from a B-25J and proved promising. Despite results from studies showing that the plane would not have been able to pass even Mach 1, orders were given to proceed with construction and further testing.

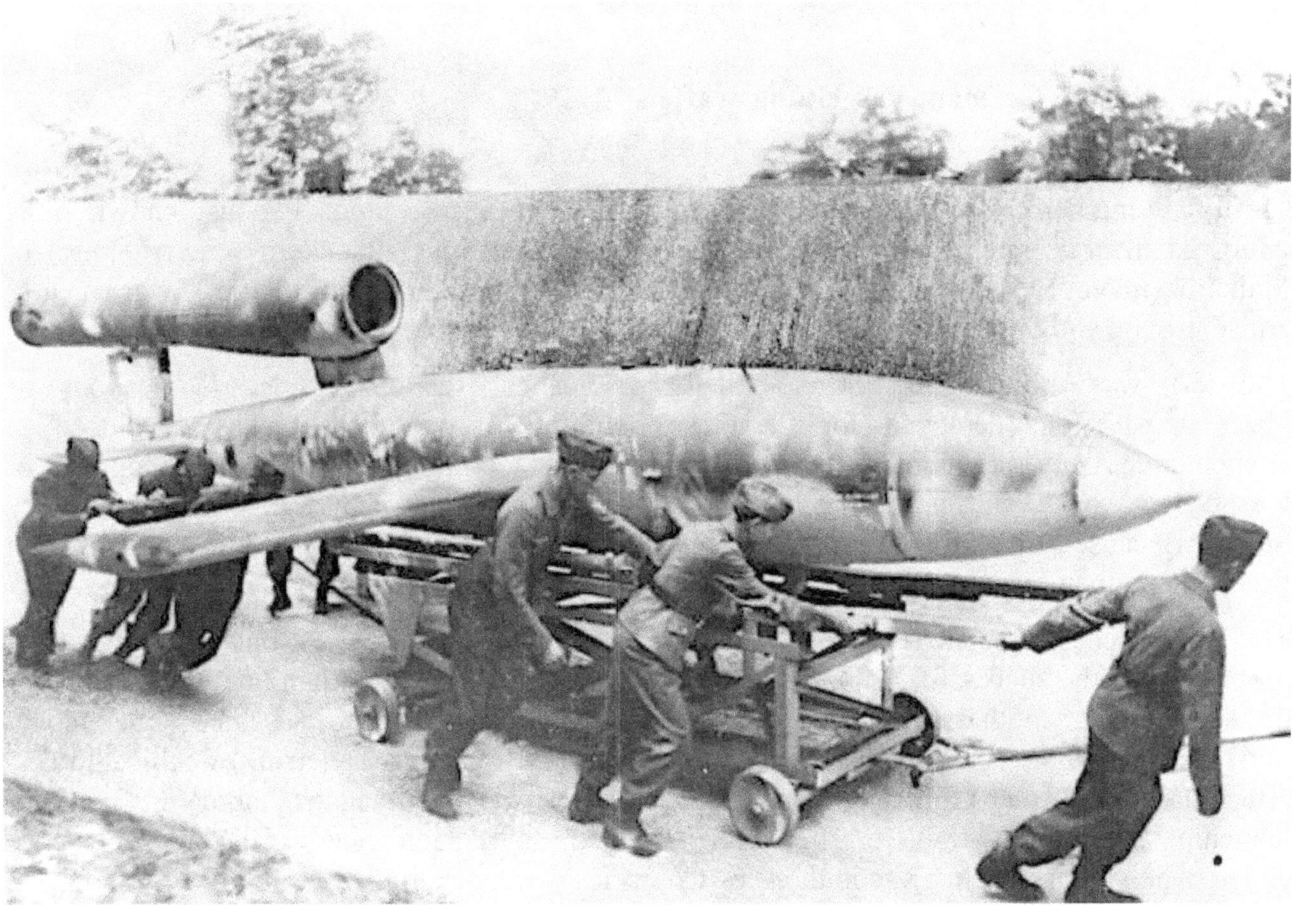

**V-1 flying bomb**

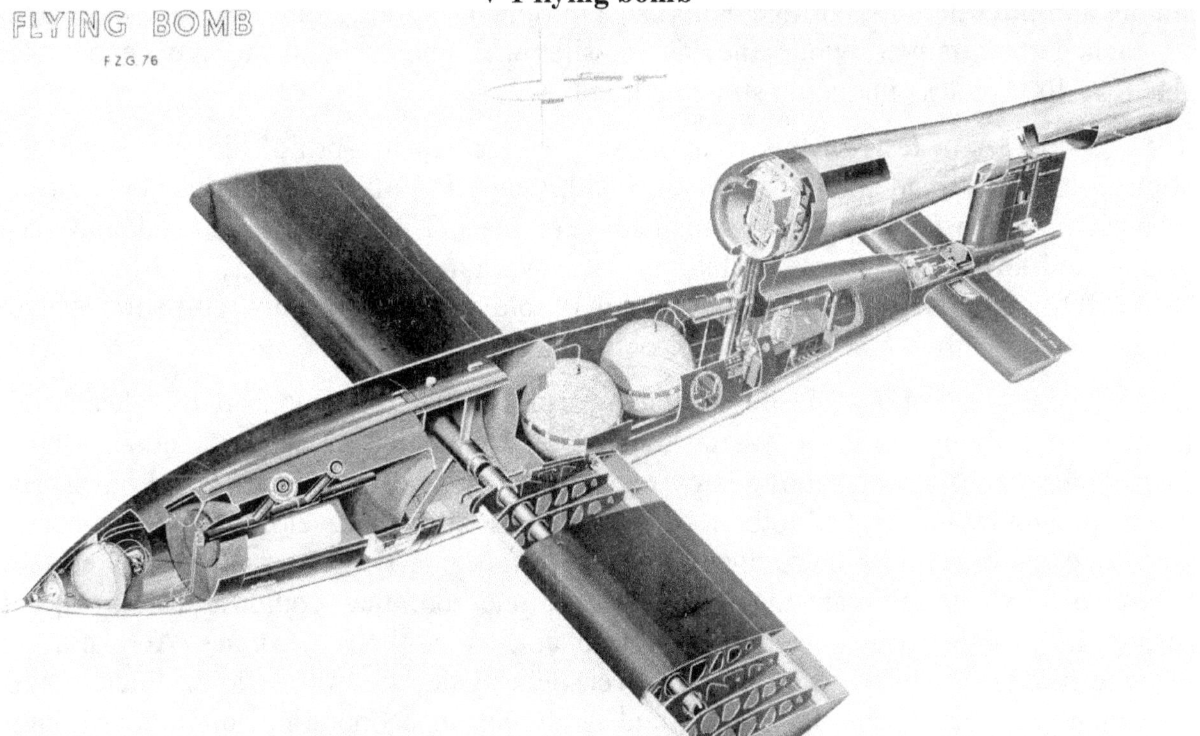

**V-1 flying bomb. German: Vergeltungswaffe 1**

The V-1 flying bomb (German: Vergeltungswaffe 1 "Vengeance Weapon 1"—also known to the Allies as the buzz bomb, or doodlebug, and in Germany as Kirschkern (cherry stone) or Maikäfer (maybug), as well as by its official RLM aircraft designation of Fi 103 —was an early cruise missile and the only production aircraft to use a pulsejet for power.

The V-1 was the first of the so-called "Vengeance weapons" series (V-weapons or Vergeltungswaffen) deployed for the terror bombing of London. It was developed at Peenemünde Army Research Center in 1939 by the Nazi German Luftwaffe at the beginning of the Second World War, and during initial development was known by the codename "Cherry Stone". Because of its limited range, the thousands of V-1 missiles launched into England were fired from launch facilities along the French (Pas-de-Calais) and Dutch coasts.

The Wehrmacht first launched the V-1s against London on 13 June 1944, one week after (and prompted by) the successful Allied landings in France. At peak, more than one hundred V-1s a day were fired at southeast England, 9,521 in total, decreasing in number as sites were overrun until October 1944, when the last V-1 site in range of Britain was overrun by Allied forces. After this, the Germans directed V-1s at the port of Antwerp and at other targets in Belgium, launching a further 2,448 V-1s. The attacks stopped only a month before the war in Europe ended, when the last launch site in the Low Countries was overrun on 29 March 1945.

As part of operations against the V-1, the British operated an arrangement of air defences, including anti-aircraft guns, barrage balloons, and fighter aircraft, to intercept the bombs before they reached their targets, while the launch sites and underground storage depots became targets for Allied attacks including strategic bombing.

In 1944, a number of tests of this weapon were conducted in Tornio, Finland. According to multiple soldiers, a small "plane"-like bomb with wings fell off a German plane. Another V-1 was launched which flew over the Finnish soldiers' lines. The second bomb suddenly stopped its engine and fell steeply down, exploding and leaving a crater around 20 to 30 metres wide. The V-1 flying bomb was referred by Finnish soldiers as a "Flying Torpedo" due to its resemblance to one from afar.

In 1935, Paul Schmidt and Professor Georg Hans Madelung submitted a design to the Luftwaffe for a flying bomb. It was an innovative design that used a jet engine, a pulse-jet engine, while previous work dating back to 1915 by Sperry Gyroscope, relied on propellers. While employed by the Argus Motoren company, Fritz Gosslau developed a remote-controlled target drone, the FZG 43 (Flakzielgerat-43). In October 1939, Argus proposed Fernfeuer, a remote-controlled aircraft carrying a payload of one ton, that could return to base after releasing its bomb. Argus worked in co-operation with C. Lorenz AG and Arado Flugzeugwerke to develop the project. However, once again, the Luftwaffe declined to award a development contract. In 1940, Schmidt and Argus began cooperating, integrating Schmidt's shutter system with Argus' atomized fuel injection. Tests began in January 1941, and the first flight made on 30 April 1941 with a Gotha Go 145. On 27 February 1942, Gosslau and Robert

Lusser sketched out the design of an aircraft with the pulse-jet above the tail, the basis for the future V-1.

Lusser produced a preliminary design in April 1942, P35 Efurt, which used gyroscopes. When submitted to the Luftwaffe on 5 June 1942, the specifications included a range of 299 km (186 miles), a speed of 700 km/h (435 mph), and capable of delivering a half ton warhead. Project Fieseler Fi 103 was approved on 19 June, and assigned code name Kirschkern and cover name Flakzielgerat 76 (FZG-76). Flight tests were conducted at the Luftwaffe's Erprobungsstelle coastal test centre at Karlshagen, Peenemünde-West.

Milch awarded Argus the contract for the engine, Fieseler the airframe, and Askania the guidance system. By 30 August, Fieseler had completed the first fuselage, and the first flight of the Fi 103 V7 took place on 10 December 1942, when it was airdropped by a Fw 200. Then on Christmas Eve, the V-1 flew 910 m (1,000 yards), for about a minute, after a ground launch. On 26 May 1943, Germany decided to put both the V-1 and the V-2 into production. In July 1943, the V-1 flew 245 kilometres and impacted within a kilometre of its target.

The V-1 was named by Das Reich journalist Hans Schwarz Van Berkl in June 1944 with Hitler's approval.

The V-1 was designed under the codename Kirschkern (cherry stone) by Lusser and Gosslau, with a fuselage constructed mainly of welded sheet steel and wings built of plywood. The simple, Argus-built pulsejet engine pulsed 50 times per second, and the characteristic buzzing sound gave rise to the colloquial names "buzz bomb" or "doodlebug" (a common name for a wide variety of flying insects). It was known briefly in Germany (on Hitler's orders) as Maikäfer (May bug) and Krähe (crow).

he Argus pulsejet's major components included the nacelle, fuel jets, flap valve grid, mixing chamber venturi, tail pipe and spark plug. Compressed air forced gasoline, from the 640 liter fuel tank, through the fuel jets, consisting of three banks of atomizers with three nozzles each. Argus' pressurized fuel system negated the need for a fuel pump. These nine atomizing nozzles were in front of the air inlet valve system where it mixed with air before entering the chamber. A throttle valve, connected to altitude and ram pressure instruments, controlled fuel flow. Schmidt's spring-controlled flap valve system provided an efficient straight path for incoming air. The flaps momentarily closed after each explosion, the resultant gas was partially compressed by the venturis, and the tapered tail pipe further compressed the exhaust gases creating thrust. The operation proceeded at a rate of 42 cycles per second.

Beginning in January 1941, the V-1's pulsejet engine was also tested on a variety of craft, including automobiles and an experimental attack boat known as the "Tornado". The unsuccessful prototype was a version of a Sprengboot, in which a boat loaded with explosives was steered towards a target ship and the pilot would leap out of the back at the last moment. The Tornado was assembled from surplus seaplane hulls connected in catamaran fashion with a small pilot cabin on the crossbeams. The Tornado prototype was a noisy underperformer and was abandoned in favour of more conventional piston-engine craft.

The engine made its first flight aboard a Gotha Go 145 on 30 April 1941.

The V-1 guidance system used a simple autopilot developed by Askania in Berlin to regulate altitude and airspeed. A pair of gyroscopes controlled yaw and pitch, while azimuth was maintained by a magnetic compass. Altitude was maintained by a barometric device. Two spherical tanks contained compressed air at 900 pounds per square inch, that drove the gyros, operated the pneumatic servo-motors controlling the rudder and elevator, and pressurized the fuel system.

The magnetic compass was located near the front of the V1, within a wooden sphere. Just before launch, the V1 was suspended inside the Compass Swinging Building (Richthaus). There the compass was corrected for magnetic variance and magnetic deviation.

The RLM at first planned to use a radio control system with the V-1 for precision attacks, but the government decided instead to use the missile against London. Some flying bombs were equipped with a basic radio transmitter operating in the range of 340–450 kHz. Once over the channel, the radio would be switched on by the vane counter, and a 400-foot aerial deployed. A coded Morse signal, unique to each V1 site, transmitted the route, and impact zone once the radio stopped transmitting.

An odometer driven by a vane anemometer on the nose determined when the target area had been reached, accurate enough for area bombing. Before launch, it was set to count backwards from a value that would reach zero upon arrival at the target in the prevailing wind conditions. As the missile flew, the airflow turned the propeller, and every 30 rotations of the propeller counted down one number on the odometer. This odometer triggered the arming of the warhead after about 60 km (37 mi). When the count reached zero, two detonating bolts were fired. Two spoilers on the elevator were released, the linkage between the elevator and servo was jammed, and a guillotine device cut off the control hoses to the rudder servo, setting the rudder in neutral. These actions put the V-1 into a steep dive. While this was originally intended to be a power dive, in practice the dive caused the fuel flow to cease, which stopped the engine. The sudden silence after the buzzing alerted listeners of the impending impact.

Initially, V-1s landed within a circle 31 km (19 miles) in diameter, but by the end of the war, accuracy had been improved to about 11 km (7 miles), which was comparable to the V-2 rocket.

The warhead consisted of 850 kg of Amatol, 52A+ high-grade blast-effective explosive with three fuses. An electrical fuse could be triggered by nose or belly impact. Another fuse was a slow-acting mechanical fuse allowing deeper penetration into the ground, regardless of the altitude. The third fuse was a delayed action fuse, set to go off two hours after launch.

The purpose of the third fuse was to avoid the risk of this secret weapon being examined by the British. It was too short to be any sort of booby trap, but was instead meant to destroy the weapon if a soft landing had not triggered the impact fuses. These fusing systems were very reliable, and there were almost no dud V-1s recovered.

Ground-launched V-1s were propelled up an inclined launch ramp by an apparatus known as a Dampferzeuger ("steam generator"), in which steam was generated when hydrogen peroxide (T-Stoff) was mixed with sodium permanganate (Z-Stoff). Designed by Hellmuth Walter Kommanditgesellschaft, the WR 2.3 Schlitzrohrschleuder consisted of a small gas generator trailer, where the T-Stoff and Z-Stoff combined, generating high-pressure steam that was fed into a tube within the launch rail box. A piston in the tube, connected underneath the missile, was propelled forward by the steam. This enabled the missile to become airborne with a strong enough air-flow allowing the pulse-jet engine to operate. The launch rail was 49 m (160 ft) long, consisting of 8 modular sections 6 m long, and a muzzle brake. Production of the Walter catapult began in January 1944.

The Walter catapult accelerated the V-1 to a launch speed of 200 mph, well above the needed minimum operational speed of 150 mph. The V-1 made British landfall at 340 mph, but accelerated to 400 mph over London, as its 150 gallons of fuel burned off.

On 18 June 1943, Hermann Göring decided on launching the V-1, using the Walter catapult, in both large launch bunkers, called Wasserwerk, and lighter installations, called the Stellungsystem. The Wasserwerk bunker measured 215m long, 36m wide, and 10m high. Four were initially to be built: Wasserwerk Desvres, Wasserwerk St. Pol, Wasserwerk Valognes, and Wasserwerk Cherbourg. Stellungsystem-I was to be operated by Flak Regiment 155(W), with 4 launch battalions, each having 4 launchers, and located in the Pas-de-Calais region. Stellungsystem-II, with 32 sites, was to act as a reserve unit. Stellungsystem-I and II had nine batteries manned by February 1944. Stellungsystem-III, operated by FR 255(W), was to be organized in the spring of 1944, and located between Rouen and Caen. The Stellungsystem locations included distinctive catapult walls pointed towards London, several "J"-shaped stowage buildings referred to as "ski" buildings, and a compass correction building. In the spring of 1944, Oberst Schmalschläger had developed a more simplified launching site, called Einsatz Stellungen. Less conspicuous, 80 launch sites and 16 support sites were located from Calais to Normandy. Each site took only 2 weeks to construct, using 40 men, and the Walter catapult only took 7–8 days to erect, when the time was ready to make it operational.

Once near the launch ramp, the wing spar and wings were attached and the missile was slid off the loading trolley, Zubringerwagen, onto the launch ramp. The ramp catapult was powered by the Dampferzeuger trolley. The pulse-jet engine was started by the Anlassgerät, which provided compressed air for the engine intake,and electrical connection to the engine spark plug, and autopilot. The Bosch spark plug was only needed to start the engine, while residual flame ignited further mixtures of gasoline and air, and the engine would be at full power after 7 seconds. The catapult would then accelerate the bomb above its stall speed of 200 mph, and ensuring sufficient ram air.

Mass production of the FZG-76 did not start until the spring of 1944, and FR 155(W) was not equipped until late May 1944. Operation Eisbär, the missile attacks on London, commenced on 12 June. However, the four launch battalions could only operate from the Pas-de-Calais area, amounting to only 72 launchers. They had been supplied with missiles, Walter catapults, fuel, and other associated equipment since D-Day. None of the 9 missiles launched on the 12th reached England, while only 4 did so on the 13th. The next attempt to start the attack occurred on the night of 15/16 June, when 144 reached England, of which 73 struck London, while 53 struck Portsmouth and Southampton. Damage was widespread and Eisenhower ordered attacks on the V-1 sites as a priority. Operation Cobra forced the retreat from the French launch sites in August, with the last battalion leaving on 29 August. Operation Donnerschlag would begin from Germany on 21 October 1944.

The first complete V-1 airframe was delivered on 30 August 1942, and after the first complete As.109-014 was delivered in September, the first glide test flight was on 28 October 1942 at Peenemünde, from under a Focke-Wulf Fw 200. The first powered trial was on 10 December, launched from beneath an He 111.

The LXV Armeekorps z.b.V. ("65th Army Corps for special deployment) formed during the last days of November 1943 in France commanded by General der Artillerie z.V. Erich Heinemann was responsible for the operational use of V-1.

The conventional launch sites could theoretically launch about 15 V-1s per day, but this rate was difficult to achieve on a consistent basis; the maximum rate achieved was 18. Overall, only about 25% of the V-1s hit their targets, the majority being lost because of a combination of defensive measures, mechanical unreliability or guidance errors. With the capture or destruction of the launch facilities used to attack England, the V-1s were employed in attacks against strategic points in Belgium, primarily the port of Antwerp.

Launches against Britain were met by a variety of countermeasures, including barrage balloons and aircraft such as the Hawker Tempest and newly introduced jet Gloster Meteor. These measures were so successful that by August 1944 about 80% of V-1s were being destroyed (Although the Meteors were fast enough to catch the V-1s, they suffered from frequent cannon failures, and accounted for only 13. In all, about 1,000 V-1s were destroyed by aircraft.

The intended operational altitude was originally set at 2,750 m (9,000 ft). However, repeated failures of a barometric fuel-pressure regulator led to it being changed in May 1944, halving the operational height, thereby bringing V-1s into range of the 40mm Bofors light anti-aircraft guns commonly used by Allied AA.

The trial versions of the V-1 were air-launched. Most operational V-1s were launched from static sites on land, but from July 1944 to January 1945, the Luftwaffe launched approximately 1,176 from modified Heinkel He 111 H-22s of the Luftwaffe's Kampfgeschwader 3 (3rd Bomber Wing, the so-called "Blitz Wing") flying over the North Sea. Apart from the obvious motive of permitting the bombardment campaign to continue after static ground sites on the French coast were lost, air launching gave the Luftwaffe the opportunity to outflank the increasingly effective ground and air defences put up by the British against the missile. To minimise the associated risks (primarily radar detection), the aircrews developed a tactic called "lo-hi-lo": the He 111s would, upon leaving their airbases and crossing the coast, descend to an exceptionally low altitude. When the launch point was neared, the bombers would swiftly ascend, fire their V-1s, and then rapidly descend again to the previous "wave-top" level for the return flight. Research after the war estimated a 40% failure rate of air-launched V-1s, and the He 111s used in this role were vulnerable to night-fighter attack, as the launch lit up the area around the aircraft for several seconds. The combat potential of air-launched V-1s dwindled during 1944 at about the same rate as that of the ground-launched missiles, as the British gradually took the measure of the weapon and developed increasingly effective defence tactics.

Late in the war, several air-launched piloted V-1s, known as Reichenbergs, were built, but these were never used in combat. Hanna Reitsch made some flights in the modified V-1 Fieseler Reichenberg when she was asked to find out why test pilots were unable to land it and had died as a result. She discovered, after simulated landing attempts at high altitude, where there was air space to recover, that the craft had an extremely high stall speed, and the previous pilots with little high-speed experience had attempted their approaches much too slowly. Her recommendation of much higher landing speeds was then introduced in training new Reichenberg volunteer pilots. The Reichenbergs were air-launched rather than fired from a catapult ramp, as erroneously portrayed in the film Operation Crossbow.

There were plans, not put into practice, to use the Arado Ar 234 jet bomber to launch V-1s either by towing them aloft or by launching them from a "piggy back" position (in the manner of the istel, but in reverse) atop the aircraft. In the latter configuration, a pilot-controlled, hydraulically operated dorsal trapeze mechanism would elevate the missile on the trapeze's launch cradle about 8 feet (2.4 m) clear of the 234's upper fuselage. This was necessary to avoid damaging the mother craft's fuselage and tail surfaces when the pulsejet ignited, as well as to ensure a "clean" airflow for the Argus motor's intake. A somewhat less ambitious project undertaken was the adaptation of the missile as a "flying fuel tank" (Deichselschlepp) for the Messerschmitt Me 262 jet fighter, which was initially test-towed behind an He 177A Greif bomber. The pulsejet, internal systems and warhead of the missile were removed, leaving only the wings and basic fuselage, now containing a single large fuel tank. A small cylindrical module, similar in shape to a finless dart, was placed atop the vertical stabiliser at the rear of the tank, acting as a centre of gravity balance and attachment point for a variety of equipment sets. A rigid towbar with a pitch pivot at the forward end connected the flying tank to the Me 262. The operational procedure for this unusual configuration saw the tank resting on a wheeled trolley for take-off. The trolley was dropped once the combination was airborne, and explosive bolts separated the towbar from the fighter upon exhaustion of the tank's fuel supply. A number of test flights were conducted in 1944 with this set-up, but inflight "porpoising" of the tank, with the instability transferred to the fighter, meant that the system was too unreliable to be used. An identical utilisation of the V-1 flying tank for the Ar 234 bomber was also investigated, with the same conclusions reached. Some of the "flying fuel tanks" used in trials utilised a cumbersome fixed and spatted undercarriage arrangement, which (along with being pointless) merely increased the drag and stability problems already inherent in the design.

One variant of the basic Fi 103 design did see operational use. The progressive loss of French launch sites as 1944 proceeded and the area of territory under German control shrank meant that soon the V-1 would lack the range to hit targets in England. Air launching was one alternative utilised, but the most obvious solution was to extend the missile's range. Thus the F-1 version developed. The weapon's fuel tank was increased in size, with a corresponding reduction in the capacity of the warhead. Additionally, the nose cones and wings of the F-1 models were made of wood, affording a considerable weight saving. With these modifications, the V-1 could be fired at London and nearby urban centres from prospective ground sites in the Netherlands. Frantic efforts were made to construct a sufficient number of F-1s in order to allow a large-scale bombardment campaign to coincide with the Ardennes Offensive, but numerous factors (bombing of the factories producing the missiles, shortages of steel and rail transport, the chaotic tactical situation Germany was facing at this point in the war, etc.) delayed the delivery of these long-range V-1s until February/March 1945. Beginning on 2 March 1945, slightly more than three weeks before the V-1 campaign finally ended, several hundred F-1s were launched at Britain from Dutch sites under Operation "Zeppelin". Frustrated by increasing Allied dominance in the air, Germany also employed V-1s to attack the RAF's forward airfields, such as Volkel, in the Netherlands.

There was also a turbojet-propelled upgraded variant proposed, meant to use the Porsche 109-005 low-cost turbojet engine with about 500 kgf (1,100 lbf) thrust.

Almost 30,000 V-1s were made; by March 1944, they were each produced in 350 hours (including 120 for the autopilot), at a cost of just 4% of a V-2, which delivered a comparable payload. Approximately 10,000 were fired at England; 2,419 reached London, killing about 6,184 people and injuring 17,981. The greatest density of hits was received by Croydon, on the south-east fringe of London. Antwerp, Belgium was hit by 2,448 V-1s from October 1944 to March 1945.

By September 1944, the V-1 threat to England was temporarily halted when the launch sites on the French coast were overrun by the advancing Allied armies. In total, 10,492 V1s were launched against Britain, with a nominal aiming point of Tower Bridge. 4,261 V-1s had been destroyed by fighters, anti-aircraft fire and barrage balloons. Approximately 2,400 V-1s landed within Greater London, inflicting 6,000 fatalities and 18,000 serious injuries. The last enemy action of any kind on British soil occurred on 29 March 1945, when a V-1 struck Datchworth in Hertfordshire.

Unlike the V-2, the V-1 was a cost-effective weapon for the Germans as it forced the Allies to spend heavily on defensive measures and divert bombers from other targets. More than 25% of Combined Bomber Offensive's bombs in July and August 1944 were used against V-weapon sites, often ineffectively. In early December 1944, American General Clayton Bissell wrote a paper that argued strongly in favour of the V-1 when compared with conventional bombers.

**V-2 ready for lunch**

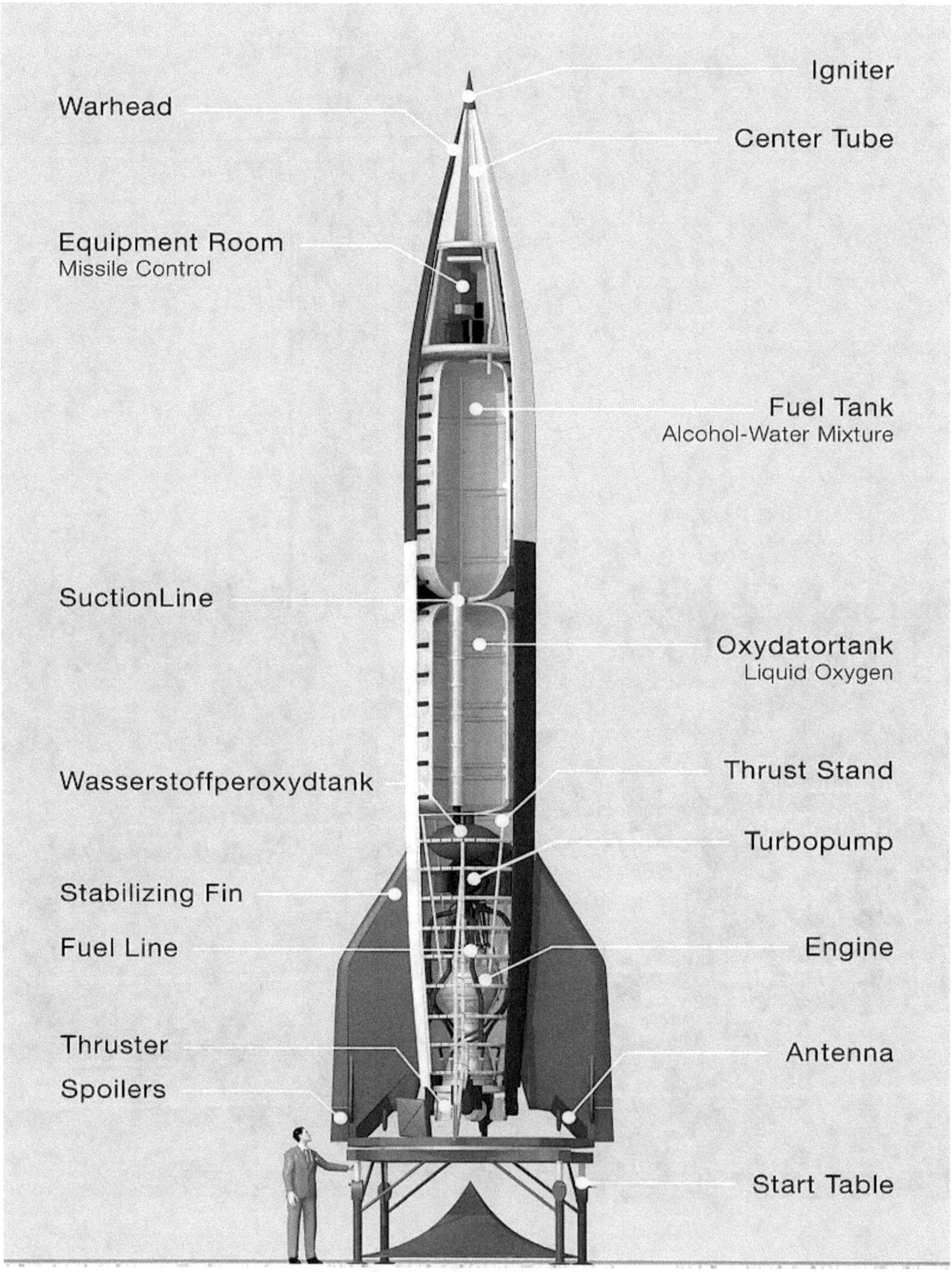


**Layout of a V-2 rocket.**

**The V-2: German: *Vergeltungswaffe 2***

The V-2 (German: Vergeltungswaffe 2, "Retribution Weapon 2"), with the technical name Aggregat 4 (A4), was the world's first long-range guided ballistic missile. The missile, powered by a liquid-propellant rocket engine, was developed during the Second World War in Germany as a "vengeance weapon" and assigned to attack Allied cities as retaliation for the Allied bombings against German cities. The V-2 rocket also became the first artificial object to travel into space by crossing the Kármán line with the vertical launch of MW 18014 on 20 June 1944.

Research into military use of long-range rockets began when the graduate studies of Wernher von Braun attracted the attention of the German Army. A series of prototypes culminated in the A-4, which went to war as the V-2. Beginning in September 1944, over 3,000 V-2s were launched by the German Wehrmacht against Allied targets, first London and later Antwerp and Liège. According to a 2011 BBC documentary, the attacks from V-2s resulted in the deaths of an estimated 9,000 civilians and military personnel, and a further 12,000 forced laborers and concentration camp prisoners died as a result of their forced participation in the production of the weapons.

The rockets travelled at supersonic speed, impacted without audible warning, and proved unstoppable, as no effective defence exist

In the late 1920s, a young Wernher von Braun bought a copy of Hermann Oberth's book, Die Rakete zu den Planetenräumen (The Rocket into Interplanetary Spaces). Starting in 1930, he attended the Technical University of Berlin, where he assisted Oberth in liquid-fueled rocket motor tests. Von Braun was working on his doctorate when the Nazi Party gained power in Germany. An artillery captain, Walter Dornberger, arranged an Ordnance Department research grant for von Braun, who from then on worked next to Dornberger's existing solid-fuel rocket test site at Kummersdorf. Von Braun's thesis, Construction, Theoretical, and Experimental Solution to the Problem of the Liquid Propellant Rocket (dated 16 April 1934), was kept classified by the German Army and was not published until 1960. By the end of 1934, his group had successfully launched two rockets that reached heights of 2.2 and 3.5 km (1.4 and 2.2 mi).

At the time, Germany was highly interested in American physicist Robert H. Goddard's research. Before 1939, German engineers and scientists occasionally contacted Goddard directly with technical questions. Von Braun used Goddard's plans from various journals and incorporated them into the building of the Aggregat (A) series of rockets, named for the German word for mechanism or mechanical system.

Following successes at Kummersdorf with the first two Aggregate series rockets, Wernher von Braun and Walter Riedel began thinking of a much larger rocket in the summer of 1936, based on a projected 25,000 kg (55,000 lb) thrust engine. In addition, Dornberger specified the military requirements needed to include a 1 ton payload, a range of 172 miles with a dispersion of 2 or 3 miles, and transportable using road vehicles.

After the A-4 project was postponed due to unfavourable aerodynamic stability testing of the A-3 in July 1936, von Braun specified the A-4 performance in 1937, and, after an "extensive" series of test firings of the A-5 scale test model, using a motor redesigned from the troublesome A-3 by Walter Thiel, A-4 design and construction was ordered 1938/39. During 28–30 September 1939, Der Tag der Weisheit (English:The Day of Wisdom) conference met at Peenemünde to initiate the funding of university research to solve rocket problems.

By late 1941, the Army Research Center at Peenemünde possessed the technologies essential to the success of the A-4. The four key technologies for the A-4 were large liquid-fuel rocket engines, supersonic aerodynamics, gyroscopic guidance and rudders in jet control. At the time, Adolf Hitler was not particularly impressed by the V-2; he pointed out that it was merely an artillery shell with a longer range and much higher cost.

In early September 1943, von Braun promised, the Long-Range Bombardment Commission that the A-4 development was "practically complete/concluded", but even by the middle of 1944, a complete A-4 parts list was still unavailable. itler was sufficiently impressed by the enthusiasm of its developers, and needed a "wonder weapon" to maintain German morale, so he authorized its deployment in large numbers.

The V-2s were constructed at the Mittelwerk site by prisoners from Mittelbau-Dora, a concentration camp where 12,000–20,000 prisoners died during the war.

In 1943 the Austrian resistance group around Heinrich Maier managed to send exact drawings of the V-2 rocket to the American Office of Strategic Services. Location sketches of V-rocket manufacturing facilities, such as those in Peenemünde, were also sent to Allied general staffs in order to enable Allied bombers to carry out air strikes. This information was particularly important for Operation Hydra. The group was gradually captured by the Gestapo and most of the members were executed.

The A-4 used a 75% ethanol/25% water mixture (B-Stoff) for fuel and liquid oxygen (LOX) (A-Stoff) for oxidizer. The water reduced the flame temperature, acted as a coolant by turning to steam and augmented the thrust, tended to produce a smoother burn, and reduced thermal stress.

Rudolf Hermann's supersonic wind tunnel was used to measure the A-4's aerodynamic characteristics and center of pressure, using a model of the A-4 within a 40 square centimeter chamber. Measurements were made using a Mach number 1.86 blowdown nozzle on 8 August 1940. Tests at Mach numbers 1.56 and 2.5 were made after 24 September 1940.

At launch the A-4 propelled itself for up to 65 seconds on its own power, and a program motor held the inclination at the specified angle until engine shutdown, after which the rocket continued on a ballistic free-fall trajectory. The rocket reached a height of 80 km (50 mi) after shutting off the engine.

The fuel and oxidizer pumps were driven by a steam turbine, and the steam was produced by concentrated hydrogen peroxide (T-Stoff) with sodium permanganate (Z-Stoff) catalyst. Both the alcohol and oxygen tanks were an aluminium-magnesium alloy.

The turbopump, rotating at 4000 rpm, forced the alcohol and oxygen into the combustion chamber at 33 gallons per second, where they were ignited by a spinning electrical igniter.

Thrust increased to 8 tons during this preliminary stage, before increasing to 25 tons, lifting the 13.5 ton rocket. Combustion gases exited the chamber at 5,100 °F (2,820 °C), and a speed of 6500 feet per second. The oxygen to fuel mixture was 1.0:0.85 at 25 tons of thrust, but as ambient pressure decreased with flight altitude, thrust increased until it reached 29 tons. The turbopump assembly contained two centrifugal pumps, one for the alcohol, and one for the oxygen, both connected to a common shaft. Hydrogen peroxide converted to steam, using a sodium permanganate catalyst powered the pump, which delivered 120 pounds of alcohol and 150 pounds of liquid oxygen per second to a combustion chamber at 210 psi.

Dr. Thiel's development of the 25 ton rocket motor relied on pump feeding, rather than on the earlier pressure feeding. The motor used centrifugal injection, while using both regenerative cooling and film cooling. Film cooling admitted alcohol into the combustion chamber and exhaust nozzle under slight pressure through four rings of small perforations. The mushroom-shaped injection head was removed from the combustion chamber to a mixing chamber, the combustion chamber was made more spherical while being shortened from 6 to 1 foot in length, and the connection to the nozzle was made cone shaped. The resultant 1.5 ton chamber operated at a combustion pressure of 220 pounds per square inch. Thiel's 1.5 ton chamber was then scaled up to a 4.5 ton motor by arranging three injection heads above the combustion chamber. By 1939, eighteen injection heads in two concentric circles at the head of the 0.12-inch thick sheet-steel chamber, were used to make the 25 ton motor.

The warhead was another source of troubles. The explosive employed was amatol 60/40 detonated by an electric contact fuze. Amatol had the advantage of stability, and the warhead was protected by a thick layer of glass wool, but even so it could still explode in the re-entry phase. The warhead weighed 975 kilograms (2,150 lb) and contained 910 kilograms (2,010 lb) of explosive. The warhead's percentage by weight that was explosive was 93%, a very high percentage when compared with other types of munition.

The protective layer was used for the fuel tanks as well and the A-4 did not have the tendency to form ice, which had plagued other early missiles (like the balloon tank-design SM-65 Atlas). The tanks held 4,173 kilograms (9,200 lb) of ethyl alcohol and 5,553 kilograms (12,242 lb) of oxygen.

The V-2 was guided by four external rudders on the tail fins, and four internal graphite vanes in the jet stream at the exit of the motor. These 8 control surfaces were controlled by Helmut Hölzer's analog computer, the Mischgerät, via electrical-hydraulic servomotors, based on electrical signals from the gyros. The Siemens Vertikant LEV-3 guidance system consisted of two free gyroscopes (a horizontal for pitch and a vertical with two degrees of freedom for yaw and roll) for lateral stabilization, coupled with a PIGA accelerometer, or the Walter Wolman radio control system, to control engine cutoff at a specified velocity. Other gyroscopic systems used in the A-4 included Kreiselgeräte's SG-66 and SG-70. The V-2 was launched from a pre-surveyed location, so the distance and azimuth to the target were known. Fin 1 of the missile was aligned to the target azimuth.

Some later V-2s used "guide beams", radio signals transmitted from the ground, to keep the missile on course, but the first models used a simple analog computer that adjusted the azimuth for the rocket, and the flying distance was controlled by the timing of the engine cut-off, "Brennschluss", ground controlled by a Doppler system or by different types of on-board integrating accelerometers. Thus, range was a function of engine burn time, which ended when a specific velocity was achieved. Just before engine cutoff, thrust was reduced to 8 tons, in an effort to avoid any water hammer problems a rapid cutoff could cause.

Dr. Friedrich Kirchstein of Siemens of Berlin developed the V-2 radio control for motor-cut-off (German: Brennschluss). For velocity measurement, Professor Wolman of Dresden created an alternative of his Doppler tracking system in 1940–41, which used a ground signal transponded by the A-4 to measure the velocity of the missile. By 9 February 1942, Peenemünde engineer Gerd deBeek had documented the radio interference area of a V-2 as 10,000 metres (33,000 feet) around the "Firing Point", and the first successful A-4 flight on 3 October 1942, used radio control for Brennschluss. Although Hitler commented on 22 September 1943 that "It is a great load off our minds that we have dispensed with the radio guiding-beam; now no opening remains for the British to interfere technically with the missile in flight", about 20% of the operational V-2 launches were beam-guided. The Operation Pinguin V-2 offensive began on 8 September 1944, when Lehr- und Versuchsbatterie No. 444 (English: Training and Testing Battery 444) launched a single rocket guided by a radio beam directed at Paris.

The painting of the operational V-2s was mostly a ragged-edged pattern with several variations, but at the end of the war a plain olive green rocket also appeared. During tests the rocket was painted in a characteristic black-and-white chessboard pattern, which aided in determining if the rocket was spinning around its longitudinal axis.

A submarine-towed launch platform was tested successfully, making it the prototype for submarine-launched ballistic missiles. The project codename was Prüfstand XII ("Test stand XII"), sometimes called the rocket U-boat. If deployed, it would have allowed a U-boat to launch V-2 missiles against United States cities, though only with considerable effort (and limited effect). Hitler, in July 1944 and Speer, in January 1945, made speeches alluding to the scheme, though Germany did not possess the capability to fulfill these threats.

While interned after the war by the British at CSDIC camp 11, Dornberger was recorded saying that he had begged the Führer to stop the V-weapon propaganda, because nothing more could be expected from one ton of explosive. To this Hitler had replied that Dornberger might not expect more, but he (Hitler) certainly did.

According to decrypted messages from the Japanese embassy in Germany, twelve dismantled V-2 rockets were shipped to Japan. These left Bordeaux in August 1944 on the transport U-boats U-219 and U-195, which reached Djakarta in December 1944. A civilian V-2 expert was a passenger on U-234, bound for Japan in May 1945 when the war ended in Europe. The fate of these V-2 rockets is unknown.

**Die Glocke"**

Among the most amazing and bizarre wonder weapons , Wunderwaffe in German, developed by the Nazis were the Glocke or "The Bell". It was a top-secret Nazi scientific technological device, secret weapon, associated with antigravity and free energy research.

The bell was created in the last stages of the Second World War (1943-1945), in the secret Nazi location known as Der Riese, or the giant, an ultra-secret experimental base located between the Owl Mountains and the Ksiaz Castle. This base consisted of 7 laboratories hidden under the mountains. The base would supposedly be built by forced laborers, supervised by men from the Shutzstafell (SS).(Die Glocke)

The bell was made of an especially heavy metal and was chained to the ground. It measured 5 meters high, by 3 meters in diameter. On its front was the Nazi symbol, had 2 rotating cylinders that contained a substance similar to mercury, called xerum 525. It is also said that this liquid was extremely radioactive, and many of the scientists who worked in the bell while it was on, They died of cancer. When it turned in the opposite direction, it gave off a violet glow.

The exterior of the artifact was lined with a ceramic material; Interestingly, NASA's space shuttles, such as the Columbus, were wrapped in its most superficial layer by a coating of ceramic tiles, which act as a thermal insulator. The original plans of the bell were lost after much of Der Riese was destroyed in 1945, after its discovery .

When it was put into operation, the Bell and the 2 rotating cylinders rotated contrary and the object was raised and could move. It was the first prototype engine against gravity and opened a new path in the path of physics and technology. In this way this technical ingenuity could serve as the propulsion system needed by the Nazi UFOs that were developing in the last phases of the war.(Nazi Bell)

The ultra-secret project of the Nazi Bell was commanded by SS General Hans Kammler, a scientific engineer who was involved in the development of V-2 missiles, jet planes, flying wings, Nazi UFOs and underground constructions, among others. Projects. The truth is that at the end of the war, it was never known about General Kammler or the Nazi Campaign. Some theories say that the Bell was moved in a cargo plane, stopping in Barcelona, Spain, towards the South American cone between Chile and Argentina, or even to the area of Atlantis.

It seems that the real secret of the Nazi campaign is that it could be a time machine, which needed to activate its system of rotating propellers to perform and to make small air movements at the same time. And, indeed, a time machine could be a great effective weapon, the ultimate weapon, to change the course of the war.

When the Soviet Army was arriving at the village of Ludwigsdorf, today called Ludwikowice, the officer of the Waffen SS, Karl Sporrenberg, by direct order of Hitler, carried out the execution of 62 Nazi scientists working on the Die Glocke project;facts for which he was subsequently tried in court as a war criminal. According to Sporrenberg, the secret prototype would have been moved to a security zone in Norway.(Die Glocke)

On December 9, 1965, an unknown flying object, acorn-shaped or bell-shaped, crashed in the vicinity of the US town of Kecksburg, Pennsylvania. This event was known in the study of Ufology as the case of Kecksburg. The artifact had strange inscriptions, like the Nazi bell, and was quickly recovered by the military forces. Many witnesses saw the strange event.

Everything suggests that the UFO of Kecksburg was the result of the development of the Nazi bellproject. In fact, the most probable hypothesis of all is that both Hans Kammler and the Nazi Campaign ended up in secret bases of the US government, protected by Project Lusty and Paperclip.

# Theodore von Kármán: The Close Encounter Man

Theodore von Kármán (11 May 1881– 6 May 1963) was a Hungarian-American mathematician, aerospace engineer, and physicist who was active primarily in the fields of aeronautics and astronautics. He was responsible for many key advances in aerodynamics, notably on supersonic and hypersonic airflow characterization. He is regarded as the outstanding aerodynamic theoretician of the 20th century.

Von Kármán belong to a group called "The Martians". A term used at the time to refer to a group of prominent Hungarian scientists (mostly, but not exclusively, physicists and mathematicians) who emigrated to the United States in the early half of the 20th century. Leó Szilárd, the father of the nuclear chain reaction, jokingly suggested that Hungary was a front for aliens from Mars. He used this term because the Hungarian emigres spoke English with a strong accent, were considered outsiders in American society, and were seemingly superhuman in intellect, spoke an incomprehensible native language, and came from a small obscure country in a far corner of Europe. This led to them being called Martians.

Kármán was born into a Jewish family in Budapest, Austria-Hungary as Kármán Tódor, the son of Helen Kohn and Mór (Maurice) Kármán. Von Kármán father was the leading pedagogue in Hungary, the secretary of the Autro-Hungarian ministry of education. He founded a model gymnasium (A kind of high school) for gifted childredn. His mother was a women of great culture that descended from a long line of scholars, like Yehuda Loew Bezael, the famous XVI Century jewish mathematician who invented a mechanical robot known as the “Golem”. At the age of 9, enrolled in his father's gymnasium where he learned advanced mathematics. This school was called the “nursery of the elite”.

Maurice von Kármán was an inflexible man that wanted to control all aspects of his son's life. He did not trust the local elementary schools, and hired private tutors. Also, he reviewed al the text books reading by young Theodore . During this time, Theodore von Kármán showed a remarkable ability for numbers', and his father became upset that his son could be labeled as an “idiot savant”. Maurice took all his son's math books away from him, and ordered him to read history, geography, and literature instead. As a result of the stress, von Kármán's father had a nervous breakdown and was interned in a mental institution. Theodore economic situation worsen, and to save money he enrolled in the Royal Joseph University of Polytehnics and Economics. To please his father, he finish a mayor in engineering. While attending the Royal Joseph, he developed a mathematical method to eliminate the clatter of engine valves.
After graduated from Royal Joseph, he served one year of compulsory service in the Austro-Hungarian Army in a artillery batallion. At the end of his service, he returned to Royal Joseph as professor of hydraulics. Here he wrote a paper on structures that became a valuable tool for the constructions of bridges, planes , and buildings. This paper was published in 1906 and gave him international recognition. He applied for a fellowship from the Hungarian Academy of Science, and sought admission at the University of Gottingen in Germany.

Von Kármán early years at Gottingen were frustrated, the inflexible social structure, and the lack of interest by the faculty on his research projects isolated him. He almost quit twice. However, 1907 the Krup armament manufacturer supply the university with a large hydraulic press. This made possible that von Kármán continued his studies, and complete his doctorate.By 1908, von Kármán ran out of money, and moved to Paris as a bohemian, drink in cafes, went to museums and attended lectures by Madame Curie.

While in Paris, von Kármán was walking home from one of his bohemian tours and by coincidence met with Margrit Veszi, the daugther of one of his friends. Veszi asked Theodore is he can come with her to an air show where the famous british aviator, Henry Farman, will try to fly the first two kilometers in Europe. Von Kármán refused to go because he has no interest to see a "box kite" flying. At the end, he capitulated, and went with her. During this time, flight was something new, Europeans had read the Wright's Brothers' invention in the newspaper, but had never seeing something like this before . Farman took his plane out of the hangar, and flew it around the airfield a couple of times. Von Kármán was so impressed by the flight that he began to investigate on his own. At that time, he contacted several airplane manufacturers in France with the idea to build, and improve better engines, but he did not receive a positive respond. He came back to Gottingen to take a laboratory assistanship with a win tunnel that was built by the Zeppelin Company. In this laboratory, young Kármán made his most important discoveries like the aerodynamic drag or "Kármán Vortex Street".

Kármán was unable to get a full professorship at Gottingen, and moved to a college in Selmeczbanya, Hungary, that was funded by the Ministry of Finance, because the mail goal of the institution was gold mining. Kármán does nor care about gold mining, but a lot about a full time job. As a result he moved to Selmeczbanya in the fall of 1912. Here he did not find what he wanted, and as soon as he could, he asked for a leave of absence. He got a position at the Technical University at Aachen in Germany, and the directorship of the Aachen Aerodynamics Institute.

Once year after moving to Aechen, WWI started, and he was drafted by the Austro-Hungarian Army with the rank of first lietenant. The war interrupted his research for the next four years in which he never received apass to go home. During this time, his father, Maurice von Kármán, died. When the war ended, he was able to returned to Hungary in 1918 with his aging mother, and sister. However, Hungary was in turnmoil as a result of the war, and in November of that year, the Austrian Eperator Charles abdicated to the throne, and the parlamente declared a republic. The new republic gave rise to a socialist regime headed by the communist Béla Kun . Theodore was named the new undersecretary of education. He agreed, and introduced new subjects as modern biology and atomic physics.However, two months later, Romanian troops invaded Hungary, and von Kármán could returned to his former post at Aachen.

By 1921, his mother and sister moved with him to his home in Vaals, Holand, that was near Aachen. At Aachen, he met with students from all over Europe. Von Kármán was fluently in Hungarian, German, French, and English, even some Yiddish. Some of his students took an interest in gliding and saw the competitions of the Rhön-Rossitten Gesellschaft as an opportunity to advance in aeronautics. Kármán engaged Wolfgang Klemperer to design a competitive glider. Josephine encouraged her brother Theodore to expand his science beyond national boundaries. They organized the first international conference in mechanics held in September 1922 in Innsbruck. Subsequent conferences were organized as the International Union of Theoretical and Applied Mechanics.

But he started to feel the symptoms of the coming economic collapse. The Great Depression was a long and extensive economic crisis, affecting most developed nations in the early and mid-1930s. The Great Depression was particularly severe in Germany, which had enjoyed five years of artificial prosperity. Unemployment hit millions of Germans, as companies shut down or downsized. Others lost their savings as banks folded.

For the next several years, von Kármán, continued his work at Aachen, but in 1926 he received an invitation from Robert Millikan, the first american to win the Nobel Prize, to move to Caltech's infant Physics Department. Millikan had requested a half million dollar grant from the Guggenheim Fund for the Promotion of Aeronautics, and was looking for a world famous expert to fill the position of Director. von Kármán wrote back expressing his interest in visiting the campus. Later that year, von Kármán and his sister arrived in New York, and stayed in Harry Guggenheim enormous mansion in Long Island. Then they traveled by car to Pasadena. At the time, Caltech was far away to resemble the european universities known by von Kármán. The Physics Department had just a faculty of five professors, and just started to award bachelor degrees.

Political climate was changing rapidly in Europe. Antisemitism was on the rise. Von Kármán saw one of his best students wearing a swastika in his buttonhole. Some students were accused to be "Hungarian Semite". Germany was secretly rearming, and the Ministry of Transporttaion warned von Kármán not to ask when German firms used the Aechen wind tunnel. Von Kármán foresaw his future in a society that will outcast jews, and the prelude of the incoming war. Apprehensive about developments in Europe, von Kármán accepted the directorship of the Guggenheim Aeronautical Laboratory at the California Institute of Technology (GALCIT). As a result, in December 1929, von Kármán, his mother and sister took an ocean liner bound to New York. Once in the United Staes, they look for a home in Pasadena, close to Caltech. Southern California became a paradise for von Kármán. Plane manufacturers like Boeign, Hughes, Curtiss-Wright, North American choose this part of the country for the weather that permited year round testing. These firms used the wind tunnel of the Guggenheim Aeronautical Lab or GALCIT for testing. In return, these firms hired Caltech students. By 1936, United Sates has become his true home. The directorship at GALCIT included provision for a research assistant, and he selected Frank Wattendorf, an American who had been studying for three years in Aachen.Also, another student Ernest Edwin Sechler took up the problem of making reliable airframes for aircraft, and with Kármán's support, developed an understanding of aeroelasticity.

By 1936, von Kármán hired the legal services of Andrew G. Haley to form the Aerojet Corporation, with his graduate students Frank Malina and their experimental rocketry collaborator Jack Parsons, to manufacture JATO rocket motors. He later became a naturalized citizen of the United States on July 24 of that year.

During World War II, German activity increased US military interest in rocket research. In early 1943, the Experimental Engineering Division of the United States Army Air Forces Material Command forwarded to Kármán reports from British intelligence sources describing German rockets capable of travelling more than 100 miles (160 km). In a letter dated 2 August 1943 Kármán provided the Army with his analysis of and comments on the German program.

In 1944 he and others affiliated with GALCIT founded the Jet Propulsion Laboratory (JPL), which is now a Federally funded research and development center managed and operated by Caltech under a contract from NASA.

**Left-to-right: Ludwig Prandtl (German scientist), Tsien Hsue-sen (Chinese), Theodore von Kármán (Hungarian-American scientist). Both, Tsien and von Karman are in military uniforms**

Technological change during World War II proceeded at a frightening pace. Developments in aircraft design, propulsion, weap-ons, and electronics contributed vitally to the outcome of events in the global conflict. At the heart of these developments were scientists, largely civilians, who worked to produce military equipment that would turn the tide of the war.

Von Karman, took the attention of Henry Harley "Hap" Arnold, Chief of the Air Corp between 1938 to 1941, in the early 30's for his work on aerodynamic. As a result of the approaching war, Arnold called civilian scientists to a meeting at the National Academy of Sciences building in Washington, D.C. Among the guess there was a team from Caltech, headed by Von Karman. Among the many problems confronting the development of airpalnes for war were: high-altitude windshield icing, developing aircraft radios and jetassisted takeoff. Kármán assigned the difficult rocket project to his most senior students at Caltech, the "suicide club." From this small project grew what is today the Jet Propulsion Laboratory near Pasadena, California.

During the closing months of WWII, Arnold now Commanding General of the U.S. Army Air Forces took advantage of the victories of the Allies and created a task force headed by von Kármán to evaluate captured German aeronautical data and laboratories for the AAF. Von Kármán team followed the steps of the advancing American, and British forces searching German laboratories, and airfileds. Arnold ordered the group to travel to many foreign countries as possible. For this task, von Kármán became an AAF consultant on scientific matters on 23 October 1944. Initially, Kármán's task force was called the AAF Consulting Board for Future Research, but AAFCBFR proved too long the name was change to the Scientific Advisory Group (SAG) on 1 December 1944. The group reported directly to General Arnold.

In April 1945, SAG group traveled to Europe searching for German laboratories. Operation

LUSTY (Luftwaffe Science and Technology), has begun. Before departured, General Arnold insisted that the SAG members investigate the most advanced information available worldwide. However, the SAG group was just an small part of a larger operation (code name LUSTY) in search of European technologies. As soon as the SAG members arrived, they packed and boxed all that they could and immediately shipped it to Wright Field, Ohio, the AAF's center for aeronautical R&D (Reserch & Development).

Perhaps the most exciting discovery during this mission was a secret aerodinamical laboratory in a pine forest near Volkenrode, a village outside the city of Braunschweig. It was the Luftfahrforschungsanstalt Herman Goering or the Herman Goering Aerodynamical Institute These facilities included an eight meter wind tunnel, a high speed wind tunnel, two supersonic wind tunnels, an armament laboratory. Many ofv the buildings were looted, but the equipment were intact. Americans used metal detectors to recover thousands of metal boxes buried with top secret documents.

This facility was a treasure trove of documents, yielded the greatest return in the field of research. SAG members arrived on the 22nd April to organize and conduct the scientific exploitation of this establishment. Dr. Von Kaman, General Arnold's personal aeronautical advisor, and his Group, remained at this place, on several occasions for periods varying from several days to a week. According to Dr. Von Karman, seventy-five to ninety per cent of the technical aeronautical information in Germany was available at this establishment, and that information on research and development which had not previously been investigated in the United States would require approximately two years to accomplish with the facilities available there. Information obtained on jet engine developments available at the Goering establishment, it was stated, would expedite the United States development by approximately six to nine months. In less than two months, one hundred and nineteen reports were written on the facilities.

A model airplane with triangular, arrow-shaped wings was found in the Luftfahrforschungsanstalt. This discovery arose a lot of discussion because just a few months earlier, an advisor working for the National Advisory Committee of Aeronautics (NACA) presented a controversial theory that claimed that such a plane could bypass the sound barrier. In 1945, scientist were dealing with the phenomenon known as sound barrier or "sonic wall". A plane approaching the speed of sounds could suddenly encounter a rapid increase in drag. In other words, a plane will hit a cone of disturbance caused by the pressure of air resistance when approaching the speed of sound. The advisor had discovered that wings swept back in a V shape could smooth the stream of supersonic flow, and even brake the sound barrier. While in America these concepts were in an infant stage, in Germany were already put in practical use. Reich scientist were years ahead of their Americans counterpart.

Members of the SAG team visited the Dora concentration camp near Nordhausen. At Dora they were called by the concentration camp survivors. These slave labours belong to all nationalities: Polish, Russians, Czech, and other groups from East Europe. Through interpreters, the survivors told that they wanted to show the Americans "something fantastic" underneath the mountain. They were referring to a rocket factory hidden under the mountain. The SAG team discovered a completed V-2, a boxcar of rocket parts. There were enough parts to assemble 75 V-2. American soldiers packed all the material in 300 large railway wagons.

However, the oficial version of Operation Lustyc did not mentioned the stange circular structure found in a a remote valley outside Lubic in Poland, occupied at that time by the Red Army. There is no official report that the Third Reich tested a new highly advanced machine known as the Glocke or the bell. Scientists like Herman Overson, and Wernher von Braun worked on this bell shaped craft that has a electromagnetic propulsion system.

Also, it is important to ask: Where did all those technological advances come from? In 1936 a 'flying saucer' allegedly crashes in the Schwarzwald (Black Forest) near Freiburg, opening the door for advanced German technology in aeronautics and space (reverse engineering). The ship and its occupants were spirited away to the dark heart of Nazi Germany, where all was dismantled and diligently studied. A resulting program was called Haunebu.

von Kármán was the best man to search for captured enemy aircraft and technology. He spoke different languages, including German. What he and his team brought back to the United Sates it is a mystery. But among the secret files already declassified, it is possible to have a comprehensive pictute.

A memo dated on May 12, 1949 from the Headquarters of the US Air Force to the Director of Special Investigations-Office of the Inspector General USAF demonstrates a clear and undeniable link between von Kármán and UFOs. In this memo, von Kármán ordered Dr. Joseph Kaplan of the Air Force's Scientific Advisory Board to "review the reports aerial phenomena of investigations and the circumstances surrounding the unidentified aerial phenomena that have been observed in this area (Kirtland Air Force Base, New Mexico) in the last five monts". According to this memo, von Kármán was aware of the UFO sightings in the area and the possible consequences. He requested to make this review two years after the Rosswell incident that occurred in the same area (New Mexico). It is important to point out that von Kármán was the leading scientist of the SAG group that traveled to Europe searching for German laboratories. In these laboratories, he could found some sort of alien technology, or parts of the UFO that crashed in the Schwarzwald (Black Forest) near Freiburg in 1936.

In 1946, von Kármán became the first chairman of the Scientific Advisory Group which studied aeronautical technologies for the United States Army Air Forces. He also helped found AGARD, the NATO aerodynamics research oversight group (1951), the International Council of the Aeronautical Sciences (1956), the International Academy of Astronautics (1960), and the Von Karman Institute for Fluid Dynamics in Sint-Genesius-Rode, south of Brussels (1956).

In 1949, von Kármán resigned his two positions of director and became professor emeritus at Caltech. He was still very active in giving advice to the U.S. airforce and NATO and played a major role in international conferences on aeronautics. Von Kármán received many honors for his outstanding contributions. He received the United States Medal for Merit in 1946, the Franklin Gold Medal in 1948, and was the first to be awarded the National Medal for Science in 1963. He also received honours from France, the Vatican, Germany, Greece, the United Kingdom, Spain and the Netherlands.

Some of the information that could shed some light on von Kármán-UFO link was censored by the FBI reviewer. Withhold information are generally marked, in the FBI File, with white boxes where something should have been in the file that is considered by the Bureau censor "sensitive". In other cases, the information has been blacking.

Von Kármán took the atention of the FBI in 1941 because some confidential information received by Bureau agents mentioned his communist sympathies. Also, his sister was considered by the FBI to be a Nazi sympathizer. Most of the information in von Kármán's FBI File deals with Soviet Agents, Nazi and Communist sympathizer, and the Von Karman's post under the Bela Kun socialist regime in Hungary during 1919. The File did not mention his whereabouts in Operation Lusty. The reason could be that this mission was so secret that even an official agency in charge of the national security of the United States, like the FBI, was forbidden to investigate. However, this File has been included in this publication.

**Some pages in this file were not included as a result of the Security Act of 1947 & the CIA Act of 1949 by the FBI censors. FBI censors focused their attention on Part.2b of von Kármán FBI's File. Seems that this part it is the most sensitive, and several pages can not be made public.**

Each individual (in this case is von Kármán) with an FBI file has a record number when the file was opened for the first time. The first two or three digit number specifies the type of offense was being investigated. Going through von Kármán's FBI File, there are found several files serial numbers. Some of these numbers belongs to the FBI regional offices. For example, in the von Kármán's FBI File, the first digit numbers found are: 39,40, 66,100, 116. According to the FBI offense code 39: is for Falsely Claiming Citizenship; 40: is for passport and Visa Matters; 65: is for Espionage. Attorney General guidelines on Foreign Counterintelligence, Internal Security Act 1950: 66 is for: Administrative Matters. This code covers such items as supplies, automobiles, salary matters and vouchers. Frecuently used as an informer file. Serial number 100 stands for Domestic Security these days. However, in the 50's this code stood for communist like Smith Act violations; 116: is for Department of Energy Applicant; Department of Energy, Employee (Formerly Atomic Energy Commission). Many investigations of Atomic Scientists were conducted under this classification.

U.S., World War II Draft Registration Cards, 1942 for Theodore Von Karman

REGISTRATION CARD—(Men born on or after April 28, 1877 and on or before February 16, 1897) 187

SERIAL NUMBER U 11

1. NAME (Print): Theodore Von Karman (First) (Middle) (Last)

ORDER NUMBER

2 PLACE OF RESIDENCE (Print): 1501 Marengo Ave Pasadena Cal.
(Number and street) (Town, township, village, or city) (County) (State)

[THE PLACE OF RESIDENCE GIVEN ON THE LINE ABOVE WILL DETERMINE LOCAL BOARD JURISDICTION; LINE 2 OF REGISTRATION CERTIFICATE WILL BE IDENTICAL]

3. MAILING ADDRESS: Same
[Mailing address if other than place indicated on line 2. If same insert word same]

4. TELEPHONE: Sy 9-3410 (Exchange) (Number)

5. AGE IN YEARS: 60

DATE OF BIRTH: May 11 1881 (Mo.) (Day) (Yr.)

6. PLACE OF BIRTH: Budapest (Town or county) Hungary (State or country)

7. NAME AND ADDRESS OF PERSON WHO WILL ALWAYS KNOW YOUR ADDRESS: Dr Josephine Von Karman 1501 Marengo Ave Pas.

8. EMPLOYER'S NAME AND ADDRESS: California Ins. of Tech 1207 California Pas.

9. PLACE OF EMPLOYMENT OR BUSINESS: 1207 California Pasadena Cal.
(Number and street or R.F.D. number) (Town) (County) (State)

I AFFIRM THAT I HAVE VERIFIED ABOVE ANSWERS AND THAT THEY ARE TRUE.

Theodore von Karman
(Registrant's signature)

D. S. S. Form 1 (Revised 4-1-42) (over) 16—21630-2

# Operation Lusty

At the beginning of the Cold War the US government found itself in the throes of a flying saucer problem. Citizens all over the country were looking up into the sky and reporting strange objects which had no easily drawn explanation. The military turned to scientists, astronomers, physicists, and engineers for answers to the unexplained phenomenon but with no physical evidence to examine, the science community almost unanimously claimed that the sightings were largely psychological in nature. Unlike other conventional wars, the Cold War did not have any singular event that set off hostilities such as the attack on Pearl Harbor which thrust the United States into World War II. Instead, the Cold War was a nebulous ideological war which pitted the United States against the Soviet Union. The roots of the Cold War can be found in several operations at the end of World War II which saw both sides repositioning themselves in an attempt to dominate the geopolitical theater in the last half of the 20th century. Many of these operations began be- fore the war ended. Both sides were en- gaged in exploitation operations in Nazi Germany while much of the fighting was still ongoing. The United States was successful in acquiring many of Germany's most distinguished atomic scientists and rocket engineers in a project undertaken by the Office of Strategic Services (OSS) called Operation Paperclip. A large portion of these scientists would go on to work on U.S. atomic weapons testing and the U.S. space program, the two projects complimented each other with the result being in later years the advent of the nuclear armed intercontinental ballistic missile.

Another aspect of Operation Paperclip was a project called Operation LUSTY which was an endeavor to capture German experimental aircraft and rockets. Intelligence operatives were able to acquire these machines which they shipped back to be examined at the Freeman Army Airfield, Indiana, by the Air Technical Intelligence team. The same team involved with crash retrievals of advanced German aircraft downed during the war. This base, and Wright-Patterson AFB would later become the home of the U.S. Government investigation into the new and unexplainable phenomenon known as flying saucers, later categorized as unidentified flying objects or UFO.

During World War II, the U.S. Army Air Forces Intelligence Service sent teams to Europe to gain access to enemy aircraft, technical and scientific reports, research facilities, and weapons for study in the United States. The Air Technical Intelligence (ATI) teams, trained at the Technical Intelligence School at Wright Field, Ohio, collected enemy equipment to learn about Germany's technical developments. The ATI teams competed with 32 allied technical intelligence groups to gain information and equipment recovered from crash sites.

As the war concluded, the various intelligence teams, including the ATI, shifted from tactical intelligence to post hostilities investigations. Exploitation intelligence increased dramatically.

On 22 April 1945, the USAAF combined technical and post-hostilities intelligence objectives under the Exploitation Division with the code name Lusty. Operation Lusty began with the aim of exploiting captured German scientific documents, research facilities, and aircraft. The Operation had two teams.

Team One, under the leadership of Colonel Harold E. Watson, a former Wright Field test pilot, collected enemy aircraft and weapons for further examination in the United States.

Team Two, under the leadership of Colonel Howard M. McCoy, recruited scientists, collected documents and investigated facilities.

By 1944, intelligence experts at Wright Field had developed lists of advanced aviation equipment they wanted to examine. Watson and his crew, nicknamed "Watson's Whizzers" and composed of pilots, engineers and maintenance men, used these "Black Lists" to collect aircraft. Watson organized his Whizzers into two sections: one collected jet aircraft while the other procured piston-engine aircraft and nonflyable jet and rocket equipment.

After the war, the Whizzers added Luftwaffe test pilots to the team, one being Hauptmann Heinz Braur. On 8 May 1945, Braur flew 70 women, children and wounded troops to Munich-Riem airport. After he landed, Braur was approached by one of Watson's men, who gave him the choice of either going to a prison camp or flying with the Whizzers; Braur thought flying preferable. Three Messerschmitt employees also joined the Whizzers: Karl Baur, the Chief Test Pilot of Experimental Aircraft, test pilot Ludwig Hoffman, and engineering superintendent Gerhard Coulis. Test pilot Herman Kersting joined later.

When the Whizzers located nine Messerschmitt Me 262 jet aircraft at Lechfeld airfield near Augsburg, these German test pilots had the expertise to fly them. It has been alleged, and partially substantiated by declassified documents, that the Whizzers recruited captured Luftwaffe personnel and pilots held at Fort Bliss, Texas, to go into what would become the British, French and Soviet controlled areas after V-E Day to fly out, hide, or otherwise remove to U.S. controlled areas all "black listed" planes, secret weapons equipment and supporting documents, some four months before Germany's surrender.

Watson's men traveled across Europe to find the aircraft on the "Black Lists." Once found, they had to be shipped to the United States. Fortunately, the British loaned them the originally American-built escort carrier HMS Reaper, first commissioned for the US Navy as the USS Winjah. The most viable harbor for docking the carrier and loading the aircraft was at Cherbourg, France.

The Whizzers flew the Me 262s and other aircraft, including an Arado Ar 234 from Lechfeld, to St. Dizier, to Melun and then to Cherbourg, on Querqueville Airfield, also known as ALG A-23C Querqueville. All the aircraft were cocooned against the salt air and weather, loaded onto the carrier and taken to the United States, where they were offloaded at Newark Army Air Field. They were then studied at their respective flight test centers by the air intelligence groups of both the USAAF, the flight test center of which was then at Wilbur Wright Field, and the U.S. Navy, which had its facility at the Patuxent Naval Air Test Center.

One of the Messerschmitt Me 262 jets was named "Marge" by the mechanics; the pilots later renamed it "Lady Jess IV."

In 1945 the enemy aircraft shipped to the United States were divided between the Navy and the

Army Air Forces. General Hap Arnold ordered the preservation of one of every type of aircraft used by the enemy forces. The air force sent their aircraft to Wright Field. When the field could not handle additional aircraft, many were sent to Freeman Field, Seymour, Indiana. In the end, Operation Lusty collectors had acquired 16,280 items (6,200 tons) to be examined by intelligence personnel who selected 2,398 separate items for technical analysis. Forty-seven personnel were engaged in the identification, inspection and warehousing of captured foreign equipment.

In 1946, when Freeman Field was scheduled to close, Air Technical Service Command had to move the aircraft. The larger aircraft were sent to Davis-Monthan Field, Arizona, and the fighter aircraft sent to the Special Depot in Park Ridge, Illinois (now O'Hare Airport), which was under the control of ATSC's Office of Intelligence. The Special Depot occupied buildings that Douglas Airplane Co. had used to build C-54 aircraft. The aircraft were stored in these two locations until they could be disposed of in accordance with General Arnold's order.

With the start of the Korean War in 1950, the air force needed the storage buildings, so the aircraft were moved outside. In 1953 some of the aircraft were moved to what would later become known as the National Air and Space Museum's Garber Restoration Facility in Suitland, Maryland, and the remaining aircraft were scrapped. It is possible that, as part of Lusty, both an American-captured example of the Junkers Ju 290 four-engined maritime patrol aircraft, and a captured prototype example of the Heinkel He 177A-7 (Werknummer 550 256), a late war development of the Luftwaffe's only operational heavy bomber, had been ferried from Europe to the Park Ridge Depot, only to both be similarly crushed flat and buried under the modern O'Hare airport runways.

Operation Lusty resulted in the survival of the sole existing examples of the Arado Ar 234 jet reconnaissance/bomber, the Dornier Do 335 twin-engined heavy fighter, and the only readily restorable example in the United States of the German Heinkel He 219 night fighter , as well as the only surviving example of the Junkers Ju 388, a Ju 388L-1 reconnaissance model bearing WkNr. 560 049; all of which are in the collection of the Smithsonian's National Air and Space Museum. These are either currently restored and on display (for the Ar 234B and Do 335A sole survivors), under restoration and partial display (for the He 219A), or still awaiting restoration at the Garber Facility in Maryland (for the Ju 388); with the first three noted examples now at the Dulles International Airport-located NASM museum facility, the Steven F. Udvar-Hazy Center, the home of the new Mary Baker Engen Restoration Hangar, the NASM's latest primary restoration workshop. However, no official disclosure about the Glocke or "The Bell" has been ever made.

According to the official account, the captured German weapons were moved to Freeman Field . This base was established in 1942 as a pilot training airfield. It was also the first military helicopter pilot training airfield. In 1944, black bomber pilots were trained at Freeman, and it was the scene of a racial incident that outraged many Americans and led to the military re-evaluating its racial policies. After the war, captured German, Italian and Japanese aircraft were brought to the base for evaluation and testing. It was closed in 1946 after de end of WWII.

Freeman Army Airfield was named in honor or Captain Richard S. Freeman. A native of Indiana and 1930 graduate of West Point, he was awarded the Distinguished Flying Cross, was awarded the Mackay Trophy, and was one of the pioneers of the Army Air Mail Service.

Captain Freeman was killed on 6 February 1941 in the crash of a B-17 Flying Fortress (B-17B 38-216) near Lovelock, Nevada while en route to Wright Field, Ohio. The aircraft was equipped with the top secret Norden bombsight and sabotage was suspected as the cause of the crash, but never was proven.

Initial surveys of the area were made in April 1942 and the present site of Freeman Municipal Airport was selected for construction. The first construction for the new airfield began in late June 1942 with construction proceeding throughout the summer. It included more than one hundred buildings, all intended to be temporary. Station buildings and streets were also constructed, the buildings consisting primarily of wood, tar paper, and non-masonry siding. The use of concrete and steel was limited because of the critical need elsewhere. Most buildings were hot and dusty in the summer and very cold in the winter. Water, sewer and electrical services were also constructed. The airfield consisted of runways in a "star" layout consisting of four 5,500 x 150' runways laid out in a north/south, northeast/southwest, east/west and a northwest/southeast direction. An extra-large parking ramp was constructed to accommodate large numbers of training aircraft, several hangars, a control tower and other auxiliary support aircraft buildings.

War Department General Order Number 10, dated 3 March 1943, announced that the airfield was to be named Freeman Army Airfield in honor of the Indiana native killed in a 1941 B-17 crash. Captain Freeman helped establish Ladd Field which is today's Fort Wainwright just outside Fairbanks, Alaska. He was Ladd Field's first commander.

The airfield was placed under the jurisdiction of the 33d Twin Engine Flying Training Group, Army Air Forces Training Command. The 447th Base Headquarters and Air Base Squadron was activated on 2 October 1942, and the airfield was activated on 1 December 1942, with the first troops began arriving on 8 December 1942.

The mission of Freeman AAF was a twin-engine advanced aircraft training school. Most of the initial staffing cadre of the faculty was drawn from Craig Army Airfield, near Selma Alabama. Five training squadrons, the 466th, 467th, 1078th, 1079th 1080th Twin-Engine Pilot were established at Freeman Field, and a total of 250 Beechcraft AT-10 Wichita trainers had arrived by the end of February 1943. The first flying cadets, who had just graduated from AAFTC advanced single-engine schools arrived on 2 March were formed as class 43-D. Night training commenced on 5 April. The first class was graduated on 29 April and the graduated went on to fly multi-engine aircraft such as the B-24 Liberator, B-17 Flying Fortress, B-29 Superfortress, and various other medium bombers and transport aircraft. Twin-engine training continued with a total of 19 classes of students being graduated from Freeman Field. The last graduates were in May 1944 (Class 44-K); 4,245 total cadets.

Twin-engine training ended in May 1944 and AAFTC initiated helicopter training at Freeman Field in June 1944. Freeman was the first helicopter base in the AAF, The first instructor pilots arrived on 30 June and preparations for the helicopter training were made in great secrecy, as in 1944 very few people had seen one and the technology was new and revolutionary. The group assigned to coordinate their arrival was known as "Section B-O". A total of six Sikorsky R-4A helicopters were assigned for training, flown directly to Freeman from the Sikorsky plant at Bridgeport, Connecticut. This was the longest long-distance flight of helicopters at the time.

The first helicopter class began training in July, graduating on 13 August. The training program continued throughout the balance of 1944, the last class (44-K) graduating on 1 February 1945. In January 1945, AAFTC moved the training to Chanute Field, Illinois, so it could consolidate the flying training operation with helicopter mechanic training.

With the end of helicopter training, Freeman Field's training mission was closed down and the facility was to be transferred as excess to Air Technical Service Command effective 1 March 1945.

On 1 February 1945 plans were changed by HQ Army Air Forces and Freeman Field was not to be inactivated. Jurisdiction of the facility was transferred to First Air Forc as an Operational Training airfield. Throughout World War II, continued pressure from African-American civilian leaders led the Army to allow blacks to train as members of bomber crews, a step that opened many more skilled combat roles to them. In response to this pressure, the mission of the base was changed to training black airmen for B-25 Mitchell medium bomber crews.

On 15 January 1944, the 477th Bombardment (later Composite) Group was activated to train African-American aviators on B-25s at Selfridge Fiel near Detroit, Michigan. On 5 May possibly out of fear of a repeat of the summer 1943 race riot in nearby Detroit, the 477th was abruptly relocated to Godman Fiel at Fort Knox, Kentucky.

Godman's was not suitable for B-25 training and to accommodate the 477th, two of the squadrons, the 618t and 619th Bombardment Squadro were moved to Atterbury Army Airfield, Indiana, in August 1944 for training. In March 1945 the 477th reached its full combat strength and the two squadrons in training at Atterbury were moved to Freeman Field to consolidate with the 616t and 617th Bombardment Squadrons that were moved to Freeman from Godman. The entire group was assembled for final group training at Freeman and it was scheduled to deploy overseas in into combat on 1 July.

The 477th ground echelon began moving by train to Freeman Field on 1 March 1945. The unit consisted of about 1,300 black airmen. The B-25 squadrons arrived at the field during the first week of March. Freeman had two officer clubs: Officer Club 1 for trainees, and Officer Club 2 for instructors. Despite Army regulations against segregation, the two officer clubs were, in practice, segregated between white officers in command and the black aviators in training, which caused much racial tension in the unit. A so-called "mutiny" at Freeman took place on 5 April 1945 when three black aviator officers attempted to enter Officer Club 2. They were placed under arrest and ordered confined to quarters. The next night, an additional 58 additional black aviator officers attempted to enter the club, which led to physical violence and over sixty personnel were arrested. In response, an investigation was made and the unit commander drafted a new regulation, Base Regulation 85-2, which confirmed segregation of club facilities, which the black aviator officers were asked to sign and acknowledge. One hundred one black officers refused to sign the regulation and were placed under arrest in quarters.

All of the arrested were transferred to Godman Field where they were held awaiting court-martial. Training of the unit at Freeman was immediately halted. Later in April, under public pressure charges were dropped against all except the original three. Of these, one was tried and fined $150 for violence against an MP.

As a result of the protest, the 477th was reassigned back to Godman Field by the end of April 1945, and two of its four bomb squadrons (the 616th and 619th) inactivated. The protests by black officers at Freeman Field against the segregated facilities made headlines throughout the nation, and helped focus a re-thinking of the racial segregation policies of the military.

With the 477th moved to Kentucky, on 2 May 1945, Freeman Field was placed on Standby Status, with jurisdiction of the facility being transferred to Air Technical Service Command on 15 May.

On 11 June, Freeman was re-activated by ATSC as the Foreign Aircraft Evaluation Center for the Air Force. After the end of the war in Europe, captured German and Italian aircraft were collected by "Operation Lusty". These aircraft were shipped to the United States for evaluation. Freeman was selected due to its inviability and large amount of empty space which could be used to store these aircraft and perform evaluation flights.

In 1945 the enemy aircraft shipped to the United States were divided between the Navy and the Army Air Forces. General Hap Arnold ordered the preservation of one of every type of aircraft used by the enemy forces.

Initially, the Air Force brought their aircraft to Wright Field, and when the field could no longer handle additional aircraft, many were sent to Freeman Field to the foreign technology evaluation center established there. Most of the foreign airplanes were German, but there were also Japanese, Italian and English planes. Nowhere in the United States would there be such large numbers of foreign aircraft, many of which were rare and incredible advanced for their time, In addition, there were warehouses full of Luftwaffe equipment. Forty-seven personnel were engaged in the identification, inspection and warehousing of captured foreign equipment. Freeman Field was also charged with the mission to receive and catalogue United States equipment for display at the present and for the future AAF museum.

The evaluation center was the last United States Air Force operation at Freeman Field. By the middle of 1946, the program was winding down and efforts began to dispose of the surplus captured equipment. The larger aircraft were sent to Davis-Monthan Field, Arizona, and the fighter aircraft sent to the Special Depot, Park Ridge, Ill. (now O'Hare Airport), which was under the control of ATSC's Office of Intelligence.

Not all of the captured planes assigned to Freeman were transferred. Some which were left at the field were destroyed or buried. Examples of aircraft that have no record of leaving Freeman Field are a Dornier Do 335 experimental interceptor; a Heinkel He 219 radar-equipped night fighter; an Arado Ar 234 twin-engined jet bomber, two Messerschmitt Me 163 rocket-powered interceptors, two Focke-Wulf Fw 190 interceptors and a Junkers Ju 88 two-engine multi-role aircraft.

In addition to the captured aircraft, there was the task of disposing all of the equipment and other surplus material at the field, including the physical buildings. Sales were held throughout 1946 for scrap lumber of torn down buildings, fence posts, barbed wire and other items which no longer had a useful need. The last airmen left Freeman Army Airfield on 27 November 1946.

Freeman Field was closed and declared surplus on 30 December 1946 and was turned over to the War Assets Administration (WAA) for disposal. Throughout 1947, buildings and equipment were sold. Freeman Field was deeded as a municipal airport to Seymour, Indiana. In July 1947, a flight training school for former servicemen was set up and over 70 students took pilot training at the field.

The WAA determined the post-war use of the land and structures: 2,241 acres (9.07 km2) for a municipal airport for Seymour; more than 240 acres (0.97 km2) for agricultural training in the Seymour Community Schools; and the Seymour Industrial Association received more than 60 acres (240,000 m2) to develop an industrial park. It was formally sold in November 1948.

Today much of the former Freeman Army Airfield is leased to farmers who grow corn and soy beans on it. The runways are still there although two are shut down. Most of the station area is an industrial park. There are about a dozen buildings that remain from the former Army Airfield. The Indiana National Guard's Company C, 38th Support Battalion (Main) also has an armory on the former base. Also, Freeman Army Air Field Museum is located near the airport office. The museum contains a large collection of memorabilia that has been collected and donated by flyers who were stationed there and other interested persons.

Without doubt, any alien technology captured by the Americans in Europe were first transfer to Freeman Airfield for storage, and never showed to the public.

Freeman Airfield Show 1945

**Freeman Airfield Show 1945**

**Freeman Airfield Show 1945**

**Freeman Airfield Show 1945**

FEDERAL BUREAU OF INVESTIGATION

# Part.1a

## SUBJECT: THEODORE VON KARMAN

## FILE NUMBER: 40-13556 AND 100-372586 SERIALS X-29

TEXT ON THIS PAGE IS ILLEGIBLE
WE HAVE LEFT THE PAGE AS REFERENCE

ND-84

RECORDED

RBS:MED

354,894
DECLASSIFIED BY SP5 JC/ltm
ON 6-26-97

TO: VISA DIVISION, DEPARTMENT OF STATE

November 28, 1941

In connection with the below entitled visa applicant case the files of the Federal Bureau of Investigation reflect the following information.

Very truly yours,

CONFIDENTIAL

J. Edgar Hoover

John Edgar Hoover
Director

Enclosure

TITLE: [redacted] Visa Applicant; [redacted] PROF. THEODORE VON KARMAN; [redacted]
Sponsors
Passports and Visas

[redacted]
Green Village, New Jersey

Relative to this individual, information is available that [redacted]

b7C

MAILED
NOV 28 1941
P.M.
FEDERAL BUREAU OF INVESTIGATION
U. S. DEPARTMENT OF JUSTICE

J-65

TEXT ON THIS PAGE IS ILLEGIBLE
WE HAVE LEFT THE PAGE AS REFERENCE



A confidential source of information reported in December, 1937, that [redacted]

b7C

PROFESSOR THEODORE VON KARMAN
University Aeronautics, Pasadena, Calif.

Information is available that he is a Hungarian Jew, who first entered the United States in October, 1926, and since that time, has made numerous trips between the United States and Europe. It was reported in May, 1941, that von Karman's sister, who lives with him, has declared herself to be a Nazi sympathizer on many occasions, and does not try to hide the fact that she is in favor of the Nazi cause. Von Karman is presently under investigation by this Bureau, along with two other individuals, all of whom are suspected of being engaged in espionage activities. (65-8943-46)

The duplicate copy of Form GH is being returned herewith.

TEXT ON THIS PAGE IS ILLEGIBLE
WE HAVE LEFT THE PAGE AS REFERENCE

ND-34

RHA:gch
40-13556

July 18, 1942

TO: VISA DIVISION, DEPARTMENT OF STATE

In connection with the below entitled visa applicant case the files of the Federal Bureau of Investigation reflect the following information.

Very truly yours,

~~CONFIDENTIAL~~

DECLASSIFIED BY 354-194 SPS JC/Dm
ON 6.26.97

J. E. Hoover

John Edgar Hoover
Director

Enclosure CIA Info. Remains unclass per letter DTD 9/23/98

SUPPLEMENTAL REPORT TITLE: [redacted] THEODORE VON KARMAN; [redacted]
Sponsors
PASSPORTS AND VISAS

PROFESSOR THEODORE VON KARMAN
University Aeronautics
Pasadena, California

b7C

Reference is made to my letter dated November 28, 1941, in connection with the visa application of [redacted] et al, in which information was furnished concerning Professor Theodore Von Karman and one [redacted]. The following information is now available concerning Von Karman.

A confidential informant advised on November 16, 1939 that Theodore Von Karman, together with other individuals [illegible] teaching at the California Institute of Technology and by virtue of such position had access to the testing facilities for airplane models of the Army and Navy. The informant did not furnish information of a [illegible] which indicated that Von Karman was engaged in any suspicious activities, but suggested that he be investigated as he was of the opinion that he possessed pro-German sympathies.

[redacted]

Mr. Tolson
Mr. E. A. Tamm
Mr. Clegg
Mr. Glavin
Mr. Ladd
Mr. Nichols
Mr. Rosen
Mr. Tracy
Mr. Carson
Mr. Coffey
Mr. Hendon
Mr. Kramer
Mr. McGuire
Mr. Quinn Tamm
Mr. Nease
Miss Gandy

INDEXED

40-13556-4

FEDERAL BUREAU OF INVESTIGATION
JUL 21 1942
U. S. DEPARTMENT OF JUSTICE

COMMUNICATIONS SECTION
(65-8943-55)
MAILED 12
JUL 18 1942
FEDERAL BUREAU OF INVESTIGATION
U. S. DEPARTMENT OF JUSTICE

1 JUL 23 1942

I-65 Suppl.

Other information advised that Von Karman was entirely reliable and was anti-Nazi in sympathy. It has been reported that a number of marked maps of the TVA and various other bridges were discovered in the davenport taken from the home of one Theodore Von Karman, who at that time was residing at 1501 South Marango Street, Pasadena, California. In this same connection, it was stated that this individual had been called in by the Federal Government as an expert on stresses and strains after the collapse of the Takoma Bridge in Washington, and that he had made a survey of all suspension bridges in this country for the government. There is conflicting evidence as to whether or not this individual is on friendly terms with one Alexander Goetz of California, concerning whom considerable derogatory information is available indicating pro-German sympathies. (65-8943-49)

Information made available indicates that Von Karman, on December 19, 1940, wrote to an individual of German extraction who was suspected of having engaged in espionage activities in this country. (65-8943-55)

Confidential information is available that Von Karman corresponded on January 10, 1941, with an individual suspected of having engaged in espionage activities. (65-8943-55)

On January 12, 1942, information was made available that an anonymous telephone call at Los Angeles, California reported that approximately one year before a man by the name of T. Kodama had contacted the informant relative to a business transaction. Kodama advised that he was employed by a Dr. Theodore Von Karman, who was an airplane designer for the United States Government and a Professor at the California Institute of Technology. The informant further advised that this individual displayed a picture of his employer, Dr. Theodore Von Karman, dressed in a robe which bore a large swastika thereon. (65-8943-54)

Information received in June of 1942 from Los Angeles, California, advises that Theodore Von Karman has had a Japanese in his employ as a chauffeur gardener and general handy man. Information is available that this individual is a Japanese named Podajiro Kodama and that he is reported to be a structural engineer who could read drawings and blueprints. According to this information, this individual has in the past had access to various blueprints and drawings which Von Karman had in his possession. Kodama, according to this information, has been removed from the Los Angeles area and is no longer in the employ of Von Karman. (65-8943-5960) b3

Von Karman is presently the subject of an espionage investigation being conducted by this Bureau.

2-24-41
Summary of above given [redacted]
along with advise
b2 [redacted] b7c
that our investigation was
closed without any action

# FEDERAL BUREAU OF INVESTIGATION

FREEDOM OF INFORMATION/PRIVACY ACTS
Section

**Subject:** Theodore Von Karman

**File:** 100-372586
Serials X-29

TEXT ON THIS PAGE IS ILLEGIBLE
WE HAVE LEFT THE PAGE AS REFERENCE

# FEDERAL BUREAU OF INVESTIGATION

Form No. 1
THIS CASE ORIGINATED AT LOS ANGELES, CALIFORNIA

FILE NO. 65-1145

| REPORT MADE AT | DATE WHEN MADE | PERIOD FOR WHICH MADE | REPORT MADE BY |
|---|---|---|---|
| CINCINNATI, OHIO | 10-6-41 | 8-30-41 | [redacted] RBR b7C |

TITLE: THEODORE VON KARMAN, with aliases, et al.

CHARACTER OF CASE: ESPIONAGE (G)

(354-894)
ALL INFORMATION CONTAINED HEREIN IS UNCLASSIFIED DATE 5-8-97 BY SP5JC

SYNOPSIS OF FACTS: THEODORE VON KARMAN was probably furnished with an old style identification pass of the War Department Air Corps Material Division, Wright Field, Ohio, which pass would take him under present regulations only to the information desk at the field, or any other air corps field, where he would be required to furnish further identification. VON KARMAN has worked at Wright Field on research problems in the aircraft laboratory wind tunnel.

2 cc's AEC (Photo) 3/9/54

R U C

b7C

REFERENCE: Report of Special Agent [redacted] Los Angeles, California, dated 8-12-41.

DETAILS:

An investigation at Wright Field, Dayton, Ohio, was requested to ascertain why an air corps identification card was issued to THEODORE VON KARMAN and to determine his connection with the air corps.

b7C

AT DAYTON, OHIO

100-372586-X Referred

[redacted]

APPROVED AND FORWARDED: SPECIAL AGENT IN CHARGE

DO NOT WRITE IN THESE SPACES

65-8943-46

RECORDED

COPIES OF THIS REPORT
5 Bureau
2 Los Angeles
2 Cincinnati

[redacted]

OCT 8 1941

b7C

# FEDERAL BUREAU OF INVESTIGATION

Form No. 1
THIS CASE ORIGINATED AT LOS ANGELES, CALIFORNIA — LA FILE NO. 65-265

| REPORT MADE AT | DATE WHEN MADE | PERIOD FOR WHICH MADE | REPORT MADE BY |
|---|---|---|---|
| LOS ANGELES, CALIFORNIA | 5-7-40 | 11-14; 12-27,29-39 4-27,29-40 | [redacted] jac |

| TITLE | CHARACTER OF CASE |
|---|---|
| THEODORE VON KARMAN; ALEXANDER GOETZ; | ESPIONAGE |

SYNOPSIS OF FACTS: THEODORE VON KARMAN, Professor of Aeronautics, California Institute of Technology is alleged to be a Hungarian Jew and very much opposed to Nazi Government. Dr. SPIRO KYROPOULOS, a Research Fellow in Physics at CIT recently submitted plans or specifications of a military nature to some U.S. Government department. Although KYROPOULOS thought this transaction confidential, ALEXANDER GOETZ, Departmental Head at CIT, admonished KYROPOULOS for not taking the matter up with him before submitting it to government. GOETZ is native of Prussia, and thought to be Nazi sympathizer, although he does not express beliefs. GOETZ is close friend of [redacted] Salesman for Adolph Frese Corp., Los Angeles. [redacted] is native of Germany who sells heat regulators and thermometers which are used by aircraft manufacturers.

[redacted] and has gone out of his way to disclaim German affiliations. Although there are several foreign Teaching Fellows in Aeronautics Department at CIT, it is not known whether they have access to the wind tunnel or confidential information obtained therefrom. [redacted] advised it is his belief that the wind tunnel at CIT is closely guarded against unauthorized admittance - this belief being substantiated by [redacted] Pasadena, California, student at CIT.

RECORDED FILES SECTION

APPROVED AND FORWARDED: [signature] SPECIAL AGENT IN CHARGE

DO NOT WRITE IN THESE SPACES

MAY 1

COPIES OF THIS REPORT

5- Bureau
1- OAI, San Francisco
1- OAI, Ft. McArthur
2- ONI, San Diego
2- Los Angeles

TEXT ON THIS PAGE IS ILLEGIBLE
WE HAVE LEFT THE PAGE AS REFERENCE

DETAILS: The following investigation was conducted by Special Agent [redacted]

[redacted] Pasadena, California, [redacted] advised the Los Angeles Division by letter dated November 15, 1939 of the following information:

[redacted] had received information that a Dr. SPIRO KYROPOULOS, a Research Fellow in Physics at the California Institute of Technology, Pasadena, recently submitted certain plans or specifications of a military nature to some United States Government department. Although this transaction was confidential, Dr. KYROPOULOS was astonished a few days later to find that Dr. GOETZ, head of one of the departments at Cit, knew of this transaction. GOETZ is alleged to have admonished KYROPOULOS for not taking the matter up with him before submitting it to the Government.

KYROPOULOS took his degree in Physics at the University of Leipzig, and came to this country in 193[redacted]

[redacted] KYROPOULOS is alleged to have been an engineer in the German submarine service during the first World War. In this same letter [redacted] furnished the names of the following [redacted] who are alleged to be pro-nazi - the comments of [redacted] are quoted:

> JOE CASPROWIACK, "40, definitely pro-Nazi. Lives at hotel. In U.S. about 12 yrs. Works as Flower Boy. Amateur photographer."
>
> [redacted] "age unknown, has final citizenship papers, works in Flower Room, pro-Nazi, known as [redacted] Amateur photographer."
>
> [redacted] "age unknown, no papers, known as possible pro-Nazi."
>
> [redacted] "age unknown, possible pro-Nazi."
>
> [redacted] "age unknown, has citizenship papers, married, supposed to __ active in, if not head of, local Bund."
>
> [redacted] "age unknown, no papers, possible pro-Nazi."

Upon interview [redacted] advised that he has studied at the California Institute of Technology for the past [redacted] years, and is personally acquainted with the majority of professors at that

-2-

institution. He stated that Dr. THEODORE VON KARMAN, Head of the Aeronautics Department at CIT. bears the reputation of being definitely anti-Nazi. [redacted] said that [redacted] who is presently [redacted] at CIT, is very anti-Nazi; that [redacted] recently advised him that VON KARMAN is a Hungarian Jew, and that on several occasions he has assisted in aiding Jewish refugees in leaving Germany. According to [redacted] VON KARMAN resides at 1501 South Morengo Avenue, Pasadena, with his sister; and his description is as follows:

| | |
|---|---|
| Name | THEODORE VON KARMAN |
| Age | 60 years |
| Height | 5' 6" |
| Weight | 160 pounds |
| Hair | Gray |
| Eyes | Dark |
| Speech | German accent |

[redacted] stated that VON KARMAN is a close friend of [redacted] the actress, and that he has never heard anything which would indicate that he is sympathetic toward the Nazi Government.

b7C
b7D

[redacted] further advised that the information which he had received relative to ALEXANDER GOETZ criticizing KYROPOULOS for sending his specifications or plans of military value to one of the departments of the United States Government at Washington, D.C. - was obtained from [redacted]

[redacted] stated that he would keep in touch with [redacted] and endeavor to develop an acquaintance with KYROPOULOS in an effort to obtain definite information relative to what plans or specifications he submitted to the government; and further to learn how GOETZ obtained the information that the plans had been submitted. [redacted] stated that while GOETZ is very close-mouthed about his political views, he is thought to be a Nazi sympathizer.

[redacted] further stated that quite some time ago, [redacted] is connected with the Soviet Embassy at [redacted] is now in Washington, D.C., employed in one of the governmental departments as a physicist.

[redacted] stated that [redacted] advised him that GOETZ is a Prussian, and was having difficulty with the Nazi Government when he left Germany. However, after arriving in the United States, GOETZ made definite efforts to obtain the good will of the Nazi Government and is undoubtedly pro-Nazi in his sympathies at the present time.

[redacted] stated that the wind tunnel at CIT is used by all of the local manufacturers of airplanes to test out models, both commercial and those being manufactured for the Army and Navy; that immediately above the wind tunnel there are several computing rooms where the confidential data relative to the performance of the planes in the wind tunnel are recorded; and even though a person did not obtain access to the wind tunnel, if he could obtain the confidential data relative to the plane's performance he would undoubtedly have a great deal of valuable information concerning the new models. [redacted] stated that he understood that a great deal of care is exercised by the officials of CIT in order to prevent students from gaining entrance to the wind tunnel and computing rooms. However, he stated, all the professors in the Aeronautics Department, and Research Fellows, could probably gain access to the wind tunnel.

[redacted] stated that the catalog for the CIT reflects that BASIL PETROVICH ANTONENKO is a Teaching Fellow in the Aeronautics Department, and that he is from the Petersburg School of Naval Aviation - probably Russia. Further that the catalog shows JOHN SHOICHI ATSUMI is a Teaching Fellow and Assistant in the Aeronautics Department at CIT; that he has a BS degree from the University of Southern California, obtained in 1932, and a MSE degree from the University of Michigan, obtained in 1935. The school catalog also reflects that GEORGE YOSHIO TSUBOTA is a Teaching Fellow and Assistant in the Aeronautics Department at CIT. TSUBOTA obtained a BS degree at CIT in 1937, and a MS degree there in 1938; and that these last two mentioned individuals are Japanese.

[redacted] stated that it is very possible that all three of the above-mentioned individuals could gain access to both the wind tunnel and computing rooms. However, he stated that he had no definite information that such was the case.

It will be recalled that this investigation was predicated upon information as set forth in reference letter to the effect that foreigners, including VON KARMAN, who were studying or teaching at CIT, had access to the wind tunnel where all new airplane models for the Army and Navy manufactured in this area are tested. In this regard it is believed that [redacted]

[redacted] CIT, could furnish information of value concerning the various individuals mentioned in this report - as well as information regarding possible access by them to the wind tunnel and computing rooms. [redacted] has in the past furnished information of value to this office, and is very cooperative.

-5-

[redacted] was mentioned the letter previously referred to, as possibly being in a position to furnish information relative to VON KARMAN. This person is undoubtedly [redacted]

[redacted] was telephonically contacted and he advised that he left CIT approximately [redacted] years ago, and is, therefore, not able to furnish any information of value relative to activities of persons at CIT. The nature of this investigation was not disclosed to [redacted]

[redacted] subsequently advised that he learned that [redacted] is a native of Germany, [redacted] is definitely pro-Nazi in his sympathies.

*****

The following investigation was conducted by Special Agent [redacted]

[redacted] was recontacted, at which time he stated that he had since ascertained that the secrecy surrounding entries into the wind tunnel building was due chiefly to keep various experiments of the several aircraft industries who make tests in the tunnel, confidential. He had also learned that the rules regarding entering the tunnel are strictly observed and that it is the most difficult building on the campus to gain entrance to. [redacted] stated that it was his opinion that VON KARMAN was entirely reliable, being anti-Nazi, a citizen of the United States, and one of the top-ranking men in the field of aeronautical science.

No further information was obtained by [redacted] regarding ALEXANDER GOETZ. Regarding SPIRO KYROPOULOS, [redacted] stated that his original informant, had been unable to obtain any further information.

As further information regarding [redacted] who contacts ALEXANDER GOETZ on the average of twice a week, [redacted] stated that he had personally had contacts with all of the aircraft industries in and about Los Angeles, and had discussed [redacted] conduct with the various officials at each place, [redacted] pointing out his suspicions regarding [redacted] and his contacts with GOETZ. No recent information regarding [redacted] had been obtained other than that [redacted] is still strongly pro-Nazi.

[redacted] stated that GOETZ and KYROPOULOS are not known personally to him. Further that he had no reason to contact VON KARMAN in his studies, and therefore did not

-c-know him. [redacted] was very cooperative, and stated that he would be on the alert for any information indicating subversive activities or espionage - and in line with that, would contact [redacted] and request him to also watch for any irregularities in the [redacted] branch of the school. The importance of strict confidential treatment of all information and inquiries was impressed on [redacted] who stated that he would be very careful when obtaining information.

[redacted] advised that by actual test on his part he has ascertained that admittance to the wind tunnel and access to any information developed from experiments therein, is extremely difficult; and that the tunnel is kept under lock and key at all times, addmittance therein being restricted only to authorized persons, and exceptions permitted only on occasions when persons have obtained a pass from the person in charge of the tunnel.

CLOSED

TEXT ON THIS PAGE IS ILLEGIBLE
WE HAVE LEFT THE PAGE AS REFERENCE

100-392586-X1
~~65-8943~~ - 49
~~REE~~:AJ

December 23, 1941

Special Agent in Charge
Los Angeles, California

RE: THEODORE VON KARMAN, with
aliases, et al;
ESPIONAGE - G.

Dear Sir:

There are transmitted herewith for your information and possible aid in the subsequent investigation of this case, photostatic copies of a confidential report received from the Military Intelligence Division of the War Department.

This report is dated October 26, 1941, and contains the results of an investigation made at Fort MacArthur, California, concerning subject.

Very truly yours,

John Edgar Hoover
Director

354-394
ALL INFORMATION CONTAINED
HEREIN IS UNCLASSIFIED
DATE 5-21-97 BY SPSJC/...

Enclosure

4 JAN 23 1942

COMMUNICATIONS SECTION
MAILED
DEC 24 1941
P. M.
FEDERAL BUREAU OF INVESTIGATION
U. S. DEPARTMENT OF JUSTICE

TEXT ON THIS PAGE IS ILLEGIBLE
WE HAVE LEFT THE PAGE AS REFERENCE

# FEDERAL BUREAU OF INVESTIGATION

Form No. 1
THIS CASE ORIGINATED AT LOS ANGELES FILE NO. 65-266

| REPORT MADE AT | DATE WHEN MADE | PERIOD FOR WHICH MADE | REPORT MADE BY |
|---|---|---|---|
| LOS ANGELES | 1/8/42 | 12/2-5, 18, 22/41; 1/1/42. | [redacted] |

| TITLE | CHARACTER OF CASE |
|---|---|
| THEODORE VON KARMAN, with aliases; ALEXANDER GOETZ, with aliases; | ESPIONAGE - G |

SYNOPSIS OF FACTS:

Informant advises subject GOETZ a friend of [redacted] Los Angeles and San Francisco, respectively. Subject GOETZ has had Japs as guests at home. [redacted] wrote letter to subject from New York, saying that she had finished the job she was sent to do, and got the information she went after. Subject receives mail from Germany on average of one or two each week. Both subject GOETZ [redacted] have made statements reflecting sympathy with the Japanese. Subject mailed three letters to Germany on Monday morning, December 8, 1941, the day after the Japanese attack on Pearl Harbor. Subject [redacted] have become friendly with a neighbor who is connected with the Coast Guard.

P.

REFERENCE:

Report of Special Agent [redacted], Los Angeles, dated August 12, 1941.
Los Angeles letter to the Bureau dated December 4, 1941.
Los Angeles letter to the Bureau dated December 16, 1941.
Los Angeles letter to Bureau dated August 15, 1941.
Bureau letter to Los Angeles dated December 23, 1941.

APPROVED AND FORWARDED: [signature] SPECIAL AGENT IN CHARGE

DO NOT WRITE IN THESE SPACES

65-[illegible]

2 FEB 3 1942

COPIES OF THIS REPORT

5 Bureau
1 G-2, San Francisco
1 G-2, Los Angeles
1 O. N. I., Los Angeles
2 Los Angeles

RECEIVED

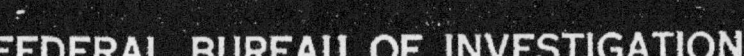

DETAILS:

Memorandum for the file, dated September 2, 1941, reflects that on August 28, 1941, information was telephonically furnished to this office by the TWA that DR. VON KARMAN was departing at 6:00 P.M. for New York City on the Stratoliner and was leaving on August 29, 1941, aboard the American Line, Trip 36, New York City, en route to Providence, Rhode Island.

Memorandum for the file dated September 8, 1941, reflects that on August 28, 1941, [redacted] Pasadena, telephonically advised Special Agent [redacted] that she had some information to divulge to the Bureau concerning a possible spy of a serious nature. She said that several months previously she had communicated with the Los Angeles Office and had furnished data concerning the activities of a certain individual in Pasadena, whose name she did not wish to divulge on the telephone. She said that at the present time she had additional information concerning the same subject but that such information was of such a serious nature that she could not reveal it unless personally contacted by a Bureau Agent. Informant was advised that she would be contacted by a Special Agent within the near future. A search of the files in the Los Angeles Field Office reveals that informant had given information concerning THEODORE VON KARMAN, L. A. File No. 65-265.

1C
1D

Memorandum for the file dated September 25, 1941, reflects that upon instructions of Assistant Special Agent in Charge [redacted] Special Agent [redacted] telephonically contacted [redacted] Pasadena, and requested an interview at her convenience. It was suggested by [redacted] had certain information which she would furnish the Bureau and he suggested that she be contacted. [redacted] suggested that Agent contact her between 10:00 and 11:00 on September 17, 1941, which request was complied with and [redacted] furnished the following information:

That the proprietor of [redacted] while doing some work for her had told her that he, while doing some [redacted] at a [redacted] residence had observed a divan in which there appeared to be a secret compartment, and that in this compartment there were a large number of railroad maps, reported to show the location of railroads in the United States, and that on these maps all bridges were marked.

[redacted] stated that she was advised by [redacted] that the residence in which he observed these maps with the bridges marked thereon was at the home of Dr. JOSEPHINE De KARMAN, who is the sister of Dr. VON KARMAN, who is employed by the California Institute of Technology. [redacted] further stated that [redacted] advised her that previous checks which have been given him in payment for [redacted] by Dr. JOSEPHINE De KARMAN had been signed Dr. JOSEPHINE VON KARMAN.

[redacted] advised that to her personal knowledge VON KARMAN was employed at the California Institute of Technology, and that he was a recognized authority on the subject of stresses and strains of bridges. She further advised that [redacted] had mentioned to her that Dr. VON KARMAN had been approached by the German Government in an effort to induce VON KARMAN to return to Germany.

2
1C
1D

It is to be noted in connection with the above memorandum that subsequent information revealed that the maps mentioned in the memorandum were in subject VON KARMAN's possession legally and rightfully. Furthermore, information furnished by Confidential National Defense Informant [redacted] known to the Bureau under Bureau cover letter dated December 23, 1941, reflects that these maps were rightfully in subject's possession.

A memorandum for the file dated October 6, 1941, reflects that Special Agent [redacted] was telephonically advised by Confidential National Defense Informant No. [redacted] that Professor GOETZ, who is purportedly on the staff of the California Institute of Technology, is an ardent Nazi sympathizer. The informant stated that this individual has, on many occasions, made pro-Nazi statements indicating sincere and ardent belief and support of the Nazi regime. The informant also stated that [redacted] in the same institution, the California Institute of Technology, can verify Professor GOETZ' sympathy and allegiance to the Nazi regime.

A card from Confidential National Defense Informant [redacted] reflects that a review of the record of subject ALEXANDER GOETZ in their files, reveals a strong German Nationalism and sympathy for the Nazi cause, and association with numerous individuals who are known to be engaged in espionage. The conclusion is drawn that subject would be a distinct threat to the National security if permitted his liberty, in the event of hostilities between the United States and Germany; reclassified as dangerous accordingly.

Memorandum for the file dated December 16, 1941, reflects that under date of December 9, 1941, an anonymous informant telephonically contacted Special Agent [redacted] and reported that about one year ago a Japanese chauffeur named T. KODAMA had contacted her relative to a business transaction; that he said he was employed by DR. THEODORE VON KARMAN, who is an airplane designer for the U. S. GOVERNMENT and a Professor at California Institute of Technology. This informant further advised that the Japanese chauffeur at the time he contacted her, displayed a picture of his employer, DR. VON KARMAN, THEODORE, dressed in a robe which bore a large Swastika thereon. The informant advised that DR. JOSEPHINE VON KARMAN, sister of THEODORE, had taught language classes last year at the University of California. THEODORE VON KARMAN resides at 1501 South Marengo, near Pasadena, and it is thought that his sister, JOSEPHINE VON KARMAN, resides with him. It was further stated by the informant that according to the telephone directory, T. KODAMA resides at 717 Cypress Street, Los Angeles.

Repeated efforts to contact T. KODAMA have been made, with negative results. The telephone number of T. KODAMA is SYcamore 35028. A lead is being set out to make further efforts to contact KODAMA for the purpose of interviewing him regarding the above information.

The Los Angeles Field Division has no record in their files concerning KODAMA.

Confidential National Defense Informant [redacted] advises that subject VON KARMAN is a Hungarian Jew, and recognized as one of the leading aeronautical experts in the world. When VON KARMAN received an offer from Germany requesting his return to Germany for military purposes, VON KARMAN jokingly asked Confidential National Defense Informant [redacted] if he shouldn't send them a picture of his profile. Informant advised that VON KARMAN had been cleared by both the office of [redacted] and [redacted] after a request by the National Defense Research Committee at California Institute of Technology, inasmuch as the Institute wanted to use VON KARMAN as a consultant. Informant advised that [redacted] investigated subject concerning the alleged finding of bridge pictures [redacted] in VON KARMAN's home. Informant stated he was sure this was in connection with a consultation concerning the Tacoma Narrows Bridge, which collapsed approximately a year ago, and at that time he was given the maps and pictures of many other bridges to check for the same possibilities. Informant further advised that each of the employees at the Institute had been required to read appropriate sections of the Espionage Act, and sign a statement saying that they had read this Act, and also furnish a great deal of history concerning themselves. Informant advised that this information was on forms which were filed at the school, and which she would be glad to produce. The forms were produced, and the information thereon appears as follows:

THEODORE VON KARMAN,
1501 South Marengo Avenue,
Pasadena, California.
Date: February 27, 1941
Marital status: Single
Position: Director, Guggenheim Aeronautical Laboratory
Date of Appointment: 1928
Former positions:
Assistant Professor, University of Göttingen, 1909 to [illegible]
Professor of Aeronautics and Director of Aeronautical Institute, University of Aachen, 1913-1930
Visiting Professor in United States, Japan, China and India, 1926 to 1929
Advisor, Guggenheim Airship Institute, Akron, Ohio, since 1930
Born May 11, 1881, Budapest, Hungary
Entered United States September, [illegible], at New York City
Naturalized July [illegible], 1936, Southern District of California
Father and mother born in Hungary
Education: University of Budapest, Hungary ([illegible])
University of Gottingen, Germany, Ph. D.
Description:
Height [illegible]
Weight [illegible] pounds
Eyes [illegible]
Hair [illegible]

- [illegible] -

UNDEVELOPED LEADS:

THE LOS ANGELES FIELD DIVISION

At Altadena, California, will ascertain the correct address of the subject ALEXANDER GOETZ.

At Pasadena, California, will investigate subject GOETZ's bank account at the bank at the corner of Madison and Colorado, Pasadena, California.

At Los Angeles, California, will interview T. KODAMA, anonymously reported to be a former chauffeur of VON KARMAN, relative to the information appearing above.

Will attempt, through confidential sources, to obtain information appearing in the cablegram sent by subject from 2400 Holliston, Altadena, California, at about 2:00 o'clock A.M. on approximately August of 1940.

Confidential National Defense Informant

Confidential National Defense Informant

TEXT ON THIS PAGE IS ILLEGIBLE
WE HAVE LEFT THE PAGE AS REFERENCE

Federal Bureau of Investigation
United States Department of Justice
Los Angeles, California
December 16, 1941

| |
|---|
| Mr. Tolson |
| Mr. E. A. Tamm |
| Mr. Clegg |
| Mr. Glavin |
| Mr. Ladd |
| Mr. Nichols |
| Mr. Tracy |
| Mr. Rosen |
| Mr. Carson |
| Mr. Coffey |
| Mr. Hendon |
| Mr. [illegible] |
| Mr. Quinn Tamm |
| Mr. [illegible] |
| Miss Gandy |
| [illegible] |

CONFIDENTIAL

Director
Federal Bureau of Investigation
Washington, D. C.

Dear Sir:

Re: THEODORE VON KARMAN, was, ET AL;
ESPIONAGE – G
CUSTODIAL DETENTION MEMORANDUM

It is respectfully suggested that subject VON KARMAN's name be deleted from the Custodial Detention Lists, inasmuch as a review of subject's file reflects no information whatsoever to the effect that he is engaged in activities inimical to the interests of the United States or has ever made statements showing sympathy to any foreign government.

On the contrary, the results of the investigation of subject VON KARMAN reflects that he is very anti-Nazi and pro-American. Subject VON KARMAN is an Hungarian Jew.

Very truly yours,

R. B. Hood

R. B. HOOD
Special Agent in Charge

WED:EEG
65-265
100-0-A

100-372586-X2

RECORDED

65-894-50

354-894
DECLASSIFIED BY SP5 JC/bgm
ON 5-9-97

FEDERAL BUREAU OF INVESTIGATION
DEC 19 1941
U. S. DEPARTMENT OF JUSTICE

7 JAN 3 1942

TEXT ON THIS PAGE IS ILLEGIBLE
WE HAVE LEFT THE PAGE AS REFERENCE

C

January 16, 1942

**MEMORANDUM**

Re: THEODORE VON KARMAN

A confidential informant advised on November 15, 1939, that Theodore Von Karman, who appears to be identical with the subject, together with other "foreigners" was studying and teaching at the California Institute of Technology, and by virtue of such position had access to the testing facilities for airplane models of the Army and Navy. The informant did not furnish information of a specific character which indicated that Von Karman was engaged in any suspicious activity, but suggested that he be investigated, as it was thought that he possessed pro-German sympathies. Other informants have advised that Von Karman is entirely reliable, is anti-Nazi in sympathy and has been active in aiding Jewish refugees in leaving Germany. [redacted] Pasadena, Calif. 65-8943-2

Information has been made available which reflects that Von Karman on December 19, 1940, wrote to an individual of German extraction who is suspected of having engaged in espionage activities in this country. (Report of [redacted] dated 12-29-41 at Los Angeles, 65-32107-)

A confidential informant advised that a subject suspected of having engaged in espionage activities had corresponded with Von Karman on January 10, 1941. (Conf. Inf. [redacted] Los Angeles, 65-32054-91)

b7C b7D

b2 b7D

100-372586-X3

(354.899)
ALL INFORMATION CONTAINED
HEREIN IS UNCLASSIFIED
DATE 5-21-92 BY

RECORDED

65-8943-5

FEDERAL BUREAU OF INVESTIGATION
4 JAN 23 1942
U.S. DEPARTMENT OF JUSTICE

TEXT ON THIS PAGE IS ILLEGIBLE
WE HAVE LEFT THE PAGE AS REFERENCE

WSC:hr

January 19, 1942

PERSONAL AND CONFIDENTIAL
BY SPECIAL MESSENGER

Honorable Adolf A. Berle, Jr.
Assistant Secretary of State
Department of State
Washington, D. C.

My dear Mr. Berle:

Reference is made to your communication dated October 14, 1941, in which you requested information concerning a number of persons connected with foreign language organizations in this country. In accordance with your request I am attaching hereto summary memoranda concerning some of the individuals whose names were included in your list, and it will be noted that my communication directed to you under date of November 14, 1941, contained the names of individuals who had been checked through the files of this Bureau, but no derogatory information which could be identified with these persons was disclosed.

A search of the files has been made in regard to the following named individuals, but no information of a derogatory character could be identified with any of the names included in this group:

Mr. Tolson
Mr. E. A. Tamm
Mr. Clegg
Mr. Glavin
Mr. Ladd
Mr. Nichols
Mr. Tracy
Mr. Rosen
Mr. Carson
Mr. Coffey
Mr. Hendon
Mr. Holloman
Mr. Quinn Tamm
Mr. Nease
Miss Gandy

COMMUNICATIONS SECTION
MAILED
JAN 20 1942
P. M.
FEDERAL BUREAU OF INVESTIGATION
U. S. DEPARTMENT OF JUSTICE

It was noted that the name of [redacted] was included in your list, and you are advised that no search has been conducted in regard to this individual.

The names of the other persons contained in your list, however, are being searched through the files, and you will be furnished with available information in regard to these persons at a early date.

Sincerely yours,

Enclosure

The following names were included in the list of memoranda forwarded under the above date.

Theodore Von Karman

TEXT ON THIS PAGE IS ILLEGIBLE
WE HAVE LEFT THE PAGE AS REFERENCE



Mr. Tolson
Mr. E. A. Tamm
Mr. Clegg
Mr. Glavin
Mr. Ladd
Mr. Nichols
Mr. Tracy
Mr. Rosen
Mr. Carson
Mr. Coffey
Mr. Hendon
Mr. Holloman
Mr. Quinn Tamm
Mr. Nease
Miss Gandy

TEXT ON THIS PAGE IS ILLEGIBLE
WE HAVE LEFT THE PAGE AS REFERENCE

# FEDERAL BUREAU OF INVESTIGATION

Form No. 1
THIS CASE ORIGINATED AT LOS ANGELES, CALIFORNIA

FILE NO. 65-265

| REPORT MADE AT | DATE WHEN MADE | PERIOD FOR WHICH MADE | REPORT MADE BY |
|---|---|---|---|
| LOS ANGELES | 6/3/42 | 1/19; 2/3,5,23; 3/2,23, 24,27,31; 4/10,13, 16,21;5/15,26; 6/2/42 | GIF |

TITLE THEODORE VON KARMAN, with aliases: Theodor Von Karman, Theodor De Karman; ALEXANDER GOETZ, with aliases, Carl Goetz, Alexander Carl Goetz, Karl Wilhelm Alexander Gustav Goetz;

CHARACTER OF CASE: ESPIONAGE (G)

SYNOPSIS OF FACTS:

File reviewed and brought up to date. Subject VON KARMAN has had a Japanese in employ as a chauffeur who was formerly reported to have been a structural engineer in Japan and to have listened to Japanese broadcasts weekly. Subject GOETZ reported to have proposed a toast "to the Bismark" a day or two after the sinking of the HMS Hood, and to have sailed around Balboa Bay with a German officer from the scuttled ship "Columbus". GOETZ further reported to have stated his interest to be in Germany rather than in the United States. Subject's bank account checked with negative results. Subject's sympathies reported definitely pro-German according to recent remarks.

\- P -

REFERENCE:

Report of Special Agent
Los Angeles 1/8/42.
Bureau letter 1/13/41 (65-8913).
Letter to Bureau 2/2/42.
Letter to El Paso 5/25/42.

DETAILS:

The following information was received under date of January 21, 1942 with reference to subject VON KARMAN:

"THEODOR VON KARMAN
1501 So. Marengo Avenue Pasadena

APPROVED AND FORWARDED: SPECIAL AGENT IN CHARGE

DO NOT WRITE IN THESE SPACES

65-18973-

COPIES OF THIS REPORT

5 Bureau
2 El Paso
1 ONI Los Angeles
1 ONI San Diego
1 G-2 Los Angeles
1 G-2 San Francisco
3 Los Angeles

JUN

"61 years, 6'1" - 240 lbs.
Black Curly Hair, Brown Eyes
Occasionally wears glasses, is nervous. Born: Budapest.
American citizen (?) Occ.: Professor of Aero-dynamics at California
    Institute of Technology
Resides with his sister, JOSEPHINE who is described as 58 yrs. of
    age, red hair (dyed).                    VON KARMAN

"Checked with the Credit Bureau who have a record since 1934. At
that time he was reported to be connected as professor and director
of the Guggenheim Aerodynamic Laboratory, receiving a salary of $9500
per year.

"Received his degree in Mechanical Engineering in Budapest in 1902.
P.H. in Gottingen in 1908. Honorary degree of Doctor of Engineering
at the University of Berlin in 1929. Privatdocent Gottingen 1910-13,
Director of Aero-Dynamic University Aacher 1913 to 1934. Honorary
advisor of the Aeronautical Department at Ising Hua University in
China in 1933. Member of Gesellschaft Der Wissen Schoften zu
Gottingen in 1925. Foreign member of Royal Academy of Science in
Torino in 1928. Rouseball lecturer at the University of Cambridge
in 1937. C.R.B. lecturer in Belgium in 1937. In 1936 newspaper
item stated that he had been elected honorary fellow in the Instruction of Aeronautical Science, stating that he was one of the
world's foremost aerodynamic experts.

"The property at his residence address was assessed to him, valuing
the land at $5350, and improvements as $3360, personal account was
$1200.
                                        JOSEPHINE
"In 1935 his sister reported that she used the name of DeKARMAN
because she had lived in Paris a number of years. She stated that
their name was originally a Hungarian name and was very long, and
explained that her brother used VON KARMAN because he had lived in
Germany many years.

"This subject has had in his employ, as a gardener, houseman, and
general handyman, for approximately the last five or six years, one
TODAJIRO KODAMA (Japanese) Alien Registration No. 4732655. Age 61
years, 5'2½" - 122 lbs. Gray hair, gray eyes (left eye slightly cocked).
Ismarried. Wife's name is CORA, white, American. Married in Tia Juana.
Address: 717 Cypress Ave., Pasadena. Telephone SY. 3-5028. He states
that he entered this country through San Francisco, and has never been
back to Japan. Has no children or living relatives.


she observed KODAMA on many occasions, in his capacity of houseman, "arranging and looking through papers on subject's desk. On many occasions subject would bring home blueprints and drawings relative to his work, which informant has seen, and she states that frequently KODAMA would be required, by this subject, to take these blueprints and drawings to Cal Tech, when subject would forget to take them with him. Our informant became very perturbed at this condition due to the fact that KODAMA had confided in her, at one time while partially under the influence of intoxicants that while he was in Japan he had been a structural engineer and could read drawings and blueprints. When informant called this condition to the attention of subject's sister JOSEPHINE she ignored the warning and said KODAMA was a harmless, ignorant Jap, and they had confidence in him.

"Our informant states that once a week, usually Thursday night, a heavy set, well dressed Japanese would call for KODAMA and then they would go to Los Angeles. When she asked KODAMA what they did he stated that they 'listened to Japan'. Our informant states that KODAMA is very well versed in current events.

[redacted] Our informant states that she was very suspicious of these two women. but due to the fact that she was very much occupied [redacted] she was unable to verify her suspicions, however, due to information in our files it is entirely possible that there is grounds for her suspicion.

"Informant also states that subject employed [redacted] we found in his billfold a membership card in The Southern California Automobile Club, issued to Dr. VON KARMAN. We inquired as to how it came into his possession, he said 'He is just a friend'.

[redacted] was interviewed at the Tujunga Canyon Detention Station subsequent to his apprehension as an enemy alien and he advised that TODAJIRO KODAMA had given instant card to [redacted] so that in the event that [redacted] ever became involved in an automobile accident he could show this card and it would assist him with the police. [redacted] advised that

TEXT ON THIS PAGE IS ILLEGIBLE
WE HAVE LEFT THE PAGE AS REFERENCE

KODAMA has about three or four such cards every year and that he had given one to [redacted] Questioned concerning what he knew about KODAMA, [redacted] advised that he knew nothing about KODAMA being a structural engineer in Japan and that he had met KODAMA at [redacted] vegetable stand at 425 South Fair Oaks In Pasadena and that the only thing he knew about him was that KODAMA was married to a white woman who was very old. He stated that he knew this only because KODAMA had told him so.

[redacted] Referenced report sets out a lead to interview KODAMA concerning information to the effect that he possessed a picture of VON KARMAN dressed in a robe with the Nazi swastika insignia thereon. The interview with KODAMA took place prior to the information received as set forth above, consequently no information was developed relative to the card which he had given [redacted] However, in view of the fact that no information was developed from [redacted] it is not deemed necessary to reinterview KODAMA. KODAMA advised that he was VON KARMAN'S chauffeur and also acted in the capacity of cook and gardener. He was asked to furnish a picture of VON KARMAN and he advised that he did not possess any pictures of him. He stated that he had been employed by VON KARMAN for about four years and that he had not returned to Japan in the last forty five years, having come to this country at that time. He stated that he was well satisfied with this country and that he did not ever want to return to Japan inasmuch as he heard that people were all poor in Japan. He stated that subject VON KARMAN was very opposed to HITLER and that he has never seen any swastika insignia in the home. He said that VON KARMAN had become a citizen about ten or twelve years ago and that VON KARMAN'S sister likewise shared subject's dislike for Germany. It is to be noted that the recent alien evacuation program has resulted in KODAMA'S being removed from this area and he is therefore no longer in the employ of VON KARMAN.

On February 21, 1942 a teletype was received from the Cleveland Office advising that subject ALEXANDER GOETZ was expected to arrive at Cleveland that night from Corning, New York and that while he was there he was expected to contact [redacted] National Carbon Company, Cleveland. The teletype further advised that the Cleveland file was closed on this case and no further investigation was contemplated unless contrarily advised. Inasmuch as subject GOETZ was on a business trip at the time in connection with his research work, it was not deemed advisable to request a surveillance of his activities.

A card dated February 21, 1942 was received from Confidential National Defense Informant [redacted] concerning subject GOETZ, [redacted] reflecting as follows:

"Subjects are friends. Subjects [redacted] relationship is accepted as one of common law marriage, and these subjects are considered pro-German and anti-British.

Subject

TEXT ON THIS PAGE IS ILLEGIBLE
WE HAVE LEFT THE PAGE AS REFERENCE

JOHN EDGAR HOOVER
DIRECTOR

Federal Bureau of Investigation
United States Department of Justice
Washington, D. C.
August 11, 1942

Mr. E. A.
Mr. Clegg
Mr. Glavin
Mr. Ladd
Mr. Nichols
Mr. Rosen
Mr. Tracy
Mr. Carson
Mr. Coffey
Mr. Hendon
Mr. Holloman
Mr. McGuire
Mr. Harbo
Mr. Quinn Tamm
Tele. Room
Mr. Nease
Miss Beahm
Miss Gandy

CAA:PGB

MEMORANDUM FOR MR. TRACY

RE: NICOLAUS KARMAN CAR GLOSZ TURA HOTEL BERN (SWITZERLAND)
THEODORE KARMAN
SUSPICIOUS MESSAGE INTERCEPTED BY CABLE CENSORSHIP

For the consideration of Mr. Kimball and Mr. Hince the Laboratory makes the following observations on the cable message cited herein. The original of this cable was returned to [redacted] by special messenger.

b7C

CONTENTS OF MESSAGE:

CCC AUG 9-42
1. SJ215 25 CABLE PASADENA CALIF 8 905P NLT
2. NICOLAUS KARMAN CARE GLOSZ TURA HOTEL BERN (SWITZERLAND)
3. BOTH ARE IN SATISFACTORY HEALTH JOSEPHINE HAS SLIGHT HEART TROUBLE WILL WRITE VIA RED CROSS
4. THEODORE KARMAN
5. MM REFERRED PER CCC 53346 ADSE & SNDR: NSL
7. WU
1129 CNY 76159 SGB

COMMENTS:

It is suspected that this message is intended for Germany. It is suggested that the sender be investigated.

354-894
ALL INFORMATION CONTAINED
HEREIN IS UNCLASSIFIED
DATE 5-21-99 BY SP5 JC

100-37256-X5

FOR DEFENSE
BUY
UNITED STATES SAVINGS BONDS AND STAMPS

Respectfully,

E. P. Coffey

19 1942

COPY IN FILE

TEXT ON THIS PAGE IS ILLEGIBLE
WE HAVE LEFT THE PAGE AS REFERENCE

COPY 2/26/51 MLS

ADDRESS REPLY TO
"THE ATTORNEY GENERAL"
AND REFER TO
INITIALS AND NUMBER

WB:DWR:FF

146-7-343

DEPARTMENT OF JUSTICE
WASHINGTON, D. C.

December 8, 1942

MEMORANDUM FOR THE DIRECTOR,
FEDERAL BUREAU OF INVESTIGATION

Re: THEODORE VON KARMAN, with aliases,
ALEXANDER GOETZ, with aliasas -
Espionage - G

Reference is made to the above-entitled case, in connection with which we have recently received copies of the following investigative reports:

1. Report of [redacted] 6-26-41 Los Angeles
2. Report of 8-12-41 Los Angeles
3. Report of 9-19-41 Washington, D. C.
4. 1-8-42 Los Angeles
5. , 6-34-2 Los Angeles
6. 6-11-42 El Paso, Texas

b7C

Since the latestin point of date of the above reports indicate the case is being carried in an active pending status, it is requested that the Criminal Division be furnished copies of all supplemental investigative reports or other data which has been acquired concerning either or both of the subjects.

Since there is a very definite indication that the subjects may be actually engaged in espionage activities, we are desirous of obtaining succeding reports as expeditiously as possible.

Respectfully,

354 199
ALL FBI INFORMATION CONTAINED
HEREIN IS UNCLASSIFIED
DATE 5-9-97 BY 575JC/...

WENDELL BERGE
Assistant Attorney General

100-372586
NOT RECORDED
82 MAR 1 1951

TEXT ON THIS PAGE IS ILLEGIBLE
WE HAVE LEFT THE PAGE AS REFERENCE

**EXCLUSION ORDER FORM**

Reference: 62-65880-208

Date of communication: JANUARY 12, 1943

Name: THEODORE VON KARMAN

Considered for individual exclusion 1-10-

~~Exclusion Order issued and served~~:

Place: LOS ANGELES FIELD OFFICE

100-372586-

~~65-8943~~

NOT RECORDED

ALL INFORMATION CONTAINED
HEREIN IS UNCLASSIFIED
DATE 5-9-97 BY SPJ JC/

C 1943 347

TEXT ON THIS PAGE IS ILLEGIBLE
WE HAVE LEFT THE PAGE AS REFERENCE

COPY 2/26/51, MLS

EAB:mva

65-8913 December 22, 1942

100-372586

SAC, Los Angeles

RE: THEODORE VON KARMAN, was, et al
ESPIONAGE (G)

Dear Sir:

The Bureau has recently received a request from Mr. Wendell Berge, Assistant Attorney General, that he be furnished with any information developed in the above-entitled case. A review of the Bureau file reflects that the latest investigative report submitted in this matter was the report of Special Agent [redacted] b7C dated June 11, 1942, at El Paso, Texas.

You are, therefore, instructed to expedite your investigation in this case and to submit a report reflecting all additional information developed by you in the very near future in order that the Department may be advised of the latest developments.

Yours truly,

John Edgar Hoover
Director

ALL INFORMATION CONTAINED
HEREIN IS UNCLASSIFIED
DATE 5-9-97

51 MAR

TEXT ON THIS PAGE IS ILLEGIBLE
WE HAVE LEFT THE PAGE AS REFERENCE

COPY 2/26/51 MLS

EAB:lm

65-8943

June 28, 1943

SAC, Los Angeles

THEODORE VON KARMAN, with aliases, et al

A review of the Bureau file in the above entitled case reflects that the last report submitted by your office was that of Special Agent [redacted], dated March 2, 1943, at Los Angeles, California.

It is desired that the remaining investigation in this case, particularly with respect to subject Goetz, be given closer attention in order that the matter may be brought up to date in the very near future.

b7C

354-899
ALL INFORMATION CONTAINED
HEREIN IS UNCLASSIFIED
DATE 5-9-97 BY SPS JC

100-372586-

NOT RECORDED
82 MAR 1 1951

51 MAR 2 1951

TEXT ON THIS PAGE IS ILLEGIBLE
WE HAVE LEFT THE PAGE AS REFERENCE

October 30, 1950

SAC, Los Angeles

Director, FBI

TODAR KARMAN
SECURITY MATTER - C
Bufile 100-372586

RECORDED
EX-29

Re New York letter October 4, 1950.

In view of the information contained in the enclosure to that letter, it is requested that you institute a thorough security investigation to determine whether this individual is a threat to the internal security of the country.

If he is employed at the California Institute of Technology, you should be guided by previous Bureau instructions with regard to investigations of persons connected with educational institutions. Should you determine that he is a Federal employee, you, of course, should cease investigation and so advise the Bureau.

Your attention is called to the report of Special Agent [redacted] dated September 27, 1950, at Cleveland in the case captioned "William Perl, aka. William Mutterperl; Espionage - R." On pages 40, 45, 46, 47, 50, and 52 of that report a Dr. von Karman is mentioned. That individual may be identical with the subject of this memorandum.

b7C

LGD:kmb

354-844
ALL INFORMATION CONTAINED
HEREIN IS UNCLASSIFIED
DATE 5-9-92 BY SP5 JC

Tolson
Ladd
Clegg
Glavin
Nichols
Rosen
Tracy
Harbo
Belmont
Mohr
Tele. Room
Nease
Gandy

MAILED 2
OCT 30 1950
COMM - FBI

52 NOV 8 1950

TEXT ON THIS PAGE IS ILLEGIBLE
WE HAVE LEFT THE PAGE AS REFERENCE

STANDARD FORM NO. 64

# Office Memor.. ndum • UNITED STA ES GOVERNMENT

TO : Director, FBI

DATE: 10/4/50

FROM : SAC, New York

SUBJECT: TODAR KARMAN, SECURITY MATTER (C)

Transmitted herewith to the Bureau is an original and one photostatic copy of a "Summary of Information" dated September 12, 1950 from Headquarters, First Army, captioned "Possible Communist, California Institute of Technology".

Enclosed also for the Los Angeles Office is one photostatic copy of referenced summary.

It will be noted that according to the Summary, KARMAN joined the Hungarian Communist Party in 1918 and subsequently was transferred to the German Communist Party when he went to reside in that country.

KARMAN is said to have given several lectures at the California Institute of Technology, Pasadena, Cal., and in 1945, was assigned to the position on the Research Staff of Army-sponsored guided missle project in Pasadena, a position which he reportedly retains to this date.

b7C The Indices of this office contain no record of KARMAN, nor of [redacted] as mentioned in the summary.

This data is being transmitted to the Bureau and Los Angeles as a matter of information for whatever action is deemed advisable.

[redacted]

b7C

Enc. (2)
JND:KW
100-0

2CC-Los Angeles (Enc.)

EX-16

372586

INDEXED

OCT 5 1950

EX-16

10-30-50

b7C

334-899
ALL INFORMATION CONTAINED
HEREIN IS UNCLASSIFIED
DATE 5-21-97 BY 385 JC

TEXT ON THIS PAGE IS ILLEGIBLE
WE HAVE LEFT THE PAGE AS REFERENCE

STANDARD FORM NO. 64

# Office Memorandum • UNITED STATES GOVERNMENT

TO : Director, FBI

DATE: 11-10-50

FROM : SAC, Los Angeles

SUBJECT: THEODORE VON KARMAN,
Aka Todar Karman,
SECURITY MATTER-C
Bufile 100-372586

Rebulet to Los Angeles dated 10-30-50.

In New York letter to the Director dated October 4, 1950, the New York Office attached a photostatic copy of a "Summary of Information" dated September 12, 1950 from headquarters, First Army, captioned "Possible Communists, California Institute of Technology".

According to summary, TODAR KARMAN joined the Hungarian Communist Party in 1918 and subsequently was transferred to the German Communist Party when he went to reside in that country.

KARMAN is said to have given several lectures at the California Institute of Technology, Pasadena, California, and in 1945 was assigned to a position on the Research Staff of the Army sponsored Guided Missile Project in Pasadena.

Reference Bureau letter instructs the Los Angeles Office to institute a security investigation to determine whether captioned individual is a threat to the internal security of the country.

Inquiry at the California Institute of Technology indicates that KARMAN is presently in Washington, D.C. and is maintaining an office in the Pentagon Building.

The Washington Field Office is requested to ascertain VON KARMAN's present employment and to notify the Los Angeles Office. Should you determine that he is a Federal employee you should cease investigation and so advise the Bureau.

RUC.

121-0-802
RKS:MWR
AMSD
CC: Washington Field Office

RECORDED - 19

100-372586-2

NOV 13 1950

ALL INFORMATION CONTAINED
HEREIN IS UNCLASSIFIED
DATE 5-21-97 BY

TEXT ON THIS PAGE IS ILLEGIBLE
WE HAVE LEFT THE PAGE AS REFERENCE

STANDARD FORM NO. 64

# Office Memorandum • UNITED STATES GOVERNMENT

TO: DIRECTOR, FBI

DATE: December 18, 1950

FROM: SAC, Chicago

G.I.R. 1

SUBJECT: Dr. THEODORE VON KARMAN
ESPIONAGE - R

On December 7, 1950 [redacted] telephonically contacted Special Agent [redacted] at which time he advised that he was passing through Chicago on his way to Washington, D.C. on business and that he formerly resided at [redacted] receiving mail at [redacted] advised that he had been previously employed [redacted] also advised that after the war he spent some time [redacted]

[redacted] advised that recently [redacted]

[redacted] also advised that [redacted]

Towards the end of the war, [redacted] had held a private meeting with VON KARMAN and that at this meeting VON KARMAN questioned him in regards to an Atomic Bomb having been exploded in the ocean. [redacted] brought up the question as to whether VON KARMAN in his capacity at Cal. Tech. should have had access to this information about the Atomic Bomb even though it was approximately one and one-half years before information regarding the Atomic Bomb had been revealed to the public.

[redacted] advised that the present whereabouts of [redacted] are unknown but that he knows [redacted] and believes that he might possibly be residing in Alabama.

MHT:ERN
65-0
cc: Los Angeles
Cleveland

RECORDED - 94
INDEXED - 94
DEC 20 1950
EX-89

COPIES DESTROYED

ALL INFORMATION CONTAINED HEREIN IS UNCLASSIFIED

TEXT ON THIS PAGE IS ILLEGIBLE
WE HAVE LEFT THE PAGE AS REFERENCE

[redacted] advised that he knows of no one in the United States who has greater access to restricted material on guided missiles and rockets than what THEODORE VON KARMAN has and believes VON KARMAN to be still employed as a top aeronautical advisor in the U. S. Air Force.

The indices of the Chicago office reflect that THEODORE VON KARMAN was a subject of an espionage G investigation with the Los Angeles office as origin in 1941 along with subjects ALEXANDER GOETZ [redacted]

WILLIAM PERL, wa. William Mutterperl, subject of an espionage - R investigation in 1950 with Cleveland as office of origin, was a technical assistant to Dr. VON KARMAN at Columbia University in 1947 and 1948 and as such received classified material in behalf of VON KARMAN who was at that time the chairman of the U. S. Air Force Scientific Advisory Board and who may still hold this position.

It is here being noted that the Chicago indices were negative [redacted]

The above is submitted for information of the Bureau for whatever action deemed necessary.

/b7C b7D

TEXT ON THIS PAGE IS ILLEGIBLE
WE HAVE LEFT THE PAGE AS REFERENCE

STANDARD FORM NO. 64

SECRET

*Office Memorandum* • UNITED STATES GOVERNMENT

DATE: January 5, 1951

TO: Director, FBI

FROM: SAC, Cleveland

SUBJECT: DR. THEODORE VON KARMAN
ESPIONAGE - R

ALL INFORMATION CONTAINED
HEREIN IS UNCLASSIFIED EXCEPT
WHERE SHOWN OTHERWISE

Re Chicago letter dated 12/18/50, Cleveland letter 8/7/50, and Bureau letter 8/18/50 in the case entitled "WILLIAM PERL, was. [redacted] b7C

Referenced Chicago letter indicates VON KARMAN while at California Institute of Technology had [redacted] b7C

This letter also noted that VON KARMAN was the subject of an Espionage - G investigation conducted by the Bureau in 1941. In so far as Cleveland files are concerned, all investigation was conducted prior to the invasion of the Soviet Union by Germany and during the Russo-German Peace Pact.

Referenced Cleveland and Bureau letters concern employees of Sverdrup and Parcel, Consulting Engineers, St. Louis, Missouri, who were working on a project for VON KARMAN. [redacted] subjects of espionage investigations: [redacted] and WILLIAM PERL. In view of these numerous references to VON KARMAN it is suggested the Bureau may desire to ascertain his present activities and in so doing inquiry might be made of [redacted] (S) b7C b1

The January 1, 1951, issue of "Time" magazine contains on pages 56 through 58 an article concerning VON KARMAN and his association with the Aerojet Engineering Corporation.

Copies of the referenced Chicago letter are enclosed for New York and Washington Field.

354-894 5-9-97
CLASSIFIED BY SP5JC/bgm
DECLASSIFY ON: 25X 6

JBO'D:CGP
65-2778

EX-46

cc: Chicago
Los Angeles
New York (Enc.)
Washington Field (Enc.)
65-2726
65-2730

RECORDED - 10 100-342586-4
JAN 8 1951
INDEXED - 104

[redacted] b7C

SECRET

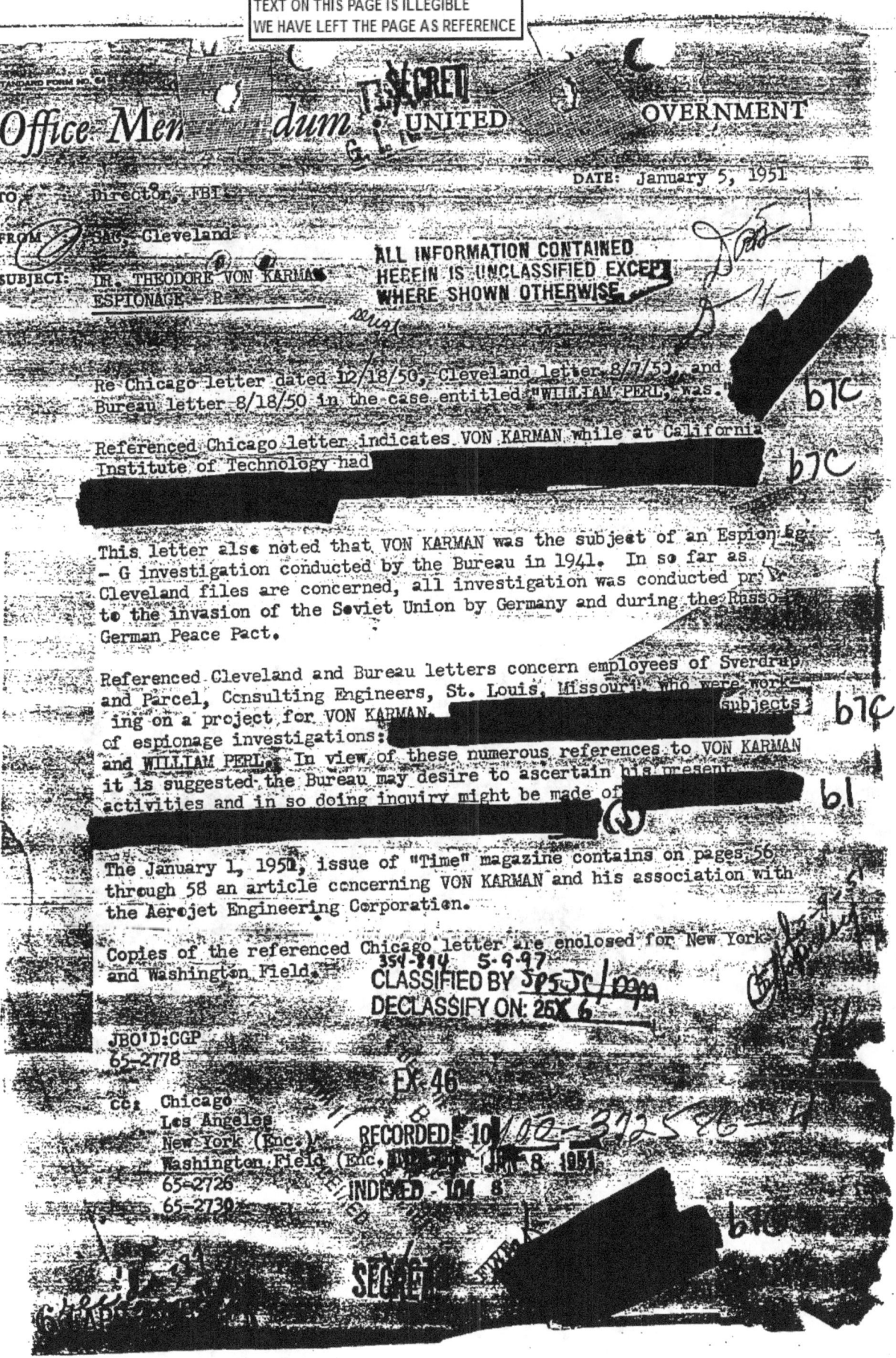

TEXT ON THIS PAGE IS ILLEGIBLE
WE HAVE LEFT THE PAGE AS REFERENCE

STANDARD FORM NO. 64

Office Memo... um • UNITED ... OVERNMENT

TO : Director, FBI DATE: January 17, 1951

FROM : SAC, Los Angeles

354-994
ALL INFORMATION CONTAINED
HEREIN IS UNCLASSIFIED
DATE 5-21-97 BY

SUBJECT: DR. THEODORE VON KARMAN
ESPIONAGE - R

Re Chicago let December 18, 1950.

As the Bureau is aware, Dr. VON KARMAN presently maintains his chairmanship of the United States Scientific Advisory Board and was last known to this office to be headquartered in the Pentagon Building, Washington, D. C.

b7C
b7D

[redacted] Informant [redacted] is identical with [redacted] who was the subject of an Internal Security - X investigation in the Los Angeles Office. The Bureau file number for [redacted] #105-11668.

In view of VON KARMAN's present position no investigation concerning him is being initiated at this time by this office unless the Bureau directs otherwise.

JHH:MES
65-265

cc: Chicago
LA #100-31377

I. R.

RECORDED - 114
INDEXED - 114

JAN 20 1951

EX-84

50 MAR 19 1951

[redacted]

b7C

TEXT ON THIS PAGE IS ILLEGIBLE
WE HAVE LEFT THE PAGE AS REFERENCE

C

SAC, Los Angeles

January 23, 1951

Director, FBI

THEODORE VON KARMAN
INTERNAL SECURITY - R

Re New York letter October 4, 1950, Los Angeles letter November 10, 1950, Chicago letter December 18, 1950, Cleveland letter January 5, 1951, and Washington Field Office teletype January 9, 1951.

The information contained in Bureau files concerning Dr. Theodore Von Karman has been made available to OSI at Washington, D. C. OSI has been requested to advise whether Von Karman is presently employed by the Air Forces.

Upon receipt of information from OSI concerning Von Karman's Federal employee status, the field will be instructed as to what further investigation is desired in this matter.

cc - New York
Chicago
Cleveland
Washington Field Office

WAK:MH

ALL INFORMATION CONTAINED
HEREIN IS UNCLASSIFIED
DATE 6-21-99 BY

RECORDED - 99 | 100-37155-6
JAN 24 1951
80

Tolson
Ladd
Clegg
Glavin
Nichols
Rosen
Tracy
Harbo
Belmont
Mohr
Tele. Room
Nease
Gandy

COMM - FBI

62 FEB 7 1951

TEXT ON THIS PAGE IS ILLEGIBLE
WE HAVE LEFT THE PAGE AS REFERENCE

Form DS-764

...ORMATION

JAN 1 6 1951

| | |
|---|---|
| TO: | FROM: SY [redacted] b7C |
| FULL NAME OF PERSON OR FIRM: von KARMAN, Theodore | DATE OF BIRTH: 5/11/81 |
| | PLACE OF BIRTH: Budap 18443 |
| ALIASES AND NICKNAMES: | RACE: |
| | SEX: |
| ADDRESS: 1501 So. Marengo, Pasadena 5, Calif. | OCCUPATION: Professor |
| | EMPLOYER: |
| TYPE OF INFORMATION DESIRED: ☐ All information ☐ Derogatory | CITIZENSHIP STATUS: US |
| NAT. CERT. NO.: 7/26/36 Calif. | MARITAL STATUS: |
| NAME OF ORGANIZATION: | HEADQUARTERS ADDRESS: |
| REPLY: ☐ Material attached ☐ No record ☐ No derogatory information ☐ Other | OSTENSIBLE PURPOSE: |
| | NAMES OF LEADERS OR SPONSORS OR AFFILIATED ORGANIZATION: |

ADDITIONAL INFORMATION

SEX

354 894
ALL FBI INFORMATION CONTAINED
HEREIN IS UNCLASSIFIED
DATE 5-12-97 BY SPS JC/TZM

SE 10

CHECKED BY

66

U. S. GOVERNMENT PRINTING OFFICE 16—60274-1

C

TEXT ON THIS PAGE IS ILLEGIBLE
WE HAVE LEFT THE PAGE AS REFERENCE

February 24, 1951

You are referred to the information furnished to the Visa Division of the Department of State on July 18, 1942 in connection with the visa application of [redacted] (40-13556-4; 40-48862)

A further review of the records of this Bureau has disclosed that the Department of State has already been furnished at various times twenty-nine reports in the case entitled "Theodore von Karman, was., Alexander Goetz, was., [redacted] Espionage - G". (65-8943)

b7C

Your attention is directed to those reports inasmuch as they appear to relate to the person inquired about. A further review of the records of this Bureau has indicated that consideration is being given to conducting an investigation of Theodore von Karman under the loyalty program pending a determination of his connection with the Federal Government. (100-372586)

The above information is furnished for your confidential use only, and is not to be distributed outside of your agency.

RECEIVED
LOYALTY SECTION
MAR 9 11 27 AM '51
F B I
U.S. DEPT. OF JUSTICE

JEFo:pam

C

TEXT ON THIS PAGE IS ILLEGIBLE
WE HAVE LEFT THE PAGE AS REFERENCE

SECRET

ALL INFORMATION CONTAINED HEREIN IS UNCLASSIFIED EXCEPT WHERE SHOWN OTHERWISE

Assistant Attorney General James M. McInerney February 3, 1951

Director, FBI

THEODORE VON KARMAN CONFIDENTIAL
INTERNAL SECURITY - R

Reference is made to your memorandum of January 18, 1951, entitled "[redacted] Espionage - IS," your reference JMM:GKN:vb.

b7C

Particular reference is made to paragraph 6 of your memorandum which requested advice as to whether the Dr. Theodore Von Karman, under whom William Perl formerly worked at Columbia University, is identical with Professor Theodore Von Karman of the California Institute of Technology, who referred subject [redacted] Your memorandum also requested advice as to whether this Bureau has any information indicating that the above matters are at all related.

b7C

Information in the files of this Bureau, furnished by reliable informants, reflects that Dr. Theodore Von Karman, who was a former superior of William Perl at Columbia University, has been Director of the Guggenheim Aeronautical Research Laboratory and Professor of Aeronautics at the California Institute of Technology since the late 1930's. He has served in various capacities with United States Government agencies.

According to the informants, Dr. Von Karman, as Director of the Guggenheim Aeronautical Research Laboratory, played an important part in causing the Air Force to set up the Jet Propulsion Laboratory at the California Institute of Technology in the early 1940's, and was an original stockholder in the Aerojet Engineering Company of Azusa, California, a private firm which was set up to manufacture pilot models developed at the Jet Propulsion Laboratory.

Because of the fact that [redacted] during a recent interview advised [redacted] it appears that the Professor Theodore Von Karman who introduced [redacted] is identical with that individual who was a superior of William Perl at Columbia University.

b7C b7D

100-372586
cc: 65-59569
65-59312

b7C

100-372586

NOT RECORDED
144 FEB 12 1951

61 MAR 15 1951

CLASSIFIED AND EXTENDED BY 2333
REASON FOR EXTENSION FCIM, II, 1-2.4.2
DATE OF REVIEW FOR DECLASSIFICATION 4-2-89

CLASSIFIED BY SPS JC/MON
DECLASSIFY ON: 25X1

APPROPRIATE AGENCIES AND FIELD OFFICES ADVISED BY ROUTING SLIP(S) OF
DATE 4/6/99

ALL INFORMATION CONTAINED HEREIN IS UNCLASSIFIED EXCEPT WHERE SHOWN OTHERWISE

SECRET

b7c

This Bureau has no information indicating that the cases of Perl and [redacted] are related other than that information which has been previously furnished you and that which is herein set out.

There is furnished for your additional information the results of a review of the files of this Bureau concerning the name Theodore Von Karman:

As of recent date, another Government agency that conducts intelligence investigations advised this Bureau that they were in possession of information concerning one Todar Karman. The information had been furnished them by letter from Vienna, Austria, dated April 1, 1948, and was originally furnished by a source evaluated as fairly reliable.

According to the source, Todar Karman joined the Hungarian Communist Party in 1918 while working as Assistant Professor of Physics at the Jozsef Nador, Technical University, Budapest, Hungary. In 1919, when the Communists seized power in Hungary, Karman was appointed Deputy Commissar of Cultural and Educational Affairs in charge of Higher Education. Karman continued to function in that capacity until late 1919 when Communists were routed by the Nationalist forces of Admiral Horthy. At that time, Karman was forced to flee from Hungary and escaped to Germany where he settled at Aachen. His membership was then transferred to the German Communist Party. Karman engaged in scientific work in Germany and was invited to lecture at the University of Aachen. In 1931 he received an invitation to lecture in the United States and was issued an entry visa to the United States from 1931 to 1933.

According to the source, Karman gave several lecture courses at the California Institute of Technology, Pasadena, California, and returned each time to Aachen after the completion of the courses. After Hitler seized power in Germany, Karman applied for an extension of his permit of residence in the United States and was subsequently granted an extended residence permit. He then became a regular Professor at the California Institute of Technology and during World War II engaged in research work in Aerodynamics for the Army Air Forces.

The source also stated that in 1945, Karman was assigned to a position on the research staff of an Army-sponsored guided missile project at Pasadena, a position which the source believed

Tolson
Ladd
Clegg
Glavin
Nichols
Rosen
Tracy
Harbo
Belmont
Mohr
Tele. Room
Nease
Gandy



SECRET

TEXT ON THIS PAGE IS ILLEGIBLE
WE HAVE LEFT THE PAGE AS REFERENCE

SECRET

he maintained as of 1948. The source further believed that Karman covered up his Communist Party membership when first applying for an entry visa to the United States in 1931.

The Chicago Office of this Bureau has recently advised that [redacted] telephonically contacted that office while passing through the City of Chicago. [redacted] advised that [redacted] He also advised that after the war [redacted]

[redacted] recalled the fact that [redacted]

b7C
b7D

[redacted] also reported that at the end of the war he had spoken with [redacted] who advised [redacted] that he had held a private meeting with Dr. Von Karman and during this meeting Dr. Von Karman questioned [redacted] regarding the atomic bomb. According to [redacted] his conversation with [redacted] brought up the question as to whether Dr. Von Karman should have had access to atomic information at a time which was approximately one and one-half years before information regarding the bomb had been revealed to the public.

The present address of [redacted] is unknown; however, he stated that he had formerly resided at [redacted] and had received mail at [redacted] advised that he believes [redacted] presently resides in Alabama. Pertinent reports

Tolson
Ladd
Clegg
Glavin
Nichols
Rosen
Tracy
Harbo
Belmont
Mohr
Tele. Room
Nease
Gandy



SECRET

SECRET

have been furnished you in connection with the investigations entitled [redacted] Internal Security - R." [redacted]

During an investigation of [redacted] conducted by this Bureau in 1945, reliable informants advised that on January 9, March 7, March 22, April 3, April 24 and 25, 1945, Dr. Theodore Von Karman, who was then associated with the Army Air Force, contacted [redacted]. The investigation of [redacted] was based on information furnished by other reliable informants to the effect that [redacted] was in frequent contact with members of the Soviet Embassy in Washington and the Soviet Consulate in New York. The informants also advised that [redacted] had been associated with Russian War Relief and the National Council for American Soviet Friendship. At that time [redacted] (S) u

b7C

b1

[redacted] (S)

In 1947 when interviewed in connection with an investigation being conducted by this Bureau, Dr. Theodore Von Karman stated that he was then Chairman of the Scientific Advisory Board of the Commanding General of the Army Air Force and a holder of the Medal of Merit.

In the January 1, 1951, issue of "Time" magazine, a photograph of Dr. Von Karman appears, together with an article which relates how he and four associates originally invested $8,700 and established the Aerojet Engineering Company of Azusa, California, as a result of Von Karman's knowledge that rockets would be an important weapon. The article states that the Aerojet Company now has a $25,000,000 backlog of orders and is planning a new $6,000,000 plant.

The present address of Dr. Theodore Von Karman is reported to be Scientific Advisory Board, Office of the Director, Research and Development, Deputy Chief of Staff, U. S. Air Force, The Pentagon.

Tolson___
Ladd___
Clegg___
Glavin___
Nichols___
Rosen___
Tracy___
Harbo___
Belmont___
Mohr___
Tele. Room___
Nease___
Gandy___



SECRET

SECRET

SECRET

There are attached for your additional information copies of the following reports which were made in connection with an investigation of which Dr. Theodore Von Karman was carried as a subject:

Report of Special Agent [redacted] dated May 7, 1940, at Los Angeles;

Report of Special Agent [redacted] dated August 12, 1941, at Los Angeles;

Report of Special Agent [redacted] dated October 6, 1941, at Cincinnati, Ohio;

Report of Special Agent [redacted] dated June 3, 1942, at Los Angeles;

Report of Special Agent [redacted] dated July 30, 1943, at Los Angeles.

b7C

Pertinent information concerning Dr. Von Karman has been furnished the Director of Special Investigations, Department of the Air Force, with the request that that agency advise whether Dr. Von Karman is presently employed by the Department of the Air Force. That agency was also requested to advise whether their files contain any information which will substantiate or disprove the recent allegations received concerning Dr. Von Karman.

You will be furnished any additional pertinent information received or developed concerning this matter.

Enclosures

Tolson____
Ladd____
Clegg____
Glavin____
Nichols____
Rosen____
Tracy____
Harbo____
Belmont____
Mohr____
Tele. Room____
Nease____
Gandy____

SECRET



SECRET

TEXT ON THIS PAGE IS ILLEGIBLE
WE HAVE LEFT THE PAGE AS REFERENCE

# FEDERAL BUREAU OF INVESTIGATION

Form No. 1
THIS CASE ORIGINATED AT LOS ANGELES, CALIF. FILE NO. 65-265.

| REPORT MADE AT | DATE WHEN MADE | PERIOD FOR WHICH MADE | REPORT MADE BY |
|---|---|---|---|
| LOS ANGELES, CALIF. | 8/12/41 | 7/24/41;8/2,4,6/41 | |

| TITLE | CHARACTER OF CASE |
|---|---|
| "CHANGED" THEODORE VON KARMAN, with aliases, Theodor Von Karman, Theodor De Karman; ALEXANDER GOETZ, with aliases, Carl Goetz, Alexander Carl Goetz, Karl Wilhelm Alexander Gustav Goetz; | ESPIONAGE - G |

SYNOPSIS OF FACTS:

Information received from that Subject GOETZ is a leading agent in his district for Fortra, Inc. GOETZ is stated to have been very friendly with the German Consul at Los Angeles and with a Japanese, and to receive many letters from Germany. Subject VON KARMAN is stated to have lost an air corps identification card issued to him by the Material Division, United States Air Corps, Wright Field, Ohio, which card will allow him to enter practically any airplane plant or defense industry, it is said. Records of Immigration and Naturalization at Los Angeles reflect VON KARMAN born May 11, 1881, Budapest, Hungary, entered the United States at New York City October 7, 1930, and became a citizen July 24, 1936, at Los Angeles. No criminal record at Los Angeles for either Subject GOETZ or VON KARMAN. Credit records of these Subjects checked, and no additional information obtained, with the exception that GOETZ is reported to have investments and residences in Germany. Results of mail cover on Subject GOETZ set out. Custodial Detention memorandum submitted as to Subject GOETZ.

- P -

REFERENCE: Report by Special Agent Los Angeles, 6/26/41.

DETAILS: AT LOS ANGELES, CALIFORNIA:

The title of this case is being changed to include the aliases of Subject VON KARMAN, THEODOR VON KARMAN, THEODOR DE KARMAN.

APPROVED AND FORWARDED: SPECIAL AGENT IN CHARGE

DO NOT WRITE IN THESE SPACES

65-9948-143

RECORDED & INDEXED

AUG 18 1941

FIVE

COPIES OF THIS REPORT

5- Bureau
2- Washington Field
2- Cincinnati
2- Boston
3- Los Angeles

U.S. GOVERNMENT PRINTING OFFICE 7-2034

"5. They are also friendly with a Japanese, apparently someone of high position. They have entertained him at dinner in the home and have taken him out to dinner. His name is not known to informant, although she has tried to learn it.

"6. They entertain many callers, apparently all German, who stay until one or two o'clock in the morning. Sometimes there are eight or ten of them at a time, and there is much conversation.

"7. [redacted] criticize President ROOSEVELT and his policy toward Germany, and they were furious about what was said by him during his last radio speech.

"8. These people give out America First literature."

Through a confidential source it was ascertained that telephone number [redacted] is listed to [redacted] Glendale. It was first ascertained from telephone operator that this 'phone had been temporarily disconnected. Inquiry among the neighbors at the above address brought forth the information that [redacted] gone away for the summer and would probably not return until the first of September. An attempt will be made at that time to contact [redacted]

A letter dated May 28, 1941, was received [redacted] Beverly Hills, California, which stated that Professor VON KARMAN, head of the Aeronautical Department of California Tech., is in a position to commit murder when it comes to secrets of the airplane industry. [redacted] VON KARMAN is a German by birth, and his sister, a spinster, lives with him. He stated that she has declared herself from time to time to be a Nazi and doesn't even try to cover up.

A memorandum in the file reflects that on July 17, 1941, [redacted] telephonically advised Special Agent [redacted] that Rooms 801-802 in the Savoy Hotel, Los Angeles, occupied by Dr. THEODORE VON KARMAN, had been burglarized on July 13, 1941, at which time a great deal of jewelry had been taken, as well as an air corps identification card issued to Dr. VON KARMAN by the Material Division, United States Air Corps, Wright Field, Ohio. [redacted] stated that this card would allow VON KARMAN to enter practically any airplane plant or defense industry.

At the Bureau of Immigration and Naturalization, Los Angeles, Petition for Naturalization No. 50558 reflected the following: THEODOR VON KARMAN, 1501 Marengo Avenue, Pasadena, occupation, Professor, born 5/11/81 Budapest, Hungary, race, Magyar, marital status, single, last foreign residence, Aachen, Germany, came to the United States from Cherbourg, France, under the name THEODOR KARMAN and entered at the port of New York October 7, 1930, via the S. S. MAJESTIC. Witnesses on the petition were [redacted] He was admitted as a citizen July 24, 1936. The file further reflected that he owns his own home and has an account in the Pasadena First National Trust and Savings Bank. It was reflected that his mother, the former HELENE KOHN, and his sister, JOSEPHINE DE KARMAN, reside with him. It was evident from the file that both the names VON KARMAN and DE KARMAN are used.

A memorandum in the file dated October 25, 1932, regarding THEODOR VON KARMAN was noted as follows: "Applicant presents German passport number 33558 in his name notated; no quota, immigration visa 1601, September 24, 1930; Professor THEODOR KARMAN, American Consulate, Budapest, admitted New York 4/9/30, Par. 2-Section 3-Act of 1924, six months; was admitted New York 9/29/31 upon presentation of re-entry permit number 704909; applicant's first entry was in October, 1926, at New York via S. S. MAURITANIA, from Cherbourg, France. His second entry was in October, 1928, at Montreal, Canada, by rail. He is unable to give the port of entry upon the Canadian border. His third entry was at New York via the S. S. ILE DE FRANCE about in October, 1930, from Cherbourg, France. The applicant states that he was an exchange professor upon his first entries."

VON KARMAN'S absences since October 7, 1930, are given as follows: Left May, 1931, from New York via the S. S. ILE DE FRANCE for Germany and returned September, 1931, same port and boat. Left November, 1932, from New York via the S. S. BREMEN for France and returned December, 1932, entering at New York via the S. S. EUROPA. Left June, 1934, and returned July, 1934, via the S. S. OLYMPIA from England. Left September, 1935, from New York via the S. S. CONTI GRANDE for Italy, returning in October, 1935, at New York via the S. S. CONTI DE SAVOI.

Special Agent [redacted] was advised by the Los Angeles County Sheriff's Office and the Los Angeles City Police Department that their respective departments had no criminal record for either Subject VON KARMAN or GOETZ.

The Los Angeles Retail Merchants Credit Association's information concerning THEODORE VON KARMAN was as follows: Age, 54 in 1936; single; professor at California Tech., also employed by Metropolitan Water District, 306 West 3rd Street, Los Angeles, Director of Guggenheim Aeronautical Laboratory at California Institute of Technology. In 1936 elected honorable fellow in Institute of Aeronautical Sciences, one of world's foremost aeronautical experts. Credit fair.

A credit report for Subject GOETZ gave his age as 40 in 1940 and reflected that [redacted] He was stated to be employed in the California Institute of Technology as an associate professor in physics. He was stated to earn $3600 per year and to have a

- 4 -

TEXT ON THIS PAGE IS ILLEGIBLE
WE HAVE LEFT THE PAGE AS REFERENCE

UNDEVELOPED LEADS:

THE WASHINGTON FIELD OFFICE:

AT WASHINGTON, D. C.:

* Will at the United States Patent Office review the application of Subject GOETZ for a patent for his liquid sterilizer, it being noted that this patent claim is Serial #317,606 on file in Division 56, Room 4735, United States Patent Office, Washington, D. C.

THE BOSTON FIELD DIVISION:

AT BOSTON, MASSACHUSETTS:

Will, at the State Street Trust Company, ascertain the nature of Subject ALEXANDER GOETZ' transactions with this bank, noting that on July 22, 1941, he received a letter from the bank post-marked July 18.

THE CINCINNATI FIELD DIVISION:

AT DAYTON, OHIO:

Will, at Wright Field in the Material Division, United States Air Corps, ascertain why an air corps identification card was issued to THEODORE VON KARMAN and will determine what his connection is, if any, with the air corps.

THE LOS ANGELES FIELD DIVISION:

AT GLENDALE, CALIFORNIA:

Will, [redacted] contact [redacted] in order to make an appointment to interview [redacted]

TEXT ON THIS PAGE IS ILLEGIBLE
WE HAVE LEFT THE PAGE AS REFERENCE

STANDARD FORM NO. 64

# Office Memorandum • UNITED STATES GOVERNMENT

TO : DIRECTOR, FBI

DATE: January 29, 1951

FROM : SAC, WFO

SUBJECT: Dr. THEODORE VON KARMAN
Aka, TODAR KARMAN
SECURITY MATTER - C
Bufile 100-372586

ALL INFORMATION CONTAINED HEREIN IS UNCLASSIFIED DATE 5-21-97 BY

Re Los Angeles letter to Director November 10, 1950, and Cleveland letter Director January 5, 1951.

On November 17, 1950, [redacted] G-2, M. D. W., advised that Dr. THEODORE VON KARMAN maintains an office in the Pentagon. This office is room 4-C-340. His phone extension is 53797. Inquiry at his office by [redacted] revealed that he was said to be employed by the Air Force Scientific Advisory Board. He was at the time in Europe, apparently for the Air Force Scientific Advisory Board, and was expected back about December 1, 1950. [redacted] further advised however that although it would appear that he was an employee of the Air Force, Air Force Personnel records show he was terminated with the Air Force on January 3, 1946. [redacted] was unable after repeated efforts to procure any more definite information concerning VON KARMAN.

After much delay a check of the office of Security and Intelligence of the Air Force revealed that that office had information available concerning VON KARMAN. A check of this record revealed that office had information concerning VON KARMAN under the caption Re: [redacted] This one page memo shows that a [redacted] of Immigration and Naturalization Service called on September 15, 1950, at 2:25 p. m. and gave information to a [redacted] apparently of OSI. [redacted] is reported as advising that Dr. THEODORE VON KARMAN, of the Air Force Scientific Advisory Board, had been attempting to contact [redacted] Dr. VON KARMAN stated he was leaving for Europe and that it was therefore very necessary that he be permitted to talk with [redacted] The Immigration authorities in Los Angeles elected to refuse Dr. VON KARMAN'S request.

[redacted]

JEH:FLH
100-22923
cc: Los Angeles ( Air Mail)
Cleveland
Chicago
New York

COPIES DESTROYED 25 APR 5 1963

G. I. R. -7

100-372586-8

RECORDED - 85 JAN 31 1951

EX-125

50 MAR 1

b7C

TEXT ON THIS PAGE IS ILLEGIBLE
WE HAVE LEFT THE PAGE AS REFERENCE



[redacted]

This report was signed by [redacted] C.I.D., O.S.I.

On January 17, 1951, Agent [redacted] C.I.D., O.S.I., advised that he had definitely determined that Dr. VON KARMAN is presently an employee of the U. S. Air Force. He is presently in Pasadena, California, but Agent [redacted] was refused information as to his exact whereabouts. VON KARMAN is expected to return to Washington, D. C., about February 1, 1951.

In absence of instructions to the contrary no further inquiry regarding this matter is contemplated by this office.

- RUC -

b7C

TEXT ON THIS PAGE IS ILLEGIBLE
WE HAVE LEFT THE PAGE AS REFERENCE

~~CONFIDENTIAL~~
VIA LIAISON

DATE: January 23, 1951
100-372586-9

RECORDED - 51

TO: Director of Special Investigations
Inspector General
Department of the Air Force
The Pentagon
Washington 25, D. C.

FROM: John Edgar Hoover - Director - Federal Bureau of Investigation

SUBJECT: THEODORE VON KARMAN
INTERNAL SECURITY - R

354-394
DECLASSIFIED BY SP5 JC/pgn
ON 5-21-97

There is furnished for your confidential information the following concerning captioned individual. Reliable sources advise that Dr. Theodore Von Karman presently maintains an office at the Pentagon in connection with employment by the Air Force.

As of recent date, another Government agency that conducts intelligence investigations advised this Bureau that they were in possession of information concerning one Todar Karman. The information had been furnished them by letter from Vienna, Austria, dated April 1, 1948, and was originally furnished by a source evaluated as fairly reliable.

According to the source, Todar Karman joined the Hungarian Communist Party in 1918 while working as Assistant Professor of Physics at the Jozsef Nador, Technical University, Budapest, Hungary. In 1919, when the Communists seized power in Hungary, Karman was appointed Deputy Commissar of Cultural and Educational Affairs in charge of Higher Education. Karman continued to function in that capacity until late 1919 when Communists were routed by the Nationalist forces of Admiral Horthy. At that time, Karman was forced to flee from Hungary and escaped to Germany where he settled at Aachen. His membership was then transferred to the German Communist Party. Karman engaged in scientific work in Germany and was invited to lecture at the University of Aachen. In 1931 he received an invitation to lecture in the United States and was issued an entry visa to the United States from 1931 to 1933.

WAK:MH
Enclosures

[redacted] 1-24-51 b7C

TEXT ON THIS PAGE IS ILLEGIBLE
WE HAVE LEFT THE PAGE AS REFERENCE

According to the source, Karman gave several lecture courses at the California Institute of Technology, Pasadena, Calif.rnia, and returned each time to Aachen after the completion of the courses. After Hitler seized power in Germany, Karman applied for an extension of his permit of residence in the United States and was subsequently granted an extended residence permit. He then became a regular Professor at the California Institute of Technology and during World War II engaged in research work in Aerodynamics for the Army Air Forces.

The source also stated that in 1945, Karman was assigned to a position on the research staff of an Army-sponsored guided missile project at Pasadena, a position which the source believed he maintained as of 1948. The source further believed that Karman covered up his Communist Party membership when first applying for an entry visa to the United States in 1931.

The Chicago Office of this Bureau has recently advised that one [redacted] telephonically contacted that office while passing through the City of Chicago. [redacted] advised that he had been [redacted] He also advised that after the war [redacted]

[redacted] recalled the fact that he had read recent [redacted]

b7C b7D

Tolson
Ladd
Clegg
Glavin
Nichols
Rosen
Tracy
Harbo
Belmont
Mohr
Tele. Room
Gandy

[redacted] also reported that at the end of the war he had spoken with [redacted] who advised [redacted] that he had held a private meeting with Dr. Von Karman and during this meeting Dr. Von Karman questioned [redacted] regarding the atomic bomb. According to [redacted] his conversation with [redacted] brought up the question as to whether Dr. Von Karman should have had access to atomic information at a time which was approximately one and one half years before information regarding the bomb had been revealed to the public.

b7C
b7D

The present address of [redacted] is unknown; however, he stated that he had formerly resided at [redacted] and had received mail at [redacted] advised that he believes [redacted] and presently resides in Alabama. Pertinent reports have been furnished you in connection with the investigations entitled "[redacted] Internal Security - R."

There are attached for your additional information copies of the following reports which were made in connection with an investigation of which Dr. Theodore Von Karman was carried as a subject:

(1). Report of Special Agent [redacted] dated May 7, 1940, at Los Angeles.
(2). Report of Special Agent [redacted] dated August 12, 1941, at Los Angeles.
(3). Report of Special Agent [redacted] dated October 6, 1941, at Cincinnati, Ohio.
(4). Report of Special Agent [redacted] dated June 3, 1942, at Los Angeles.
(5). Report of Special Agent [redacted] dated July 30, 1943, at Los Angeles.

b7C

Your attention is called to the fact that the recent allegations received which apparently refer to Dr. Theodore Von Karman have not been verified by independent investigation of this Bureau. The information is not to be disseminated outside your Agency.

It is requested that you advise whether Dr. Theodore Von Karman is presently employed by the Air Force in order that a determination may be made as to further investigation based on the information furnished you. It is also requested that you advise whether your files contain any information which will substantiate or disprove the information furnished you in this letter.

Tolson ____
Ladd ____
Clegg ____
Glavin ____
Nichols ____
Rosen ____
Tracy ____
Harbo ____
Belmont ____
____
Tele. Room ____
____

TEXT ON THIS PAGE IS ILLEGIBLE
WE HAVE LEFT THE PAGE AS REFERENCE

STANDARD FORM NO. 64

# Office Memorandum • UNITED STATES GOVERNMENT

TO : A. H. BELMONT

SECRET

DATE: January 22, 1951

FROM : C. E. HENNRICH

b7C [redacted]

SUBJECT: THEODORE VON KARMAN
INTERNAL SECURITY - R

354-894 6-13-97
CLASSIFIED BY SP5 JC/
DECLASSIFY ON: 25X 6

PURPOSE:

Subject born May 11, 1881, Hungary, entered United States 1930 and naturalized 1936. Since entry has been employed as Director of Guggenheim Aeronautical Research Laboratory at California Institute of Technology. As one of World's leading Aerodynamicists, has served as consultant to National Advisory Committee on Aeronautics and in 1947 was Chairman of the Scientific Advisory Board of the Commanding General of the Army Air Forces and the holder of a medal of Merit.

Subject presently maintains offices in the Pentagon with Air Force Scientific Advisory Board although Air Force personnel records indicate his employment was terminated in 1946. Subject has had access to material of the highest classification.

Recent report received from G-2 reflects that in 1948 a CIC investigation in Europe determined information from a source "fairly reliable - possibly true" that one Todar Karman, who is apparently identical with subject, was Commissar of Higher Education in Hungary after the Communist uprising in 1919. According to the source, Karman fled to Germany the same year and continued as a member of the German Communist Party. Bufiles reflect subject investigated in 1941 on basis of report that German aliens at Cal. Tech had access to restricted area. No subversive activity established. [redacted] (S) b1

ALL INFORMATION CONTAINED HEREIN IS UNCLASSIFIED EXCEPT WHERE SHOWN OTHERWISE

It is recommended that information in Bufiles re subject be furnished OSI by letter and that other information be furnished orally. It is also recommended that a loyalty investigation of subject be conducted in the event it is established that he is a Government employee and if not, that an Internal Security - R investigation be conducted.

SECRET

WAK:MH (vjm)
100-372586
Attachments

RECORDED - 52

100-372586-9

MAR 13 1951

INDEXED - 52

34

COPIES DESTROYED
78 APR 5 1963

HANDLED BY ... 3/1

TEXT ON THIS PAGE IS ILLEGIBLE
WE HAVE LEFT THE PAGE AS REFERENCE

SECRET

BACKGROUND:

Personal History

INS records checked August, 1941, by the Los Angeles Office and reflect Theodor Von Karman was born May 11, 1881, Budapest, Hungary and entered the United States from Cherbourg, France, under the name Theodor Karman at the Port of New York on October 7, 1930. His occupation was stated as professor and his last foreign residence, Aachen, Germany. He was admitted to citizenship in 1936. Prior to 1930, Von Karman had entered the United States as an exchange professor in 1926, 1928, and 1930. (65-8943-43)

Education

1902 - Graduated University of Budapest
1908 - Graduated from Gottengin University
1929 - Received Dr. of Engineering degree, University of Berlin
1937 - Received Dr. of Science degree, University of Brussels

Employment

1913 to 1934 - Professor of Mechanics and Aerodynamics University of Aachen
1924 to 1929 - Consultant and advisor for airplane corporations throughout the world
1927 to 1929 - Kawanishi airplane works, Japan
1939 - General Electric Company
1935 - 1940 - U. S. Bureau of Reclamation
1930 - 1941 - Director of the Guggenheim Aeronautical Research Laboratory and Professor of Aeronautics, Cal. Tech.
(G-2 investigation October 26, 1941 Bufile 65-8943-41)

Bufiles reflect Von Karman has apparently continued as Director of the Guggenheim Aeronautical Research Laboratory and Professor at Cal. Tech since 1941; that he was special advisor to [redacted] the Air Force in 1939; has served as consultant to various firms; and has held important positions with the Air Force and NACA. In 1947, when interviewed in connection with an investigation, Von Karman stated he was then Chairman of the Scientific Advisory Board of the Commanding General of the Army Air Forces and holder of the medal of Merit. His present address is believed to be Scientific Advisory Board, Office of the Director of Research and Development, Deputy Chief of Staff, U. S. Air Force, the Pentagon.

b7C

SECRET

The Air Force has advised that Karman is employed as captioned above but, in view of Karman's other work, it is not known if he is employed within the purview of Executive Order 9835 or if he is serving only in some Consultant capacity.

The Air Force has advised its files contain no information concerning the above-mentioned allegations but that all available background information concerning Todar Karman is being obtained from Europe, which information will be made available to the Bureau.

RECOMMENDATION:

It is recommended that the Liaison Section ascertain from the Department of the Air Force if Von Karman is an employee of the U. S. Government within the purview of Executive Order 9835, and, if so, it should be determined whether any action is desired concerning Von Karman under Executive Order 9835.

SECRET

In the January 1, 1951, issue of "Time" magazine, a photograph of Dr. Von Karman appears together with an article which relates how Von Karman with four associates invested $8700 and established the Aerojet Engineering Corporation of Azusa, California. As a result of Von Karman's knowledge that rockets would be an important weapon, the article states that the Aerojet Company now has a $25,000,000 backlog of orders and is planning a new $6,000,000 plant. It further states that much of Aerojet's experimental work is secret and that the firm presently has 1600 employees.

Recent Allegations received concerning Von Karman

By letter dated October 4, 1950, the New York Office furnished the Bureau and Los Angeles information which had been furnished them by G-2 who advised that in view of a news article indicating Bureau interest toward scientists of questionable political tendencies at Cal. Tech they were forwarding the information which had been extracted from their case on [redacted] b7C
(Bufiles negative)

The extracted information reflected that CIC in Vienna, Austria, had forwarded a letter dated April 1, 1948, which contained information concerning Todar Karman that had been received from a source rated as "fairly reliable - possibly true." According to the source, Todar Karman joined the Hungarian Communist Party in 1918 while working as Assistant Professor of Physics at a Technical University in Budapest, Hungary. In 1919, when the Communists seized power in Hungary, Karman was appointed Deputy Commissar of Cultural and Educational Affairs in charge of Higher Education. He functioned in that capacity until late 1919 when the Communists were routed by the Nationalist forces of Admiral Horthy. According to the source, Karman then fled to Germany where he settled at Aachen and his membership was transferred to the German Communist Party. Karman then lectured at the University of Aachen and in 1931 began trips to the United States to give short lecture courses at the California Institute of Technology. After Hitler seized power in Germany, Karman took up permanent residence in the United States and became a regular Professor at Cal. Tech. During the war, Karman engaged in research work in Aerodynamics for the U. S. Army Air Forces and in 1945 was assigned to a position on the research staff of an army-sponsored guided missile project, a position which he retains to this date. It was the source's belief that Karman covered up his Communist Party membership when applying for a visa to the United States in 1931.

SECRET

TEXT ON THIS PAGE IS ILLEGIBLE
WE HAVE LEFT THE PAGE AS REFERENCE

C

SECRET

On the basis of the foregoing, Los Angeles was requested to institute a thorough security investigation and was advised that the investigation should be ceased and the Bureau advised if it is determined that Theodore Von Karman, whom the information apparently related to, is a Federal employee. By letter dated November 10, 1950, Los Angeles advised that Von Karman presently maintains an office in the Pentagon and requested Washington Field Office to determine his Federal employee status.

On December 18, 1950, the Chicago Office advised that [redacted] telephonically contacted that office and stated that he had been [redacted] also reported that [redacted] had told him that Von Karman has questioned [redacted] concerning the atomic bomb before information had been revealed to the public.

b7C
b7D

By teletype dated January 9, 1951, WFO advised that Von Karman maintains an office in the Pentagon with the Air Force Scientific Advisory Board but that Air Force personnel records show he terminated employment January 3, 1946. WFO is attempting to clarify Von Karman's status.

Review of Bufiles re Von Karman

(1). Bureau Investigation

During the early 1940's Von Karman was one of several subjects of an espionage investigation which was based on an allegation that foreigners, including Von Karman, had access to a classified area at Cal Tech. Investigation of Von Karman failed to show that he was disloyal and revealed that the classified area was adequately guarded. (65-8943 Serial 2)

In September, 1940, the investigation was reopened on the basis of an allegation received that one of the subjects was pro-Nazi. The entire case file is devoted to the investigation of that subject with the exception of some background data determined regarding Von Karman and information furnished

SECRET

the Bureau [redacted] that Von Karman's Auto Club membership card was found on the person of [redacted] Japanese national, at the time [redacted] The Japanese, when questioned regarding the card, would only state that he was a friend of Von Karman's. Other information which appears in the file reflects that [redacted] had stated that a Japanese, T. Kodama, was Von Karman's gardner even though he was a structural engineer by profession. [redacted] stated that Von Karman brought home blue prints from Cal. Tech and that the prints disappeared for days at a time and that she had seen Kodama looking through Von Karman's work and at the blue prints. The file reflects that Von Karman was, at this time, a consultant for the National Defense Research Committee at Cal. Tech. ( 100-64877 - 65-8943 )

b7C
b7D

(2). [redacted] (S)

[redacted]

b1

(3) Contact with [redacted] (S)(U)

Investigation [redacted] was conducted by the Bureau in 1945, at which time [redacted] The investigation reflected that [redacted] was in frequent contact with members of the Soviet Embassy in Washington and the Soviet Consulate in New York. He had also been associated with Russian War Relief and the National Council for American Soviet Friendship. The investigation further reflected that on January 9, March 7, March 22, April 3, April 24, and 25, 1945, [redacted] was in contact with Dr. Theodore Von Karman who was then associated with the Army Air Forces. (S)(U)

(100-292259 Serials 45-84-109 and 118)

b7C

(4). Association with [redacted]

As you are aware, a reliable informant of the Los Angeles Office has advised that [redacted] were members of the

Communist Party in Pasadena, California, in 1939. A deportation hearing concerning [redacted] is pending at Los Angeles as a result of information determined in connection [redacted] at Cal. Tech who, in 1936, became interested in jet propulsion as a military weapon. The group [redacted] engaged in private research at Cal. Tech under the direct supervision of Von Karman. In 1939, Von Karman, as special advisor to [redacted] caused the Air Force to set up the Committee for Air Corps Research of the National Academy of Sciences to sponsor the development of rockets. Subsequently, a special laboratory was set up under the direct sponsorship of the Guggenheim Aeronautical Laboratory at Cal. Tech and became known as the Jet Propulsion Laboratory.

b7C

Under Air Force sponsorship the laboratory grew and in 1942 the Aerojet Engineering Company was formed to manufacture the pilot models. [redacted]

By letter dated October 30, 1950, Los Angeles furnished a transcript of a conversation which took place between Von Karman and [redacted] on September 15, 1950. The conversation was the result of a telephone call placed by Von Karman from his Pentagon Office [redacted] (100-164610 Serial 8 65-58574 Serial 5 and 122)

(5). Possible Association with [redacted]

*Classified per CIA letter dated 9-8-98

[redacted] is presently the subject of an Internal Security - R investigation based on information furnished the Bureau Liaison representative in England. [redacted]

b1
b3
(S)

b7C Dunn and Bradstreet records, New York City, reflect that [redacted] the Institution for Muscle Research, 270 Park Avenue, New York City, and that Von Karman is on the Scientific Advisory Board of that institution.

(40-84216 Serial 11)

(6). Association with William Perl

As you are aware, Perl is the subject of an espionage investigation based on his associations with Julius Rosenberg, Morton Sobell, and Joel Barr. [redacted] (S) b1

Bureau investigation of Perl reflects that he was Special Assistant to Von Karman in New York City in 1947 and 1948 and as such was entitled to confidential material of the NACA which was furnished Von Karman. On July 22, 1947, Von Karman, while in Paris, forwarded a letter to NACA which requested NACA to send information to Perl who was his technical assistant. In April, 1948, Perl, using Von Karman's stationery, requested NACA to furnish a document entitled "Index of NACA Classified Publications." The documents are described as a compilation of titles of material and papers helpful in determining the advanced areas of studies that have been explored in Aeronautical Research. During the latter part of 1950, Von Karman was interviewed regarding his association with Perl and stated that it was almost entirely related to his lectures at Columbia University and Perl's studies. Von Karman stated he had no reason to question Perl's loyalty. Perl was also employed by Von Karman for a brief period at St. Louis on unclassified research for a private concern in 1947.

(65-59312 Serial 5
65-58236 Serial 304)

b7C [redacted]

RECOMMENDATIONS:

(1). That the attached letter be furnished OSI advising them of recent allegations received concerning Von Karman.

(2). That Liaison orally advise OSI as follows concerning William Perl and his employment under Von Karman:

William Perl is the subject of a Bureau pending espionage investigation which has determined that he was a classmate at the

SECRET

College of the City of New York of Julius Rosenberg, Morton Sobell, and Joel Barr. Perl is known to have continued his association with these persons after leaving CCNY through meetings at an apartment which Perl rented in New York City. The Rosenberg espionage parallel is known to have been comprised principally of Rosenberg's fellow classmates at CCNY. Rosenberg and Sobell are presently in custody in New York City awaiting trial on espionage charges. Barr left this country in January, 1948, and is strongly suspected of having been a Soviet espionage agent. It is noted that on July 23, 1950, Vivian Glassman, the former fiancee of Joel Barr, visited Perl in Cleveland, Ohio, furnished him instructions and offered him $2,000 to leave the United States and to flee to Europe by way of Mexico. At the time Perl informed the Bureau regarding this incident he denied he had accepted the money and claimed no knowledge as to the purpose of the contact or the identity of the person who sent him the instructions. It is recalled that David Greenglass has stated that Rosenberg gave him similar instructions and furnished him with $5,000 to leave the country. The investigation of Perl and Glassman is being continued. During the investigation, it has been ascertained that Perl worked for Von Karman in 1947 when Von Karman was a special consultant for Sverdrup and Parcel on an unclassified Aeronautical Research contract. It has also been determined that in 1947 and 1948 Perl worked under Von Karman at Columbia University during which time Perl had access to classified NACA material which was sent Von Karman. Also that Perl requested certain classified material from NACA using Von Karman's stationery. It is noted that Von Karman has been interviewed both as a reference for Perl and in connection with Perl's investigation. He advised his association with Perl was almost entirely related to lectures at Columbia University and Perl's studies there. Von Karman states he had no reason to question Perl's loyalty. There has been determined no reason during the investigation to believe that Von Karman is aware of any subversive activity in which Perl may have engaged.

b7C [redacted]

It is also recommended that Liaison orally furnish OSI the information in items 2, 3, and 5 hereinbefore set out in this memorandum.

(3). That upon receipt of information that Von Karman is or is not employed by the U. S. Government, the following investigation of him be conducted:

a. If Von Karman is employed by the Government, a loyalty investigation of him be conducted on the basis of recent allegations.

SECRET

b. If he is not employed by the Government, it is recommended that a discreet Internal Security - R investigation of Von Karman be conducted for the purpose of verifying or disproving the allegation that he was a former member of the Hungarian and German Communist Party. The investigation will be requested through G-2 who furnished the original allegation. Investigation of Von Karman's present activities and contacts will be confined to the use of reliable sources and discreet investigative techniques such as mail cover and toll call checks. In view of Von Karman's position, it is not recommended that open inquiries concerning him be made except through established sources until such time as his membership in the Communist Party has been established.

OSI investigating Europe

(4). That the attached letter be sent the field advising them of the action taken and informing them that they will be requested to conduct the appropriate investigation after Von Karman's Federal employee status has been determined.

TEXT ON THIS PAGE IS ILLEGIBLE
WE HAVE LEFT THE PAGE AS REFERENCE

STANDARD FORM NO. 64

# Office Memorandum • UNITED STATES GOVERNMENT

SECRET

TO : A. H. BELMONT

FROM : C. E. HENNRICH

DATE: February 5, 1951

SUBJECT: THEODORE VON KARMAN
INTERNAL SECURITY - R

[redacted] b7C

Tolson, Ladd, Clegg, Glavin, Nichols, Rosen, Tracy, Harbo, Belmont, Mohr, Tele. Room, Nease, Gandy

ALL INFORMATION CONTAINED HERE IS UNCLASSIFIED EXCEPT WHERE SHOWN OTHERWISE

PURPOSE:

OSI advises that Von Karman is presently employed by the Air Force as Chairman of the Scientific Advisory Board, Room 4C-340, Pentagon. Von Karman is considered one of the world's leading aerodynamicists and has been employed at California Institute of Technology and United States Air Force since late 1930s. A recent report received from G-2 alleges that Todar Karman who is apparently identical with Theodore Von Karman, was Commissar of Higher Education in Hungary in 1919, and later a member of the German Communist Party. Bufiles reflect subject has been associated in aeronautical research with espionage subjects. However, no information has been developed that his association was connected with their espionage activity. It is recommended that this matter be referred to the Loyalty Section in view of subject's status as a government employee.

BACKGROUND:

Reference is made to my memorandum dated January 22, 1951, which furnished in detail information recently received concerning subject and information developed during the course of investigations involving persons who have been associated with subject in aeronautical research.

My memorandum advised that subject was born May 11, 1881, Hungary; entered the United States in 1930; and was naturalized in 1936. Since his entry into the United States, subject has been employed as Director of the Guggenheim Aeronautical Research Laboratory at the California Institute of Technology and as one of the world's leading aerodynamicists. He has served as a consultant to the National Advisory Committee on Aeronautics and as Chairman of the Scientific Advisory Board of the Commanding General of the Army Air Force. He is also a holder of the Medal of Merit.

My memorandum advised that the Bureau had received a recent report from G-2 which reflects that in 1948, a CIC investigation

CLASSIFIED BY
DECLASSIFY ON: 25X

HANDLING DESK 3/19

WAK:mes
100-372586

RECORDED - 52 100-372586-10

MAR 15 1951
34

SECRET

51 MAR 28 1951

SECRET

in Europe determined information from a source "fairly reliable - possibly true" that one Todar Karman, who is apparently identical with subject was Commissar of Higher Education in Hungary after the Communist uprising in 1919. According to the source, Karman fled to Germany the same year and continued as a member of the German Communist Party. He then came to the United States where he associated as a Professor with the California Institute of Technology and engaged in research work for the United States Army Air Force.

My memorandum noted that Bufiles reflect that in 1941, subject was investigated on the basis of a report that German aliens at Caltech had access to restricted areas. No subversive activity was established. [redacted] (S) b1

Bufiles further reflect that subject has associated in aeronautical research [redacted] b7C

[redacted] It has also (S) b1 been [redacted] Perl advised that he had taken the documents in order that he might have the benefit of information contained therein in preparing a necessary paper [redacted] Perl stated he was introduced to [redacted] by Dr. Von Karman. He emphasized that [redacted] did not ask him for classified information. b7C

- 2 -

SECRET

TEXT ON THIS PAGE IS ILLEGIBLE
WE HAVE LEFT THE PAGE AS REFERENCE

No evidence has been determined during the above investigations that Von Karman is engaged in espionage activity.

My memorandum recommended the furnishing of pertinent information in Bufiles to OSI with a request that OSI advise if subject is employed by that Agency. It also recommended that in the event subject is employed by OSI that a Loyalty investigation of him be conducted and in the event he is not so employed, that the Bureau institute a discreet Internal Security - R investigation.

By letter dated January 30, 1951, OSI advised that subject is presently employed by the Air Force as Chairman of the Scientific Advisory Board, Room 4C-340, Pentagon. They also advised that an electronic communication had been dispatched to Europe requesting all available background data pertaining to Todar Karman who is apparently identical with subject.

By memorandum dated February 3, 1951, pertinent information concerning Von Karman was furnished the Department in answer to a request by the Department as to whether the Bureau had any information indicating that the cases of [redacted] Perl were related and whether the Von Karman in those cases was identical. b7C

RECOMMENDATION:

In accordance with the information set out in my memorandum of January 22, 1951, and in view of the fact that no evidence of espionage activity on the part of Von Karman has been developed in the various Bureau cases in which his name is mentioned, it is recommended that this matter be referred to the Loyalty Section for their consideration as to whether a Loyalty investigation of Von Karman should be conducted in view of his employment with the United States Government.

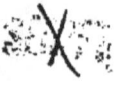

TEXT ON THIS PAGE IS ILLEGIBLE
WE HAVE LEFT THE PAGE AS REFERENCE

STANDARD FORM NO. 64

# Office Memorandum • UNITED STATES GOVERNMENT

SECRET

TO : Mr. A. H. Belmont

DATE: February 17, 1951

FROM : C. H. Stanley

SUBJECT: THEODORE VON KARMAN
Chairman
Scientific Advisory Board
Department of the Air Force
Washington, D.C.
LOYALTY OF GOVERNMENT EMPLOYEES

Tolson, Ladd, Clegg, Glavin, Nichols, Rosen, Tracy, Harbo, Belmont, Mohr, Tele. Room, Nease, Gandy

ALL INFORMATION CONTAINED HEREIN IS UNCLASSIFIED EXCEPT WHERE SHOWN OTHERWISE

PURPOSE:

To request that the Liaison Section ascertain from the Department of the Air Force if Von Karman is an employee of the U. S. Government within the purview of Executive Order 9835, and, if so, it should be determined whether any action is desired concerning Von Karman under the provisions of Executive [redacted]

BACKGROUND: [redacted] b7C

Von Karman, after his entry into the United States in 1930, was employed as Director of the Guggenheim Aeronautical Research Laboratory at the California Institute of Technology and is one of the World's leading Aerodynamicists. Prior to 1947, he served as a Consultant to the National Advisory Committee for Aeronautics and in 1947 he was made Chairman of the Scientific Advisory Board of the Commanding General of the Department of the Air Force and he is the holder of the Medal of Merit.

HANDLED IN STOP DESK 3/17

Information was recently received from G-2 indicating that one Todar Karman was Commissar of Higher Education in Hungary after the Communist uprising in 1919, and was later a member of the Communist Party in Germany. This information was furnished to the Air Force by Letter dated January 23, 1951.

Air Force was also orally advised that information is contained in the files of the Bureau indicating Von Karman has associated in aeronautical research at the California Institute of Technology [redacted] b7C

(S) b1

WDC:dba

100-372576-11

RECORDED - 52

MAR 15 1951

CLASSIFIED BY
DECLASSIFY ON: 25X

TEXT ON THIS PAGE IS ILLEGIBLE
WE HAVE LEFT THE PAGE AS REFERENCE

SAC, Los Angeles | SECRET | March 14, 1951

RECORDED - 52 100-372586-12

Director, FBI

SECRET
CLASSIFIED BY SP5 JC/1DW 154894 6-13-97
DECLASSIFY ON: 25X 6

THEODORE VON KARMAN
INTERNAL SECURITY - R

Reference is made to Bulet dated January 23, 1951, which advised that information in Bureau files concerning subject had been made available to OSI at Washington and the Field would be furnished instructions concerning the investigation of subject upon receipt of information from OSI as to subject's Federal employee status.

On March 7, 1951, the Bureau was advised by [redacted] Counterintelligence Division, OSI, that Von Karman, as Chairman of the Scientific Advisory Board, Department of the Air Force, maintains an office in the Pentagon Building at Washington. According to [redacted] Von Karman is paid on a contract basis and is therefore not on the Air Force payroll or subject to Loyalty investigation under Executive Order 9835. [redacted] has further advised that subject is still employed by the California Institute of Technology and requested that the Bureau conduct an Internal Security - R investigation of subject. [redacted] has also advised that OSI is conducting immediate investigation in Europe for the purpose of developing background information concerning Todar Karman for the purpose of attempting to definitely establish that Todar Karman is identical with subject.

b7C

ALL INFORMATION CONTAINED HEREIN IS UNCLASSIFIED EXCEPT WHERE SHOWN OTHERWISE

Information available to the Bureau concerning Theodore Von Karman reflects that he has been a Professor of Aeronautics at the California Institute of Technology since his arrival in the United States in 1930 with the exception of short periods of employment in other parts of the United States. Since 1936, he has been associated closely in aeronautical research [redacted]

b7C

(S) b1

HANDLE BY STOP DESK

MAILED 10
MAR 14 1951

Tolson
Ladd
Clegg
Glavin
Nichols
Rosen
Tracy
Harbo
Belmont
Mohr

100-372586

SECRET

cc - Washington Field (Attachment)
New York (Attachment)
Chicago
Cleveland

WAK:mes:njf

SECRET

SECRET

b1 [redacted]

b7D b7C

[redacted] Bureau files further reflect that [redacted] during a recent interview conducted [redacted] advised that he had been sent to [redacted] Theodore Von Karman for the purpose of [redacted] According to [redacted] Von Karman had recommended [redacted] as an old friend. It is noted that [redacted] and [redacted] are the subjects of Los Angeles security investigations.

As you are aware, G-2 has now furnished information concerning one Todar Karman, which alleges that Todar Karman was appointed Deputy Commissar of Cultural and Educational Affairs in charge of higher education after the Communist uprising in Hungary during 1919. The information also alleges that Todar Karman later fled from Hungary to Germany where he continued his membership in the Communist Party. On the basis of information furnished by the Los Angeles Office, as a result of an INS record check, made by Los Angeles in August of 1941 in connection with a previous investigation of Von Karman, it appears that Todar Karman and Theodore Von Karman are identical.

On the basis of the foregoing information, Los Angeles is being designated office of origin and is instructed to conduct an immediate and thorough Internal Security - R investigation of Theodore Von Karman. The investigation is to be discreet and confined at this time to the use of such discreet sources as toll call checks, mail covers, spot physical surveillances, and interviews with established sources of information only. All reports are to be submitted promptly and are to be prepared in accordance with existing regulations concerning dissemination.

The Washington Field Office is to conduct the same type investigation of Von Karman during his presence in Washington, D. C. In the event it is subsequently determined that Von Karman spends the greater part of his time in Washington, the Washington Field Office will be designated by the Bureau as office of origin. It is noted that the Washington Field Office is presently in the process of interviewing Theodore Von Karman in connection with the

SECRET

SECRET

C

TEXT ON THIS PAGE IS ILLEGIBLE
WE HAVE LEFT THE PAGE AS REFERENCE

SECRET SECRET

investigation of William Perl. The Bureau does not desire that the interview with Von Karman concerning Perl be held in abeyance as a result of the independent investigation of Von Karman which is now being instituted.

New York is to immediately contact G-2 Headquarters, New York City, for the purpose of determining the identity of the CIC informant who furnished the information concerning Todar Karman in order that the informant can be reinterviewed by Bureau sources or OSI in Europe for all information in his possession concerning Todar Karman or Theodore Von Karman. New York is to also determine from G-2 whether the investigation of [redacted] mentioned in New York letter dated October 4, 1950, is in any way related to the investigation of Von Karman. There is attached for New York a copy of the G-2 report concerning Von Karman, which New York forwarded the Bureau in connection with its letter of October 4, 1950. A photostatic copy is also attached for the information of the Washington Field Office.

b7C

On the basis of a previously conducted review of the Bureau files, it appears that Los Angeles is in the possession of all pertinent information concerning Theodore Von Karman. A current review of Bureau files is, however, being made and any additional pertinent information not available to Los Angeles will be furnished.

A check of Central Office records of INS at Washington is being made by the Bureau concerning Todar Karman to determine whether it is possible that Todar Karman and Theodore Von Karman are not identical. It is noted that INS records concerning Theodore Von Karman have already been checked by Los Angeles in connection with their previous investigation of subject. A photograph of Von Karman which appeared in the January 1, 1951, issue of Time magazine is being copied at the Bureau and will be furnished Los Angeles and interested offices.

The Bureau is also determining from its files the identity of persons who are known to have held official positions in the Hungarian Communist Government of 1919 and if deemed appropriate, will set out leads requesting the interview of those persons concerning subject. The results of the OSI investigation now being conducted in Europe will be made available when received at the Bureau.

SECRET - SECRET

STANDARD FORM NO. 64

# Office Memorandum • UNITED STATES GOVERNMENT

TO : Mr. A. H. Belmont

FROM : V. P. Keay

DATE: February 28, 1951

SUBJECT: THEODORE VON KARMAN
Chairman
Scientific Advisory Board
Department of the Air Force
Washington, D. C.
LOYALTY OF GOVERNMENT EMPLOYEES

Tolson___
Ladd___
Clegg___
Glavin___
Nichols___
Rosen___
Tracy___
Harbo___
Belmont___
Mohr___
Tele. Room___
Nease___
Gandy___

By memorandum dated February 17, 1951, addressed to you by Mr. C. H. Stanley, it was recommended that the Liaison Section ascertain from the Department of the Air Force if Von Karman is an employee of the U. S. Government within the purview of Executive Order 9835 and, if so, it should be determined whether any action is desired concerning Von Karman under Executive Order 9835.

b7C [redacted] This m[redacted] discussed by Special Agent [redacted] with [redacted] OSI Headquarters. [redacted] requested that an investigation be made of Von Karman but requested that the investigation be under the heading of Internal Security rather than the Loyalty of Government Employees. This request was based on the fact that Von Karman is connected with the California Institute of Technology and is Chairman of the Scientific Advisory Board. ~~In connection with his duties as Chairman of the Scientific Advisory Board he attends conferences in Washington approximately twice each year and is paid on a consultant basis.~~ b7C [redacted] stated that there is some doubt at this time as to whether it is proper to investigate Von Karman under Executive Order 9835 and stated that in any event, if possible, it would preferable for the investigation to be made under the Internal Security character. In this connection they noted that Von Karman has access to practically all classified information in Air Force Headquarters and is an outstanding technician. They pointed out that to conduct the investigation under 9835, which may not be appropriate the information developed would of necessity be passed to Air Force through the Civil Service Commission and many individuals not directly concerned would have access to the results of the investigation.



ESS:bsh

RECORDED - 52

MAR 15 1951

[redacted] b7C

C

RECOMMENDATION:

It is recommended that this memorandum be referred to the Loyalty Section for its information and then to the Internal Security Section for appropriate investigation.

b7C

[redacted] requested that every effort be made to trace Theodore Von Karman's immigration and naturalization records in order that they can be compared with the immigration and naturalization records of Todar Karman, who was Commissioner of Higher Education in Hungary, in order that it can be determined whether the two individuals are or are not the same.

3-7-51

b7C

[redacted] OSI stated Von Karman maintains office in Pentagon and spends a considerable amount of time there but is paid on a contract basis and is therefore not on the Air Force payroll and not subject to E.O. 9835.

E.S.S.

TEXT ON THIS PAGE IS ILLEGIBLE
WE HAVE LEFT THE PAGE AS REFERENCE

STANDARD FORM NO. 64

# Office Mem[illegible]dum • UNITED [illegible] OVERNMENT

TO : DIRECTOR, FBI DATE: February 6, 1951

FROM : SAC, WFO

SUBJECT: THEODORE VON KARMAN
INTERNAL SECURITY - C
Bufile 100-372586 and 65-8943

From a review of the information presently available to the WFO, it would appear that the THEODORE VON KARMAN, subject of Bufile 100-372586, and the THEODORE VON KARMAN, subject of Bufile 65-8943, are probably identical.

This is being brought to the Bureau's attention as this office is not aware as to whether or not this identification has been made. RUC

cc: Los Angles
65-1936

JEH:dep
100-22923

RECORDED - 14

[redacted]

354-894
ALL INFORMATION CONTAINED
HEREIN IS UNCLASSIFIED
DATE 5-21-97 BY

[redacted]

b7C

66 MAR 22 1951

TEXT ON THIS PAGE IS ILLEGIBLE
WE HAVE LEFT THE PAGE AS REFERENCE

Mr. Ladd
Mr. Clegg
Mr. Glavin
Mr. Nichols
Mr. Rosen
Mr. Tracy
Mr. Harbo
Mr. Belmont
Mr. Mohr
Tele. Room
Mr. Nease
Miss Gandy

JEH:cl
100-22923

FBI WASHINGTON FIELD 1-9-51 12:15 PM DEFERRED

DIRECTOR, FBI

ALL INFORMATION CONTAINED
HEREIN IS UNCLASSIFIED
DATE 5-22-97 BY

THEODORE VON KARMAN, SM - C. (BUFILE 100-372586) RE LOS ANGELES LETTER, NOV. 10, 1950, AND CLEVELAND LETTER JAN. 5, 1951. FILES OSI, AIR FORCE, PENTAGON, WASHINGTON, D.C., SHOW THAT ON SEPT. 15, 1950, [redacted] OF INS, LOS ANGELES, CONTACTED [redacted] OSI, LOS ANGELES, RE [redacted] ADVISING VON KARMAN ATTEMPTING CONTACT [redacted] STATING VON KARMAN LEAVING FOR EUROPE AND VERY NECESSARY THAT HE BE PERMITTED TO TALK WITH [redacted] INS REFUSED THIS REQUEST. [redacted] VON KARMAN MAINTAINS OFFICE IN PENTAGON, WITH AIR FORCE SCIENTIFIC ADVISORY BOARD, WHICH ADVISED NOV. 17, 1950 THAT HE WAS IN EUROPE FOR THEM. HOWEVER, AIR FORCE PERSONNEL RECORDS SHOW TERMINATED JAN. 3, 1946. EFFORTS TO CLARIFY STATUS CONTINUING.

b7C

HOTTEL

CC - Chicago by Mail
CC - Los Angeles by Mail
CC - New York by Mail
CC - Cleveland by Mail

RECORDED - 63 100-372586
INDEXED - 63 MAR 28 1951

COPIES DESTROYED
278 APR 5 1963

cc: Mr Belmont

TEXT ON THIS PAGE IS ILLEGIBLE
WE HAVE LEFT THE PAGE AS REFERENCE

SERVICE UNIT b7C 4-22a
SEARCH SLIP

Supervisor [redacted] Room 4708

Subj: Todar Karman

✓Exact Spelling
All References
Subversive Ref.
Main File
Restricted to Locality of

Searchers
Initial
Date 11-16

| FILE NUMBER | SERIALS |
|---|---|
| ✓100-372586 | |

File swept.

358894
ALL INFORMATION CONTAINED
HEREIN IS UNCLASSIFIED
DATE 5-23-97 BY

Initialed

FEDERAL BUREAU OF INVESTIGATION

Part. 1b

# SUBJECT: THEODORE VON KARMAN

# FILE NUMBER: 40-13556 AND 100-372586 SERIALS X-29

C

TEXT ON THIS PAGE IS ILLEGIBLE
WE HAVE LEFT THE PAGE AS REFERENCE

SERVICE UNIT b7C 4-22a
SEARCH SLIP

Supervisor [redacted] Room 4708

Subj: Theodore Karman

✓ Exact Spelling
✓ All References
Subversive Ref.
Main File
Restricted to Locality of (384-899)
on move

Searchers
Initial
Date 1-16

ALL INFORMATION CONTAINED
HEREIN IS UNCLASSIFIED
DATE 5-22-97 BY

| FILE NUMBER | SERIALS |
|---|---|
| 65-59312 | 129 p5-5 |
| 7-10, 13, 14, 41 | 43, 46; |
| (Duplicate) 100-3 [illegible] 86 | |
| 116-160113 | 12 |
| 40-84216 | 11 p5 |
| 65-59589 | 3 |
| 65-58574 | 22 |
| 65-59312 | 136, 159, 129 p5-5 |
| 7-10, 13, 14, | 41, 43, 46; 16 |
| p54, 64, 81; | 17 p5; 86 |
| 49; 5; | 164 p33, 37, 63, 69 |
| 70, 71, 72, 73; | 180; 20; |
| 59; 147 p | 40, 45-47, 50 |

Initialed

TEXT ON THIS PAGE IS ILLEGIBLE
WE HAVE LEFT THE PAGE AS REFERENCE

SERVICE UNIT 4-22a
SEARCH SLIP

Supervisor ____________ Room ______

Subj: Theodore Karman

✓ Exact Spelling
✓ All References
___ Subversive Ref.
___ Main File
___ Restricted to Locality of ____________

Searchers
Initial ______
Date ______

| FILE NUMBER | SERIALS |
|---|---|
| ✓ 65-58236 | 304 |
| ✓ ~~65-12313~~ | ~~3~~ |
| ✓ 126-163450 | 5 |
| ✓ 65-58574 | 114, 5 ✓ |
| Theodore Von Karman | |
| ✓ 65-8943 | |
| ~~65-8943~~ | |
| ✓ ~~100-341759~~ | ~~11~~ |
| ~~65-59312~~ | ~~129 p. 2, 3, 4, 5,~~ |
| ~~7, 8, 9~~ | ~~10, 13, 14, 41, 43, 46~~ |
| ~~65-8943~~ | |
| ✓ 40-13556 | |
| ✓ ~~40-48862~~ | |

written

Initialed

TEXT ON THIS PAGE IS ILLEGIBLE
WE HAVE LEFT THE PAGE AS REFERENCE

SERVICE UNIT 4-22a
SEARCH SLIP

Supervisor ____________ Room ______

Subj: Theodore Von Karman

✓ Exact Spelling Searchers
✓ All References Initial
Subversive Ref. Date 1/16/57
Main File
Restricted to Locality of

ALL INFORMATION CONTAINED ... EXCEPT ... WISE

FILE NUMBER SERIALS

CLASSIFIED BY
DECLASSIFY ON: 25X (354-894)

100-372 - DECLAS
46-1355 - 4
116-163450 - 5
65-59312 - 183, 164 p.33,
37, 62, 69, 70, 71, 72, 73
65-57312 - 49, 129 p.2,3,
4, 5, 7, 8, 9, 10, 13, 14, 4, 45, 46
116-168173 - 12
65-58574 - 5
b1 [redacted] 227, p.10
65-59312 - 159, 136
65-22489 - 7
100-64877 - 8

SECRET

Initialed

C



SERVICE UNIT 4-22a
SEARCH SLIP

SECRET Supervisor ____________ Room ______

Subj: Theodore Von Karman

✓ Exact Spelling — Searchers
✓ All References — Initial
___ Subversive Ref. — Date 1/16/51
___ Main File
___ Restricted to Locality of

| FILE NUMBER | SERIALS |
|---|---|
| ✓ 65-58574 | 114 |
| ✓ 100-64877 | 5 |
| ✓ 65-5725 | 1 |
| ✓ 100-2 | 43 |
| ✓ 65-14415 | 2 |
| ✓ 62-23533 | 7259 |
| ~~65-57312~~ | ~~59~~ |
| ✓ 105-10038 | 1 |
| ✓ 96-0 | 234 |
| ✓ 65-32107 | 5 |
| ✓ 100-292259 | 125 |
| ✓ 65-32054 | 91 |
| ✓ 100-47852 | 14 p.5 |

SECRET

Initialed

TEXT ON THIS PAGE IS ILLEGIBLE
WE HAVE LEFT THE PAGE AS REFERENCE

SERVICE UNIT 4-22a
SEARCH SLIP

SECRET

Supervisor ______________ Room______

Subj: Theodore Von Karman

✓ Exact Spelling — Searchers
✓ All References — Initial
Subversive Ref. — Date 1/16/51
Main File
Restricted to Locality of

| FILE NUMBER | SERIALS |
|---|---|
| ✓100-203581 | 4723 |
| ✓100-164610 | 8 |
| ✓65-33716 | 213, p.14 |
| ✓64-4102 | 483 |
| ✓65-58574 | 122 |
| ~~65-59312~~ | ~~20~~ |
| [redacted] | b1 |
| 105-12313 | 3 (S) |
| ✓40-84216 | 11 p.5 |
| ✓65-59312 | 86 |
| 65-8943 | 73 |
| ✓65-59294 | 100 p.18 |
| ~~100-344159~~ | ~~22~~ |

SECRET

Initialed

TEXT ON THIS PAGE IS ILLEGIBLE
WE HAVE LEFT THE PAGE AS REFERENCE

SERVICE UNIT
SEARCH SLIP
4-22a

SECRET

Supervisor ________ Room ________

Subj: Theodore Von Karman

✓ Exact Spelling
✓ All References
___ Subversive Ref.
___ Main File
___ Restricted to Locality of ________

Searchers JD
Initial
Date 1/16

| FILE NUMBER | SERIALS |
|---|---|
| 100-292259 | 118 |
| ~~65-59589~~ | ~~3~~ |
| 100-292259 | 109; 84; 73; 45 |
| 62-65880 | 208 |
| ~~65-59312~~ | ~~5, 16 p. 54, 69, 81~~ |
| 65-58236 | 304 |
| 65-33716 | 200 |
| ~~65-59312~~ | ~~17 p. 5~~ |

SECRET

Initialed

TEXT ON THIS PAGE IS ILLEGIBLE
WE HAVE LEFT THE PAGE AS REFERENCE

Karman.

~~65-59689-5~~ K-2

65-59312-159, 164, 136 K-2-K-4

~~100-292259-123, 118, 109, 45~~ ~~K-7-K-5~~

~~100-164610~~ ~~K-6~~

~~[illegible]~~6

Very sp. locate | 1-19 | 1-19
1-18 | 9:30 | 4:45
3:40

TEXT ON THIS PAGE IS ILLEGIBLE
WE HAVE LEFT THE PAGE AS REFERENCE

1-15-51

To - Mr Hennrich

354-894
ALL INFORMATION CONTAINED
HEREIN IS UNCLASSIFIED
DATE 5-21-97 BY SPS JC/[illegible]

fireworks.

Carl — this
man Von Karman
is possible
Esp. agt. I
think you will
want to handle

JEH

STATES DEPARTMENT OF JUST[illegible] CC-150

To: COMMUNI N.

March 22, 1951 URGENT

Transmit the following message to: SAC, NEW YORK

TEXT ON THIS PAGE IS ILLEGIBLE
WE HAVE LEFT THE PAGE AS REFERENCE

THEODORE VON KARMAN, IS - R. REBULET MARCH FOURTEEN LAST. OSI HAS INFORMED BUREAU THAT THEY HAVE LOCATED CIC AGENT IN GERMANY WHO PREPARED REPORT ON [redacted] WHICH ALLEGED THAT TODAR KARMAN WAS FORMER MEMBER OF CP IN HUNGARY AND GERMANY. OSI WILL CONDUCT APPROPRIATE INVESTIGATION IN EUROPE. NEW YORK DISREGARD REQUEST IN REFERENCED LET TO CONTACT G-2.

HOOVER

b7C

100-372586

CC: LOS ANGELES (BY MAIL)
WASHINGTON FIELD (BY SPECIAL MESSENGER)

WAK:mes

The above information was furnished telephonically by liaison agent [redacted] at 1:15 PM on 3-22-51. OSI is conducting the foreign investigation as subject is Chairman of the Scientific Advisory Board of the Air Force.

b7C

354-899
ALL INFORMATION CONTAINED
HEREIN IS UNCLASSIFIED
DATE 5-22-97 BY SP5JC/dgm

Tolson___
Ladd___
Clegg___
Glavin___
Nichols___
Rosen___
Tracy___
Harbo___
Mohr___
Tele. Room___
Nease___
Gandy___

COPIES DESTROYED
.28 APR 5

RECORDED - 106

MAR 22 1 20 PM '51

SENT VIA ___ 5-51 P. Per ___

FD-654 (12-2-83)

TEXT ON THIS PAGE IS ILLEGIBLE
WE HAVE LEFT THE PAGE AS REFERENCE

Date 3/28/51

Classification of Mail:

- ☐ Unclassified
- ☐ Confidential
- ☐ Secret
- ☑ Top Secret*
- ☐ SCI*

Mail Category:

| | | | |
|---|---|---|---|
| Letter | ✓ | Airtel | |
| LHM | | Memo | |
| Report | | Other | |
| Teletype | | | |

FD-501 Number HQ 86-7731 FD-502 Number

Subject Theodore Van Karman

Date of Mail 3/28/51

Description of Material Letter: co. FBIHQ: Los Angeles
(include identity of originating office or agency)

This serial has been removed and placed in:

☑ Special File Room, Room 5991, FBIHQ

☐ ______
(Field Office - Room, Cabinet, or other location where material is stored)

This action taken based upon authority of:

☐ TS/SCICO, FBIHQ, 62-116065

☐ Field Office Manager — 100-372586-
File and Serial number

354 894
ALL INFORMATION CONTAINED
HEREIN IS UNCLASSIFIED
DATE 9 10 91 BY SP5 JC

(Signature and Title of Approving Official)

Date

*requires special handling

PERMANENT SERIAL CHARGE-OUT

FBI/DOJ

TEXT ON THIS PAGE IS ILLEGIBLE
WE HAVE LEFT THE PAGE AS REFERENCE

SAC, LOS ANGELES

March 28, 1951

354-894
ALL INFORMATION CONTAINED
HEREIN IS UNCLASSIFIED
DATE 5-22-97 BY SPS

DIRECTOR, FBI

THEODORE VON KARMAN
INTERNAL SECURITY - R

INDEXED - 97
RECORDED - 97
100-372586-16

Rebulet March 14, 1951.

b7C

[redacted] Central Office of Immigration and Naturalization Service, pursuant to a request, caused a check of the indices of that Service to be made for information concerning the above individual. That check disclosed Central Office file C-4052565 on Theodore Von Karman.

Examination of the file disclosed that Dr. Theodore Von Karman made application to the American Consular Service in Budapest, Hungary, on September 24, 1930, for a non-quota immigration visa. His application reflected that he was born on May 11, 1881, in Budapest, Hungary; and except for several trips to the United States, from 1913 to 1930, he resided in Aachen, Germany, from 1913 to 1930, and in Budapest, Hungary, from September 1, 1930 to September 24, 1930. His mother's name was given as Ilka Karman, nee Kohn, of Budapest, Hungary. His father was deceased.

At the time of his application, Theodore Von Karman stated he intended to enter the United States at New York City, destined for Pasadena, California, to take up permanent residence in order to continue his vocation. He indicated he had been appointed to the directorship of the Aeronautical Laboratory at the California Institute of Technology in Pasadena, California. An endorsement thereon disclosed that he entered the United States on the SS Majestic on October 7, 1930, through New York City. Subsequently, he was naturalized in the District Court of the United States at Los Angeles on July 24, 1936, under the name of Theodore Von Karman. His Certificate No. is C-4052565. The witnesses to the petition were [redacted] Pasadena, California, and [redacted] Pasadena, California.

b7C

b7C

[redacted] advised that a check of the indices of her Service failed to reveal any record of Todar Karman.

100-372586
Attachments

WAK:mes

MAILED 10
MAR 28 1951
COMM - FBI

HANDLED BY STOP DESK

Tolson
Ladd
Clegg
Glavin
Nichols
Rosen
Tracy
Barbo
Belmont
Mohr
Tele. Room
Nease
Gandy

66 APR 13 1951

U.S. DEPT. OF JUSTICE
F B I
RECEIVED - MAIL ROOM

Relative to the information appearing in the naturalization record of Dr. Theodore Von Karman indicating he had made several trips to the United States between 1913 and 1930, [redacted] pointed out that the Central Office of INS would not have any record of these trips inasmuch as they were of short duration. Any record as to the trips would be maintained by the Immigration and Naturalization Service at the port of entry.

b7C

There are attached for your information two copies of a photograph of subject which appeared in the January 1, 1951, issue of Time magazine as well as a photostatic copy of an article concerning him which appeared in the same issue of Time.

There are also attached copies of the following reports in which subject is mentioned:

Atlanta report dated 10-8-40, entitled [redacted] Espionage."

Washington Field Office report dated 1-29-45, entitled [redacted] Internal Security - R."

Washington Field Office report dated 3-22-45, entitled [redacted] Internal Security - R."

Washington Field Office report dated 4-13-45, entitled [redacted] Internal Security - R."

b7C

Washington Field Office report dated 5-9-45, entitled [redacted] Internal Security - R."

New York report dated 2-10-50, entitled [redacted] Internal Security - R and HU."

St. Louis report dated 8-2-50, entitled "William Perl, Espionage - R."

Additional information concerning subject can be found in the following reports which are in the possession of your office:

Los Angeles report dated 10-5-39, entitled [redacted] wa., Espionage."

Tolson____
Ladd____
Clegg____
Glavin____
Nichols____
Rosen____
Tracy____
Harbo____
Belmont____
Mohr____
Tele. Room____
Nease____
Gandy____

- 2 -

Los Angeles report dated 1-29-41, entitled [redacted] wa., Espionage - G." (65-32107-4)

Los Angeles report dated 3-27-41, entitled [redacted] wa., Espionage." (65-3210725)

Los Angeles report dated 1-26-42, entitled [redacted] Internal Security - J, Alien Enemy Control." (100-64877-5)

Los Angeles report dated 6-3-42, entitled [redacted] Espionage - G." (65-22489-7)

Los Angeles report dated 10-14-42, entitled "Survey of Hungarian Activities in the Los Angeles Field Division, Internal Security - (H)," page 11. (100-89-27-1)

Los Angeles report dated 11-28-42, entitled [redacted] wa., Internal Security - R, Custodial Detention." (100-164610-1)

San Antonio report dated 6-11-43, entitled [redacted] Foreign Travel Control - G." (100-50430-12)

Newark report dated 4-13-45, entitled [redacted] - Internal Security - R," Page 7. (100-292259-105)

Los Angeles report dated 8-14-45, entitled [redacted] Los Angeles, Internal Security - R," (65-33716-213) Page 14.

Los Angeles report dated 4-5-49, entitled [redacted] was., Espionage - R," Page 8. (100-359682-25)

Los Angeles report dated 7-26-49, entitled [redacted] wa., Internal Security - R." (100-164610-8)

Tolson
Ladd
Clegg
Glavin
Nichols
Rosen
Tracy
Harbo
Belmont
Mohr
Tele. Room
Mease
Gandy

b7C

Los Angeles report dated 8-29-49, entitled [redacted] Espionage - R." (65-58574-5)

Los Angeles report dated 1-27-50, entitled [redacted] AEA-A." (116-163450)

Washington Field Office report dated 6-18-50, entitled [redacted] Junkers Aircraft Co. Inc., Espionage." (65-18126-1)

New York report dated 8-7-50, entitled "William Perl, wa., Espionage - R," Pages 54, 64, and 81. (65-59312-16)

Albany report dated 8-7-50, entitled "Alfred Epaminondas Sarant, was., Espionage - R," Pages 32 and 34. (65-59242-77)

Cleveland report dated 8-7-50, entitled "William Perl, aka., Espionage - R," Page 5. (65-59312-17, page 5

Cleveland letter dated 8-7-50, entitled "William Perl, aka., Espionage - R." (65-59312-49)

Washington Field Office report dated 9-21-50, entitled "William Perl, wa., Espionage - R." (65-59312-129)

Cleveland report dated 9-27-50, entitled "William Perl, aka., Espionage - R," Pages 40, 45, 46, 47, 50, 51. (65-59312-147)

Cleveland report dated 9-27-50, entitled "William Perl, aka., Espionage - R." (65-59312-147)

Washington Field Office letter dated 10-17-50, entitled [redacted] wa., Espionage - R." (65-58574-114)

Cleveland report dated 10-20-50, entitled [redacted] Espionage - R," Page 18. (65-59294-100)

Tolson____
Ladd____
Clegg____
Glavin____
Nichols____
Rosen____
Tracy____
Harbo____
Belmont____
Mohr____
Tele. Room____
Nease____
Gandy____

b7C

TEXT ON THIS PAGE IS ILLEGIBLE
WE HAVE LEFT THE PAGE AS REFERENCE

New York report dated 10-26-50, entitled
"William Perl, wa., Espionage - R."
Pages 33, 37, 63, 69, 70, 71, 72, 73.
(65-59312-164)

Albany report dated 10-31-50, entitled
"Julius Rosenberg, Espionage - R."
Pages 35, 37.
(65-58236-563)

Washington Field Office report dated 11-30-50,
entitled "William Perl, wa., Espionage - R."
(65-59312-180)

Los Angeles report dated 12-7-50, entitled
b7C [redacted] Espionage - IS."
(65-59589-3)

Cleveland report dated 1-5-51, entitled
"William Perl, wa., Espionage - R."
Page 4.
(65-59312-200)

Tolson
Ladd
Clegg
Glavin
Nichols
Rosen
Tracy
Harbo
Belmont
Mohr
Tele. Room
Nease
Gandy

TEXT ON THIS PAGE IS ILLEGIBLE
WE HAVE LEFT THE PAGE AS REFERENCE

STANDARD FORM NO. 64

# Office Memorandum • UNITED STATES GOVERNMENT

TO : MR. V. P. KEAY

FROM : [redacted] b7C

SUBJECT: THEODORE VON KARMAN

DATE: March 20, 1951

354-894
ALL INFORMATION CONTAINED HEREIN IS UNCLASSIFIED DATE 5 22 97 BY SP5

Tolson, Ladd, Clegg, Glavin, Nichols, Rosen, Tracy, Harbo, Belmont, Mohr, Tele. Room, Nease, Gandy

[redacted] the Central Office of Immigration and Naturalization Service, pursuant to a request, caused a check of the indices of that Service to be made for information concerning the above individual. That check disclosed Central Office file C-4052565 on Theodore Von Karman. Examination of the file disclosed that Dr. Theodore Von Karman made application to the American Consular Service in Budapest, Hungary, on September 24, 1930, for a non-quota immigration visa. His application reflected that he was born on May 11, 1881, in Budapest, Hungary; that he resided in Aachen, Germany, and Budapest, Hungary, except for several trips to the United States, from 1913 to 1930. Actually he resided in Aachen, Germany, from 1913 to 1930, and only resided in Budapest, Hungary, from September 1, 1930, to September 24, 1930. His mother, who was then living, was given as Ilka Karman, nee Kohn, of Budapest, Hungary. His father was deceased. At the time of his application, Theodore Von Karman stated he intended to embark at Liverpool-Quebec and intended to enter the United States at New York City destined for Pasadena, California, to take up permanent residence in order to continue his vocation. He indicated he had been appointed to the directorship of the Aeronautical Laboratory at the California Institute of Technology in Pasadena, California. An endorsement thereon disclosed that he entered the United States on the SS Majestic on October 7, 1930, through New York City. Subsequently, he was naturalized in the District Court of the United States at Los Angeles on July 24, 1936, under the name of Theodore De Karnan, having changed it at the same time from Theodore Von Karman. [redacted] The witnesses to the petition were [redacted] Pasadena, California, and [redacted] Pasadena, California.

b7C [redacted] advised that a check of the indices of her Service failed to reveal any record of Todar Karman.

3 ENCL

Relative to the information appearing in the naturalization record of Dr. Theodore Von Karman indicating he had made several trips to the United States between 1913 and 1930, [redacted] pointed out that the Central Office of INS would not have any record of these trips inasmuch as they were of short duration. Any record as to the trips would be maintained by the Immigration and Naturalization Service at the port of entry. It would be necessary, of course, to ascertain the port of entry before a record could be checked. b7C

RECOMMENDATION: RECORDED - 97

This memorandum be routed to [redacted] for his information.

JEFo:ejj HANDLED BY STOP DESK b7C

TEXT ON THIS PAGE IS ILLEGIBLE
WE HAVE LEFT THE PAGE AS REFERENCE

SECRET SERVICE UNIT b7C 4-22a
SEARCH SLIP

Supervisor [redacted] Room 1732

Subj: Katman, Todar

✓ Exact Spelling
✓ All References
___ Subversive Ref.
___ Main File
___ Restricted to Locality of

Searchers Initial JCI
Date 3-15

| FILE NUMBER | SERIALS |
| --- | --- |
| ~~100-372586~~ | |

354894 9-22-97
CLASSIFIED BY SP5 JC/DQ
DECLASSIFY ON: 25X 1

No reference
Re Ransom

ALL INFORMATION CONTAINED
HEREIN IS UNCLASSIFIED EXCEPT
WHERE SHOWN OTHERWISE

SECRET

Initialed

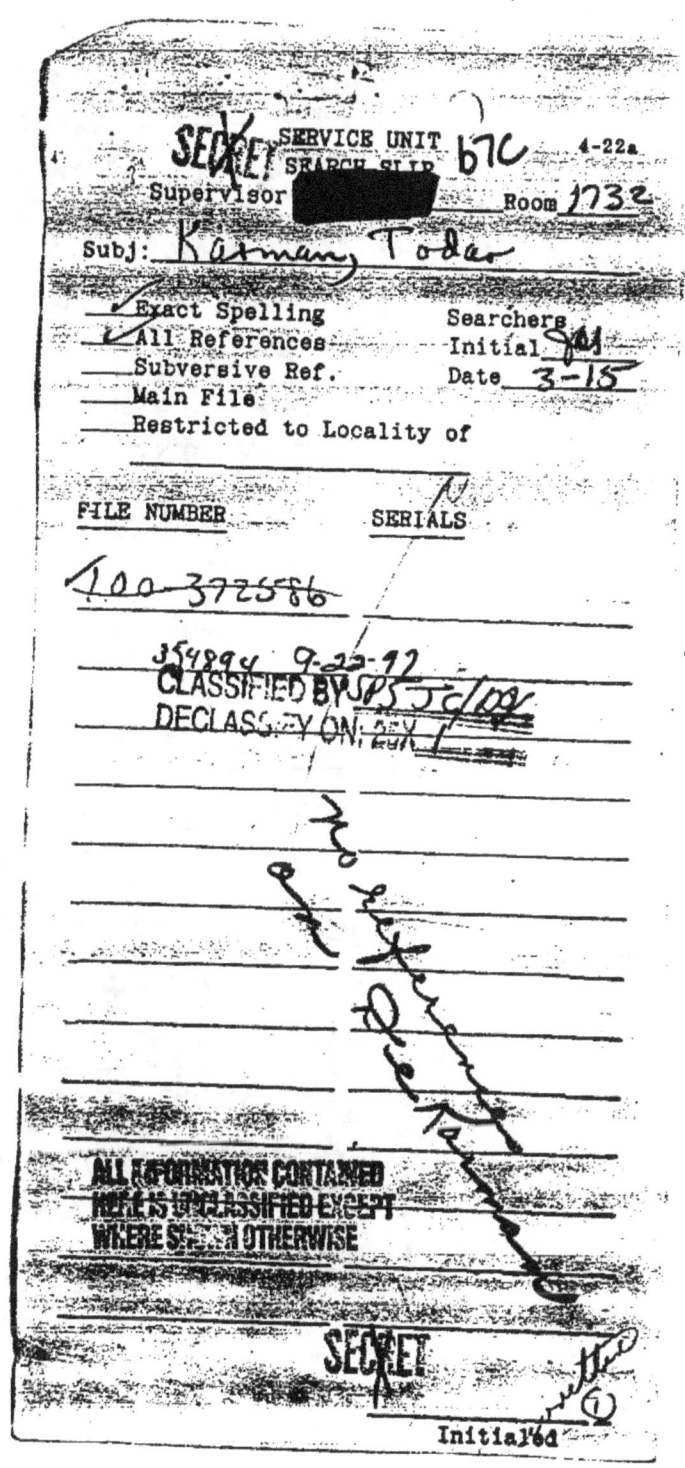

TEXT ON THIS PAGE IS ILLEGIBLE
WE HAVE LEFT THE PAGE AS REFERENCE

SERVICE UNIT 4-22a

SEARCH SLIP

Supervisor [redacted] b7C Room 1732

Subj: Von Karman, Theodore

SECRET

✓ Exact Spelling
✓ All References
___ Subversive Ref.
___ Main File
___ Restricted to Locality of

Searchers
Initial
Date 3-15

| FILE NUMBER | SERIALS |
|---|---|
| ~~65-8943~~ | |
| ~~40-13556~~ | |
| ~~40-48862~~ | |
| ~~100-372586~~ LT | |
| ~~100-64879-5,~~ | |
| ~~65-75253,~~ | |
| ~~100-2-43,~~ | |
| ~~65-14415-2,~~ | |
| ~~62-23533-7259,~~ | |
| ~~65-59318-59,~~ | |
| ✓ ~~105-10038-1,~~ | |
| ~~96-0-234,~~ | |
| ~~65-32107-5,4,6,7~~ | |
| ~~100-292257-125,~~ | |

SECRET

Initialed written

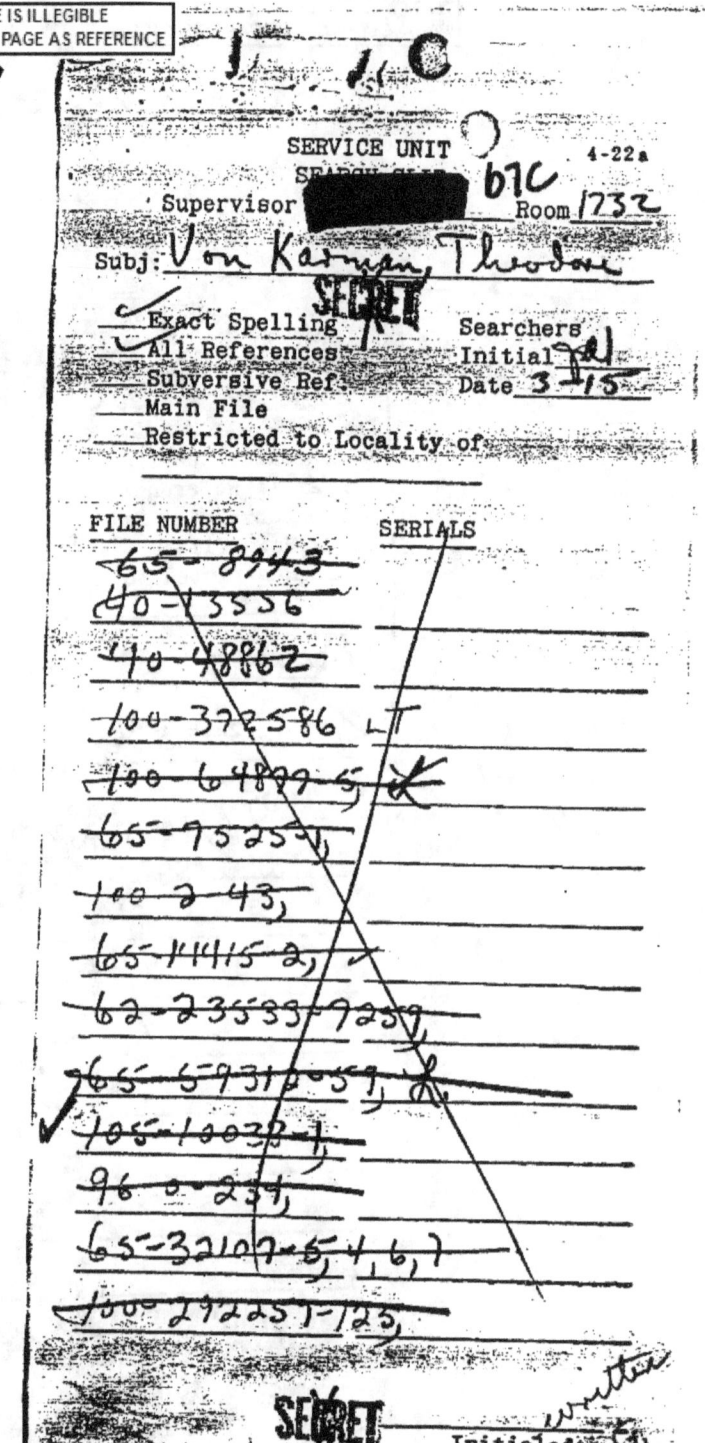

TEXT ON THIS PAGE IS ILLEGIBLE
WE HAVE LEFT THE PAGE AS REFERENCE

SERVICE UNIT b7C 4-22a
SEARCH SLIP

Supervisor [redacted] Room 1732

Subj: Von Karman, Theodore

SECRET

✓ Exact Spelling
✓ All References
___ Subversive Ref.
___ Main File
___ Restricted to Locality of

Searchers
Initial
Date 3-15

| FILE NUMBER | SERIALS |
|---|---|
| 65-32054-91; | |
| 100-47852-14p5; | |
| 100-203581-4723; | |
| 100-164610-8 | |
| 65-33716-213p14; | |
| 64-4102-483; | |
| 65-58574-122; | |
| 65-59312-30, 86; | |
| [redacted] | b1 |
| 105-12313-3; | (S) |
| 40-84216-11p5; | |
| 65-59294-100p18; | |
| 100-341759-22; | |

SECRET

Initialed (3)

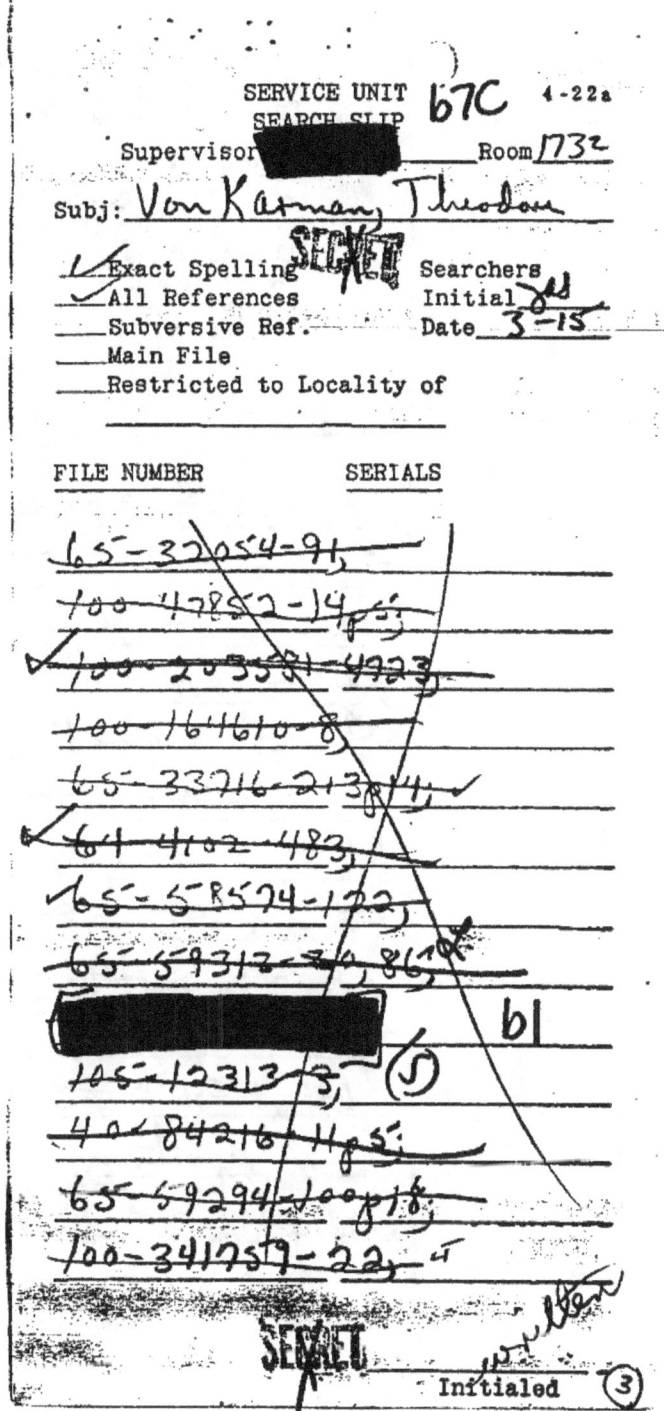

TEXT ON THIS PAGE IS ILLEGIBLE
WE HAVE LEFT THE PAGE AS REFERENCE

SERVICE UNIT b7C 4-22a
SEARCH SLIP

Supervisor [redacted] Room 1732

Subj: Von Karman, Theodore

SECRET

✓ Exact Spelling
✓ All References
___ Subversive Ref.
___ Main File
___ Restricted to Locality of

Searchers
Initial
Date 3-15

FILE NUMBER SERIALS

~~100-292259-118, 129, 84, 73, 45,~~
✓ ~~65-59589-3,~~
~~62-65880-208,~~
~~65-59312-5, 16, 54, 64, 81,~~
✓ ~~65-58236-204,~~
~~65-59312-200, 4, 79, 180,~~
~~65-33716-209,~~ ✓
~~65-56402-621,~~
~~40-13556-4 (Summary)~~ LT
~~116-163450-5,~~ LT
~~65-59312-164, 33, 37, 63, 69,~~
~~70, 71, 72, 73, 49, 129, 214,~~
~~116-160113-12,~~

SECRET

Initialed (4)

TEXT ON THIS PAGE IS ILLEGIBLE
WE HAVE LEFT THE PAGE AS REFERENCE

SERVICE UNIT b7C 4-22a
SEARCH SLIP

Supervisor [redacted] Room 1732

Subj: Von Karman, Theodore

✓ Exact Spelling
✓ All References
___ Subversive Ref.
___ Main File
___ Restricted to Locality of

SECRET

Searchers
Initial JOS
Date 3-18

| FILE NUMBER | SERIALS |
|---|---|
| ~~65-58574-5, 114~~ | |
| [redacted] (S) b1 | |
| (SWIF) | |
| ~~65-59312-159, 136~~ | |
| ~~65-22489-2~~ | |
| ~~100-64877-8~~ | |
| Theodore H. | |
| ~~105-12313-3~~ | LT |
| Von Karman, Theodore | |
| ~~65-59312-231, 16~~ (SWIF) | |
| Von Karmian, Theodore | |
| ~~65-58236-211~~ | |
| ~~65-59312-16, 54, 64, 81~~ | LT |
| Von Karmon, Ome | |
| ✓ 65-5928-11 | |

SECRET

Initialed (S)

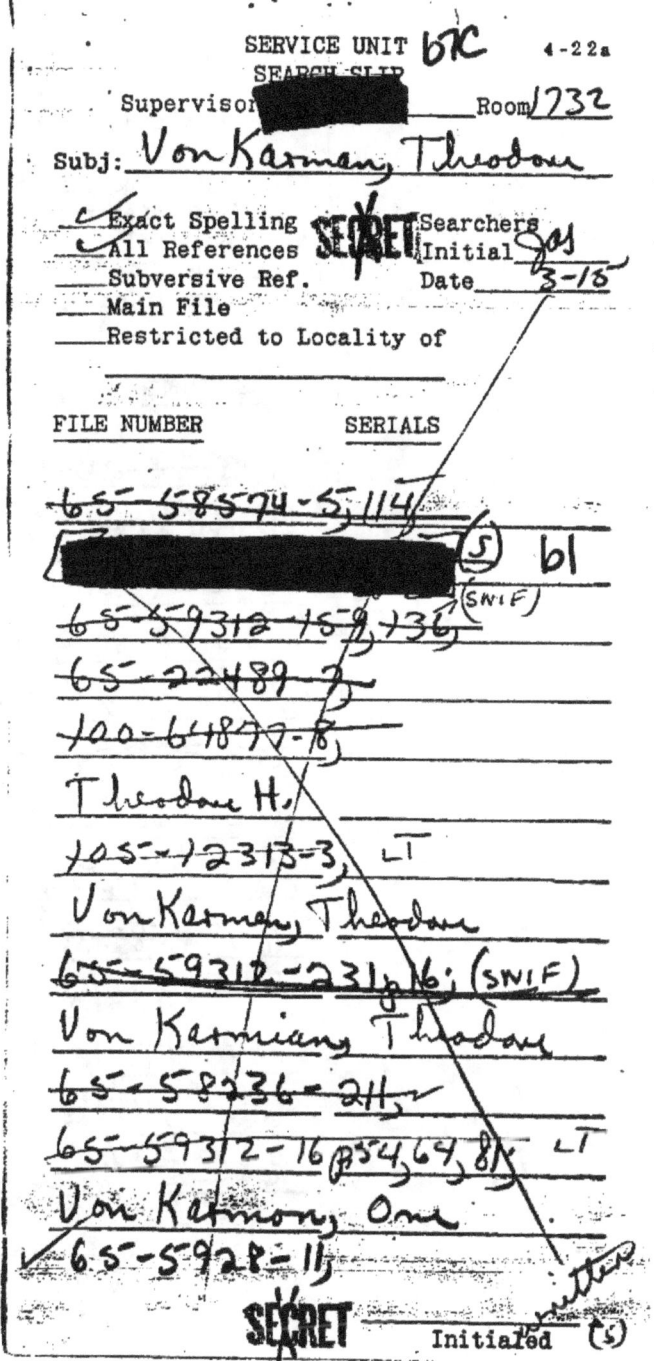

TEXT ON THIS PAGE IS ILLEGIBLE
WE HAVE LEFT THE PAGE AS REFERENCE

SERVICE UNIT b7C 4-22a
SEARCH SLIP
Supervisor [redacted] Room 1732

Subj: Von Karman, Ona

✓ Exact Spelling SECRET Searchers
✓ All References Initial
___Subversive Ref. Date 3-15
___Main File
___Restricted to Locality of

FILE NUMBER SERIALS

~~65-18126-1~~
Von Karman, Ona
~~65-59312-102, 117,~~
~~105-8090-149 5p243,~~
~~100-359682-25p8,~~
~~65-59242-775p32,34,~~
~~100-164610-1,~~
~~65-14415-3,~~
~~65-58236-563p35,37,~~
62-73361-392x5,
~~100-119070-9,~~
~~65-58574-124,~~
~~65-55316-55,~~

SECRET Initialed (c)

SERVICE UNIT b7C 4-22a
SEARCH SLIP

Supervisor [redacted] Room 732

Subj: Von Karman, T.

SECRET

✓ Exact Spelling
All References
Subversive Ref.
Main File
Restricted to Locality of

Searchers
Initial JLS
Date 3-4-5

| FILE NUMBER | SERIALS |
| --- | --- |
| ~~121-18540-16,~~ | |
| Th. | |
| ~~105-8090-149 Ep 144,~~ LT | |
| T. H. | |
| ~~65-32127-6, 7, 4,~~ | |
| ~~100-54674-2,~~ | |
| Theo | |
| [redacted] (5) b1 | |
| Theodor | |
| ~~100-341759-11,~~ | |
| ~~65-59312-129p(2, 3, 4, 5, 7, 8, 9,~~ | |
| ~~10, 13, 14, 41, 43, 46,~~ LT | |

SECRET

Initialed written (7)

TEXT ON THIS PAGE IS ILLEGIBLE
WE HAVE LEFT THE PAGE AS REFERENCE

SERVICE UNIT b7C 4-22a
SEARCH SLIP

Supervisor [redacted] Room 1732

Subj: Von Karman, Theodore

✓ Exact Spelling SECRET Searchers
All References Initial
Subversive Ref. Date 3-15
Main File
Restricted to Locality of

FILE NUMBER SERIALS

Karman, Theodore
~~100-372586~~ LT
~~116-160113-12~~, LT
~~40-84216-11 p5~~
~~65-59589-3~~,
65-58574-723, 114, 5
LT ~~65-59312-136, 159, 129, 16 p 54,~~
~~64, 81; 17 p 5, 86, 49, 5, 164 p 33, 37,~~
~~63, 69, 70, 71, 72, 73; 214, 180, 20,~~
~~57,~~
~~65-58236-304~~,
~~105-12513-3~~, LT
~~116-163450-5~~, LT

SECRET Initialed (8)

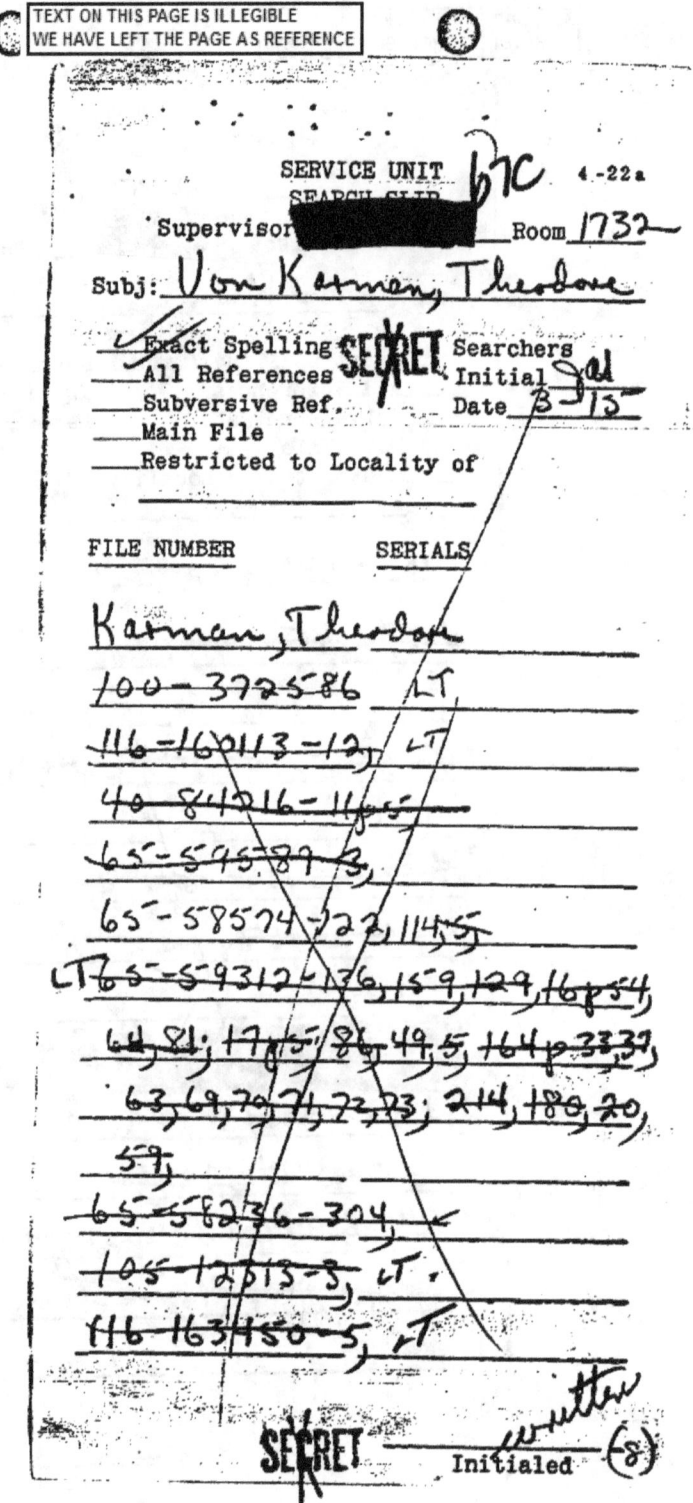

TEXT ON THIS PAGE IS ILLEGIBLE
WE HAVE LEFT THE PAGE AS REFERENCE

SERVICE UNIT b7C 4-22a

Supervisor [redacted] Room 1732

Subj: Karman, Theodore

✓ Exact Spelling SECRET Searchers
✓ All References Initial Jal
Subversive Ref. Date 3-13
Main File
Restricted to Locality of

FILE NUMBER SERIALS

~~100-89-27-1,~~
~~100-50430-12,~~
~~100-164610-8,~~
~~65-59294-100p18,~~ LT
Theodore Bar
~~100-146964-593, 572,~~
Theodore H.
~~105-12313-3,~~ LT
Theodore V.
~~65-59312-147p 40, 45, 46, 47,~~
~~50, 51,~~
Theodore Van
~~100-292259-155,~~

SECRET Initialed

TEXT ON THIS PAGE IS ILLEGIBLE
WE HAVE LEFT THE PAGE AS REFERENCE

SERVICE UNIT b7C 4-22a
SEARCH

Supervisor [redacted] Room 1732

Subj: Karman, Theodore Von

✓ Exact Spelling SECRET Searchers
✓ All References Initial JAL
___Subversive Ref. Date 3-15
___Main File
___Restricted to Locality of

FILE NUMBER SERIALS

~~40-18867~~
~~40-48862~~ LT
~~40-135556~~ LT
~~40-135556-4 (Summary)~~ LT
~~100-64877-5,~~ LT
~~105-10058-1,~~ LT
~~96-0-234,~~ LT
~~65-32107-5,~~ LT
~~65-57225-1,~~
65-14415-2,
~~65-32054-91,~~ LT
~~62-23533-725,~~
~~100-47852-14p5,~~ LT

SECRET written (10)
Initialed

TEXT ON THIS PAGE IS ILLEGIBLE
WE HAVE LEFT THE PAGE AS REFERENCE

SERVICE UNIT b7C 4-22a
SEARCH SLIP

Supervisor [redacted] Room 1732

Subj: Karman, Theodore Von

✓ Exact Spelling SECRET Searchers
✓ All References Initial
___ Subversive Ref. Date 3-15
___ Main File
___ Restricted to Locality of

FILE NUMBER SERIALS

~~100-3 43,~~
~~65-22489-9,~~ LT
✓ ~~100-64877-8,~~
~~62-65880-208,~~
~~100-292259-40, 93, 84, 109,~~
~~118, 125,~~
✓ ~~65-33716-200, 213 p14;~~
~~100-341759-92, 11,~~
[redacted] b1
~~64-4102-483,~~
~~100-203581-4723,~~
~~65-56402-621,~~ LT
✓ [redacted] b1
Theodore
~~65-59312-200 p4,~~ LT

SECRET Initialed

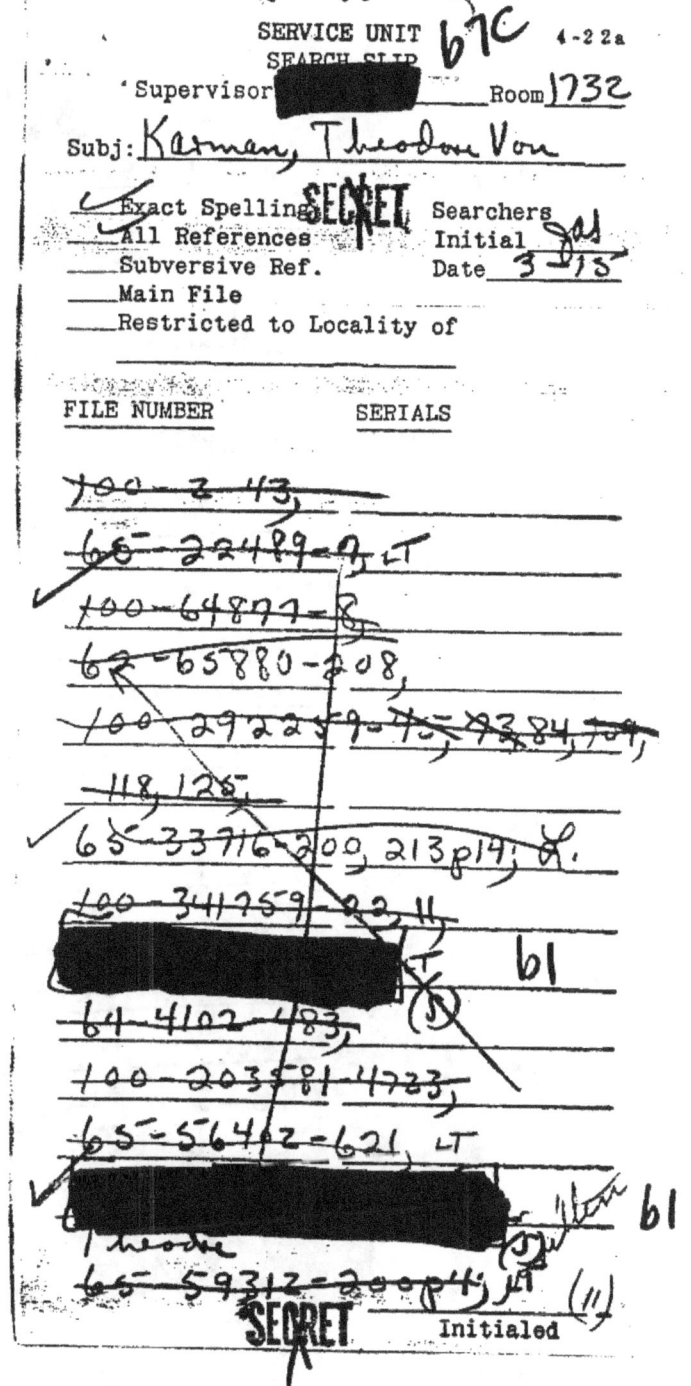

TEXT ON THIS PAGE IS ILLEGIBLE
WE HAVE LEFT THE PAGE AS REFERENCE

SERVICE UNIT b7C 4-22a
SEARCH SLIP

Supervisor [redacted] Room 1732

Subj: Karman, T.

SECRET

✓ Exact Spelling
✓ All References
___ Subversive Ref.
___ Main File
___ Restricted to Locality of

Searchers
Initial
Date 5-15

FILE NUMBER SERIALS

121-18540-16, LT
65-1312-149, [illegible]
52, LT
T. H. Von
65-32107-6, 7, LT
T. Van
100-272251-199, 155,
Th.
65-8393-1445, 441, LT
Th. Von
100-54674-2, LT
65-32107-4, LT
Thea. [illegible]
[redacted] (S) b1

SECRET Initialed

TEXT ON THIS PAGE IS ILLEGIBLE
WE HAVE LEFT THE PAGE AS REFERENCE

TEXT ON THIS PAGE IS ILLEGIBLE
WE HAVE LEFT THE PAGE AS REFERENCE

C

THEODORE VON KARMAN

COPIED FROM
1/1/51 ISSUE OF
TIME MAGAZINE.

SEE SER. #16 OF
100-372586

TEXT ON THIS PAGE IS ILLEGIBLE
WE HAVE LEFT THE PAGE AS REFERENCE

111

SAC, NEW YORK    (S) SECRET    April 2, 1951

DIRECTOR, FBI

WILLIAM PERL, aka
William Mutterperl    (S) SECRET
ESPIONAGE - R;
PERJURY
New York 65-15387

61

[redacted]

(S)

In accordance with referet inquiry was made of [redacted]

Referred

The Bureau is in receipt of a letter from [redacted]

65-59312
cc: Cleveland
Los Angeles

ALL INFORMATION CONTAINED
HERE IS UNCLASSIFIED EXCEPT
WHERE SHOWN OTHERWISE

EFE:hc

cc: (VON KARMAN)

100-372

354-194 9-9-97
CLASSIFIED BY SP5SC/09m
DECLASSIFY ON: 25X 6

NOT RECORDED
144 APR 1951

ORIGINAL COPY FILED IN 65-59312-260

Tolson
Ladd
Clegg
Glavin
Nichols
Rosen
Tracy
Harbo
Belmont
Mohr
Tele. Room
Nease
Gandy

241

65 APR 30 1951

(S) SECRET

DUPLICATE YELLOW

(S) SECRET

C

TEXT ON THIS PAGE IS ILLEGIBLE
WE HAVE LEFT THE PAGE AS REFERENCE

SAC, LOS ANGELES — April 9, 1951

DIRECTOR, FBI

CONFIDENTIAL

THEODORE VON KARMAN, was.,
INTERNAL SECURITY - R

G. I. R. -1

ALL INFORMATION CONTAINED HEREIN IS UNCLASSIFIED EXCEPT WHERE SHOWN OTHERWISE

Re New York let October 4, 1950, entitled, "Todar Karman, Security Matter - C" and Bulet March 14, 1951.

There are attached for New York two photographs of subject which appeared in the January 1, 1951, issue of Time magazine. New York is to exhibit the photograph of subject to [redacted] in view of the allegation contained in referenced New York let that subject, as Todar Karman, was formerly a member of the German Communist Party. [redacted] are also to be questioned for any information in their possession concerning subject and for the purpose of determining the identity of other reliable individuals in the United States who may be in a position to furnish information concerning subject's past activities in Europe. (U)

b7C
b7D
L

A review of Bureau files concerning [redacted] (New York Confidential Informant [redacted], and [redacted] reflects that both may be in a position to furnish information concerning subject's activities in Hungary under Bela Kun. Bureau files also reflect that both have been interviewed on numerous occasions by New York. It is therefore requested that [redacted] be contacted concerning subject providing that New York believes that such contacts can be made without compromising the investigation of subject. [redacted] are not to be advised of subject's presence in the United States or of his position as Chairman of the Scientific Advisory Board, Department of the Air Force. (U)

b2
b7C
b7D

Classified by ... 10-26-83
Declassify on: OADR

By memorandum dated April 5, 1951, OSI, Washington, furnished the Bureau with results of an interview with [redacted] of Aachen, Germany. [redacted] advised that he was formerly very close to the Von Karman family and that both Von Karman's mother and an individual, Von Fakla, advised him that Von Karman was the Minister of Culture in Hungary under Bela Kun while the latter was in power for a few months in Hungary. Von Fakla, according to [redacted] is reported to have assisted Von Karman and his mother and sister in escaping to Germany after the fall of the Bela Kun Government. (U)

b7C
b7D

DECLASSIFIED BY ... 6-13-97

100-372586-17

RECORDED - 50

APR 13 1951

80

EX-59

RECEIVED READING ROOM F B I U.S. DEPT OF JUSTICE APR 13 3 17 PM '51

100-372586

cc - New York (Attachments)

WAKames

Tolson
Ladd
Clegg
Glavin
Nichols
Rosen
Tracy
Harbo
Belmont
Mohr
Tele. Room
Nease
Gandy

COMM - FBI
APR 10 1951
MAILED 18

495

65 APR 19 1951

CONFIDENTIAL

CONFIDENTIAL

The report reflects that the surname of Von Karman at the time of birth was Von Szoellosstcictak. The investigation of subject in Europe by OSI is continuing. (C) (4)

It is desired that New York conduct the investigation requested herein in an expeditious manner.

Tolson_______
Ladd_______
Clegg_______
Glavin_______
Nichols_______
Rosen_______
Tracy_______
Harbo_______
Belmont_______
Mohr_______
Tele. Room_______
Nease_______
Gandy_______



CONFIDENTIAL

TEXT ON THIS PAGE IS ILLEGIBLE
WE HAVE LEFT THE PAGE AS REFERENCE

UNITED STATES DEPARTMENT OF JUSTICE

To: COMMUNICATIONS SECTION. April 16, 1951 URGENT

Transmit the following message to: SAC, LOS ANGELES
WASHINGTON FIELD (BSM)

THEODORE VON KARMAN, INTERNAL SECURITY - R. REBULET MARCH FOURTEEN LAST. OSI ADVISES THAT THEIR INVESTIGATION IN EUROPE HAS DETERMINED THAT [redacted] IS CIC SOURCE OF INFORMATION IN NINETEEN THIRTY EIGHT G-TWO REPORT WHICH ALLEGED TODAR KARMAN WAS FORMER COMMISSAR UNDER BELA KUHN AND LATER MEMBER OF GERMAN CP. OSI HAS REQUESTED, AND BUREAU IS AUTHORIZING, EARLY INTERVIEW OF [redacted] FOR ALL INFORMATION IN HIS POSSESSION REGARDING SUBJECT'S ACTIVITIES. IN RESPONSE TO THEIR REQUEST, OSI IS BEING ADVISED THAT BUREAU HAS NO OBJECTION TO [redacted] ATTENDING THE INTERVIEW WITH [redacted] AS AN OBSERVER. [redacted] IS CLOSE CONTACT OF BUREAU AND IS HANDLING OSI END OF INVESTIGATION. [redacted] IS SUBJECT OF CLOSED INTERNAL SECURITY - R AND HU INVESTIGATION CONDUCTED BY WFO IN NINETEEN FORTY NINE AT WHICH TIME HE WAS EMPLOYED BY [redacted] WFO IS TO ADVISE WHETHER [redacted] IS PRESENTLY IN WASHINGTON SO ARRANGEMENTS CAN BE MADE BY BUREAU LIAISON FOR [redacted] OF OSI TO BE PRESENT DURING INTERVIEW.

HOOVER

b7C
b7D

CC: WASHINGTON FIELD (BY SPECIAL MESSENGER)
NEW YORK BY MAIL

100-372586
cc - 100-354543
KAK:mes

INITIALED
DIRECTOR'S OFFICE

100-372586-18

RECORDED - 33
EX-8C

APR 17 1951

ALL INFORMATION CONTAINED HEREIN IS UNCLASSIFIED DATE 5-22-97 BY

HANDLED BY STOP DESK

62 APR 23 1951

COPIES DESTROYED
APR 5 1963

SENT VIA 11:43 A M Per

SAC, LOS ANGELES

DIRECTOR, FBI

April 9, 1951

THEODORE VON KARMAN, was.,
INTERNAL SECURITY - R

AIR MAIL - SPECIAL DELIVERY
REGISTERED MAIL

Rebulet March 28, 1951.

There are attached for your information and assistance in connection with captioned investigation a copy of OSI letter dated April 5, 1951, concerning subject, and a copy of OSI report dated March 20, 1951, which was furnished the Bureau as an attachment to the above letter.

OSI has advised that the investigation of subject in Europe is continuing. Additional information received at the Bureau will be immediately made available to you.

In view of subject's position as Chairman of the Scientific Advisory Board of the Air Force, the Bureau desires that this investigation be given preferred and expeditious handling.

Your initial report in this investigation is to reach the Bureau by April 28, 1951.

RECORDED - 26 100-372586-19

EX. - 118

100-372586 - 2

Attachments

WAKsmes

359-544
ALL INFORMATION CONTAINED
HEREIN IS UNCLASSIFIED
DATE 5-22-97 BY SP5JC/agm

APR 9 11 23 AM '51
RECEIVED MAIL ROOM
FBI
U.S. DEPT. OF JUSTICE

APR 9 12 28 PM '51
U.S. DEPT. OF JUSTICE
497787 F B I
RECEIVED-MAIL ROOM

MAILED 13
APR -9 1951
COMM - FBI

62 MAY 12 1951

TEXT ON THIS PAGE IS ILLEGIBLE
WE HAVE LEFT THE PAGE AS REFERENCE

SERVICE UNIT
SEARCH SLIP
b7C
F-19a

Supervisor [redacted] Room 1732

Subj: Von Szellacteutek

___Exact Spelling
___All References
___Subversive Ref
___Main File
___Restricted to Locality of

Searchers
Initial McCallum
Date 4-6-57

| FILE NUMBER | SERIALS |
|---|---|
| NR | |
| Szellacteutek | |
| NR | |

354-894
ALL INFORMATION CONTAINED
HEREIN IS UNCLASSIFIED
DATE 3-22-97 SDS/JC/Dop

Initialed

TEXT ON THIS PAGE IS ILLEGIBLE
WE HAVE LEFT THE PAGE AS REFERENCE

STANDARD FORM NO. 64

# Office Memorandum • UNITED STATES GOVERNMENT

TO : MR. A. H. BELMONT

DATE: April 16, 1951

FROM : V. P. KEAY

SUBJECT: THEODORE VON KARMAN

ALL INFORMATION CONTAINED HEREIN IS UNCLASSIFIED DATE 5-22-92

Von Karman is the Chairman of the Air Force Scientific Advisory Board, and information has been received indicating he was formerly connected with the Communist regime in Hungary.

OSI has contacted the CIC Agent in Austria who originally furnished this information, and it has been determined that the CIC Agent received his information from [redacted]

b7C
b7D

The Air Force is extremely interested in this case, inasmuch as Von Karman has had access to practically all scientific developments of the Air Force and is closely associated with top Air Force officials. OSI has conducted a considerable portion of this investigation, which of necessity had ramifications in Europe.

Efforts of the Bureau and OSI have been exerted to definitely determine whether Theodore Von Karman, who is connected with the Air Force, is identical with Todar-Karman, who reportedly was connected with the Communist regime of Hungary. Other investigation in Europe by OSI has for all practical purposes determined that they were identical. OSI has now requested that [redacted] of OSI Headquarters, who is completely familiar with all aspects of this case, be allowed to accompany a Bureau Agent when [redacted] is interviewed.

It is believed desirable that [redacted] be permitted to accompany a representative of the Bureau when [redacted] is interviewed inasmuch as he is familiar with all aspects of this case, particularly with the European aspects, and it is believed that his assistance would be of considerable value. He is one of the prime contacts of the Liaison Section at Air Force Headquarters and is extremely friendly and cooperative. It is believed that to deny OSI this request in a case in which the Air Force is so vitally concerned would seriously affect the cordial relations which presently exist. It is understood, however, that the contact with [redacted] would be strictly a Bureau contact and that [redacted] would be present as an observer for the purpose of making available all of his background concerning the European phases of this case.

b7C
b7D

ESS:hke

RECORDED - 73
INDEXED - 73
EX-92

TEXT ON THIS PAGE IS ILLEGIBLE
WE HAVE LEFT THE PAGE AS REFERENCE

C

*RECOMMENDATION:*

*It is recommended that [redacted] be allowed to accompany as an observer the Bureau representative at the time [redacted] is interviewed.*

*Inasmuch as this is probably the most important case in which OSI is presently engaged, it is suggested that this matter be given the most expeditious handling and that arrangements be made through Special Agent [redacted] of the Liaison Section for [redacted] and a Bureau representative to get together.*

*ADDENDUM: (April 16, 1951)*

*The Espionage Section agrees that [redacted] be interviewed concerning information furnished by him to CIC, concerning Todar Karman who is undoubtedly identical with subject. The Espionage Section also agrees that [redacted] of OSI be allowed to attend the interview because of the extreme OSI interest due to subject's position and the fact that OSI is jointly investigating subject with the Bureau. As noted in this memorandum, Bureau refusal may seriously affect our cordial relations with OSI.*

*Bureau files reflect [redacted] arrived in the United States in [redacted] An investigation was conducted by the Bureau during which numerous persons advised that [redacted] was anti-Communist. He has been interviewed by the Bureau at which times, he appeared cooperative. (100-354543)*

b7C
b7D

*In the event you agree, there is attached an appropriate teletype with instructions to WFO.*

OK

TEXT ON THIS PAGE IS ILLEGIBLE
WE HAVE LEFT THE PAGE AS REFERENCE

SAC, LOS ANGELES — April 18, 1951

DIRECTOR, FBI

THEODORE VON KARMAN
INTERNAL SECURITY - R

Rebutel April 16, last.

There are attached for the completion of the WFO files, two copies of a photograph of subject which appeared in the January 1, 1951, issue of Time magazine.

cc - Washington Field - Attachments

WAK:mes

G.I.R.-8

354-894
ALL INFORMATION CONTAINED
HEREIN IS UNCLASSIFIED
DATE 5-22-97 BY 5050

RECORDED - 43 100-372586-21

APR 21 1951

STANDARD FORM NO. 64

# Office Memorandum • UNITED STATES GOVERNMENT

TO : DIRECTOR, FBI

DATE: APRIL 26, 1951

FROM : SAC, LOS ANGELES

SUBJECT: THEODORE VON KARMAN
INTERNAL SECURITY - R
(Bufile 100-372586)

ALL INFORMATION CONTAINED
HEREIN IS UNCLASSIFIED
DATE 5-22-90 BY

G. I. R. 3

Rebufile 100-372586 and Bulet 3/14/51 in above-captioned matter requesting a discreet limited investigation of the subject including the use of spot physical surveillance as a source of information.

The attention of the Bureau and Washington Field Division is called to the current consideration being reportedly given by authorities in Washington to furnishing the subject with a constant bodyguard as a security measure.

According to information recently furnished this office by OSI, Los Angeles, California, an unknown individual has recently appeared at the VON KARMAN residence located at 1501 S. Marengo Street, Pasadena, California, inquiring about subject's whereabouts and claiming to have been acquainted with VON KARMAN in Hungary. This matter accordingly caused Brigadier General STACE, Commanding General, Western Air Procurement District, Los Angeles, California, to have apprehension for the personal safety of Doctor VON KARMAN. As a result thereof, a survey of subject's residence for security measures was made on March 27, 1951 by [redacted] Intelligence Section for the Western Procurement District, Air Material Command, Los Angeles, California, and a representative of OSI.

[redacted] subsequently advised this office that in view of an apparent lack of proper and adequate security measures at subject's residence, for his personal safety and the safety of his papers, a conference was held in Los Angeles on March 30, 1951 between [redacted] Research and Development Division, Headquarters, U. S. Air Force, Washington, D.C., and [redacted] Los Angeles Air Force Engineering Field Office, Air Materiel Command, Los Angeles, California, as to whether or not VON KARMAN should be furnished with a bodyguard.

On April 9, 1951 [redacted] advised that no recommendation was made as a result of the above conference, and that a final

7C

105-863
JPA:ldb

cc: Washington Field (100-22923)

RECORDED - 95
INDEXED - 95

APR 30 1951
17

[redacted]

b7C

COPIES DESTROYED
.78 APR 5 1963

C



recommendation, if any, would have to be made by officials in Washington, D. C. At the above conference, however, it was suggested by [redacted] that a more secure situation could be had by letting Doctor VON KARMAN maintain his office and papers at the Jet Propulsion Laboratory of Caltech or on the Caltech campus, or he could even share a portion of [redacted] own office.

With regard to subject's papers, [redacted] pointed out that no documents with a higher rating than "Confidential" are ever maintained at the VON KARMAN residence overnight.

[redacted] stated also that the identity of the unknown visitor had not been determined.

b7C

A subsequent limited inquiry by this office as to the identity of the above visitor was also made with negative results.

It is suggested that the Bureau attempt to determine what decision, if any, has finally been reached in this matter which, as indicated above, was originally under consideration by [redacted] of the U. S. Air Force.

As a result of current investigation in this case, it has been determined that subject is currently in Europe on a business and pleasure trip with his sister, JOSEPHINE DE KARMAN visiting Algiers, Paris, and Switzerland. He is expected back in Washington, D. C. sometime in May or June.

5-15-51
no further consideration has been given to this. Von Karman has been in Europe. OSI will advise if anything further along this line.
E.S.

SAC, LOS ANGELES

May 23, 1951

DIRECTOR, FBI

THEODORE VON KARMAN, was.,
INTERNAL SECURITY - R

Re Los Angeles let April 26, 1951.

OSI, Washington, has advised that no further consideration has been given to the question of furnishing subject with a bodyguard. OSI will advise the Bureau in the event any decision is made to furnish protection to subject.

In the event you feel for any reason that spot-check surveillance of subject is inadvisable, you should so advise the Bureau.

RECORDED - 38
100-372586 - 22
EX-130
WAK:mes



Tolson
Ladd
Clegg
Glavin
Nichols
Rosen
Tracy
Harbo
Alden
Belmont
Laughlin
Mohr
Tele. Room
Nease
Gandy



MAY 26 1951

TEXT ON THIS PAGE IS ILLEGIBLE
WE HAVE LEFT THE PAGE AS REFERENCE

WASHINGTON FROM WASHINGTON FIELD 4/21/51 1P

DIRECTOR URGENT

THEODORE VON KARMAN, IS DASH R. RE WFO TEL APRIL TWENTY FIFTY ONE [redacted] IN INTERVIEW BY AGENT WFO AND [redacted] OSI, DENIES FURNISHING INFORMATION RE SUBJECT TO OIC WHEN INTERVIEWED IN EUROPE. STATES HE HAS KNOWN OF SUBJECT BY REPUTATION AS A GREAT SCIENTIST FOR MANY YEARS AND KNEW SLIGHTLY SUBJECT'S YOUNGER BROTHER, NAME NOT RECALLED, AND HIS FATHER MOR KARMAN. ADMITS HAVING HEARD GENERAL RUMORS IN BUDAPEST THAT SUBJECT LEFT HUNGARY AFTER KUN REVOLUTION DUE TO POPULAR ANIMOSITY TOWARD SEMITIC PERSONS AT THE TIME AS WELL AS SOME SUPPOSED SYMPATHY WITH COMMUNISM. [redacted] NOT AWARE OF ANY PART PLAYED BY SUBJECT IN KUN REVOLUTION OR ANY OFFICIAL OR HONORARY POSITION HELD DURING THAT REGIME. [redacted] DOES NOT KNOW OF ANY CP AFFILIATION OF SUBJECT IN HUNGARY OR AACHEN, ALTHOUGH ACQUAINTED WITH FACT HE TAUGHT AT LATTER PLACE. ONLY TIME THEY MET WAS ABOUT ONE YEAR AGO AT WASHINGTON APT. OF [redacted] WHO HAD INVITED SEVERAL HUNGARIANS [redacted] DURING THAT EVENING, SUBJECT NOTED IN CONVERSATION THAT QUOTE [redacted] UNQUOTE. WHEN SOMEONE PRESENT SAID QUOTE [redacted] UNQUOTE HE REPLIED QUOTE [redacted] UNQUOTE. [redacted] FAILED TO IDENTIFY TIME MAGAZINE PHOTO OF SUBJECT UNTIL ADVISED AS TO ITS IDENTITY. HE REFERRED TO SUBJECT EXCLUSIVELY AS TODOR KARMAN DURING INTERVIEW. REPORT FOLLOWS.

STRN

ALL INFORMATION CONTAINED
HEREIN IS UNCLASSIFIED

RECORDED 13
INDEXED 13

TEXT ON THIS PAGE IS ILLEGIBLE
WE HAVE LEFT THE PAGE AS REFERENCE

FEDER... REAU OF...

SEE REVERSE SIDE FOR ADD DISSEMINATION

LOS ANGELES

[redacted] b7C

THEODORE VON KARMAN, was Theodor Karman, Theodor Von [redacted] b7C

INTERNAL SECURITY - R

AGENCY
REQ. REC'D
REP'T FORW.
BY

SYNOPSIS OF FACTS: EXCEPT WHERE SHOWN OTHERWISE.

Doctor THEODORE VON KARMAN, world renowned Aerodynamicist, was born in Budapest, Hungary on May 11, 1881. He entered the U. S. for permanent residence on October 7, 1930 and was naturalized in U. S. District Court, Los Angeles, California, on July 21, 1936. Employed as Director of Guggenheim Aeronautical Laboratory, California Institute of Technology, Pasadena, California, from 1930 to 1942, when placed on leave of absence to be a full time consultant for the U. S. Air Force. From 1942 to date, VON KARMAN has been affiliated with the National Advisory Committee for Aerodynamics, Washington, D.C. Currently he is engaged as Chairman of the Scientific Advisory Board, Department of the Air Forc[e] and maintains an office in the Pentagon Buil[ding] Washington, D.C. Beginning in 1936 VON K[ARM]AN was associated at California Institute of Technology with a group of graduate students interested in the military application of jet propulsion and rockets. In 1942 he was instrumental in founding AEROJET ENGINEERING CORPORATION, Azusa, California, to manufacture rockets for military use. [redacted] b7C

SPECIAL AGENT IN CHARGE

DO NOT WRITE IN THESE SPACES

COPY IN FILE

Bureau (100-372586) (AMSD)
Washington Field (100-2292...)
New York
OSI, District 18, Maywood
Los Angeles

APR 30 1951

RECORDED
EX

FBI—This confidential report and its contents are loaned to ... agency to which loaned.

CLASSIFIED AND EXTENDED BY ...
REASON FOR EXTENSION ...
DATE OF REVIEW FOR DECLASSIFICATION

[redacted]
another Government Agency, reports that VON KARMAN in 1919 was Minister of Culture in Hungary under BELA KUN, while latter was in power for few months, and was thereafter assisted in escaping to Germany after the fall of the BELA KUN Government. (u)

- P -

TABLE OF CONTENTS

TEXT ON THIS PAGE IS ILLEGIBLE
WE HAVE LEFT THE PAGE AS REFERENCE



SECRET

DETAILS:

## I. BACKGROUND AND PERSONAL HISTORY

The records of Immigration and Naturalization Service, Los Angeles, California, reflect that Dr. THEODORE VON KARMAN was born on May 11, 1881 in Budapest, Hungary. He entered the United States for permanent residence at the Port of New York on October 7, 1930, under the name of THEODOR KARMAN. He was naturalized in the District Court of the United States at Los Angeles, California on July 24, 1936, under the name of THEODORE VON KARMAN, and was issued Certificate No. C-4052565.

The Central Records of Immigration and Naturalization Service, Washington, D.C., reflect further that except for several trips to the U. S., from 1913 to 1930, VON KARMAN resided in Aachen, Germany during that period. His mother's name was given as ILKA KARMAN, nee KOHN, of Budapest, Hungary. His father was deceased. At the time of his application for a non quota immigration visa, VON KARMAN stated that he intended to enter the U. S. at New York City, destined for Pasadena, California, to take up permanent residence in order to continue his vocation. He indicated he had been appointed to the Directorship of the Aeronautical Laboratory at CALIFORNIA INSTITUTE OF TECHNOLOGY, Pasadena, California.

"Who's Who in America", for 1944-1945, carries the following information regarding VON KARMAN:

"von KARMAN, Theodore, aeronautical engr.; b. Budapest, Hungary, May 11, 1881; s. Prof. Maurice and Helene (Konn) von K.; M.E., Royal Tech. U., Budapest, 1902; Ph.D., U. of Goettingen, Germany, 1909; hon. D. Eng., Tech. U., Berlin, 1929; hon. D.Sc., University of Brussels, 1937; LL.D., University of California, 1942; unmarried. Came to U.S., 1930. Mechanical engr. Ganz Co., Budapest, 1903-06; asst. prof. U. of Goettingen, 1909-12; prof. aeronautics and dir. Aeronautical Inst., U. of Aachen, 1913-30; visiting prof. in U.S., Japan, China and India, 1926-29; adviser Junkers Airplane Works, 1922-28; prof. of aeronautics and dir. Guggenheim Aeronautics Lab., Calif. Inst. of Tech., since 1930; adviser Guggenheim Airship Inst. since 1930; adviser to Tsung Hua U. since 1933; visiting prof. C.R.B. Foundation in Belgium; Rouse Ball lecturer Cambridge U., Eng.; Wilbur Wright lecturer Royal Aeron. Soc., London, 1937; Gibbs lecturer at Am. Mathematics Society, 1939. Awarded American Society Mechanical



SECRET

Engineers medal, 1941, Sylvanus Reed award of Institute of Aeronautical Sciences, 1941. Served as 1st lieut. Austrian-Hungarian Army, 1915-18. Honorary fellow Inst. Aeronautical Sciences; mem. Goettingen Acad. Sciences, Royal Acad. Sciences (Torino, Italy), Am. Soc. M.E., Nat. Acad. Science, Am. Philos. Soc., Am. Soc. C.E., Tau Beta Pi. Club: Athenaeum. Editor of books on aerodynamics in German lang. Author: (with J.M. Burgers) General Aero-dynamic Theory (2 vols.), 1924; (with M.A. Biot) Mathematical Methods in Engineering, 1940. Contbr. scientific articles to jours. Home: 1501 S. Marengo Av., Pasadena, Calif."

b7C b7D

[redacted] AEROJET ENGINEERING CORPORATION, Azusa, California, in June, 1949 furnished Special Agents [redacted] the following background information regarding VON KARMAN and his association with CALIFORNIA INSTITUTE OF TECHNOLOGY, hereinafter referred to as CIT, and AEROJET ENGINEERING CORPORATION:

b7C

Early in 1936 a group of graduate students of CIT, Pasadena, California, became interested in the field of jet propulsion as a possible military weapon. [redacted]

These students, relying on a small grant from a private citizen, engaged in research on the CIT campus for a number of years, and in the course of so doing, were working under the direct supervision of Dr. THEODORE VON KARMAN, who was regarded as the world's outstanding aerodynamicist.

In about 1939 VON KARMAN, who was then Special Adviser to [redacted] of the U. S. Air Force, realized the military significance of this research, and it was through his instigation that [redacted] set up the Committee for Air Corps Research of the National Academy of Sciences to sponsor development of rockets. As a result of this small start, a special laboratory was set up in the nearby hills under the direct sponsorship of the Guggenheim Aeronautical Laboratory of CIT. It was in this manner that the present Jet Propulsion Laboratory obtained its original code name of GALCIT, which is an abbreviation for the Guggenheim Aeronautical Laboratory of CIT.

b7C

Under Army Air Force sponsorship the laboratory grew and considerable research was done along the lines of rocket and jet propulsion theory.

In the early part of 1942 it became apparent that the pilot models developed at the laboratory would have to be manufactured. Inasmuch as it was against the policy of CIT to engage in manufacturing of any type, AEROJET ENGINEERING CORPORATION, Azusa, California, was formed at the instigation of VON KARMAN, who had the sponsorship of the Air Force in the form of contractual commitments.

[redacted] National Advisory Committee of Aeronautics, 1724 F Street, N.W., Washington, D.C., advised Special Agent [redacted] of the Washington office, in July, 1950, in connection with another matter, that Dr. THEODORE VON KARMAN was in 1947 and 1948, and presently may remain, Chairman of the U. S. Air Force Scientific Advisory Board; and that during that period and until January 1, 1950, he was a member of the Aerodynamics Committee of the National Advisory Committee for Aeronautics, hereinafter referred to as NACA, which Committee meets in Washington. As a member of that Committee, he was entitled to all classified material pertinent to the work conducted by that Committee; that such classified material was sent to VON KARMAN by registered mail; that VON KARMAN likewise was sent NACA classified publications not dealing directly with the work of that Committee. [redacted] stated that because of VON KARMAN'S chairmanship of the Air Force Scientific Advisory Board, he probably also received information, including material relating to the U. S. Air Force, as well as military scientific studies.

The records of NACA in July, 1950 also reflected the following information:

VON KARMAN was placed on the Committee on Aerodynamics, a sub-committee of the NACA, on March 13, 1943. At this time his address was the Guggenheim Aeronautical Laboratory, CIT, Pasadena, California.

On October 29, 1943, his first name was changed from THEODOR to THEODORE. He was a member of the NACA Technical Sub-Committee on Air Craft Structure, from February 19, 1942 to January 27, 1944. During this period, he continued to be located at CIT. From February 19, 1942 to February 25, 1942, he was a member of the NACA Special Sub-Committee to direct research in applied structures. VON KARMAN was placed on the restricted monthly list to receive papers and releases of a classified nature from November 22, 1940 to May 24, 1945. He was custodian of restricted publications at CIT for the same perio[redacted] b7C

A temporary address from November 17, 1944 to March 1, 1946 was Headquarters, Army Air Force, Chief of Air Staff, Scientific Advisory Group, Room 4D 1070, Pentagon Building, Washington, D.C. A receipt for material returned by VON KARMAN to the NACA in Washington, dated September 26, 1947, indicated a change of address from 570 Lexington Avenue, Room 711, to COLUMBIA UNIVERSITY, Pupin Physics Laboratory, New York City. At this time he was Chairman of the U. S. Air Force Scientific Advisory Board. As of September 13, 1948, he was listed as having changed his address back to the Guggenheim Aeronautical Laboratory, Pasadena, California.

"Time" magazine of January 1, 1951, under the "Business" section column, labeled "Corporations", carried an article concerning Dr. THEODORE VON KARMAN and his association with AEROJET ENGINEERING CORPORATION, Azusa, California. A portion of this article, which was accompanied by a photograph of VON KARMAN, is as follows:

> "Until World War II, most Americans thought that rockets were useful only for Fourth of July celebrations and trips to the moon. But not Dr. Theodore von KARMAN, the cigar-smoking, eager boss of the famed Guggenheim Aeronautical Laboratory at CalTech. With Air Force and private funds, Dr. von KARMAN had been experimenting enough with rockets to know they could be an important weapon. And since he was well acquainted with the work of the top Axis aerodynamicists, he knew what fast progress they were making with rockets. But when Dr. von KARMAN tried to get U. S. corporations interested in going into the rocket business in 1941, he was turned down flat. So Scientist von KARMAN decided to make them himself.
>
> "The next year, with four associates, an $8,700

investment, and five employees, he set up the AEROJET ENGINEERING CORP. of Azusa, Calif. Its product: Jato units, 10-in. thick, 3-ft. long rockets to give big planes an extra push to get them off short runways or aircraft carriers.

"In no time at all, the Navy and Air Force began firing orders at AEROJET and the company took off with a whoosh itself. Within 18 months, it got six Government loans to expand, still needed more cash. It got it from GENERAL TIRE & RUBBER CO. (which liked AEROJET so much that it now owns 81% of its stock).

"$185 a Bottle. During the war, AEROJET turned out some $10 million worth of Jato units, became one of the biggest U. S. rocket manufacturers. As AEROJET began to rise, VON KARMAN stepped down from the presidency, became the company's chief research consultant. CalTech's imaginative physicist Dr. FRITZ ZWICKY became active research chief."

The "Columbia Report" of January, 1951 carries the following item regarding VON KARMAN:

"The Kelvin Medal, one of the highest international honors in the field of engineering, was recently awarded to Dr. THEODORE von KARMAN, internationally renowned expert in the field of aerodynamics. Dr. von KARMAN holds one of the rare honorary professorships at COLUMBIA - in the field of mechanical engineering."

b2

[On March 7, 1951, a representative of [redacted] a Government Agency, conducting security investigations, advised that the subject is currently engaged as Chairman of the Scientific Advisory Board, Department of the Air Force, on a contract basis, and maintains an office at the Pentagon Building at Washington, D.C. (U)

[redacted] advised Special Agent [redacted] on April 12, 1951, during the course of another matter, that in early 1942 Dr. THEODORE VON KARMAN was placed on leave of absence from the Institute and spent his full time as a consultant with the U. S. Air Force.

b7C
b7D

Residence:

Subject, single, presently maintains a residence at 1501 South Marengo Street, Pasadena, California, where he resides with his sister, JOSEPHINE De KARMAN, about 60, also single. A small separate building on the premises is used by VON KARMAN as his office, which is managed by his secretary, [redacted] a Government employee [redacted] has advised that VON KARMAN is currently in Europe with his sister on a combined business and pleasure trip, and will visit Algiers, Paris and Switzerland before returning to Washington some time during May or June. His foreign mailing address is: CALIFORNIA HOTEL, Paris, France. b7C

## II. ACTIVITIES AND ASSOCIATES

General:

b2 [redacted] another Government Agency conducting security investigations, advised on April 5, 1951 that a representative of that agency had on March 19, 1951, interviewed [redacted] of Aachen, Germany. [redacted] advised that he was formerly very close to the VON KARMAN family and that VON KARMAN'S mother and an individual named Herr VON FAKLA, advised him that VON KARMAN in 1919 was the Minister of Culture in Hungary under BELA KUN, while the latter was in power for a few months. VON FAKLA, according to [redacted] is reported to have assisted VON KARMAN and his mother and sister, JOSEPHINE, in escaping to Germany after the fall of the BELA KUN Government. (U)

b7C b7D

[redacted] stated further that [redacted] VON KARMAN from shortly after World War I until VON KARMAN left for the U. S. in 1932. After graduating from the University of Budapest, where his father was head of the Department of Philosophy, VON KARMAN entered the University of Goettingen; and shortly before World War I he came to the University of Aachen where he became the head of the Mechanical Science and Aerodynamics Department. During World War I he served in the Austrian Army with the rank of Captain.

b2 [redacted] indicated also that the surname of VON KARMAN at the time of birth was VON SZOELLOESTCICTAK X(U)

[redacted]

b7C

As noted previously, [redacted]

TEXT ON THIS PAGE IS ILLEGIBLE
WE HAVE LEFT THE PAGE AS REFERENCE



SECRET

[redacted] became closely associated with VON KARMAN [redacted]

b7C

b2
b7C
b7D

[redacted] of known reliability [redacted] who had access to the [redacted]

b7C
b7D

[redacted] advised Special Agents [redacted] of the Albany office, in a signed statement, dated March 9, 1951, at Albany, New York, that he recalls [redacted]

b7C
b7D

It is observed tha [redacted]

[redacted]

b7D b7C

As indicated previously, [redacted] became closely associated with VON KARMAN. [redacted]

[redacted]



SECRET

TEXT ON THIS PAGE IS ILLEGIBLE
WE HAVE LEFT THE PAGE AS REFERENCE



[redacted] On December 2, 1950 [redacted] advised Special Agent [redacted] that he had originally gone to [redacted] on the advice of Dr. THEODORE VON KARMAN, an old acquaintance of his, who had recommended [redacted] as an old friend. [redacted] added that he himself had known VON KARMAN for many years, having been associated with him [redacted]

b7C b7D

[redacted] an admitted [redacted] stated in 1942 that [redacted] mentioned above under the [redacted] matter, was known by that informant to have in the past associated with various Soviet officials in Los Angeles, California, and to have been [redacted]

b7C

WILLIAM PERL
104 East Thirty-Eighth Street
New York, New York

[redacted] National Advisory Committee for Aeronautics, 1724 F Street, N.W., Washington, D.C., advised Special Agent [redacted] of the Washington Office, in July, 1950, in connection with another matter, that WILLIAM PERL was engaged as Technical Assistant to Dr. THEODORE VON KARMAN at the Pupin Physics Laboratory, COLUMBIA UNIVERSITY, at New York City, from about February, 1947 to June, 1948. During VON KARMAN'S absence, PERL handled certain of VON KARMAN'S affairs which included receiving classified material on behalf of the latter, which had been disseminated and prepared by the NACA in Washington. PERL also had access to VON KARMAN'S private safe at COLUMBIA UNIVERSITY.

b7C b7D [redacted] SVERDRUP and PARCEL, CONSULTING ENGINEERS, Syndicate Trust Building, 915 Olive

TEXT ON THIS PAGE IS ILLEGIBLE
WE HAVE LEFT THE PAGE AS REFERENCE



b7C

Street, St. Louis, Missouri, advised Special Agent [redacted] of the St. Louis Office, on August 1, 1950, that Dr. THEODORE VON KARMAN, whom he described as a world renowned aerodynamicist, had been employed by his company in 1947 as a Special Consultant engaged to work on a theoretical problem pertaining to high speed air flows. [redacted] stated that Dr. VON KARMAN employed his own staff on the project and as a general rule paid his staff personally from funds which had been provided him by the company. Among the six employees and a secretary so engaged by VON KARMAN, were (1) WILLIAM PERL, whose addresses were furnished as 570 Lexington Avenue, Room 711, New York City, and Graduate School of Aeronautical Engineering, CORNELL UNIVERSITY, Ithaca, New York [redacted] added that his company has had special Air Force contracts for a number of years but that the above project was not considered classified.

b7C b7D

On March 20, 1951, during the course of another matter, Dr. THEODORE VON KARMAN, 1501 South Marengo Street, Pasadena, California, advised Special Agent [redacted] that in 1946, while VON KARMAN was a visiting professor at COLUMBIA UNIVERSITY, New York City, that WILLIAM PERL had been assigned to him by [redacted] to assist him in the gathering of research material needed by VON KARMAN in connection with a series of lectures that he was then delivering. PERL acted in this capacity for VON KARMAN for some time and also collaborated to some extent with him in connection with consulting work which VON KARMAN was then doing for the GENERAL ELECTRIC CORPORATION.

b7C

In 1947, VON KARMAN continued, he visited Europe for a year or so and during the period that he was gone, PERL remained in the U. S. where he helped assemble scientific data necessary for the lectures and papers which VON KARMAN delivered at various scientific conferences he attended.

Dr. THEODORE VON KARMAN was previously interviewed at his office at the Air Force Scientific Advisory Board, Pentagon Building, Washington, D.C., at which time he admitted that he had lent a 1935 Plymouth automobile to WILLIAM PERL, but that it was actually owned by his sister, Dr. JOSEPHINE De KARMAN, who was then temporarily residing in Paris, France. VON KARMAN explained that PERL requested the use of this car in April or May, 1948 before he, VON KARMAN, left for Europe. However, due to the influence of his sister who disliked the idea of PERL keeping the car for a long period of time, he had requested PERL, in the Fall of 1948, to return the car to a designated garage for storage.

TEXT ON THIS PAGE IS ILLEGIBLE
WE HAVE LEFT THE PAGE AS REFERENCE



It is here observed that on March 15, 1951 WILLIAM PERL, above, was apprehended in New York City after being indicted under the Perjury Statute in connection with the testimony he gave before the Grand Jury in 1950, denying any acquaintance with JULIUS ROSENBERG and MARTIN SOBELL, both of whom have recently been convicted and sentenced in New York City for espionage by obtaining and transferring to Russia secret atomic information. PERL is currently awaiting trial.

At the time of his arrest, WILLIAM PERL was Physics Instructor at COLUMBIA UNIVERSITY, New York City, and was described in a United Press Dispatch, datelined New York on March 14, 1951, as the nation's second ranking aerodynamic engineer.

[redacted] was closely associated with VON KARMAN [redacted]

b7C
b7D

[redacted] furnished a signed statement on March 9, 1951 to Special Agents [redacted] of the Albany Office, wherein he stated that [redacted]

[redacted]

As indicated previously [redacted] the field of jet propulsion and rocket missiles which was actually sponsored by Dr. THEODORE VON KARMAN, who was then Director of the Guggenheim Aeronautical Laboratory at CIT. b7C

[redacted] advised further in August, 1949 that VON KARMAN was regarded as one of the world's outstanding aerodynamicists and since before the war had headed the National Advisory Committee for Aeronautics. Possibly, by reason of this original association - and together with the fact that [redacted] b7C b7D

Also, as noted above, [redacted] VON KARMAN in 1947 when he was hired by SVERDRUP and PARCEL, Consulting Engineers, St. Louis, Missouri, as a Special Consultant to work on a theoretical problem involving high speed air flows. b7C

b2 b7C [redacted] conducting security investigations, [redacted], another Government Agency advised that it had been informed that Dr. THEODORE VON KARMAN, of the Air Force Scientific Advisory (u)

TEXT ON THIS PAGE IS ILLEGIBLE
WE HAVE LEFT THE PAGE AS REFERENCE



SECRET

Board, had attempted - several days prior to September 15, 1950 - to contact [redacted] VON KARMAN indicated that he was leaving for Europe and that it was, therefore, very necessary for him to be permitted to contact [redacted]

b7C

[redacted] telephone call [redacted] received a person-to-person [redacted] from the office of Dr. THEODORE VON KARMAN, Air Force Advisory Board, Washington, D.C.

b2
b7C
b7D

[redacted]

b7C
b7D

b1

III. DESCRIPTION

The following description of the subject has been obtained from available records:



SECRET

TEXT ON THIS PAGE IS ILLEGIBLE
WE HAVE LEFT THE PAGE AS REFERENCE

LA 105-863

SECRET

| | |
|---|---|
| Name: | Dr. THEODORE VON KARMAN |
| Age: | 70 |
| Born: | 5/11/81; Budapest, Hungary |
| Height: | 5'8" |
| Weight: | 165 lbs. |
| Hair: | Thick, dark-gray |
| Eyes: | Hazel |
| Eyebrows: | Heavy |
| Ears: | Wears hearing aid on right ear |
| Glasses: | Wears reading glasses. |
| Citizenship status: | Naturalized July 24, 1936, Los Angeles, California, Certificate No. C-4052565 |
| Marital Status: | Single |
| Occupation: | Aerodynamicist |
| Present Employment: | Chairman, Scientific Advisory Board, Department of the Air Force, Pentagon Building, Washington, D.C. |
| Home Address: | 1501 South Marengo Street, Pasadena, California |
| Photograph: | Available |

- PENDING -



SECRET

SECRET

ADMINISTRATIVE PAGE

b2 [redacted] another Government Agency, conducting Security Investigations, advised in September, 1950 that information had been furnished to them in April, 1948 which indicated that one TODAR KARMAN joined the Hungarian Communist Party in 1918 while working as Assistant Professor of Physics at the JEZSEF NADOR TECHNICAL UNIVERSITY of Budapest, Hungary. In 1919, when the Communists seized power in Hungary, KARMAN was appointed Deputy Commissar of Cultural and Educational Affairs in charge of higher education (high schools and universities). KARMAN continued to function in that capacity until late in 1919, when the Communists were routed by the nationalist forces of Admiral HORTHY. At that time KARMAN was forced to flee Hungary; he escaped to Germany, where he settled at Aachen. Simultaneously, according to informant, KARMAN'S membership was transferred to the German Communist Party. KARMAN engaged in scientific work in Germany and was invited to lecture at the UNIVERSITY OF AACHEN. In 1931 KARMAN received an invitation to lecture in the United States; on the basis of this invitation he was issued an entry visa to the U. S. from 1931 to 1933. He reportedly gave several short lecture courses at the California Institute of Technology, Pasadena, California, returning each time to Aachen after the completion of these courses. After HITLER'S seizure of power, however, KARMAN applied for an extension of his permit of residence in the U. S. on the ground that it was dangerous for him, a Jew, to expose himself to Nazi racial persecution. KARMAN was subsequently granted an extended residence permit, and he became a regular professor at the California Institute of Technology. During the war, KARMAN reportedly engaged in research work in aerodynamics for the U. S. Army Air Forces. Informant stated that in 1945 KARMAN was assigned to a position on the research staff of an Army-sponsored guided missile project at Pasadena, a position which KARMAN reportedly retains to this date. Informant indicated to [redacted] belief that KARMAN covered up his Communist Party membership when first applying for an entry visa to the U. S. in 1931. It is not known, however, whether KARMAN has continued his membership in the Communist Party and whether or not his membership has been transferred to the American Communist Party. (U) b2



SECRET

[redacted] of known reliability, advised that the following have attempted to contact VON KARMAN in the recent past:

1) [redacted]
New York 4, New York

2) [redacted]
Paris, France

3) Fiat Societe for Czoloni
Division Technico Propellatine
Torino, Italy

4) [redacted]
Massachusetts Institute of Technology
77 Massachusetts Avenue
Cambridge, Massachusetts

5) Royal Aeronautical Society
4 Hamilton Place
London, England

6) Royal Society
Burlington House
London, England

7) [redacted]
Bern, Switzerland

8) [redacted]
New York 21, New York

9) [redacted]
Houston, Texas

Regarding [redacted] Massachusetts Institute of Technology, Cambridge, Massachusetts, mentioned above, the records of this office reflect that information was furnished by Special Agent [redacted] Boston, Massachusetts, in a report dated March 31, 1950, and captioned, [redacted] INTERNAL SECURITY - R", to the effect that the staff directory of MIT listed one [redacted]

TEXT ON THIS PAGE IS ILLEGIBLE
WE HAVE LEFT THE PAGE AS REFERENCE



No information had been received from confidential sources of the Boston Office, reflecting disloyalty on his part. [redacted]

b7C

b2 b7D [redacted] of known reliability, advised that VON KARMAN had been in contact with the following individuals in the recent past:

1) [redacted]
New York, New York
[redacted]

b7C 2) [redacted]
Columbia University
New York, New York
[redacted]

WILLIAM PERL:

b2 b7D [redacted] of known reliability, has identified WILLIAM PERL, Bureau file 65-59312, as a Soviet Agent. (u)

b7C [redacted]

b7C b2 b7D On March 20, 1951, [redacted] of known reliability, advised that [redacted] Bureau file 100-345440, [redacted]

b1

b7C [redacted]

b2 [redacted] of known reliability, advised that Dr. THEODORE VON KARMAN was visited at his office in the War Department, Army Air Forces Operation Commitment Requirements, Pentagon Building, (u)



SECRET

TEXT ON THIS PAGE IS ILLEGIBLE
WE HAVE LEFT THE PAGE AS REFERENCE



Washington, D.C., on the following dates by [redacted] Bureau file 100-138643. [redacted]

b7C

SECRET

[1/ 9/45 4/ 3/45 4/24/45
3/ 7/45 4/ 4/45 4/25/45
5/ 2/45]

X(u)

Each of the above visits lasted either for the entire day or a greater portion of the day. The visit on January 9, 1945 was continued that evening at VON KARMAN'S Washington Hotel.

X(u)

The Visitor's Register, maintained at [redacted] was observed in early 1945 by former Special Agent [redacted] of the Newark Office, to contain the name, "Mr. T. VON KARMAN, War Department", listed on December 30, 1944. He was accompanied by [redacted] USNR.

With reference to [redacted] it is observed, as commented in Bureau letter to Newark, dated April 11, 1946, that this matter was under investigation from July, 1944 to that time, but that to date no specific information had been developed which indicated that [redacted]

b7C

X(X)(u)

MISCELLANEOUS:

Regarding the variation in the spelling of the last name as VON KARMAN by the subject and De KARMAN by his sister, JOSEPHINE [redacted] dated January 21, 1942, set forth the information that in 1935 subject's sister had reported that she used the name De KARMAN because she had lived in Paris a number of years. She explained further that the family name was originally a Hungarian name (not given) and very long. She explained that her brother, THEODORE, had used VON KARMAN because he had lived in Germany many years.

b7D

I.N.S. records at Los Angeles, California reflected also that witnesses of subject's naturalization petition were listed as:



SECRET

LA 105-863

(1) [redacted]
Pasadena, California
[redacted]

SECRET

(2) [redacted]
Pasadena, California
[redacted]

b7C

Indices of this office contain no pertinent information regarding the above individuals.



SECRET

TEXT ON THIS PAGE IS ILLEGIBLE
WE HAVE LEFT THE PAGE AS REFERENCE



SECRET

LEADS

NEW YORK OFFICE

At New York, New York: Will review indices for any pertinent information regarding the following New York contacts of the subject, as reported by [redacted] and [redacted] (4) b2 b7D

b7C

1) [redacted]
New York, New York

2) [redacted]
New York, New York

3) [redacted]
New York, New York

4) [redacted]
Columbia University
New York, New York

LOS ANGELES OFFICE

At Los Angeles, California: Will report the results of the contemplated interview with [redacted] regarding subject's alleged former Communist Party membership and association with the BELA KUN Government in Hungary. b7C b7D

Will ascertain additional information and activities of the subject as furnished by confidential informants.

SECRET

TEXT ON THIS PAGE IS ILLEGIBLE
WE HAVE LEFT THE PAGE AS REFERENCE

LA 105-863

INFORMANTS SECRET

[redacted]
Counter Intelligence Division
Office of Special Investigations
Washington, D. C.

[redacted] - OSI Report by Special Agent [redacted] dated March 20, 1951.

[redacted] who furnished information to Special Agent [redacted] on February 16 and February 23, 1942.

[redacted] Security and Intelligence Office of the Air Force, Washington, D.C., as reflected in Washington Field letter to the Bureau, dated January 29, 1951, in instant matter.

[redacted] (S)

[redacted] Report from Headquarters, First Army, Governors Island, New York 4, New York, as reflected in the "Summary of Information", dated September 12, 1950, captioned, "Possible Communist, CIT", originally furnished to the New York Office.

[redacted] - Mail cover on subject's residence, 1501 South Marengo Street, Pasadena, California.

[redacted] - Confidential Source [redacted] covering the period October 26, 1950 to March 26, 1951.

[redacted] (S)

[redacted]

[redacted] Surveillance by agents of the Washington Office as reflected in reports of Special Agent [redacted] dated January 29, 1945, March 22, 1945, April 13, 1945, and Special Agent [redacted] dated May 9, 1945, all captioned [redacted] INTERNAL SECURITY-R"

- 22 -

SECRET

b1 b2 b7C b7D

TEXT ON THIS PAGE IS ILLEGIBLE
WE HAVE LEFT THE PAGE AS REFERENCE



Copies of this report are being furnished the Washington Field Division in view of their active current interest in this matter inasmuch as the subject maintains his headquarters in that area.

SECRET

REFERENCE: Bureau File 100-372586
Bureau letter to Los Angeles, dated April 4, 1951.

SECRET

TEXT ON THIS PAGE IS ILLEGIBLE
WE HAVE LEFT THE PAGE AS REFERENCE

SECRET AIR COURIER

Date: May 9, 1951

To: Legal Attache
Paris, France

From: John Edgar Hoover - Director
Federal Bureau of Investigation

Subject: THEODORE VON KARMAN, was.,
INTERNAL SECURITY - R

Subject, who is a world-renowned Aerodynamicist, was born in Budapest, Hungary, on May 11, 1881. In 1930, subject entered the United States and was naturalized at Los Angeles, California, on July 24, 1936. He is presently employed as Director of the Guggenheim Aeronautical Laboratory, California Institute of Technology, Pasadena, California. He is also employed as Chairman of the Scientific Advisory Board, Department of the Air Force, and as such, has continual access to classified information.

The investigation of subject is based on reports received from informants of unknown reliability which allege that subject was Minister of Culture in Hungary under the Communist regime of Bela Kun during 1919.

Investigation of subject reflects that he has of a recent date, been in contact with [redacted] Paris, France.

b7C

It is requested that you have your sources identify [redacted] and that pertinent information concerning [redacted] be furnished the Bureau at an early date.

CC - Foreign Service Desk

WAK:mes
100-372586

DECLASSIFIED BY [illegible] on 6-16-97

TEXT ON THIS PAGE IS ILLEGIBLE
WE HAVE LEFT THE PAGE AS REFERENCE

FD FORM NO. 64

42109

# Office Memorandum • UNITED STATES GOVERNMENT

TO : DIRECTOR, FBI DATE: 4/26/51

FROM : SAC, Los Angeles

SUBJECT: THEODORE VON KARMAN, was.
Theodor Karman, Theodor Von Szoelloestcictak
INTERNAL SECURITY - R

[redacted] Reference is made to the report of Special Agent [redacted] dated April 26, 1951, in the above-captioned matter, wherein it is reflected that subject was contacted in the recent past by [redacted] Paris, France.

It is suggested that through appropriate sources in Europe the above-named individual is identified.

It is further suggested that the Bureau give consideration to an interview with [redacted] Woods Hole, Massachusetts, regarding subject's activities in Hungary under BELA KUN in 1919, and his alleged Communist Party membership in Hungary and Germany.

As noted in Boston letter to the Bureau dated April 11, 1951, captioned [redacted]

As to Dr. THEODORE VON KARMAN, it is recalled that G-2 has recently furnished information concerning one TODAR KARMAN which alleges that TODAR KARMAN was appointed Deputy Commissar of Culture and Educational Affairs in charge of Higher Education, after a Communist uprising in Hungary in 1919. This information also alleges that TODAR KARMAN later fled from Hungary to Germany where he continued his membership in the Communist Party.

OSI has further advised on 4/5/51 that a representative of that agency has interviewed one [redacted] Aachen, Germany on 3/19/51, and who described himself as a former, very close friend of the subject.

AMSD
105-863
JPA:ams
cc: Boston

ALL INFORMATION CONTAINED HEREIN IS UNCLASSIFIED DATE 5-30-97

RECORDED - 56
INDEXED - 56

100-373586-2

APR 30 1951

17

G.I.R.-10

b7C
b7D

TEXT ON THIS PAGE IS ILLEGIBLE
WE HAVE LEFT THE PAGE AS REFERENCE

42110



and his family since about 1919. He advised that he had been informed by subject's mother and also one VON FAKLA that subject had been Minister of Culture in Hungary under BELA KUN while the latter was in power for a few months.

b7C

In the event that this interview with [redacted] is approved by the Bureau, it is requested that the Boston office be so advised.

STANDARD FORM NO. 64

# Office Memorandum • UNITED STATES GOVERNMENT

TO : Director, FBI DATE: May 2, 1951

FROM : SAC, New York

SUBJECT: THEODORE VON KARMAN
ISR
Bufile 100-372586

Rebulet 3/14/51 which designated Los Angeles office of origin in the above captioned case.

A thorough review of the New York files reflects the Los Angeles Division is in possession of all pertinent information re VON KARMAN with the possible exception of information received from one [redacted] by the Washington Field Office in July 1940. This information is set forth in WFO letter to Bureau 7/18/40 captioned [redacted] ESPIONAGE," photostat copy of which is enclosed for Los Angeles together with copy of this letter.

b7C

It is also noted that "Who's Who in America," Volume 25, 1948 Edition (covering 1948 and 1949) on page 2559 reveals a background sketch concerning VON KARMAN. This information is not set forth herein since it is in all probability available to the Bureau and the Los Angeles Division.

In the event instant investigation re VON KARMAN produces information which may be pertinent to the case entitled "WILLIAM PERL, Was, ESP-R, PERJURY," New York origin, (Bufile 65-59312, Los Angeles file 65-5075, New York file 65-15387) the Los Angeles Office is requested to report same under the PERL caption. RUC

2 cc Los Angeles (1-Von Karman
1-65-5075)
Enc-1)

MWC:IM
65-6747
cc - NY 65-15387

354 899
ALL INFORMATION CONTAINED
HEREIN IS UNCLASSIFIED
DATE 5-22-97 BY SP5 JC/dm

RECORDED - 92

INDEXED - 92 100-372586-27

MAY 3 1951

65 MAY 8

TEXT ON THIS PAGE IS ILLEGIBLE
WE HAVE LEFT THE PAGE AS REFERENCE

STANDARD FORM NO. 64

# Office Memorandum • UNITED STATES GOVERNMENT

TO : DIRECTOR, FBI

DATE: May 3, 1951

FROM : SAC, WASHINGTON FIELD

SUBJECT: THEODORE VON KARMAN
INTERNAL SECURITY - R

b7C

Re report of Special Agent [redacted] dated May 3, 1951, in above captioned case wherein is noted leads for the conducting of interviews by the Boston, Baltimore, New York, and Washington Field Offices. It is requested that the Bureau advise the respective offices of the permissibility of conducting such interviews.

It is further suggested that the Bureau, through their liaison facilities, may wish to recheck with the Office of Special Investigations, Department of the Air Force or CIC concerning the accuracy of the reportage by which certain information concerning subject and his activities in Hungary has been attributed to and subsequently denied by [redacted]

b7C
b7D

65-1936
RLS:dtk
CC:Los Angeles
Baltimore
Boston
New York

354-894
ALL INFORMATION CONTAINED
HEREIN IS UNCLASSIFIED
DATE 5-30-97 BY

RECORDED - 131

100-372586-28
MAY 4 1951

EX-100

62 MAY 31 1951

HANDLED BY
STOP DESK

TEXT ON THIS PAGE IS ILLEGIBLE
WE HAVE LEFT THE PAGE AS REFERENCE

4-20-51

FBI WASH FIELD

20 10:30a

DIRECTOR

URGENT

THEODORE JON KARMAN, IS DASH R. [redacted] TO BE INTERVIEWED BY [redacted] OSI AND AGENT OF WFO THIS EVENING.

b7C
b7D

STEIN

RLS: lm

65-1936

554-894
ALL INFORMATION CONTAINED
HEREIN IS UNCLASSIFIED
DATE 5-30-97 BY

SE 12

100-37256-

APR 25 1951

RECORDED - 1

EX-65

HANDLED BY
STOP DESK

[redacted]

b7C

FEDERAL BUREAU OF INVESTIGATION

Part. 2a

# SUBJECT: THEODORE VON KARMAN

# FILE NUMBER: 100-372586 SERIALS 30-END OF FILE

TEXT ON THIS PAGE IS ILLEGIBLE
WE HAVE LEFT THE PAGE AS REFERENCE

1-72
(1-10-49)

# FEDERAL BUREAU OF INVESTIGATION

FORM NO. 1
THIS CASE ORIGINATED AT LOS ANGELES     SEE REVERSE SIDE FOR ADD. DISSEMINATION.     FILE NO. 65-1936

| REPORT MADE AT | DATE WHEN MADE | PERIOD FOR WHICH MADE | REPORT MADE BY |
|---|---|---|---|
| WASHINGTON, D. C. | MAY 8 1951 | 4/20/51 | [redacted] b7C RLS:DTK |

| TITLE | CHARACTER OF CASE |
|---|---|
| THEODORE VON KARMAN | INTERNAL SECURITY - R |

CONFIDENTIAL

AGENCY ICC [redacted] b2
REQ. REC'D 12/20/54
REP'T FORW. 1/5/55

SYNOPSIS OF FACTS: [redacted] advises he heard unverified rumors that subject left Budapest after overthrow of Kun Government in 1919 due to general animosity towards Semitic persons and his supposed sympathy with Communism. Subject not known to have been active in Kun Government or to hold position therein. No Communist Party affiliations known. [redacted] met KARMAN only once about one year ago at which time he appeared to be "somewhat sympathic to Communism". [redacted] denies furnishing information re subject to Informant [redacted] in Europe.

b7C b7D

AGENCY ICC
REQ. REC'D 6-26-56
REP'T FORW. 7-13-56

ICC OSI LIASON VIA 5-9-51

- P -

AGENCY
REQ. REC'D 1-15-58
REP'T FORW.

DETAILS: AT WASHINGTON, D. C.

SEE REVERSE SIDE FOR ADD. DISSEMINATION.

[redacted] was interviewed by the writer and [redacted] Office of Special Investigations, United States Air Force, at which time there was displayed to [redacted] two pictures of subject, one taken apparently when he was approximately twenty-five years of age and the other published in January by Time Magazine and apparently recently taken. [redacted] was not advised as to the name of the individual depicted in these photographs and stated that he could not recall ever having seen the person before nor was he acquainted with the subject of the photographs. When

b7C b7D

DECLASSIFIED BY SP5 JC 6-16-97

APPROVED AND FORWARDED: [signature] SPECIAL AGENT IN CHARGE

DO NOT WRITE IN THESE SPACES

COPY IN FILE

100-372586-30

RECORDED - 107
INDEXED - 107

1951

COPIES OF THIS REPORT
5 - Bureau (100-372586)
3 - Los Angeles
2 - Baltimore
2 - Boston
2 - New York
2 - Washington Field

CONFIDENTIAL

TEXT ON THIS PAGE IS ILLEGIBLE
WE HAVE LEFT THE PAGE AS REFERENCE



it was explained to him that the photographs were those of subject he advised that it was his recollection that subject would resemble the more recent photograph but due to his very slight acquaintance with him he did not immediately recall him from the picture. [redacted] stated that he had known the brother of TODOR KARMAN (by which name he repeatedly referred to subject) in Budapest around 1922 at which time they both were [redacted] in that city. He also noted that he had met MOR KARMAN, the father of subject, a well known teacher in Budapest. According to [redacted], he knew TODOR by reputation as a teacher at the Jozef Nador University, and one of the foremost authorities in hydrodynamics but that he never personally met him.

[redacted] recalled that subject left Hungary after the Kun Government was overthrown and that he subsequently went to Aachen, Germany, where he taught in the University and evidently continued his scientific work. Subsequently KARMAN came to this country and has evidently been engaged in the scientific field in California. According to [redacted] he had never known subject having been referred to as VON KARMAN, stating that in Hungary the name has simply been TODOR KARMAN. [redacted] could not recall, other than by attributing his statements to general rumor at the time, facts concerning subject's fleeing from Budapest and stated that it was his recollection that he had supposedly left the country due to the fact that after the Kun Regime there was a wave of anti-semitism throughout Hungary and that furthermore subject had apparently evidenced or expressed some sympathy toward Communism or the Kun Regime in particular. [redacted] however, stated that he did not know nor had he heard rumors to the effect that subject had been active in the Kun Government or that he had ever attained or served in any official or honorary capacity under that Government.

It was further related that [redacted] had no knowledge concerning any Communist activity or membership in the Communist Party by subject in Hungary, Germany, the United States, or elsewhere. [redacted] was unacquainted with facts concerning subject's entry into the United States and details concerning his activities and associations subsequent to his arrival here.

Pursuant to an invitation from [redacted] along with several other individuals of Hungarian descent, was about a year or a year and a half ago invited to [redacted] home in Washington [redacted] subject who was at that time visiting in the city. The

/b7C b7D

TEXT ON THIS PAGE IS ILLEGIBLE
WE HAVE LEFT THE PAGE AS REFERENCE



evening was of a social nature, the conversation being generally innocuous, although at one juncture it turned toward the subject of Communism and in particular the present Communist controlled government of Hungary. In reference thereto the subject stated that [redacted] This remark was recalled by [redacted] who stated that in context it was an implication that KARMAN was speaking favorably of the fact that the Hungarian people were presently living under a Communist Government and apparently voluntarily so doing. In answer to subject one of the other guests remarked that [redacted] and in reply thereto the subject merely shrugged and stated, [redacted] Due to the fact that most of the individuals present during the evening were in some field of scientific endeavor the conversation also concerned itself with general scientific talk. [redacted] noted that subject was accompanied that evening by a lady who he subsequently recalled to be probably his sister, JOSEPHINE.

Concerning [redacted] it is noted that Confidential Informant [redacted] who has previously furnished reliable information and is a [redacted]

[redacted] advised that among the individuals present at the apartment were [redacted] Baltimore, and [redacted] Washington, both of whom were described by him as being anti-Communist. [redacted] noted that [redacted] had informed him that in the Spring of 1945, subject had been in Budapest and had also visited Moscow to attend the three hundredth jubilee of the Moscow Academy of Science. [redacted] did not know the facts concerning this trip of subject.

[redacted] informed that he had been interviewed by Informant [redacted] a government agency which conducts security investigations, in Europe in 1948 and that he had made available such information as he possessed concerning Communist activities and persons of Communist sympathies in

/b2 b7C b7D

TEXT ON THIS PAGE IS ILLEGIBLE
WE HAVE LEFT THE PAGE AS REFERENCE



CONFIDENTIAL

Hungary at that time but that he did not give any information concerning subject nor was he questioned relative thereto. He further stated that had he been questioned concerning subject, he could have offered little information of value due to the fact that he was not personally acquainted with him and that his knowledge of him and his activities was simply derived from unverified rumors. This information concerning subject's reasons for leaving Hungary after the Kun Government's overthrow has been set forth above.

- P E N D I N G -

CONFIDENTIAL

TEXT ON THIS PAGE IS ILLEGIBLE
WE HAVE LEFT THE PAGE AS REFERENCE

WFO 65-1936

LEAD PAGE

It is requested that all of the following leads be held in abeyance pending advice from the Bureau concerning the permissibility of the indicated interviews being made.

BALTIMORE DIVISION

AT BALTIMORE, MARYLAND

Will interview [redacted] concerning his knowledge of subject and in particular any information concerning his political activities in Hungary in 1918 and 1919.

BOSTON DIVISION

AT WOODS HOLE, MASSACHUSETTS

Will interview [redacted] for his information concerning subject and in particular the latter's political activities in Hungary during the Bela Kun Regime.

b7C

NEW YORK DIVISION

AT NEW YORK, NEW YORK

Will interview [redacted] reported to be connected with the [redacted] concerning his knowledge of subject and the latter's activities in Hungary.

WASHINGTON FIELD DIVISION

AT WASHINGTON, D. C.

Will interview [redacted] concerning any information in his possession concerning subject.

TEXT ON THIS PAGE IS ILLEGIBLE
WE HAVE LEFT THE PAGE AS REFERENCE

WFO 65-1936

**LEAD PAGE**

For the information of Baltimore and Boston, a report from CIC dated April, 1948, reflected that TODOR KARMAN had joined the Hungarian Communist Party in 1918, while an Assistant Professor of Physics at Jozef Nador Technical University in Budapest. When the Communist seized power under Bela Kun in 1919, KARMAN was appointed Deputy Commissar of Cultural and Educational Affairs remaining as such until the Kun Government was overthrown in 1919, at which time he fled to Germany and settled in Aachen, transferring his Communist Party membership. He subsequently came to this country and during the war worked on research in aerodynamics for the United States Army Air Forces.

b7C
b7D

The above information is reportedly given to CIC by [redacted] It is noted that subject is one of the foremost aerodynamists in the world and is known to have been closely associated in scientific research with Communist Party members.

INFORMANT PAGE

[redacted] b7D b2 [redacted] b2      b7C b7D [redacted] CIC, United States Army.

REFERENCES: Bureau Letter dated March 14, 1951
Bureau Teletype dated April 16, 1951

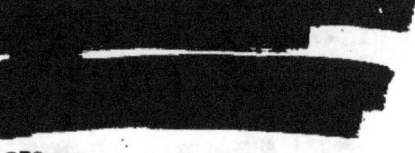

TEXT ON THIS PAGE IS ILLEGIBLE
WE HAVE LEFT THE PAGE AS REFERENCE

May 25, 1951

DEFERRED

SAC, KNOXVILLE

JULIUS ROSENBERG; ESP-R. b7C b7D

INFORMANT [redacted] NY HAS RECENTLY ADVISED THAT ON HOLIDAY WEEKEND WILLIAM PERL, ACCORDING TO ROSENBERG, REMOVED CERTAIN CONFIDENTIAL PAPERS FROM PUPIN LABORATORY, COLUMBIA UNIVERSITY, WHICH PAPERS SUBSEQUENTLY PHOTOGRAPHED AT ROSENBERG APARTMENT. BY REASON PREVIOUS STATEMENT DAVID GREENGLASS THAT IN FORTY EIGHT ROSENBERG CLAIMED TO HAVE RECEIVED MATHEMATICS ON NUCLEAR ENERGY FOR AIRPLANES IDENTIFIED AS NEPA PROJECT, CHECK BEING MADE TO DETERMINE WHETHER COPY "LEXINGTON REPORT" OR OTHER NEPA REPORTS FURNISHED THEODORE VON KARMAN, PUPIN LABORATORY, COLUMBIA UNIVERSITY. PERL KNOWN TO HAVE SERVED AS ASSISTANT TO VON KARMAN AND HAD ACCESS TO VON KARMAN'S PAPERS. REQUEST IMMEDIATE CHECK AT NEPA, OAK RIDGE, TO DETERMINE WHETHER "LEXINGTON REPORT" OR OTHER NEPA PAPERS FURNISHED VON KARMAN AND IF SO, DATE AND IDENTITY SUCH REPORT. SUTEL.

86-1840CV

ALL INFORMATION CONTAINED
HEREIN IS UNCLASSIFIED
DATE 7/22/86 BY 3042PWT/RWS/lmw

EFK:hs HOOVER

cc: New York (By Mail) 354891 SRSJC/bp 5-30-97

65-58236

100-372586-V
NOT RECORDED
98 1951 MAY 31

cc: 65-59312 (Perl)
100-372586 (Von Karman) ✓

[redacted] b7C

Tolson
Ladd
Clegg
Glavin
Nichols
Rosen
Tracy
Harbo
Belmont
Mohr
Tele. Room
Nease
Gandy

85 JUN 18 1951

HANDLED
STOP

TEXT ON THIS PAGE IS ILLEGIBLE
WE HAVE LEFT THE PAGE AS REFERENCE

FEDERAL BUREAU OF INVESTIGATION
U. S. DEPARTMENT OF JUSTICE
COMMUNICATIONS SECTION

MAY 9 1951

TELETYPE

ALL INFORMATION CONTAINED
HEREIN IS UNCLASSIFIED
DATE 5-30-97 BY

WASH AND WASH FLD 32 LOS ANGELES1 FROM NEW YORK 9 [redacted]

DIRECTOR AND SACS DEFERRED

b7C

THEODORE VON KARMAN, WAS, IS-R. REBUTEL MAY SEVEN LAST. THOROUGH SEARCH OF RECORDS OF COLUMBIA UNIVERISTY LIBRARY, INCLUDING MASTERS AND DOCTORS DEGREES THESES FROM EIGHTEEN NINETYONE TO PRESENT, REVEAL NO THESIS ON BELA KUN COUP IN HUNGARY. ONLY ITEMS LOCATED RE THIS SUBJECT WERE FOUR BOOKS INCLUDING A VOLUME OF BOUND PAMPHLETS ENTITLED QUOTE WHAT IS COMMUNISM, END OF QUOTE, WRITTEN BY BELA KUN, PREFACE BY KISHKA, PRINTED BERLIN, GOSUDARST, NINETEEN TWENTY, IN THE RUSSIAN LANGUAGE, TRANSLATED FROM GERMAN. ANOTHER BOOK ENTITLED, QUOTE THE MOST BURNING QUESTION DASH UNITY OF ACTION, END OF QUOTE, WRITTEN BY BELA KUN, PUBLISHED BY WORKERS LIBRARY PUBLISHERS, NYC, NINETEEN THIRTYFOUR. THIS BOOK MISSING FROM COLUMBIA LIBRARY SINCE AUGUST FIFTY. ANOTHER BOOK, ENTITLED QUOTE OTTO BAUER-S WEG, UNQUOTE, WRITTEN BY BELA KUN, IN GERMAN LANGUAGE, PUBLISHED BY MUNCHEN PROMETHEUS - VERLAG, NINETEEN THIRTYFOUR. ANOTHER BOOK ENTITLED, QUOTE REVOLUTIONARY ESSAY, UNQUOTE, REPRINTED IN ENGLISH LANGUAGE FROM PRAVDA, LONDON, NINETEEN EIGHTEEN, BY BELA KUN. REVIEW OF LATTER

RECORDED - 141 100- 32
INDEXED - 141
MAY 12

END OF PAGE ONE

TWO COPIES WFO

TEXT ON THIS PAGE IS ILLEGIBLE
WE HAVE LEFT THE PAGE AS REFERENCE

PAGE TWO

BOOK REVEALED NO REFERENCE TO SUBJECT. SEARCH OF GENERAL INDICES OF COLUMBIA LIBRARY RE NAME AND ALIASES OF SUBJECT REFLECTS NUMEROUS REFERENCES TO HIM AS AUTHOR OF VARIOUS SCIENTIFIC BOOKS AND PAPERS BUT NEGATIVE RE ANY ASSOCIATION WITH BELA KUN OR HIS REGIME. SUGGEST BUREAU RECONTACT OSI FOR EXACT TITLE AND OR AUTHOR OF THESIS OR THESES REFERRED TO IN BUTEL AS FURTHER SEARCH AT COLUMBIA NOT FEASIBLE WITHOUT SAME. FOR INFORMATION REBUTEL APRIL NINE, LAST [redacted] NOT ACQUAINTED WITH SUBJECT. [redacted] INTRODUCED SOCIALLY TO SUBJECT IN HOLLYWOOD, CALIFORNIA, ABOUT NINETEEN THIRTYSEVEN, BUT DOES NOT KNOW PRESENT ACTIVITIES OR WHEREABOUTS, AND DOES NOT RECALL HIS PRESENCE IN EUROPE SPECIFICALLY DURING BELA KUN REGIME, AND THEREAFTER. THIS INFORMANT WAS ACQUAINTED WITH GYORGY LUKACS, WHO WAS COMMISSAR OF CULTURAL AND EDUCATIONAL AFFAIRS UNDER BELA KUN, AND WHO IS NOW FUNCTIONARY OF HUNGARIAN DASH COMMUNIST REGIME. [redacted] ADVISED HE HEARD OF SUBJECT AS ASSISTANT TO PROFESSOR RADO KOVESLIGHETY, A MATHEMATICS PROFESSOR AT THE JOZSEF NADOR TECHNICAL UNIVERISTY

END OF PAGE TWO

b2
b7D

OF BUDAPEST, ALTHOUGH HE DID NOT KNOW HIM PERSONALLY. INFORMANT SAID THAT SUBJECT AND SEVERAL OTHER ASSISTANTS OF ABOVE PROFESSOR JOINED THE BELA KUN REGIME IN HUNGARY, AND IN SO DOING, WERE SWAYED BY PROFESSOR [illegible]SLIGHETY. SUBJECT LATER CAME TO US, AND WAS ASSOCIATED AT CALTECH, ACCORDING TO INFORMANT. INFORMANT SUGGESTED FURTHER INFO MIGHT BE OBTAINED FROM [redacted] WASHINGTON, D.C. BUREAU REQUESTED TO ADVISE WFO IF THIS CONTACT DESIRED. [redacted] ADVISED HE CONTACTED SUBJECT IN A [illegible] NINETEEN FORTY FIVE SHORTLY AFTER SUBJECT RETURNED TO THE [illegible] FROM A TRIP TO HUNGARY, AT WHICH TIME SUBJECT DISCUSSED [illegible] CONDITIONS IN HUNGARY. INFORMANT SAID THAT FROM ABOVE [illegible], INFORMANT WAS IMPRESSED WITH SUBJECT-S FAVORABLE REACTION [illegible] COMMUNIST DOMINATION OF HUNGARY. FOR THIS REASON, INFORMANT NEVER RECONTACTED SUBJECT. CONFIDENTIAL INFORMANT [redacted] HE DID NOT KNOW VON KARMAN IN HUNGARY, ALTHOUGH HE [illegible] WITH MANY BELA KUN FUNCTIONARIES. NYO SUGGESTS CONTACT COULD BE HAD WITH CONFIDENTIAL INFORMANTS [redacted] IN EUROPE, AND [redacted] PRESENTLY IN BOSTON.

END [illegible]

b2 b7C b7D

TEXT ON THIS PAGE IS ILLEGIBLE
WE HAVE LEFT THE PAGE AS REFERENCE

PAGE FOUR

b7C b7D

HOWEVER, IN VIEW OF ABOVE INFORMATION FROM OTHER INFORMANTS, AND SINCE [redacted] NOT READILY AVAILABLE, NO ATTEMPT TO CONTACT THEM WILL BE MADE WITHOUT SPECIFIC INSTRUCTIONS FROM BUREAU OR LA.

RE LA REPORT APRIL TWENTYSEVEN, LAST, NYO INDICES REVEAL NO IDENTIFIABLE DATA RE PERSONS REPORTED AS CONTACTS OF SUBJECT. REPORT FOLLOWS.

SCHEIDT

44

HOLD

CC: Mr [redacted]

b7C

FEDERAL BUREAU OF INVESTIGATION
UNITED STATES DEPARTMENT OF JUSTICE

To: COMMUNICATIONS SECTION.

May 12, 1951 DEFERRED

Transmit the following message to: SAC, NEW YORK
WASHINGTON FIELD (BSM)

TEXT ON THIS PAGE IS ILLEGIBLE
WE HAVE LEFT THE PAGE AS REFERENCE

THEODORE VON KARMAN, IS - R. RE NY TEL MAY NINE LAST. OSI HAS BEEN REQUESTED TO FURNISH FURTHER INFORMATION RE THESES AT COLUMBIA UNIVERSITY IN THE EVENT THEY DESIRE FURTHER REVIEW MADE. NY IS AUTHORIZED TO INTERVIEW [redacted] AND WFO TO INTERVIEW [redacted] NY IS TO ADVISE WHEN [redacted] RETURNS TO US. DECISION RE INTERVIEW OF HER WILL BE THEN MADE. THE FACT THAT SUBJECT IS UNDER INTENSIVE INVESTIGATION SHOULD NOT BE REVEALED DURING INTERVIEWS.

b7C
b7D

HOOVER

WAK:Mes

CC: WASHINGTON FIELD (BY SPECIAL MESSENGER)

CC: LOS ANGELES (BY MAIL)

RECEIVED READING ROOM
FBI
U S DEPT. OF JUSTICE

RECORDED - 141

Note: Bufiles describe [redacted] He has been interviewed concerning prominent Bureau subjects and was recommended by Informant [redacted] He is presently being considered for a permanent informant symbol.

EX. - 85

b7C
b7D

Bufiles reflect [redacted] has, since 1948, been a source of information on Hungarian matters in the WFO. [redacted] and has been described by WFO as thoroughly anti-Communist and loyal to the U.S.

Tolson
Ladd
Clegg
Glavin
Nichols
Rosen
Tracy
Harbo
Alden
Tele. Room
Nease
Gandy

FEDERAL BUREAU OF INVESTIGATION
U. S. DEPARTMENT OF JUSTICE
COMMUNICATIONS SECTION
MAY 12 1951
TELETYPE

ALL INFORMATION CONTAINED
HEREIN IS UNCLASSIFIED
DATE 5-30-97

HANDLED BY
STOP DESK

DESTROYED
APR 5 1963

60 MAY 23 1951

113 PM Per

TEXT ON THIS PAGE IS ILLEGIBLE
WE HAVE LEFT THE PAGE AS REFERENCE

SAC, LOS ANGELES

May 9, 1951

DIRECTOR, FBI

THEODORE VON KARMAN, was.,
INTERNAL SECURITY - R

Re Los Angeles report dated April 27, 1951.

There are attached for the information of the Los Angeles and Washington Field Offices copies of OSI investigative reports dated April 16, 1951. The reports were furnished the Bureau by memorandum dated April 27, 1951, from OSI and reflect the results of investigation by that Agency in Europe concerning subject.

In a recent memorandum to the Bureau, [redacted] Office of Special Investigations, Department of the Air Force, requested that the investigation of subject be expedited in view of the fact that subject, as Chairman of the Scientific Advisory Board, Department of the Air Force, has continual access to information pertaining to highly sensitive aeronautical research.

b7C

The investigation of subject is to be given preferred handling and the result of all investigation is to be submitted promptly to the Bureau for transmission to OSI.

Attachment

cc - Washington Field - Attachment
New York

100-372586 - 33
WAK:mes

RECORDED - 137
EX-65

Mr. Tolson
Mr. Ladd
Mr. Clegg
Mr. Glavin
Mr. Nichols
Mr. Rosen
Mr. Tracy
Mr. Harbo
Mr. Belmont
Mr. Mohr
Tele. Room
Mr. Nease
Miss Gandy

354894
ALL INFORMATION CONTAINED
HEREIN IS UNCLASSIFIED
DATE 5-31-97 BY

MAY 9 3 24 PM '51
RECEIVED READING ROOM
FBI
U.S. DEPT OF JUSTICE

HANDLED BY
SPOT DESK

COMM - FBI
MAY 10 1951
MAILED 19

65 MAY 23

TEXT ON THIS PAGE IS ILLEGIBLE
WE HAVE LEFT THE PAGE AS REFERENCE

Assistant Attorney General
James M. McInerney

May 9, 1951

Director, FBI

CONFIDENTIAL

THEODORE VON KARMAN, was.,
INTERNAL SECURITY - R

Reference is made to our memorandum dated February 3, 1951, concerning captioned individual.

There is attached for your further information a copy of the report of Special Agent [redacted] b7C dated April 27, 1951, at Los Angeles, California.

Attachment

WAK:mes

ALL INFORMATION CONTAINED
HEREIN IS UNCLASSIFIED
DATE 5-30-97 BY

Mr. Tolson
Mr. Ladd
Mr. Clegg
Mr. Glavin
Mr. Nichols
Mr. Rosen
Mr. Tracy
Mr. Harbo
Mr. Belmont
Mr. Mohr
Tele. Room
Mr. Nease
Miss Gandy

RECORDED - 135
EX-130
100-372586
MAY 12 1951

MAY 10 1951
COMM - FBI

HANDLED BY

MAY 9 3 53 PM '51

66 MAY 19 1951

May 7, 1951 URGENT

SAC, NEW YORK
WASHINGTON FIELD (BSM)

THEODORE VON KARMAN, INTERNAL SECURITY DASH R. RELAREP APRIL TWENTY-SEVEN LAST. OSI ADVISES THAT THESES ON FILE QUOTE IN THE STACKS UNQUOTE AT COLUMBIA UNIVERSITY LIBRARY, CONCERNING BELA KUN COUP IN HUNGARY, MAY REFLECT INFORMATION CONCERNING SUBJECT. BUREAU DESIRES THAT ABOVE THESES BE REVIEWED IMMEDIATELY AND ANY PERTINENT INFORMATION CONCERNING SUBJECT BE FURNISHED BY TELETYPE. NEW YORK ALSO SUBMIT IMMEDIATELY REPORT COVERING LEADS SET OUT IN BULET APRIL NINE LAST AND REFERENCED REPORT.

HOOVER

100-372584

CC - LOS ANGELES (BY MAIL)
WASHINGTON FIELD (BY SPECIAL MESSENGER)

WAK:LJB

354-894
ALL INFORMATION CONTAINED
HEREIN IS UNCLASSIFIED
DATE 9-30-92 BY SPS JC/bgn

NOTE: Subject is Chairman of the Scientific Advisory Board, Department of the Air Force, and has continuous access to highly sensitive research. OSI investigation in Europe verifies allegation that subject was an official during the Bela Kun Regime in Hungary, in 1919. Because of subject's position, [redacted] in letter to Bureau requests that investigation be expedited.

b7C

OSI had also suggested that Hungarian and Russian newspapers at the New York Public Library may furnish further information concerning subject. In view of the fact that OSI has verified subject's participation under Bela Kun, and in view of the tremendous work involved in reviewing Russian and Hungarian newspapers for the year 1919, this lead is not being set out at the present time.

COPIES DESTROYED
18 APR 5 1963

Tolson
Ladd
Clegg
Glavin
Nichols
Rosen
Tracy
Harbo
Belmont
Mohr
Tele. Room
Nease
Gandy

FEDERAL BUREAU OF INVESTIGATION
U. S. DEPARTMENT OF JUSTICE
COMMUNICATIONS SECTION
MAY 7 - 1951
TELETYPE

RECORDED - 133
EX-130
100-372586-35
MAY 1951

66 MAY 19 1951

HANDLED BY
STOP DESK

TEXT ON THIS PAGE IS ILLEGIBLE
WE HAVE LEFT THE PAGE AS REFERENCE

100-372586

May 12, 1951

CONFIDENTIAL
VIA LIAISON

To: Director of Special Investigations (I.G.)
Department of the Air Force
The Pentagon
Washington 25, D.C.

From: John Edgar Hoover, Director
Federal Bureau of Investigation

Subject: THEODORE VON KARMAN, was.
INTERNAL SECURITY - R

Reference is made to your memorandum dated April 27, 1951, your reference 33-3676. Your memorandum noted that an OSI representative abroad had furnished information indicating that further details concerning subject's connection with the Bela Kun uprising in Hungary could be found in theses concerning the Bela Kun coup, at the Columbia University Library.

The New York Office of this Bureau has made a thorough search of the records of the Columbia University Library including the theses for Masters' and Doctors' degrees from the year 1901 to the present date. This search revealed no thesis which concerned the Bela Kun coup in Hungary.

In addition to the above, a book entitled "Revolutionary Essay" reprinted in the English language from Pravda, London, 1918, and written by Bela Kun was reviewed. This review failed to reveal any information concerning subject.

In the event you desire a further check of information contained in the Library of Columbia University, it is requested that you recontact your representative in Europe for the exact titles or the authors of the theses recalled by him.

WAK:LJB

RECORDED - 41 MAY 17 1951

100-372586-36

DECLASSIFIED BY [redacted]

Mr. Tolson
Mr. Ladd
Mr. Clegg
Mr. Glavin
Mr. Nichols
Mr. Rosen
Mr. Tracy
Mr. Harbo
Mr. Alden
Mr. Belmont
Mr. Laughlin
Mr. Mohr
Tele. Room
Mr. Nease
Miss Gandy

HANDLED BY STOP DESK

MAY 23 1951

TEXT ON THIS PAGE IS ILLEGIBLE
WE HAVE LEFT THE PAGE AS REFERENCE

*In connection with the investigation of subject, several reliable informants who have knowledge of the activities of the German Communist Party, and who were present in Hungary during the Bela Kun Regime have been contacted. One of the informants has advised that he has heard of subject as having been a former assistant to Professor Rado Kovesligheti of the Jozsef Nador Technical University of Budapest, Hungary. The informant, although he does not know subject personally, has heard that subject and several other assistants of the above professor joined the Bela Kun Regime in Hungary as a result of Professor Kovesligheti's influence over them. The informant is unable to furnish any further information.*

*A second reliable informant advised that he contacted subject in 1945 after subject had returned to this country from a trip to Hungary. During this contact the informant discussed conditions in Hungary with subject and states that he was impressed with subject's favorable reaction to the Russian Communist domination of Hungary. As a result, the informant states that he has not since been in contact with subject.*

*A third informant has advised that he was personally acquainted with Gyorgy Lukacs who was Commissar of Cultural and Educational Affairs under Bela Kun, and who is now a functionary of the Hungarian Communist Regime, and although the informant was present in Hungary during the Bela Kun Regime, he knows of no connection of Von Karman with Bela Kun.*

*The foregoing information is furnished you in confidence and it is requested that no dissemination be made outside the Office of Special Investigations. A detailed report covering the above matters will be made available to you in the very near future. You will also be furnished any additional pertinent information developed concerning subject.*

TEXT ON THIS PAGE IS ILLEGIBLE
WE HAVE LEFT THE PAGE AS REFERENCE

Assistant Attorney General
James M. McInerney

May 11, 1951

Director, FBI

CONFIDENTIAL

THEODORE VON KARMAN
INTERNAL SECURITY - R

Reference is made to our memorandum dated May 9, 1951, concerning captioned individual.

There is attached for your further information a copy of the report of Special Agent [redacted] dated May 3, 1951, at Washington, D. C.

b7C

Attachment

WAK:mes
100-372586

RECEIVED-READING ROOM
MAY 11 7 05 PM '51
FBI
U.S. DEPT OF JUSTICE

DECLASSIFIED BY 5P5 JC/...
ON 5-30-97

RECORDED - 124

100-372586
MAY 16 1951
80

EX-24

MAY 12 1951
COMM - FBI

60 MAY 23 1951

TEXT ON THIS PAGE IS ILLEGIBLE
WE HAVE LEFT THE PAGE AS REFERENCE

SAC, WASHINGTON FIELD May 15, 1951

DIRECTOR, FBI

THEODORE VON KARMAN, was., BY SPECIAL MESSENGER
INTERNAL SECURITY - R

OSI has advised this date that subject, after returning to the Pentagon from a European trip on May 14, 1951, contacted the Vice Chief of Staff of the Air Force and advised him that while in Europe, he had determined that he was being investigated by OSI. Subject also advised the Air Force that he had not belonged to the Communist Party in Germany but did not volunteer any information concerning his connection with the Bela Kun regime in Hungary.

OSI has requested that Bureau interview subject and that [redacted] OSI Counter Intelligence Division, be permitted to attend interview. Bureau has authorized the interview and participation by [redacted]

WFO Agent [redacted] to whom investigation is assigned, is to immediately contact Bureau Liaison Agent [redacted] in order that arrangements for interview can be made.

During interview, subject is to be specifically questioned regarding his former position as Commissar under Bela Kun and regarding any knowledge he may have of Communist Party membership or subversive activity on the part of [redacted] Subject is also to be questioned concerning association with [redacted] to whom [redacted] was referred by subject. Questioning concerning [redacted] is to be conducted in a manner that will not enable subject to conclude that [redacted] is presently under investigation by the Bureau.

Information concerning all above associates set out in Los Angeles report dated April 27, 1951, concerning subject.

cc - New York
Los Angeles

WAK:mes

b7C

RECORDED - 100-372586-38

RECEIVED DIRECTOR F B I U.S. DEPT. OF JUSTICE MAY 16 1951

HANDLED BY STOP DESK

RECEIVED READING ROOM F B I MAY 16 2 54 PM '51

MAILED 10 MAY 16 1951 COMM - FBI

65 MAY 25 1951

TEXT ON THIS PAGE IS ILLEGIBLE
WE HAVE LEFT THE PAGE AS REFERENCE

SAC, LOS ANGELES

May 16, 1951

DIRECTOR, FBI

THEODORE VON KARMAN, was.,
INTERNAL SECURITY - R

94-11-1
845-1

Rebulet May 9, 1951.

There is attached for your information a copy of OSI report dated April 26, 1951, OSI file number 33-49 which concerns captioned subject.

You will be furnished additional information received from OSI as a result of their continuing investigation.

100-372586

Attachment

WAK:mes

HANDLED BY
STOP DESK

ALL INFORMATION CONTAINED
HEREIN IS UNCLASSIFIED
DATE 5-26-97 BY

100-372586-39

RECORDED - 81
MAY 19 1951

MAILED 10
MAY 16 1951

U.S. DEPT. OF JUSTICE
FBI
RECEIVED—MAIL ROOM

Tolson
Ladd
Clegg
Glavin
Nichols
Rosen
Tracy
Harbo
Alden
Belmont
Laughlin
Mohr
Tele. Room
Nease
Gandy

TEXT ON THIS PAGE IS ILLEGIBLE
WE HAVE LEFT THE PAGE AS REFERENCE

SAC, LOS ANGELES

DIRECTOR, FBI

May 11, 1951

SECRET

THEODORE VON KARMAN
INTERNAL SECURITY - R

Re WFO report May 3, 1951.

b7D [redacted] New York is authorized to interview [redacted] in accordance with the leads set out in referenced report. Prior to conducting the interview, New York is to review its files concerning [redacted] for the purpose of determining whether they are in the possession of any information not previously made available to the Bureau which makes such an interview inadvisable.

[redacted] WFO is also authorized to interview [redacted] subject, [redacted] concerning ; after a similar review of their files.

b7C b7D The interview of [redacted] is not being authorized at this time, because of the fact that [redacted] New York City. Bureau files also reflect that [redacted] Bureau files described as [redacted] has been reliably [redacted] has been cooperative during several recent interviews, [redacted] and although he he has failed to fully volunteer information concerning [redacted]

Bureau files reflect that by memorandum dated [redacted] (S) On the basis of that information, authority to interview [redacted] is not being granted at this time. b1 b7C

RECORDED - 81

100-372586

MAY 16

cc - Washington Field
Baltimore
Boston
New York

EX-30

CLASSIFIED BY
DECLASSIFY ON: 25X
Classified per CIA Letter

:mes

SECRET

STANDARD FORM NO. 64

# Office Memorandum • UNITED STATES GOVERNMENT

TO : DIRECTOR, FBI    DATE: May 12, 1951

FROM : SAC, LOS ANGELES

SUBJECT: THEODORE VON KARMAN
INTERNAL SECURITY - R

G.I.R.-3

Rebufile 100-372586 in above captioned matter.

Re New York letter dated 3/22/51 captioned, [redacted] Internal Security - R reporting the results of a detailed interview with [redacted] in Paris, France in January, 1951.

It is observed therein that [redacted] was apparently officially connected with the Communist regime of BELA KUN in Hungary in 1919. [redacted] indicated that he had resided in Hungary from at least 1905 to 1920 including attendance at law school at the University of Budapest from [redacted] military service in the Austrian-Hungarian army during 1913, 1915 and 1916, and employment after the war as [redacted]

b7D

[redacted] stated also that after his duties with [redacted] terminated in 1919, the Democratic Government in Hungary was overthrown and the Communist regime came in. He advised that he worked in the [redacted] under the Communist regime, the latter of which was BELA KUN. He was thereafter mobilized for the army as a Captain in charge of an artillery group when the Roumanian and Czechoslovakian armies invaded Hungary. He served in this position with the army until the end of the war in August, 1919.

[redacted] In view of the above information indicating participation by [redacted] in the Communist regime of BELA KUN in Hungary in 1919, it is suggested that the Bureau consider the advisability of having GIRARTI interviewed specifically concerning subject's activities in Hungary under BELA KUN in 1919.

As to Dr. THEODORE VON KARMAN, it is recalled that G-2 has furnished information concerning one TODAR KARMAN who was appointed Deputy Commisar of Cultural and Educational Affairs, in charge of higher education after the Communist uprising in Hungary during 1919 under the leadership of BELA KUN. This information also revealed that TODAR KARMAN later fled from Hungary to Germany where he continued his membership in the Communist Party.

JPA:res
105-863

100-372586

MAY 16 1951
10

ALL INFORMATION CONTAINED
HEREIN IS UNCLASSIFIED
DATE 6-25-97 BY

COPIES DESTROYED

b7C
b7D

CSI has further advised on 4/5/51 that a representative of that agency has interviewed one [redacted] of Achen, Germany on 3/19/51 and who described himself as a former very close friend of the subject and his family since about 1919. He advised that he had been informed by subject's mother and also one VON FAKLA that subject had been Minister of Culture in Hungary under BELA KUN in 1919 while the latter was in power for a few months.

TEXT ON THIS PAGE IS ILLEGIBLE
WE HAVE LEFT THE PAGE AS REFERENCE

SAC, NEW YORK June 1, 1951

DIRECTOR, FBI

THEODORE VON KARMAN, was.,
INTERNAL SECURITY - R

354-994
ALL INFORMATION CONTAINED
HEREIN IS UNCLASSIFIED
DATE 6/16/91 BY SP5...

Re New York report May 21, 1951.

b2
b7D

Pages 2 and 3 of referenced report reflect an interview with New York Confidential Informant [redacted] concerning subject. That part of the interview reported on page 3 states as follows:

"This meeting with the subject occurred in a local hotel, at which time the subject told the informant that Hungary was in good shape; that everything there was 'just fine', and generally impressed the informant by his Communistic and pro-Russian views concerning Hungary. The informant advised that because of his estimate of subject, resulting from the above conversation, he has never recontacted the subject."

While it is clear that the statement that subject generally impressed the informant by his Communistic and pro-Russian views concerning Hungary is an opinion of the informant, the report fails to reflect that the informant was questioned for further specific statements made by the subject which gave the informant the impression that subject had Communistic and pro-Russian views concerning Hungary.

The New York Office is to set out in a corrected page 3 any further specific information the informant may be able to furnish concerning his conversation with subject that supports the informant's opinion as reported above. In the event the informant, when interviewed, was requested to furnish additional information to support his opinion and was unable to do so, that fact should be stated in the report.

A corrected page 3 is to be furnished the Bureau and offices to whom referenced report was furnished at an early date.

100-372586-41

cc - Boston
Los Angeles
Washington Field

Note: Pertinent information in ref. report was previously furnished OSI by memorandum based on a NY tel.

100-372586-41

WAK:mes

EX-120

COMM - FBI
JUN 1 1951
MAILED 25

TEXT ON THIS PAGE IS ILLEGIBLE
WE HAVE LEFT THE PAGE AS REFERENCE

FD-72 (1-10-48)

# FEDERAL BUREAU OF INVESTIGATION

SECRET

FORM No. 1
THIS CASE ORIGINATED AT LOS ANGELES

NY FILE NO. 65-6747 GN

| REPORT MADE AT | DATE WHEN MADE | PERIOD FOR WHICH MADE | REPORT MADE BY |
|---|---|---|---|
| NEW YORK | 5/21/51 | 5/2,5,7,8,9,10,12/51. | [redacted] b7C |

TITLE

THEODORE VON KARMAN, was., Theodor Karman,
Theodr Von Szoelloestcictak

CHARACTER OF CASE

INTERNAL SECURITY - R

SEE REVERSE SIDE FOR ADD. DISSEMINATION.

AGENCY [redacted] b2
REQ. REC'D
REP'T FORW.
BY

SYNOPSIS OF FACTS:

CI advised acquaintance with subject by reputation, and knew him to be assistant to a professor at Jozsef Nador Technical University, of Budapest, Hungary, who joined BELA KUN Regime and probably took assistant professors, including subject, with him. Another CI states that in 1945, in NYC, sucject described Hungary with approval and impressed informant with Communistic and pro-Russian views. [redacted] who was acquainted with Commissar of Cultural and Educational Affairs in Hungary under BELA KUN, does not associate subject with that regime. Search of Columbia University Library records, NYC, for information concerning BELA KUN's association with subject, negative. Info concerning [redacted] [redacted] contact of subject, set out.

b2 b7D

AGENCY
REQ. REC'D
REP'T FORW.
BY

b7C

1 cc. with corrected page sent 6-25-51 via liason 6-25-51 WAK.

6-1-51 WAK:mcc

[redacted] b7C

CLASSIFIED BY
DECLASSIFY ON: 25X

APPROVED AND FORWARDED: Edward Schmidt SPECIAL AGENT IN CHARGE

DO NOT WRITE IN THESE SPACES

2 cc - CSC
8-28-64

COPIES OF THIS REPORT

5 Bureau (100-372586)
2 Boston
3 Los Angeles (105-8659)
2 Washington Field (65-1936)
3 New York

COPY IN FILE

MAY 23 1951

RECORDED - 52
INDEXED - 52

EX-59

PROPERTY OF FBI—This confidential report and its contents are loaned to you by the FBI and are not to be distributed outside of agency to which loaned.

ALL INFORMATION CONTAINED HERE IS UNCLASSIFIED EXCEPT WHERE SHOWN OTHERWISE

SECRET

DETAILS:

Confidential Informant [redacted] of known reliability, advised that he knew the subject in this country, although he never personally met him either in the United States or in Hungary. The informant advised that he knew all of the prominent persons in the BELA KUN Regime in Hungary, and that to the informant's knowledge the subject was not prominent, although the informant believed he was an Assistant Professor at the Jozsef Nador Technical University, in Budapest, under one Professor RADO KOVESLIGHETY, who was a Professor of Mathematics. b2 b7D

The informant stated that Professor KOVESLIGHETY joined the BELA KUN Regime and probably took his assistant professors, including the subject, with him. The informant did not know where the subject went after leaving Hungary, at the downfall of the BELA KUN Government, although he understood that he was later associated with the California Institute of Technology, Pasadena, California.

The informant continued that in 1945 or 1946 he discussed the subject with [redacted] Washington, D. C., and at that time the informant and [redacted] subject THEODORE VON KARMAN, should he try to approach them. This decision was reached after concluding that the subject [redacted] b7C b7D

[redacted] according to the informant, is a prominent Hungarian, who is well versed in the activities of Hungarian Nationals in this country, and is friendly with many former members of the Horthy Government in Hungary, which deposed BELA KUN.

Confidential Informant [redacted] of known reliability, advised that in 1945 after the subject returned to this country from a trip to Hungary, the informant contacted the subject on behalf of a local relief society b2 b7D

TEXT ON THIS PAGE IS ILLEGIBLE
WE HAVE LEFT THE PAGE AS REFERENCE



for the purpose of learning means of sending needed supplies, such as sulfa drugs, into Hungary. This meeting with the subject occurred in a local hotel, at which time the subject told the informant that Hungary was in good shape; that everything there was "just fine", and generally impressed the informant by his Communistic and pro-Russian views concerning Hungary. The informant advised that because of his estimate of subject, resulting from the above conversation, he has never recontacted the subject. Informant advised he could recall no further specific statements by subject which gave him this impression. He explained his conversation with subject was very brief and occurred six years ago.

b2 b7D

Confidential Informant [redacted] of known reliability, identified a recent photograph of the subject and stated that he was introduced to the subject in Hollywood, California, during 1937, at which time the informant went to Hollywood on a social visit. The informant did not recall the identity of the person who introduced him to VON KARMAN, but was told that VON KARMAN was an outstanding engineer in what he now recalls as aeronautics, and that he had held highly responsible positions with the United States Government. This informant is unaware of VON KARMAN'S present whereabouts.

Aside from the above social meeting, the informant subsequently met VON KARMAN from time to time in various Hungarian Restaurants, in New York City. The informant stated that he never met VON KARMAN in Hungary, and knew nothing of his background there, nor could the informant recall his name in connection with events during the BELA KUN Regime. The informant indicated, however, that during this commune he was acquainted with GYORGY LUKACS, the Commissar of Cultural and Educational Affairs, who is also a functionary of the present Hungarian Communist Regime.

According to information received at the Bureau from the Office of Special Investigations, United States Air Force, there was reported to be on file in the stacks at Columbia University, New York City, theses concerning the BELA KUN Coup, in Hungary, which may reflect information concerning the subject.

Special Agent (A) [redacted] through the cooperation of the Chief Librarian at Columbia University, made a thorough search of the records of that university library, which included Master and Doctors Degree theses, from 1891 to the present time. This search revealed no thesis on the BELA KUN Coup, in Hungary, nor any information which associated the subject with that regime. However, four items were located during this search, which are being listed for possible future use.

b7C

1. Volume of bound pamphlets entitled, "What is Communism," written by BELA KUN, preface by KISHKA, printed in Berlin, Gosudarst, 1920, in the Russian language, translated from German.

2. A book entitled, "The Most Burning Question - Unity of Action," written by BELA KUN, published by Workers Library Publishers, New York City, 1934. This book has been missing from Columbia Library since August, 1950.

3. A book entitled, "Otto Bauer's Weg", written by BELA KUN in the German language, published by Munchen Prometheus - Verlag, 1934.

4. A book entitled, "Revolutionary Essay", reprinted in the English language from "Pravda", London, England, 1918, by BELA KUN.

A review of the last book listed, the only one of the above list which was written in the English language, revealed no reference to the subject.

A search of the general indices of the Columbia Library concerning the name and known aliases of the subject reflected numerous references to the subject as the author of various scientific books and papers, but did not reveal any association of the subject with BELA KUN or his regime.

Confidential Informants [redacted] both of known reliability and who are generally acquainted with Communist activities in Germany during the 1920s, advised that they are not acquainted with the subject.

Confidential Informant [redacted] of known reliability, who is generally acquainted with German and Hungarian Communist activities during the 1920s, stated that he did not know THEODORE VON KARMAN, although he was acquainted with many BELA KUN functionaries.

Confidential Informant [redacted] of known reliability, advised that the subject had recently been in communication with one [redacted] New York 4, New York, and one [redacted] New York 21, New York.

No derogatory information was available in the files of the New York Office, which could be identified with these individuals. It was noted, however, that the current Manhattan Telephone Directory reflects that one [redacted]

Confidential Informant [redacted] of known reliability, advised that the subject also was recently in contact with a [redacted] New York City, and with a [redacted] Columbia University, whose home is in Danbury, Connecticut. No derogatory information is available in the files of the New York Office which can be identified with [redacted]

Concerning [redacted] who was contacted at [redacted] Confidential Informant [redacted] of known reliability, [redacted]

b2
b7D
b2
b7C
b7D

TEXT ON THIS PAGE IS ILLEGIBLE
WE HAVE LEFT THE PAGE AS REFERENCE



b1

[redacted] (S)

[redacted] (S)

[redacted] (S)

[redacted] (S)

* classified by letter dated 9-8-9?

b2 b7D

Confidential Informant [redacted] was thereafter interviewed by Agents of the New York Office, [redacted] (S)

b1 * classified per letter dated ?-?-98

TEXT ON THIS PAGE IS ILLEGIBLE
WE HAVE LEFT THE PAGE AS REFERENCE

SECRET

NY 65-6747

[redacted] (S)

b1 *classified per CIA letter dated 9-8-97

Confidential Informant [redacted] further stated that during his various associations with both [redacted] neither had indicated any Communist or pro-Russian sympathies to him.

b2 b7C b7D

- PENDING -



SECRET

TEXT ON THIS PAGE IS ILLEGIBLE
WE HAVE LEFT THE PAGE AS REFERENCE

XET

NY 65-6747

ADMINISTRATIVE PAGE

The Confidential Informants mentioned in the report of SA [redacted] dated 5/21/51 at New York, are identified as follows:

[redacted] [redacted] contacted by SA [redacted] on May 8 and 9, 1951.

[redacted] [redacted] contacted by SA [redacted] on May 9, 1951.

[redacted] [redacted] contacted by SA [redacted] on May 9, 1951.

[redacted] [redacted] contacted by SA [redacted] on May 11 and 12, 1951.

[redacted] [redacted] contacted by SA [redacted] on May 12, 1951.

[redacted] [redacted] He requested that his identity be kept confidential.

[redacted] Mail cover placed on the subject's residence at 1501 South Marengo Street, Pasadena, California, as set forth in the report of SA [redacted] 4/27/51, at Los Angeles.

[redacted] Confidential Source [redacted] as set forth in the report of SA [redacted] 4/27/51, at Los Angles.

[redacted] Confidential Source [redacted]



XET

b2 b7C b7D

TEXT ON THIS PAGE IS ILLEGIBLE
WE HAVE LEFT THE PAGE AS REFERENCE

SECRET

NY 65-6747

ADMINISTRATIVE PAGE

b1
b2
b7C
b7D

[redacted] (S) contacted by SA [redacted], on 5/15/51.

[redacted] contacted by SA [redacted] during the investigation of the case entitled, [redacted] was.; ATOMIC ENERGY ACT", NY file 117-128.

b1

[redacted] (S)

Classified per CIA letter dated 9-8-98

- 9 -

SECRET

SECRET

NY 65-6747

## LEADS

TO ALL OFFICES:

The Bureau has instructed that investigation in this case is to be given preferred handling and results to be submitted promptly for transmission to OSI. Further that the fact subject is under intensive investigation should not be revealed to persons interviewed.

BOSTON OFFICE

At Cambridge, Massachusetts

Will interview [redacted] Cambridge, Massachusetts, who is reported to be [redacted]

For the information of the Boston Office, by teletype dated May 12, 1951, the Bureau authorized this contact with [redacted] b7D

[redacted] has been contacted on several occasions on a confidential basis by SA [redacted] and former SA [redacted] of the New York Office, and he has furnished detailed information concerning [redacted] b7C

[redacted] is a close friend of [redacted] a confidential informant of this office. b7D

(Lead previously set forth in New York teletype, May 12, 1951, instant case.)



SECRET

SECRET

NY 65-6747

LEADS (CONT'D)

WASHINGTON FIELD OFFICE

At Washington, D. C.

Will interview [redacted] Washington, D. C., in accordance with Bureau instructions received in Bureau teletype of May 12, 1951. b7C b7D

NEW YORK OFFICE

At New York, New York

Will interview [redacted] in accordance with Bureau authority set forth in Bureau letter dated May 11, 1951. b7D

Will advise the Bureau of the return of confidential informant [redacted] from Europe, at which time the Bureau will give consideration to authorizing an interview with her concerning the subject's activities. b7C b7D

REFERENCE: Bureau letter to Los Angeles, 4/11/51.
Report of SA [redacted] 4/27/51, at Los Angeles. b7C
Report of SA [redacted] 5/3/51, at Washington, D. C.
Bureau teletype to New York, 5/7/51.
New York teletype to the Bureau, 5/9/51.
New York teletype to the Bureau, 5/12/51.
Bureau teletype to New York, 5/12/51.
Bureau letter to Los Angeles, 5/11/51

X

TEXT ON THIS PAGE IS ILLEGIBLE
WE HAVE LEFT THE PAGE AS REFERENCE

SECRET AIR COURIER

RECORDED - 35

Date: May 22, 1951

DECLASSIFIED BY 5055JC/pgs ON 6-19-97

To: Legal Attache
Paris, France

From: John Edgar Hoover - Director
Federal Bureau of Investigation

Subject: THEODORE VON KARMAN, was.,
INTERNAL SECURITY - R

Rebulet May 9, 1951.

There are attached for your information a copy of the report of Special Agent [redacted] dated April 27, 1951, and a recent photograph of subject which appeared in the January, 1951, issue of "Time" magazine. b7C

It will be noted that pages 8 and 16 of the attached report reflect that subject was Minister of Culture during the Bela Kun regime of 1919 in Hungary. It will also be noted on page 16 that subject is alleged to have transferred his Communist Party membership to the German Communist Party after fleeing Hungary during the same year.

A review of information recently received at the Bureau reflecting the results of an interview with [redacted] reveals that [redacted] was apparently officially connected with the Communist regime of Bela Kun in Hungary in 1919, and had worked in [redacted] under that Communist regime.

b7D

It is requested that you interview [redacted] at an early date for any information in his possession concerning subject's activity under the Bela Kun regime and concerning any knowledge that he may have of subversive activity on the part of subject.

Attachments
RAK:mes
100-372586
cc - Foreign Service Desk

BY SPL MSGR.
MAY 24 1951
COMM - FBI

STANDARD FORM NO. 64

TEXT ON THIS PAGE IS ILLEGIBLE
WE HAVE LEFT THE PAGE AS REFERENCE

# Office Memorandum • UNITED STATES GOVERNMENT

TO : MR. A. H. BELMONT

FROM : V. P. KEAY

SUBJECT: THEODORE VON KARMAN
INTERNAL SECURITY - R

DATE: May 15, 1951

Tolson, Ladd, Clegg, Glavin, Nichols, Rosen, Tracy, Harbo, Belmont, Mohr, Tele. Room, Nease, Gandy

354894
ALL INFORMATION CONTAINED
HEREIN IS UNCLASSIFIED
DATE 6-16-97 BY

Theodore Von Karman is presently Chairman of the Scientific Advisory Board of the Air Force and an investigation has been conducted by the Bureau, assisted by the Air Force, which has determined that he was Minister of Culture in Hungary [redacted] during the Communist Bela Kun regime some 32 years ago. The Bureau is presently conducting an internal security case concerning Von Karman and this investigation has, to date, failed to develop any current activities which would indicate Von Karman is engaging in espionage. b7C

Inquiries in this case were made in Europe by OSI. Von Karman, on May 14, 1951, returned to his office in the Pentagon Building, contacted the Vice Chief of Staff of the Air Force, and advised him that while in Europe he had determined that he was being investigated by the Air Force. Von Karman advised the Vice Chief of Staff that he had not belonged to the Communist Party in Germany, where he went after leaving Hungary, but apparently did not volunteer any information concerning his connection with the Bela Kun regime in Hungary.

[redacted] of OSI, has suggested that inasmuch as Von Karman is now aware of the investigation being made concerning him that it would in all probability be advisable, if the Bureau has no objections, to interrogate Von Karman at this time in connection with his past known Communist connections. In this connection, [redacted] noted that this investigation is, of course, within the Bureau's jurisdiction but that this case is probably the most important case OSI has at this time and that he [redacted] would appreciate it if the Bureau would allow [redacted] OSI Counterintelligence Division, to sit in with the Bureau Agent on the interrogation of Von Karman. It was noted by [redacted] that [redacted] is familiar with the Von Karman case and its ramifications in Europe. He is also familiar with Von Karman's work and relationship with the Air Force.

b7C

RECOMMENDATION:

RECORDED - 49
INDEXED - 49
MAY 25

It is recommended that Special Agent [redacted] of the Washington Field Office, be designated to interrogate Von Karman

ESS:jmr

HANDLED BY
STOP DESK

JUN 2 1951

inasmuch as [redacted] has previously handled this investigation in the Washington area, and it is further recommended that [redacted] of OSI Headquarters, be allowed to sit in on the interrogation as suggested by [redacted] Such interrogation would not interfere with the present investigation of Von Karman inasmuch as Von Karman is presently aware that such investigation is being conducted. It is felt that to allow [redacted] to sit in on this interrogation will contribute further to the close liaison between the Bureau and OSI, and will result in the Air Force being completely satisfied with the results of this investigation. It will allow the Air Force to cover any points which may be of interest to the Air Force which would not necessarily be apparent to the Bureau representatives.

ADDENDUM: May 15, 1951 WAK:mes

As you are aware, subject is considered the world's leading aerodynamicist. He has been associated with the Air Force in an advisory capacity since 1939. It is noted that in 1945, when applying for a re-entry permit, his sister, Josephine, gave as references [redacted] In addition to information hereinbefore set out, the investigation of subject is based on the fact that subject, in the early 1940's [redacted] working under him William Perl, a known Soviet agent. [redacted]

b7C

The Espionage Section agrees that an interview of subject is appropriate at this time as he is aware of the pending investigation and therefore little likelihood exists that he will continue subversive activity if ever so engaged. In addition, no allegation has been received that subject is engaged in subversive activity and as subject is Chairman of the Air Force Scientific Advisory Board, an interview may clarify his activities enabling the Air Force to make a determination as to his loyalty.

It is noted that subject has been interviewed on numerous occasions by the Bureau, most recently concerning William Perl. At that time subject advised he was completely unaware of any subversive activity on the part of Perl.

In view of the importance of this investigation to OSI, the close relationship which exists between the Bureau and that organization, and the fact that it does not appear that the presence of [redacted] OSI, a former Bureau Agent, will interfere with our interview, it is recommended that the joint interview be authorized.

RECOMMENDATIONS:

1. That WFO be advised of this new development in the investigation of subject, and that WFO be instructed to interview subject and be informed that authorization for [redacted] OSI to be present during the interview has been granted.

2. That WFO be instructed to specifically interview subject concerning the allegation that he was Minister of Culture under Bela Kun in Hungary in 1919 and that subject be also interviewed concerning his knowledge of Communist Party membership or subversive activity [redacted]

3. That subject be also interviewed concerning his association with [redacted] Because of the fact that [redacted] is presently under investigation, WFO should be instructed not to reveal the Bureau's intense interest in [redacted]

If you agree, there is attached an appropriate ~~teletype~~ Memo. to WFO.

Attachment

OK. b7C

- 3 -

TEXT ON THIS PAGE IS ILLEGIBLE
WE HAVE LEFT THE PAGE AS REFERENCE

Mr. Tolson
Mr. Ladd
Mr. Clegg
Mr. Glavin
Mr. Nichols
Mr. Rosen
Mr. Tracy
Tele. Room
Mr. Nease
Miss Gandy

WASHINGTON AND NEW YORK AND LOS ANGELES FROM WASH FIELD 17 6:50P.

DIRECTOR AND SACS DEFERRED

THEODORE VON KARMAN, WAS, IS DASH R. REBULET MAY FIFTEENTH, LAST. [redacted] OSI, ADVISES SUBJECT RETURNED LA MAY FIFTEENTH, AND NOT REVISITING D.C. UNTIL FALL THIS YEAR. [redacted] REQUESTS [redacted] OSI, LA, BE PERMITTED PARTICIPATE IN INTERVIEW OF SUBJECT BY BUREAU AGENTS IN LA. [redacted] FORWARDING COPIES OF OSI FILE RE SUBJECT TO [redacted] FOR THIS PURPOSE. LA AWAIT BUREAU INSTRUCTIONS BEFORE INTERVIEWING SUBJECT.

b7C

STEIN

RLS:MO'B

100-22923

354-894
ALL INFORMATION CONTAINED
HEREIN IS UNCLASSIFIED
DATE 6-16-97

RECORDED - 49

HANDLED BY
STOP DESK

100-37258-44

MAY 25 1951

5-18-51
Tel to L.A. + WFO
cc N.Y.

MAY 29

[redacted]

b7C

FEDERAL BUREAU OF INVESTIGATION
UNITED STATES DEPARTMENT OF JUSTICE

CC-150

TEXT ON THIS PAGE IS ILLEGIBLE
WE HAVE LEFT THE PAGE AS REFERENCE

To: COMMUNICATIONS SECTION.

May 18, 1951 URGENT

Transmit the following message to: SAC, LOS ANGELES
WASHINGTON FIELD (BSM)

THEODORE VON KARMAN, WAS., INTERNAL SECURITY - R. REBULET TO WFO MAY FIFTEEN LAST WITH COPY TO LA, AND WFO TEL MAY SEVENTEEN LAST. LA IS TO INTERVIEW SUBJECT IN ACCORDANCE WITH REFERENCED BULET. THE PRESENCE OF [redacted] OSI, DURING INTERVIEW IS AUTHORIZED UNLESS LA RELATIONSHIP WITH [redacted] IS NOT CORDIAL AND LA THEREBY OBJECTS. IN SUCH CASE, FULL FACTS ARE TO BE FURNISHED BUREAU. INTERVIEW IS TO BE CONDUCTED BY EXPERIENCED AGENT. SUTEL RESULTS.

b7C

HOOVER

CC: WASHINGTON FIELD (BY SPECIAL MESSENGER)

CC: NEW YORK (BY MAIL)

100-372586

WAK:mea

ALL INFORMATION CONTAINED HEREIN IS UNCLASSIFIED DATE 6-16-97

Note: Authority for interview recommended by memo from Keay to Belmont, May 17, 1951, and approved by Director. Same memo also authorized [redacted] OSI Counterintelligence Division, Washington, to attend interview at request of [redacted] As noted in referenced tel, subject departed from Washington on same date interview requested and authorized. It is noted that OSI, at that time, advised Liaison Agent [redacted] that subject would be in Washington for interview on May 17, 1951, although subject comes and goes as he pleases. As a joint interview of subject has already been authorized, it does not appear that Bureau should object to the replacement of [redacted] by [redacted] if LA relationship with [redacted] is cordial.

b7C

COPIES DESTROYED

APR 5 1963

Tolson, Ladd, Clegg, Glavin, Nichols, Rosen, Tracy, Mohr, Tele. Room, Gandy

HANDLED BY STOP DESK

INITIALED DIRECTOR'S OFFICE

RECORDED - 49 MAY 25 1951

100-372586

MAY 29 1951

M Per

100-372586

FEDERAL BUREAU OF INVESTIGATION
U. S. DEPARTMENT OF JUSTICE
COMMUNICATIONS SECTION

MAY 16 1951

TELETYPE

TEXT ON THIS PAGE IS ILLEGIBLE
WE HAVE LEFT THE PAGE AS REFERENCE

8-25 PM

WASHINGTON 7 AND NEW YORK 4 FROM BOSTON 5-16

DIRECTOR AND SAC DEFERRED

[redacted] b7C

THEODORE VON KARMEN, WAS, IS DASH R. RENYTEL MAY TWELVE LAST. [redacted] ON INTERVIEW THIS DATE STATED SUBJECT COMPLETELY UNKNOWN TO HIM AND THAT SO FAR AS HE IS AWARE HE HAS NEVER HEARD MENTION OF SUBJECT-S NAME. [redacted] WAS UNACQUAINTED WITH INDIVIDUALS ACTIVE IN CP AT AACHEN, GERMANY, WITH EXCEPTION OF ONE [redacted]

b7C
b7D

REPORT FOLLOWS.

THORNTON RECORDED-19

HOLD

ALL INFORMATION CONTAINED HEREIN IS UNCLASSIFIED DATE 5-26-98 BY

MAY 25 1951

50 JUN 1 1951

HANDLED BY STOP DESK

SAC, LOS ANGELES

May 15, 1951

DIRECTOR, FBI

THEODORE VON KARMAN, was.,
INTERNAL SECURITY - R

TEXT ON THIS PAGE IS ILLEGIBLE
WE HAVE LEFT THE PAGE AS REFERENCE

Re Los Angeles report dated April 27, 1951, which reflects that subject has been in contact with [redacted] New York, New York, [redacted]

The attention of Los Angeles and New York is called to the New York report dated July 17, 1950, entitled [redacted] was., AEA," a copy of which is in the possession of the Los Angeles Office (Los Angeles file 117-83; New York file 117-126).

New York is to determine if [redacted] mentioned in referenced report, is identical with Bureau subject [redacted]

100-372586

cc - New York

WAK:mes

ALL INFORMATION CONTAINED
HEREIN IS UNCLASSIFIED
DATE 6-16-92 BY SPS JC/ajn

b7C

MAY 15 1951
COMM - FBI

RECORDED-19
EX-130

MAY 17 1951
80

JUN 1 1951

TEXT ON THIS PAGE IS ILLEGIBLE
WE HAVE LEFT THE PAGE AS REFERENCE

MR. [illegible]

May 26, 1951

MR. [illegible]

[illegible], was.
[illegible] - R

[illegible]

[redacted]

Referred

DETAILS

[redacted] teletype 5/23/51 advised that, according to [redacted] Rosenberg made statement that on holiday weekend, which he felt was July 4th of last year, Perl removed secret files from Laboratory at Columbia University, took them to Rosenberg's apartment where [illegible], Perl, a man from out of town whom [redacted] believed to be [redacted] and a fourth man spent 17 hours with two cameras photographing the material so that Perl could return it.

b7C
b7D

Cleveland teletype 5/24/51 pointed out that on basis of check of Perl's and [redacted] leave records there appeared little likelihood of this being done on July 4th in 1949 or 1950. However, this teletype suggested that it could have been done on July 4, 1949, as both Perl and [redacted] had leave over this period.

Referred

[redacted]

65-[illegible]
cc: 65-[illegible] (Perl)
100-[illegible] ([illegible])

100-[illegible]
NOT RECORDED
45 JUN [illegible] 1951

[illegible]

Attachment (Tel to Knoxville)

[redacted] b7C



ORIGINAL FILED IN

TEXT ON THIS PAGE IS ILLEGIBLE
WE HAVE LEFT THE PAGE AS REFERENCE

[redacted]

Referred

RECOMMENDATION

It is recommended that the attached teletype be sent to Knoxville requesting an immediate check at NEPA in Oak Ridge to determine whether they furnished to Von Neumann either the "Lexington Report" or any confidential reports on the NEPA Project.

It further recommend that through Liaison a similar check be made at the U. S. Air Force to determine whether they may have made available any such reports to Von Neumann.

TEXT ON THIS PAGE IS ILLEGIBLE
WE HAVE LEFT THE PAGE AS REFERENCE

MAY 12 1951

TELETYPE

CONF WASHINGTON 30 AND BOSTON 3 FROM NEW YORK 12 645 P

DIRECTOR AND SAC DEFERRED

ALL INFORMATION CONTAINED
HEREIN IS UNCLASSIFIED
DATE 6-16-97 BY

THEODORE VON KARMAN, WAS, THEODOR KARMAN, THEODOR VON SZOELLOESTCICTAK, ISR. REBUTEL MAY TWELVE INST. INFO OBTAINED MAY TWELVE THAT CI [redacted] IS STILL IN EUROPE AND DATE OF RETURN INDEFINITE. NYO WILL ADVISE BUREAU WHEN SPECIFIC INFO RE HER RETURN OBTAINED. [redacted] ADVISED MAY TWELVE THAT [redacted] IN VIEW THEREOF BOSTON REQUESTED TO INTERVIEW [redacted] FOR ALL INFO RE VON KARMAN. FOR INFO BOSTON, [redacted] HAS BEEN CONTACTED ON CONFIDENTIAL BASIS SEVERAL TIMES BY SA [redacted] AND FORMER SA [redacted] OF NYO AND HAS FURNISHED NYO DETAILED INFO RE [redacted] IS CLOSE FRIEND OF [redacted] A CI OF THIS OFFICE. RE VON KARMAN, BOSTON REFER REPT SA [redacted] MAY THREE INST, WASH, DC, PAGE SIX, FOR BACKGROUND INFO. NOTED FURTHER SUBJECT IS SEVENTYSIX YEAR OLD WORLD RENOWNED AERODYNAMIST WHO CAME TO THIS COUNTRY IN NINETEEN THIRTY AND FROM NINETEEN THIRTY TO FORTYTWO EMPLOYED AS DIRECTOR OF GUGGENHEIM AERONAUTICAL LAB, CALTECH, PASADENA, CALIF. LATER ACTED AS CONSULTANT FOR NATIONAL ADVISORY COMMITTEE FOR AERONAUTICS AND CURRENTLY IS

b7C
b7D

RECORDED 19
MAY 25 1951

56 JUN 8 1951

HANDLED BY

END PAGE ONE

cc: [redacted]

b7C

PAGE TWO

CHAIRMAN OF SCIENTIFIC ADVISORY BOARD, DEPT. OF AIR FORCE, PENTAGON BLDG, WASH, DC. AS SUCH HE HAS CONTINUAL ACCESS TO INFO PERTAINING TO HIGHLY SENSITIVE AERO RESEARCH. BUREAU HAS INSTRUCTED INVESTIGATION THIS CASE TO BE GIVEN PREFERRED HANDLING AND RESULTS TO BE SUBMITTED PROMPTLY TO BUREAU FOR TRANSMISSION TO OSI. FURTHER THAT THE FACT THAT SUBJECT IS UNDER INTENSIVE INVESTIGATION SHOULD NOT BE REVEALED DURING INTERVIEW. FOR INFO BUREAU, NYO HOLDING INTERVIEW OF [redacted] IN ABEYANCE UNTIL BUREAU AUTHORITY RECD. LA ORIGIN. SUTEL AND SUREP.

b7D

Sent.

SCHEIDT

END, AAD PLS

WA $ NY R 30 WA JD

BS NY R 3 BS NER

DEPARTMENT OF JUSTICE
COMMUNICATIONS SECTION

MAY 24 1951

TELETYPE

TEXT ON THIS PAGE IS ILLEGIBLE
WE HAVE LEFT THE PAGE AS REFERENCE

ALL INFORMATION CONTAINED
HEREIN IS UNCLASSIFIED
DATE 6-16-97 BY

WASH AND WFO 1 FROM LOS ANGELES 23 /24/ 9-45 PM

DIRECTOR, FBI AND SAC, WASHINGTON FIELD DEFERRED [redacted] b7C

THEODORE VON KARMAN, IS-R, BUFILE ONE HUNDRED DASH THREE SEVEN TWO FIVE EIGHT SIX. REBUTEL MAY EIGHTEEN LAST. SUBJECT INTERVIEWED MAY TWENTY-THIRD INSTANT BY SA [redacted] AT LA OFFICE IN THE PRESENCE OF [redacted] OSI, AT WHICH TIME HE ADMITS SUBSTANTIALLY AS FOLLOWS CONCERNING HIS AFFILIATION WITH THE COMMUNISTS BELA KUN REGIME IN HUNGARY IN NINETEEN NINETEEN. SUBJECT IN NINETEEN TWELVE WAS APPOINTED PROFESSOR OF AEURONAUTICS AT AACHEN, GERMANY. IN NINETEEN FOURTEEN, HOLDING A RESERVE COMMISSION, HE WAS CALLED BACK INTO THE AUSTRO DASH HUNGARIAN ARMY AND WAS ENGAGED IN AIR FORCE RESEARCH AND DEVELOPMENT UNTIL DESITERGRATION OF THE ARMY IN LATE NINETEEN EIGHTEEN. ABOUT DEC. NINETEEN EIGHTEEN, BEING STILL ON LEAVE OF ABSENCE FROM UNIVERSITY OF AACHEN, HE BECAME PART TIME ADVISOR TO EUGENE GONCI, ASST. SECRETARY OF EDUCATION UNDER COUNT MICHAEL KAROLYI, PRES. OF THE INDEPENDENT REPUBLIC OF HUNGARY. GONCI-S SUPERIOR AND MINISTER OF EDUCATION WAS SIEGMEND KUNFI. SUBJECT ALSO THEN GAVE A COURSE OF LECTURES AT THE JOZSEF NADOR TECHNICAL UNIVERSITY AT BUDAPEST. UPON THE SURRENDER OF THE GOVT. BY KAROLYI TO COMMUNIST BELA KUN IN MARCH NINETEEN NINETEEN, GONCI TELEPHONED SUBJECT TO STAY ON IN HIS POSITION TO WHICH SUBJECT REPLIED THAT HE WOULD TRY AND DID REMAIN. KUNFI AND GONCI WERE BOTH TEMPORARILY CARRIED OVER BY THE BELA KUN REGIME, BUT REPLACED AFTER ABOUT TWO MONTHS BY GEORGE LUKACS, WHO WAS A COMMUNIST AND WHOSE TITLE

RECORDED - 127 100-37286-4
EX. - 120 MAY 31 1951

78 APR 5 1964

JUN 9 1951

TWO COPIES

HANDLED BY

WAS PEOPLES COMMISSARIATE FOR EDUCATIONAL AFFAIRS. SUBJECT CONTINUED HIS DUTIES AS QUOTE ADVISOR UNQUOTE UNDER THE BELA KUN REGIME TO BOTH KUNFI, GONCI, AND THEIR SUCCESSOR LUKACS UNTIL THE COLLAPSE OF THE BELA KUN REGIME AT THE END OF JULY, NINETEEN NINETEEN. SUBJECT WITH THE TITLE OF GROUP LEADER HAD AN OFFICE IN THE MINISTRY BLDG. OF BUDAPEST AND HIS DUTIES CONSISTED OF PLANNING FOR UNIVERSITY EDUCATION, CHOOSING PROFESSORS AND PREPARING COURSES OF STUDY FOR BOTH SCIENCE AND ENGINEERING. AFTER ABOUT ONE MONTH IN THE BELA KUN REGIME, HIS DUTIES INCREASED SO THAT HE WAS THEREAFTER SO ENGAGED FULL TIME AL-THOUGH ALSO DOING SOME LECTURING AT THE SAME TIME. WHILE SO ENGAGED SUBJECT BELIEVES THAT HE RECEIVED COMPENSATION FROM THE BELA KUN REGIME AND ALSO WAS COMPENSATED AS AN ARMY OFFICER AND FROM HIS LECTURING. UPON THE COLLAPSE OF THE BELA KUN REGIME, SUBJECT REMAINED IN BUDAPEST ABOUT A WEEK AND THROUGH FRIENDS IN THE AIR FORCE WAS TRANSPORTED TO VIENNA AND THENCE TO AACHEN, LEAVING HIS MOTHER AND SISTER BEHIND. HIS PURPOSE IN HASTILY LEAVING WAS TO AVOID NECESSARY EXPLANATIONS. SUBJECT ATTEMPTS TO EXPLAIN HIS FORMER AFFILIATION WITH THE BELA KUN REGIME AS PROMPTED BY, ONE DASH INFLUENCE OF FRIENDS AT THE UNIV. OF BUDAPEST WHO PREVALED UPON HIM TO PARTICIPATE FOR THE PRESERVATION OF THE HUNGARIAN SYSTEM OF EDUCATION. TWO DASH HIS OWN DESIRE TO PREVENT

THE COMMUNIST INFLUENCE FROM DESTROYING THE COUNTRY-S EDUCATIONAL SYSTEM. THREE DASH HIS BELIEF THAT THE COMMUNIST CONTROL WAS ONLY A TEMPORARY THING. FOUR DASH HIS ADMITTED DESIRE TO PRESERVE HIS OWN LIFE, THAT OF HIS FAMILY, PRESERVATION OF FAMILY PROPERTY AND FATHERS LIBRARY. SUBJECT DENIES ANY PAST OR PRESENT INTEREST IN COMMUNISM, DENIES THAT HE WAS A MEMBER OF THE CP UNDER THE BELA KUN REGIME PRIOR OR SINCE, AND WAS NEVER ASKED OR REQUIRED BY THE BELA KUN GOVT. TO BE A MEMBER. HE HAD NO PERSONAL DEALINGS WITH BELA KUN AND HAD NEVER SEEN HIM. SUBJECT STATED THAT HE DID NOT CONSIDER HIMSELF AS HAVING BEEN ASSOCIATED WITH THE BELA KUN REGIME, BUT CONSIDERED HIMSELF RATHER AS AN OUTSIDE ADVISOR ALTHOUGH HE HAD AN OFFICE IN THE MINISTRY BLDG. HE NEVER RECEIVED ANY INSTRUCTIONS TO PUT COMMUNIST PROPAGANDA INTO THE SCHOOLS AND ASSOCIATED WITH REGULAR CIVIL SERVICE PEOPLE, VERY FEW OF WHOM WERE COMMUNIST EXCEPT AT THE VERY TOP. SUBJECT REMARKED THAT HE ONCE TOLD THE BELA KUN AUTHORITIES THAT HE WAS IN AN INDEPENDENT POSITION, WAS AGAINST THEIR THEORIES AND THAT SUBJECT WAS CALLED QUOTE MR. PROFESSOR UNQUOTE AND NEVER QUOTE COMRADE UNQUOTE. SUBJECT ADDED THAT IF ONE IS UNDER THE COMMUNIST REGIME FOR FOUR MONTHS AS HE WAS, QUOTE YOU ARE IMMUNIZED FOR LIFE UNQUOTE. SUBJECT STATED THAT HIS IDENTIFICATION WITH THE COMMUNIST BELA KUN GOVT. IN NINETEEN NINETEEN HAS NEVER BEEN RAISED EXCEPT ON ONE OCCASION IN ABOUT NINETEEN TWENTY DASH TWENTYONE

END PAGE THREE

TEXT ON THIS PAGE IS ILLEGIBLE
WE HAVE LEFT THE PAGE AS REFERENCE



WHEN HE WAS A MEMBER OF THE GERMAN EQUIVALENT OF THE SCIENTIFIC SOCIETY FOR AERONAUTICS AT BERLIN. AT THAT TIME HE WAS QUESTIONED BY ABOVE S SOCIETY, EXPLAINED CIRCUMSTANCES, AND ALSO EXHIBITED TO THEM A LETTER FURNISHED BY ALEXANDER IMRI, MINISTER OF EDUCATION IN THE GOVERNMENT SUCCEEDING THE BELA KUN REGIME WHEREIN SUBJECT WAS COMMENDED FOR PROTECTING THE EDUCATIONAL SYSTEM OF HUNGARY BY HIS EFFORTS. SUBJECT ALSO ADVISED THAT UPON HIS RECENT RETURN TO THE PENTAGON FROM EUROPE WHERE HE LEARNED OF A CURRENT INVESTIGATION RE HIM, HE PERSONALLY CONTACTED [redacted] VICE CHIEF, U.S. AIR FORCE, WASH. D.C. AND INFORMED HIM OF HIS ABOVE ASSOCIATION WITH BELA KUN GOVT. SUBJECT CLAIMS HE HAS NEVER BEEN APPROACHED BY UNAUTHORIZED INDIVIDUALS FOR SECRET INFO. ON BEHALF OF A FOREIGN POWER. ALSO CLAIMS NO FIRST HAND KNOWLEDGE OF CP MEMBERSHIP OR SUBVERSIVE ACTIVITIES [redacted] IT IS OBSERVED THAT SUBJECT WAS VERY COOPERATIVE BUT EXPRESSED A DESIRE THAT ANY EMBARRASSMENT TO HIM OR THE U.S. AIRFORCE BY NEWSPAPER PUBLICITY BY THIS DISCLOSURE BE AVOIDED. FOR INFO. OF WFO RECORDS OF LA PUBLIC LIBRARY INDICATE THE COMMUNIST BELA KUN REGIME WAS IN POWER FROM THREE TWENTYTWO NINETEEN TO SEVEN THIRTYONE NINETEEN, WAS GRANTED SAFE CONDUCT BY ALLIES TO ¢ GERMANY, REACHED PETROGRAD, RUSSIA ON EIGHT FOURTEEN NINETEEN WHERE A RECEPTION WAS GIVEN IN HIS HONOR ON EIGHT NINETEEN NINETEEN BY SOVIET OFFICIALS. REPORT FOLLOWS.

HOOD

HOLD

b7C

b7C

CC [redacted]

b7C

TEXT ON THIS PAGE IS ILLEGIBLE
WE HAVE LEFT THE PAGE AS REFERENCE

STANDARD FORM NO. 64

# Office Mem... ..um • UNITED STAT... GOVERNMENT

TO : Director, FBI DATE: June 1, 1951

FROM : SAC, Los Angeles

SUBJECT: THEODORE VON KARMAN, was.
INTERNAL SECURITY - R
(Bufile 100-372586)

G.I.R.-1

Rebulet dated May 23, 1951.

In view of subject's detailed explanation of his connection with the Communist Bela Kun Regime in 1919, as furnished by him upon interview on May 23, 1951, results of which were reported in Los Angeles teletype of the same date, a spot surveillance of the subject is not considered advisable, and is not contemplated by this office at this time.

JPA:mkm
105-863

RECORDED - 119 ... 372586-50
JUN 7 1951
10

FIVE 10 [redacted]
b7C

50JUN25 1951
61

ALL INFORMATION CONTAINED
HEREIN IS UNCLASSIFIED
DATE 6-11-97 BY ...

TEXT ON THIS PAGE IS ILLEGIBLE
WE HAVE LEFT THE PAGE AS REFERENCE

SAC, NEW YORK

June 26, 1951

DIRECTOR, FBI

THEODORE VON KARMAN, was.,
INTERNAL SECURITY - R

Reurlet June 7, 1951.

You are authorized to interview [redacted] for any information in her possession concerning possible membership or activity in the Communist Party on the part of subject.

b7C
b7D

The interview is to be conducted in a manner that will not embarrass the Bureau.

RECORDED - 61

100-372586 51

cc - Los Angeles

WAK:mes

Subject is presently Chairman of the Scientific Advisory Board of the Department of the Air Force. He is being investigated at the request of the Air Force on the basis of an allegation that he was Commissar of Education during the short-lived Bela Kun uprising in Hungary during 1918 and 1919. Subject has been interviewed and he has admitted occupying an official position in the Beh Kun Government, but has denied Communist Party membership. The original allegation in this matter also alleges that subject, after leaving Hungary in 1919 was a member of the German Communist Party. It will be noted that [redacted] and has been frequently interviewed by New York during which interviews she has been cooperative. [redacted] it is logical that she be interviewed concerning subject.

b7C
b7D

Tolson
Ladd
Clegg
Glavin
Nichols
Rosen
Tracy
Harbo
Alden

359-894
ALL INFORMATION CONTAINED
HEREIN IS UNCLASSIFIED
DATE 6-16-97 BY SPS

COMM - FBI
JUN 27 1951

# Office Memorandum • UNITED STATES GOVERNMENT

TO : Director, FBI DATE: June 7, 1951

FROM : SAC, New York

SUBJECT: THEODORE VON KARMAN, was; IS - R (Bufile 100-372586)

ALL INFORMATION CONTAINED HEREIN IS UNCLASSIFIED DATE 6-16-92

Rebulet 6/1/51.

Attached hereto are five copies of a Corrected page 3 to be substituted for page 3 of N.Y. report dated 5/21/51. Appropriate copies of this page are enclosed for those offices reviewing copies of this letter.

For the information of the Bureau and Los Angeles, [redacted] has advised that he does not know THEODORE VON KARMAN under his true name or known aliases, nor could he identify a photo of subject. He stated that he has a faint recollection of a Professor KARMAN in Budapest who was an old man thirty years ago and if this individual was in any way connected with subject, he must have been subject's father. However, he could give no further information concerning this Professor KARMAN, or whether he in fact had a son or other relative who could have been identified with subject. b7D

It should be noted that [redacted] advised he was in March, 1919, [redacted] the MIHALY KAROLYI government in Hungary and in such capacity [redacted] of BELA KUN and a number of other Communist leaders of that regime. He stated that he was thus well acquainted with the various top level functionaries but could not recall specifically who were the Commissar or Deputy Commissars of Cultural and Educational Affairs, and definitely did not associate subject's name with these offices. According to the [redacted] issue of "Amerikai Magyar Nepszava", a Hungarian language newspaper published in New York City, [redacted] b7D

RECORDED - 8

100-372586-51

Encls (5)
cc-Boston (Encls (2))
cc-Los Angeles (Encls 3)
cc-Washington Field (2) Encls)

JUN 8 1951

MWC:LEW
65-6747

HANDLED BY STOP DESK

Letter to Director
NY 65-6747

[redacted] b7D

b2 b7C b7D

For the additional information of the Bureau, CI [redacted] advised this office on 6/6/51 that [redacted] returned to NYC from Europe on [redacted]. In accordance with instructions in Butel 5/12/51, the Bureau is requested to advise this office if it desires that [redacted] be contacted concerning the subject.

FEDERAL BUREAU OF INVESTIGATION

ORIGIN: LOS ANGELES

BS File No. 65-1838 RMT

| MADE AT: | DATE: | PERIOD: | MADE BY: |
|---|---|---|---|
| BOSTON, MASS. | 6-8-51 | 5/15,19/51 | [redacted] b7C |

| TITLE: | CHARACTER: |
|---|---|
| THEODORE VON KARMAN | INTERNAL SECURITY - R |

SYNOPSIS:

[redacted] stated on May 15, 1951, that the Subject is unknown to him and he is not aware of ever having heard reference to the Subject's name. [redacted] advised the reign of terror initiated by the regime succeeding the Hungarian Bela Kun Government in 1919, was equally anti-Semitic and anti-Communistic.

AGENCY ICC [redacted] b2
REQ. REC'D
REP'T FORW. 1/5/55
BY

AGENCY ICC State
REQ. REC'D 6-26-56
REP'T FORW. 7-13-56
BY ALF

SEE REVERSE SIDE FOR ADD. DISSEMINATION. - RUC -

AGENCY
REQ. REC'D 1-15-
REP'T FORW. 1-2
BY

DETAILS:

[redacted] interviewed on May 15, 1951, stated he did not know VON KARMAN by his true name or by the name of those aliases which are known to this office. He stated he was not aware of ever having heard information regarding the Subject.

b7D

Concerning activities within Hungary following the overthrow of the Bela Kun Government, [redacted] advised the succeeding Social Democrats found it politically expedient to institute a reign of terror which was equally directed against Semitics as well as Communists. This policy, according to [redacted] caused hundreds to flee because of the racial discrimination, and he cautioned that all those who fled Hungary at that time could not accordingly be classified as political refugees.

ICC OSI via liaison 6-25-51 WAK

1cc McInerney 6/29/57 WAK

- REFERRED UPON COMPLETION TO THE OFFICE OF ORIGIN -

APP. & FOR. J E Thornton SAC

DO NOT WRITE IN THESE SPACES

RECORDED - 126

INDEXED - 126

JUN 11 1951

COPIES:
5 - Bureau (100-372586)
3 - Los Angeles (65-1936)
1 - Washington Field (100-22923) (Info.)
1 - New York (Info.)

TEXT ON THIS PAGE IS ILLEGIBLE
WE HAVE LEFT THE PAGE AS REFERENCE



Reference

New York teletype to Bureau and Boston Office dated May 12, 1951.

SAC, LOS ANGELES June 2, 1951

DIRECTOR, FBI

THEODORE VON KARMAN, was.,
INTERNAL SECURITY - R

Rebulet 5-22-51.

There is attached for your information a copy of OSI report dated May 1, 1951, concerning subject.

Pertinent information which appears in the attachment is to be set out in your next investigative report.

100-372586 - 53

Attachment
WAK:mes

TEXT ON THIS PAGE IS ILLEGIBLE
WE HAVE LEFT THE PAGE AS REFERENCE

FD-77

# FEDERAL BUREAU OF INVESTIGATION

Form No. 1
THIS CASE ORIGINATED AT LOS ANGELES

SEE REVERSE SIDE FOR ADD. DISSEMINATION

FILE No. 105-863

| REPORT MADE AT | DATE WHEN MADE | PERIOD FOR WHICH MADE | REPORT MADE BY |
|---|---|---|---|
| LOS ANGELES | 6/13/51 | 5/23,29,31;6/1/51 | [redacted] b7C |

| TITLE | CHARACTER OF CASE |
|---|---|
| CHANGED: THEODORE VON KARMAN, was., Theodore De Karman, Todor Karman, Todor Szolloskislaki Karman, Theodor Karman, Theodor Von Karman, Theodor Karman Von Szolloskistak | INTERNAL SECURITY - R |

SYNOPSIS OF FACTS:

AGENCY ICC [redacted] b2
REQ. REC'D 12/20/54
REP'T FORW. 1/5/55
BY

Dr. THEODORE VON KARMAN interviewed on 5/23/51 and 5/29/51 at which time he admitted having been formerly associated with the Communist BELA KUN government in Hungary from March to July, 1919 as an Advisor with the title of Group Leader in the People's Commissariat for Educational Affairs. Attempts to explain action as a required matter of expediency to help preserve educational system of Hungary, to preserve his own life and that of his family, and to preserve family property. Denies he was then or has ever been a member of the Communist Party or that he has furnished or been requested to furnish classified information to any unauthorized person. Details furnished and set out. Disclaims any personal knowledge of Communist Party membership or subversive activity [redacted] Biographical sketch of BELA KUN set out. Former European associates affirm subject's association with BELA KUN government. b7C

AGENCY Photo USAF
REQ. REC'D 1-15-58
REP'T FORW. 1-24-58
BY

AGENCY State
REQ. REC'D 6-26-56
REP'T FORW. 7-13-56
BY

DETAILS:

The title of this report is being marked changed in order to reflect subject's correct name as currently used and variations ascertained from interview and available records.

SEE REVERSE SIDE FOR ADD. DISSEMINATION.

ALL INFORMATION CONTAINED HEREIN IS UNCLASSIFIED DATE 6-16-97 BY

HANDLED BY

APPROVED AND FORWARDED: SPECIAL AGENT IN CHARGE

DO NOT WRITE IN THESE SPACES

100-372586-54

SE

PROPERTY OF FBI
This confidential report and its contents are loaned to you by the FBI and are not to be distributed outside of agency to which loaned -

RECORDED - 39
JUN 19 1951
INDEXED - 39

COPIES OF THIS REPORT
6 - Bureau (100-372586)
3 - Washington Field (100-22923)
2 - Boston
2 - Cincinnati
2 - New York (65-6747)
2 - OSI, District 18, Maywood (Enc.)
5 - Los Angeles

50 JUN 28

U. S. GOVERNMENT PRINTING OFFICE 16-57982-1

TEXT ON THIS PAGE IS ILLEGIBLE
WE HAVE LEFT THE PAGE AS REFERENCE



TABLE OF CONTENTS

I. INTERVIEW WITH DR. THEODORE VON KARMAN

Dr. THEODORE VON KARMAN, Chairman, Scientific Advisory Board, Department of the Air Force, 1501 South Marengo Avenue, Pasadena, California, was interviewed by the writer on May 23 and May 29, 1951 at the Los Angeles Office in the presence of [redacted] U. S. Air Force, Maywood, California. He furnished substantially the following information after first being informed that he was not required to make any statement whatever and that he had a right to be represented by counsel.

b7C

He was born on May 11, 1881 at Budapest, Hungary and received his early education there. During 1902-03, he served the required one year of military duty in the Austrian-Hungarian Army and then attended Jozsef Nador Technical University in Budapest from 1903 to 1906. In 1906 he entered the University of Goettingen at Goettingen, Germany, from which he received a Ph.D in 1909. From 1909 to 1912 he was engaged as a lecturer at the University of Goettingen.

In 1912 he was appointed Professor and Director of the Aeronautical Laboratory at the University of Aachen at Aachen, Germany. In August, 1914, holding a Reserve commission in the Austrian-Hungarian Army, although a German citizen, he was called back into service where he was engaged as a Department Head in the Air Force Research and Development Division. He held the rank of First Lieutenant and developed, among other things, the first helicopter and the first sealed gas tank. He served in this capacity until the disintegration of the Army in late 1918.

About December, 1918, being still on leave of absence from the University of Aachen, and because of Armistice conditions it was impossible for him to return to occupied Aachen, he became a part time Advisor to his friend EUGENE GONCI who was then Assistant Secretary of Education under Count MICHAEL KAROLYI, President of the Independent Republic of Hungary. At the same time he gave a course of lectures on Aeronautics at the Jozsef Nador Technical University in Budapest. GONCI'S superior and Minister of Education was SIEGMUND KUNFI.

Upon the surrender of the government by Count KAROLYI to Communist BELA KUN in March, 1919, GONCI personally telephoned the subject and requested him to stay on in his position to which VON KARMAN replied that he "would try" and in fact, did remain.

Both SIEGMUND KUNFI and EUGENE GONCI, who were non-Communists, were temporarily carried over by the BELA KUN regime, but GONCI resigned later and after about two months, it was believed, KUNFI was replaced by GEORGE LUKACS, who was definitely a Communist, and whose title was People's Commissar for Educational Affairs. LUKACS' immediate assistant was EMERIC FOGARASI, who, of course, was also a Communist.

VON KARMAN continued his duties as Advisor under the BELA KUN regime to KUNFI, GONCI and their successors LUKACS and FOGARASI until the collapse of the BELA KUN government near the end of July, 1919. He had a title of Group Leader in the People's Commissariat for Educational Affairs and had an office in the Ministry Building in Budapest. He never had any other title.

Subject's duties as Advisor consisted of planning for University education and included the choosing of professors and the preparation of curricula of study in the Science and Engineering fields in cooperation with the universities. After about one month in the BELA KUN regime, his former part time duties gradually increased so that he was actually thereafter so engaged full time, although he was also able to do some lecturing.

While so engaged as Advisor, he believes that he received compensation from the BELA KUN Government for his services, although he did not pay attention to the financial aspect because the money issued by the Communists was practically worthless. In addition, for some time thereafter he continued receiving regular Army pay as an Army officer, and he also received compensation from his lecturing.

Upon the collapse of the BELA KUN regime, VON KARMAN remained in Budapest approximately one week and then, with the assistance of STEPHEN FAKLA, an old Army officer friend with whom he had served in the Imperial Air Force, he was able to leave Hungary. FAKLA was then still an active Air Force officer in 1919 although disapproving of the Communist government. Upon the overthrow of the BELA KUN regime, FAKLA arranged to get an army plane and transport the subject to the Austrian frontier. From there subject crossed the frontier with a regular passport and then proceeded to Aachen, Germany. His mother and sister remained in Budapest where they continued to reside until 1930.

Subject explained that he left Budapest in order to return to his work at the University of Aachen and also to avoid a lot of explaining that might naturally have been required. His prior fears and concern for the life of his mother and sister, left behind, and the preservation of family property did not still exist inasmuch as he felt that the Allies

TEXT ON THIS PAGE IS ILLEGIBLE
WE HAVE LEFT THE PAGE AS REFERENCE



who would follow could well maintain a good government. He returned to Hungary in 1921 on a Hungarian passport, had no trouble whatever, and did not consider himself as a refugee.

VON KARMAN gave the following explanation and reasons for his connection with the BELA KUN Government:

1. He stated that friends at the University of Budapest prevailed upon him to stay with the Ministry of Education in order to preserve the Hungarian system of education. In this regard he pointed out that he was very well known there and that his father MAURICE KARMAN had previously been a Professor at the University of Budapest until his death in 1915. His father had also been an Advisor to the Minister of Education from 1909 to 1915 under the Royal regime of Count APPONYI.

2. He stated that he had a personal desire to prevent the Communist influence from destroying the country's educational system and believed that cooperation could best make this possible.

3. He stated that it was his personal belief that Communist control of the country was only a temporary and passing influence and that conditions would shortly be returned to normal.

4. He stated also that it was his personal desire to preserve his own life, that of his family, and to preserve the family property including his father's large library, and believed that remaining in the Ministry could best achieve these results.

Subject claimed also that he was not then nor has he ever been a member of the Communist Party. He stated that he had never been asked or required to be a member of the Communist Party by the BELA KUN Government. He recalls advising the BELA KUN authorities on several occasions that he was against their theories and was in an independent position. He was therefore called "Mr. Professor" and never "Comrade." In this regard VON KARMAN remarked that if one is under a Communist regime for four months as he was, a person is immunized against Communism for life.

As to BELA KUN himself, he had no personal dealings with him and in fact, had never seen him. He had never received any instructions to put Communist propaganda into the universities and his dealings were generally with the Civil Service people, very few of whom were Communists except at the very top.

VON KARMAN carefully differentiated and explained that he did not consider himself as having been a "part of," "connected" or "associated with" the BELA KUN Government, but considered himself rather as having been an outside "Advisor" who was "identified" with that regime.

VON KARMAN indicated that he believed that he had rendered a service to his native country. In this regard he pointed out that after the fall of the BELA KUN Government and his return to Germany, he had received a personal letter of commendation from ALEXANDER IMRI, the succeeding Minister of Education for Hungary, wherein he was commended for his efforts in protecting the educational institutions of Hungary during that period. This letter may still be among his personal effects and an effort will be made by him to locate it.

The subject did produce however a typewritten letter in German on the letterhead of Prof. Dr. L. PRANDTL, Goettingen, Den, dated June 28, 1920. It was addressed to "Professor Dr. v. KARMAN, Aerodynamisches Institut der Techn. Hochschule, Aachen," and read as follows, according to a translation previously prepared by the subject on his own letterhead. A photostatic copy of the above letter is being retained in the files of this office:

"Dear Colleague,

"Have my best thanks for your detailed letter of June 16; I was especially glad to have the statements concerning the Hungarian matter. I was very glad because I believe that the justification of your way of action will be much more perfectly established, than it seemed possible before. I myself know you too well to have any different opinion of you; however for such persons who are less acquainted with you, it is very useful that you have the opportunity to speak up yourself.

"I forwarded immediately your statement to the W.G.L. (Scientific Society for Aeronautics) and attached a copy of the letter of the Hungarian Minister of Education."

Concerning GEORGE LUKACS, People's Commissar for Educational Affairs under BELA KUN, and with whom subject dealt primarily, VON KARMAN stated that he would be approximately 60 years of age now. Upon the collapse of the BELA KUN regime he had returned to the Soviet Union where he was employed at the Soviet Academy. According to information contained in current Hungarian newspapers, he is now believed to be a Professor of Philosophy at the University of Budapest. He is also reported to be

TEXT ON THIS PAGE IS ILLEGIBLE
WE HAVE LEFT THE PAGE AS REFERENCE



currently in disfavor with the present Communist Hungarian government for not being sufficiently Communistic.

As to the other Communist officials in the BELA KUN Government, VON KARMAN recalls a Dr. EUGENE VARGA who was believed to be Commissar of Economics. In 1945 while in Moscow to attend the 220th anniversary of the Academy of Science of the USSR, he met VARGA at the United States Embassy in Moscow at which time he was then a representative of the Soviet Union to a Reparations Conference.

Other officials that he recalls only from newspaper accounts of that day include ALEXANDER GARBAI, who was believed to be nominal president although BELA KUN of course was the actual head of the government. GARBAI was in fact a Trade Union Leader in the Imperial Regime and was merely brought in and used by the BELA KUN Government to rally the people. Also in the government were one ______ PUGANY and one ______ SZANTO, who were Commissars of War and Commerce, respectively. Nothing is known concerning them.

Regarding the position taken by other professors at the University of Budapest and Jozsef Nador Technical University (where he had been a visiting professor from 1908 to 1909, including the period of Communist control) subject stated that other professors, names not specifically recalled, also found it necessary and expedient to cooperate with the BELA KUN regime in order to preserve the educational system and their own physical property which was being seized and turned over to the peasants. He did recall Prof. RADO KOVESLIGHETY who was Director of the Seismology Department, who though not a real Communist, also found it necessary to cooperate. He was believed to be on the staff of the University of Budapest at that time.

As to STEPHEN FAKLA, mentioned above, subject advised that his present whereabouts is unknown. He last heard from him during 1930-35 when he was believed to be an Instructor in the Air Force. After his return to Germany, VON KARMAN invited FAKLA to the University of Aachen where he completed his studies and thereafter was his assistant for a time. If alive today, FAKLA would be about 50 to 55 years of age and would probably be somewhere in the Western Zone of Germany.

Upon returning to Aachen, Germany in 1919, VON KARMAN continued, he resumed his former professorship at the University of Aachen where he remained until 1926. In 1926 he made his first trip to the United States to the Guggenheim Foundation at Pasadena, California. From 1926 to 1930 he spent considerable time both in the United States and in Germany.

TEXT ON THIS PAGE IS ILLEGIBLE
WE HAVE LEFT THE PAGE AS REFERENCE



In 1930 he immigrated to the United States to become Director of the Guggenheim Aeronautics Laboratory at the California Institute of Technology, Pasadena, California. He became a citizen in Los Angeles in 1936. In 1944, at the request of [redacted] U. S. Army Air Force [redacted] he became Advisor to the U. S. Air Force and also became affiliated with the National Advisory Committee on Aeronautics. He is currently engaged as Chairman of the Scientific Advisory Board, Department of the Air Force, with an office in the Pentagon Building, Washington, D.C. He also is Professor Emeritus at the California Institute of Technology, Pasadena, California. b7C

As to the above disclosure of his association with the BELA KUN Government, VON KARMAN stated that he has never made any attempt to conceal this matter and believed, in fact, that it was generally known. However, he indicated that he had never volunteered this information to government authorities in this country, except as hereinafter noted, nor had he ever been previously questioned regarding it by anyone anywhere except in Germany in 1920-21 when he was associated with "Wissenschaftliche Gesellschaft fur Luftfahrt" (Scientific Society for Aeronautics). The President of this society was Prince HENRY, brother of the Imperial Kaiser WILHELM. At that time subject explained the circumstances as given above and also furnished them the previously mentioned letter of commendation sent him by ALEXANDER IMRI. This apparently satisfied all concerned and no other questions were ever raised. At that time Dr. ADOLPH BAUMKER, now at Wright-Patterson Air Force Base, Dayton, Ohio, was in the Air Ministry in Berlin, Germany and worked with the subject. It is possible, subject stated, that he may know and recall the circumstances of this questioning and the results.

Subject stated that while in Europe recently he was advised of a current investigation of him there by Prof. NICHOLAS SCHEUBE of the University of Darmstadt in the American Zone of Germany. SCHEUBE had been offered a three month Information Trip to the United States by the American Military Government and SCHEUBE had visited him in Paris to inquire as to where he should visit in the United States. At this same time he informed the subject that he had been questioned by an American officer concerning subject's association with the BELA KUN Government in 1919. VON KARMAN explained that SCHEUBE had been a former student of his at the University of Aachen and was his assistent from 1923 to 1926.

b7C

Upon his return to this country on May 8, 1951, VON KARMAN thereafter, on May 11, 1951, contacted [redacted] of the U. S. Air Force at the Pentagon Building, and informed him of the investigation and furnished him the circumstances of his prior association with the BELA KUN regime. This was the first disclosure to any U. S. Government authority.

TEXT ON THIS PAGE IS ILLEGIBLE
WE HAVE LEFT THE PAGE AS REFERENCE



As to the latter mentioned trip abroad which extended from late March, 1951 to May 8, 1951, subject stated that it was a combined official business and pleasure trip.

He visited Algiers, North Africa where he attended a Scientific Conference. He then proceeded to the Sahara Desert where he inspected a French Guided Missle Project. Thereafter he went to Tunis, North Africa, and Rome, Italy for pleasure. Finally, he proceeded to Paris, France regarding the setting up of an Air Force Research and Development Organization for the combined North Atlantic Treaty Nations forming NATO (North Atlantic Treaty Organizations).

Concerning the previously mentioned attendance in Moscow in 1945 on the 220th anniversary of the Academy of Science of the USSR, subject stated that he was one of approximately sixteen United States scientists who had been invited. At that time he was already in Europe on a military mission. At the conclusion of the conference he then proceeded to Budapest to visit his brother and has not been there since.

Subject stated further that he has never furnished classified information to any unauthorized person, American or foreign, and to his knowledge has never been approached by any unauthorized person requesting such information. In this latter regard, VON KARMAN claimed also that at the above mentioned meeting in Moscow in 1945, VON KARMAN was not only not approached for information, but to the contrary, Russian scientists were apparently prohibited from contacting him for fear of his attempting to get information from them.

Regarding [redacted] referred to previously in this investigation, VON KARMAN advised that he had no personal knowledge that they were Communist Party members or otherwise engaged in subversive activities. He added that he was, of course, now aware of such former activity [redacted]

b7C

Of the above mentioned individuals, he was most surprised to learn that [redacted] was a Communist Party member. Subject admitted having telephonically contacted [redacted] while the latter was [redacted]

As to [redacted] also previously referred to in this investigation, subject explained that he

b7C

had been acquainted with [redacted] since about 1938 and has known [redacted] socially for the past three or four years. VON KARMAN identified as [redacted] Some time ago [redacted] first contacted VON KARMAN concerning [redacted] Subject disapproved and the plan did not materialize.

Several months ago when [redacted] approached him with aspirations of [redacted] subject referred him to [redacted] The latter, a retired businessman, is now believed by the subject to be financing [redacted] on a new invention, details of which are not known to him.

Subject explained that his name is now properly designated as THEODORE VON KARMAN. On occasions in the past he has used the name of THEODORE DE KARMAN, a French designation which is normally used by his sister. The correct Hungarian version had been TODOR KARMAN. His honorary Hungarian geographical designation of "SZOLLOSKISLAKI" indicating a land owner, was available to his family making his name TODOR SZOLLOSKISLAKI KARMAN, but such a designation is rarely used he added, except by the "snooty" and that "Von" is used as its substitute.

As indicated previously, subject's father MAURICE KARMAN was a former professor at the University of Budapest and died in 1915. His mother HELEN came to the United States in 1930, resided with him in Pasadena until her death in 1941. His sister, Dr. JOSEPHINE DE KARMAN came to the United States at the same time and is currently residing with him.

His brother NICHOLAUS KARMAN, married, about 67, now resides in Budapest. He formerly was a vice-president of a bank in Budapest until it was nationalized about two years ago and is retired on a small pension. A brother FERENCZ KARMAN, a former high school teacher in Budapest, died there in 1940 when about 52 years of age. His brother ELEMER KARMAN, a lawyer, died in Budapest in 1925 when about 24 years of age.

## A. STATEMENT

The following statement, incorporating substantially the above pertinent information concerning subject's association with the Communist BELA KUN Government, was carefully read and corrected in detail by VON KARMAN on May 29, 1951. At the conclusion though he advised that he preferred not to sign it at this time inasmuch as he did not know the legal implications thereof nor did he know the uses to which the statement might be put. However, he admitted it was correct "in general". The statement, in its final revised form, with insertions made by the subject in his own handwriting being here underlined, is as follows:

"Los Angeles, California
May 29, 1951

"I, THEODORE VON KARMAN, make the following voluntary statement to SA [redacted] who has identified himself to me as a Special Agent of the Federal Bureau of Investigation. I have been advised that I need not make any statement and that I have the right to be represented by counsel.

b7C

"I was born in Budapest, Hungary, on May 11, 1881, and reside at 1501 South Marengo Avenue, Pasadena, California.

"Concerning my identification with the Communist BELA KUN government in Hungary in 1919, I desire to state as background that in 1912 I had been appointed Professor of Aeronautics at the University of Aachen at Aachen, Germany. In 1914, holding a reserve commission, I was called back into the Austro-Hungarian Army and was engaged in Air Force research and development until the disintegration of the Army in late 1918.

"About December, 1918, being still on leave of absence from the University of Aachen, (because of armistice conditions it was impossible for me to return to occupied Aachen) I became a part time advisor to EUGENE GONCI, Assistant Secretary of Education under Count MICHAEL KAROLYI, who was then President of the Independent Republic of Hungary. The Minister of Education was then SIEGMUND KUNFI. During this time I also gave a course of lectures on Aeronautics at the JOZSEF NADOR TECHNICAL UNIVERSITY at Budapest.

"Upon the surrender of the Independent Government by KAROLYI to Communist BELA KUN in March, 1919, EUGENE GONCI telephoned me to stay on in my position, to which I replied that 'I would try,' and I did remain.

"Both SIEGMUND KUNFI and EUGENE GONCI, who were non-Communists, were temporarily carried over by the BELA KUN regime, but GONCI resigned later after about two months and I believe KUNFI was replaced by GEORGE LUKACS, who was definitely a Communist and whose title was People's Commissar for Educational Affairs.

"I continued my duties as Advisor under the BELA KUN regime to both KUNFI, GONCI, and their successor LUKACS until the collapse of the BELA KUN Government near the end of July, 1919. I had a title of Group Leader in the People's Commissariat for Educational Affairs, and had an office in the Ministry Building in Budapest.

"My general duties consisted of planning for University Education and included the choosing of professors and the preparation of curricula of study in the science and engineering fields in cooperation with the universities. After about one month in the BELA KUN regime, my former part-time duties gradually increased so that I was actually thereafter so engaged full time although I was also able to do some lecturing.

"While so engaged as advisor, I believe that I received compensation from the BELA KUN Government. I did not pay attention to the financial aspect, because the money issued by the communists was practically worthless. For some time I continued receiving compensation as an Army officer and also from my lecturing.

"Upon the collapse of the BELA KUN regime, I remained in Budapest about a week and then, through former fellow-officers in the Air Force, I was transported near the Austrian frontier, passed the frontier with regular passport and then went to Aachen. My reason in leaving was not because of fear for my life or liberty but to return to my work in Aachen and also to avoid a lot of explaining that might have been required.

"My reasons for working with the BELA KUN Government as indicated above are as follows:

"(1) The influence of friends at the University of Budapest who prevailed upon me to stay with the Ministry in order to preserve the Hungarian system of education.

"(2) My own personal desire to prevent the Communist influence from destroying the country's educational system.

TEXT ON THIS PAGE IS ILLEGIBLE
WE HAVE LEFT THE PAGE AS REFERENCE



"(3) My personal belief that Communist control of the Country was only a temporary condition.

"(4) My personal desire to preserve my own life, that of my family, and the preservation of family property, including my father's large library.

"I desire to state that I was not then nor have I ever been a member of the Communist Party. I was never asked or required to be a member of the Communist Party by the BELA KUN Government. I recall advising the BELA KUN authorities on several occasions that I was against their theories and was in an independent position. I was therefore called 'Mr. Professor' and never 'Comrade.' In this regard, I wish to add that if one is under a Communist regime for four months as I was, you are immunized against Communism for life.

"I wish to state also that I do not consider myself as having been associated with the BELA KUN regime, but consider myself rather as having been an outside advisor who was identified with that regime. I had no personal dealings with BELA KUN, and, in fact, never saw him. I never received any instruction to put Communist propaganda into the universities and my dealings were with regular civil service people, very few of whom were Communists except at the very top.

"I also desire to add that I have never furnished classified information to any unauthorized person, American or foreign, nor to my knowledge have I ever been approached by any unauthorized person requesting such information.

"I have read this statement consisting offour typewritten pages. After having had an opportunity to make any corrections, additions, or deletions, I have initialed each page and voluntarily signed below.

_______________________

"Witnesses:

_______________________

_______________________

"On May 29, 1951, Dr. THEODORE VON KARMAN read and corrected the above statement, indicated that it was correct generally, although he preferred not to sign it at this time.

b7C "/s/ [redacted] Special Agent, FBI, Los Angeles
"/s/ [redacted] USAF."

## II. IDENTITY OF BELA KUN

The following information was obtained from literature on file at the Los Angeles Public Library.

The 1948 edition of Webster's Biographical Dictionary published by G. C. Merriam Company, Springfield, Massachusetts, contains the following biographical sketch of BELA KUN: "KUN, BELA. 1885- . Hungarian-Jewish Communist; born in Transylvania. Journalist in Cluj; fought in Austrian Army in World War; captured by Russians (1915); became Bolshevist; sent to Hungary (1918) by Communist leaders, headed Red News (1918-19); organized Communist revolution in Budapest (1919); succeeded KAROLYI as Premier (March 22 to July 31, 1919); introduced radical changes in government; failed to control Slovakian peasants. In counter revolution was defeated with aid of Rumanians (1919); fled to Vienna and later (1920) to Russia; re-appeared in Vienna (April 1928), briefly imprisoned, and deported to Russia."

The Statesman's Year Book of 1920 published by MacMillan Company, New York, contains the following information regarding the historical aspect of the above pertinent period in the Hungarian Government: "On October 31, 1918, a revolution broke out in Hungary with the object of establishing a Republic and making the country independent of Austria. On November 13, 1918, King CHARLES issued a letter of abdication and on November 16, 1918 Hungary was proclaimed an independent Republic (Hungarian People's Republic) of which Count MICHAEL KAROLYI became Provisional President.

"The KAROLYI regime continued until March 22, 1919 when the Count resigned in consequence of an Entente note in reference to the boundary between Hungary and Rumania. Count KAROLYI'S Cabinet was succeeded by a Soviet government which proclaimed a dictatorship of the proletariat and called upon the whole Hungarian people to aid in the establishment of socialism and the freedom of the country. An opposition government, however soon was set up at Arad and Szeged which, with the assistance of the Rumanian Army, swept away the Soviet government, and on August 7, 1919, a National Government was again in the capital. Elections were held in January and February of 1920 and as a result a bloc composed of parties of the Right were returned to power with Admiral NICHOLAS VON HORTHY as Regent."

The New International Year Book of 1919 published by Dodd, Mead and Company, New York, indicated that on March 22, 1919 the KAROLYI Ministry resigned and was succeeded by a Bolshevist Ministry composed as follows: President - ALEXANDER GARBAI; People's Commissar for Home Affairs - EUGENE LANDLAR; People's Commissar for Finance - BELA SZEKELY; People's Commissar for Education - SIEGMUND KUNFI; People's Commissar for Foreign Affairs - BELA KUN; People's Commissar for Agriculture - EUGEN HAMBURGER. Of the above named individuals, subject stated that he had no knowledge whatever concerning LANDLAR, SZEKELY, or HAMBURGER.

The New York Times of August 3, 1919 reflected that BELA KUN resigned on July 31, 1919 and was granted safe conduct out of the country by the Allies. The New York Times of August 19, 1919 indicated that he was allowed to leave Germany in order to proceed to Petrograd, USSR, where he arrived on August 14, 1919. A reception was then held in his honor in Petrograd by Soviet officials on August 19, 1919.

## III. INTERVIEWS WITH FORMER ASSOCIATES IN EUROPE

A. [redacted]

b2
b7D

[redacted] another government agency conducting security investigations, advised on April 26, 1951 that a representative of that agency had on April 12 and 13, 1951 interviewed [redacted] the Georg August University at Goettingen, Germany, [redacted] at Badenweiles, Schwarzwald, French Zone, Germany. [redacted] furnished substantially the following information:

He first became acquainted with the subject in 1906 and has corresponded with him frequently until 1945. Upon receiving his doctorate degree, subject became a member of the faculty of the Georg August University where he remained until about 1913. Subject then accepted the Directorship of the Department of Mathematics and Aerotechnics at the University of Aachen.

He was then drafted into the Austrian Army and served as an officer until the war ended, during which time he was in charge of a project to develop some type of observation aircraft which would be least vulnerable to ground fire. As a result he successfully developed a helicopter before the war ended.

b7D

[redacted] continued that subject accepted the position as Minister of Culture in the Communist coup under BELA KUN. He believed, however,

TEXT ON THIS PAGE IS ILLEGIBLE
WE HAVE LEFT THE PAGE AS REFERENCE



that subject accepted this position not for political reasons, but to aid in supervising the educational system in Hungary. Subject had related to him that Communist officials in the BELA KUN Government tried to direct him to make changes in the educational system but that subject would tell them he "would take care of any changes were there any to be made." Subject was very independent and would not allow anyone to influence him in the field of education and told [redacted] that they, the Communists, did not understand anything about education.

b7D

Later, when subject returned to Germany and to the University of Aachen, it was brought to the attention of the Ministry of Education in Germany that the subject had been a member of the BELA KUN Government and that subject was a Communist. Subject denied ever being a convinced Communist and produced a letter of praise from the succeeding Minister of Culture in Germany. This letter stated that the subject had made no changes in the educational system and praised the subject for adherence to accepted principles of education. This letter satisfied all concerned that the subject was not a radical Communist and no reference was made again to the subject's activities with BELA KUN.

B. [redacted]

[redacted] also advised on April 16, 1951 that [redacted] presently employed as [redacted] Aachen, Germany, was reinterviewed on April 10, 1951 by a representative of [redacted] above, at which time he reiterated his previous information to the effect that subject's mother and one VON FAKLA had informed him that the subject was Minister of Culture under BELA KUN in Hungary in 1919 and that reportedly VON FAKLA had helped him escape from Hungary after the fall of the BELA KUN Government. [redacted] added that on April 1, 1951, he had written the subject a note congratulating him on his 70th birthday.

b2
b7C
b7D

C. [redacted]

[redacted] advised on April 16, 1951 that [redacted] University of Aachen, Aachen, Germany, had also been interviewed on April 10, 1951 at which time he advised that he had been acquainted with the subject from 1919 until 1933 and that the subject had been Minister of Culture under BELA KUN in 1919. He had become a Minister in the government in order to save his rich family from financial ruin.

## IV. MISCELLANEOUS

[redacted] above, also advised that the records of the Georg August University, Goettingen, Germany, reflect that the subject registered there on November 9, 1906, received his doctorate in Philosophy on February 23, 1909, and had been associated as assistant professor to Dr. Prof. PRANDTL from 1909 to 1913.

[redacted] advised that the records of the University of Aachen, Aachen, Germany, reflect that the subject was employed as a member of the faculty on April 1, 1913 and was carried as a member until April 1, 1934. On April 15, 1930 he was given a leave of absence to Pasadena, California. On November 20, 1930 this leave was extended to five years on the condition that he return to AACHEN and teach one semester each year. On April 1, 1934 subject, on his own request, was released as a member of the faculty.

b2

[redacted] reported also that the files of the Austrian Ministry of the Interior, Vienna, Austria, reflect that the subject served as a First Lieutenant in the Austrian-Hungarian Army under the name of Dr. THEODOR KARMAN VON SZOLLOSKISTAK during World War I (1914-18) with Aircraft Defense and Air Force Replacement Troops.

[redacted] of known reliability, advised that the subject had recently been in contact with [redacted] Columbia University, New York City, [redacted] and also [redacted] Houston, Texas.

b7C

The records of the New Haven Office covering Danbury, Connecticut, contain no information pertaining to [redacted] The records of the Houston Office contain no derogatory information concerning [redacted]

b2

[redacted] stated that the subject has recently been in correspondence with the following individuals:

1. [redacted] Washington, D.C.
2. [redacted] MIT, Gas Turbine Laboratory, Cambridge, Massachusetts
3. B. KLEINMAN, 222 East 202nd Street, New York 58.
4. [redacted] Princeton University, Princeton, New Jersey.

b7C

It is observed that [redacted] above, has previously been identified in this investigation.

b2

[redacted] has also advised that the subject has been in correspondence with the following who reside abroad:

b7C

1. [redacted] Zurich, Switzerland
2. Dienst Ministerie, Van der Keen en Waterstaat, Amsterdam, Holland
3. [redacted] Torino, Italy
4. [redacted]oteborg, Sweden
5. [redacted] Paris 16, France
6. F. N. SCHEUBE, 156 Dieburger Str., Darmstadt, Deutschland.

It is believed that the last named individual above is identical with the NICHOLAS SCHEUBE who was identified by the subject at the time of his interview as being his former student and assistant at the University of Aachen, who recently informed him in Paris of a current investigation regarding him.

ENCLOSURE: OSI, District 18, Maywood

Photostatic copy of a letter in German dated June 28, 1920 from Prof. Dr. L. PRANDTL and translation of same, made available by subject.

P E N D I N G

TEXT ON THIS PAGE IS ILLEGIBLE
WE HAVE LEFT THE PAGE AS REFERENCE

LA 105-863

ADMINISTRATIVE PAGE

b2 [redacted] OSI reports by Special Agent [redacted] b7C dated April 16, 1951 and April 26, 1951, OSI file No. 33-49.

[redacted] Mail cover on subject's residence at 1501 South Marengo Avenue, Pasadena, California, as reflected in the report of SA [redacted] dated April 27, 1951 at Los Angeles.

b7C

Serial 35

LA 105-863

## LEADS

TO ALL OFFICES:

The Bureau has instructed that this investigation is to be given preferred handling and the results submitted promptly to the Bureau for transmission to OSI. Further, the fact that the subject is under intensive investigation should not be revealed to persons interviewed.

BOSTON OFFICE:

At Cambridge, Massachusetts: Will review office records for any pertinent information regarding the identity and activities of [redacted] MIT, Gas Turbine Laboratory, who recently was in correspondence with the subject.

b7C

Will report the results of the Bureau authorized interview with [redacted] previously set out in the New York report of SA [redacted] dated May 21, 1951.

b7D

b7C

CINCINNATI OFFICE:

At Dayton, Ohio: Will interview [redacted] concerning subject's association with the BELA KUN regime in 1919 [redacted]

b7D

For the information of the Cincinnati Office, this investigation is based on information originally furnished by G-2 on September 12, 1950 to the effect that a CIC report dated April 1, 1948 reflected that one TODAR KARMAN had joined the Hungarian Communist Party in 1918 while an Assistant Professor of Physics at the Jozsef Nador Technical University at Budapest, Hungary. When the Communists seized power under BELA KUN in 1919, KARMAN was appointed Deputy Commissar of Cultural and Educational Affairs in charge of Higher Education (high schools and universities). He reportedly remained in this capacity until the BELA KUN Government was overthrown in late 1919, after which he fled to Germany where he settled in Aachen. He subsequently came to this country, became associated with the California Institute of Technology and during the war reportedly engaged in research work in aerodynamics for the U. S. Army Air Force.

TEXT ON THIS PAGE IS ILLEGIBLE
WE HAVE LEFT THE PAGE AS REFERENCE



NEW YORK OFFICE:

At New York City, New York: Will review office records for any pertinent information regarding the identity and activities of B. KLEINMAN, 222 East 202nd Street.

b7D [redacted] Will report the results of the Bureau authorized interview with [redacted] previously set out in New York report of SA [redacted] dated May 21, 1951.

b7C

WASHINGTON FIELD OFFICE:

At Washington, D.C.: Will review office records for any pertinent information regarding the identity and activities of [redacted] who recently corresponded with the subject. b7C

Will report the results of the interview with [redacted] in accordance with Bureau authorization granted in Bureau letter dated May 11, 1951. b7C

Will also report the results of the interview with [redacted] in accordance with Bureau authorization granted by Bureau teletype dated May 12, 1951. b7D

LOS ANGELES OFFICE:

At Los Angeles, California: Will continue to report additional information and activities concerning the subject as furnished by confidential informants.

REFERENCE: Los Angeles teletype to the Bureau and Washington Field dated May 23, 1951
Bureau teletype to Los Angeles dated May 11, 1951
b7C Report of SA [redacted] dated April 27, 1951 at Los Angeles.

TEXT ON THIS PAGE IS ILLEGIBLE
WE HAVE LEFT THE PAGE AS REFERENCE

Assistant Attorney General
James M. McInerney

Director, FBI

June 26, 1951

CONFIDENTIAL

THEODORE VON KARMAN, was.,
INTERNAL SECURITY - R

47588

Reference is made to our memorandum dated May 11, 1951, concerning captioned individual.

There is attached for your additional information a copy of the report of Special Agent [redacted] dated June 13, 1951, at Los Angeles, California.

b7C

Attachment

WAK:mes
100-372586

ALL INFORMATION CONTAINED
HEREIN IS UNCLASSIFIED
DATE 6-16-97 BY

RECORDED - 22

JUN 29 1951

F B I

COMM - FBI

STANDARD FORM NO. 64

# Office Memorandum • UNITED STATES GOVERNMENT

TO : DIRECTOR, FBI

DATE: May 7, 1951

FROM : SAC, WASHINGTON FIELD

47589

SUBJECT: THEODORE VON KARMAN
INTERNAL SECURITY - R
(Bufile 100-372586)

5-1
1-1

Rerep SA [redacted] dated 5/3/51, Washington, D. C.

b2
b7C
b7D

It is noted that the next to last line of the Synopsis should reflect that [redacted] denies furnishing information re subject to Informant [redacted] in Europe," instead of [redacted] as it appears. WFO copies of this report are being changed accordingly and it is requested that offices receiving copies of this letter note such change on copies in their files.

It is further requested that mail in this case directed to WFO bear the WFO file number, 100-22923.

RLS/wl
100-22923

cc: Los Angeles
Baltimore
Boston
New York

5-11 Change made on disseminated copies & those retained. Wak

ALL INFORMATION CONTAINED HEREIN IS UNCLASSIFIED DATE 6-16-97

RECORDED - 66

EX-176

TEXT ON THIS PAGE IS ILLEGIBLE
WE HAVE LEFT THE PAGE AS REFERENCE

STANDARD FORM NO. 64

# Office Memorandum • UNITED STATES GOVERNMENT

TO : Director, FBI. DATE: June 28, 1951

FROM : SAC, CINCINNATI

SUBJECT: THEODORE VON KARMAN, was
INTERNAL SECURITY - R
(Bufile 100-372586)

Reference is made to the report of SA [redacted] dated at Los Angeles, 6-13-51, in which a lead was set out to interview one [redacted]

It has been determined that [redacted] is presently on extended leave and will not return [redacted] until on or about August 1, 1951.

[redacted] supervisor at that [redacted] has advised that [redacted] has gone to someplace in Colorado to visit friends or relatives, and t hat upon the arrival at his destination, he will furnish his address to [redacted]

Unless otherwise advised [redacted] will be interviewed upon his return [redacted]

cc: Los Angeles (105-863)

HDS:MAH
65-1145

b7C
b7D

354-994
ALL INFORMATION CONTAINED
HEREIN IS UNCLASSIFIED
DATE 6-16-97 BY

56

RECORDED - 88
INDEXED - 88
JUN 30
EX. - 97

b7C [redacted]

76 JUL 5 1951

TEXT ON THIS PAGE IS ILLEGIBLE
WE HAVE LEFT THE PAGE AS REFERENCE

THE FOREIGN SERVICE
OF THE
UNITED STATES OF AMERICA

SECRET

American Embassy
2 Avenue Gabriel
Paris 8, France

SECRET - AIR COURIER

Date: June 25, 1951

To: Director, FBI

From: Legal Attache, Paris

Subject: THEODORE VON KARMAN, was.
INTERNAL SECURITY - R

[redacted] ReBulet May 22, 1951, requesting this office to interview [redacted] for any information in his possession concerning the above captioned who was reportedly an official connected with the Communist regime of BELA KUN in Hungary in 1919.

Accordingly, [redacted] was interviewed on June 14, 1951. A photograph of the subject was exhibited to him and [redacted] was unable to identify it.

b7D

Neither did [redacted] know anyone by the name of THEODORE VON KARMAN, nor was he able to say that any individual by that name was connected with the BELA KUN regime. [redacted] stated that he doubted very much whether one THEODORE VON KARMAN was an important official during the BELA KUN regime in 1919 for the reason that he, [redacted] himself was a young officer in the Hungarian Army in the BELA KUN regime and he did not recall anyone by the name of VON KARMAN. If the subject had been an important personality in Hungary during that period, it is [redacted] contention that he would certainly remember him.

b1

Reliable and established sources in the [redacted] have been requested to furnish this office with any data concerning the subject they may have, and the Bureau will be advised if any such information is forthcoming.

ROL:AM

ALL INFORMATION CONTAINED
HEREIN IS UNCLASSIFIED EXCEPT
WHERE SHOWN OTHERWISE

1 cc. Los Angeles
via R/S
7-5-51
wak

RECORDED - 57
INDEXED - 57

100-372586-57

JUN 30 1951

SECRET

CLASSIFIED BY SP5JC/kmr

FEDERAL BUREAU OF INVESTIGATION
U. S. DEPARTMENT OF JUSTICE
COMMUNICATIONS SECTION

JUN [illegible] 1951

TELETYPE

Mr. Tolson
Mr. Ladd
Mr. Clegg
Mr. Glavin
Mr. Nichols
Mr. Rosen
Mr. Tracy
Mr. Harbo
Mr. Alden
Mr. [illegible]
Mr. [illegible]
Mr. Mohr
Tele. Room
Mr. Nease
Miss Gandy

##

WASH 18 AND WFO FROM LOS ANGELES 12 4-21 PM

DIRECTOR, SAC DEFERRED

b7C [redacted]

THEODORE VON KARMAN, WAS, IS DASH R. BUFILE ONE HUNDRED DASH THREE SEVEN TWO FIVE EIGHT SIX. SUBJ NOW REPORTED TO BE IN THE EAST TO ATTEND A REGULAR MEETING OF THE SCIENTIFIC ADVISORY BOARD AT WANGTON, AND ALSO TO DELIVER A COMMENCEMENT ADDRESS AT AN UNNAMED NEW ENGLAND UNIVERSITY. ABOVE FOR INFORMATION ONLY. REPORT COVERING INTERVIEW WITH SUBJ BEING SUBMITTED.

HOOD

HOLD PLS

ALL INFORMATION CONTAINED
HEREIN IS UNCLASSIFIED
DATE 6-16-92 BY [illegible]

RECORDED - 79
EX - 120

100-37258

76 JUL 9 1951

HANDLED BY
STOP DESK

TEXT ON THIS PAGE IS ILLEGIBLE
WE HAVE LEFT THE PAGE AS REFERENCE

FEDERAL BUREAU OF INVESTIGATION
U.S. DEPARTMENT OF JUSTICE
COMMUNICATIONS SECTION

JUN 22 1951

TELETYPE

ALL INFORMATION CONTAINED
HEREIN IS UNCLASSIFIED
DATE 6-16-97 BY

Mr. Tolson
Mr. Ladd
Mr. Clegg
Mr. Glavin
Mr. Nichols
Mr. Rosen
Mr. Tracy
Mr. Harbo
Mr. Belmont
Mr. Mohr
Tele. Room
Mr. Nease
Miss Gandy

WASH 69 FROM LOS ANGELES 22 8-43 PM

DIRECTOR, FBI DEFERRED

THEODORE VON KARMAN, WAS., IS DASH R. REURTEL JUNE TWENTYTWO, FIFTYONE

REPORT SUBMITTED JUNE THIRTEEN LAST.

HOOD

HOLD

RECORDED - 42 100-372586

JUN 28 1951

56 JUL 12 1951 HANDLED BY STOP DESK

TEXT ON THIS PAGE IS ILLEGIBLE
WE HAVE LEFT THE PAGE AS REFERENCE

JUNE 22, 1951 [illegible]

SAC, LOS ANGELES

THEODORE VON KARMAN, WAS, INTERNAL SECURITY DASH R. REURTEL [illegible]
LAST. SUBMIT REPORT IMMEDIATELY. HOOVER

WAK:dmd

47581

Note: Subject was interviewed May 23, 1951, and an OSI Colonel was present. OSI desires report on interview so they may make determination concerning subject's continued employment with Air Force.

ALL INFORMATION CONTAINED
HEREIN IS UNCLASSIFIED
DATE 6/6/97

EX. - 37
RECORDED - 36
100-37258

HANDLED BY
STOP DESK

FEDERAL BUREAU OF INVESTIGATION
U. S. DEPARTMENT OF JUSTICE
COMMUNICATIONS SECTION
JUN 22 1951
TELETYPE

62 JUL 9

TEXT ON THIS PAGE IS ILLEGIBLE
WE HAVE LEFT THE PAGE AS REFERENCE

FEDERAL BUREAU OF INVESTIGATION
U. S. DEPARTMENT OF JUSTICE
COMMUNICATIONS SECTION

JUN 22 1951

TELETYPE

47585

LOS ANGELES 12 FROM WASH DC 22 627 PM

SAC D E F E R R E D

THEODORE VON KARMAN, WAS, INTERNAL SECURITY DASH R. REURTEL JUNE TWELVE LAST. SUBMIT REPORT IMMEDIATELY.

HOOVER

HOLD PLS

354-894
ALL INFORMATION CONTAINED
HEREIN IS UNCLASSIFIED
DATE 6-16-97 BY

TO : Director, FBI

FROM : SAC, Los Angeles

SUBJECT: THEODORE VON KARMAN
INTERNAL SECURITY - R
(Bufile 100-372586)

DATE: ly 5, 1951

TEXT ON THIS PAGE IS ILLEGIBLE
WE HAVE LEFT THE PAGE AS REFERENCE

b7C

Reference is made to the report of [redacted] dated June 13, 1951 in the above captioned matter.

It is recalled that upon subject's recent interview he carefully corrected and amended a prepared statement of his association with the Communist Bela Kun Government in Hungary in 1919. He admitted that the facts contained therein were true but he declined to sign it "at this time". he indicated that he desired "to think the matter over", and agreed to advise this office later of his final decision. It was pointed out that this was purely a voluntary matter on his part and that it was entirely his privilege to sign or to decline to sign this statement. However, a definite expression of his ultimate choice, whatever it might be, would be appreciated in the immediate future. To date the subject has not contacted this office.

A contemplated recontact with the subject as to his possible oversight in this matter is currently being delayed in view of the sudden death of his sister, JOSEPHINE DE KARMAN, on July 2, 1951 as a result of a heart attack. It is felt that the subject should not be contacted at this time because of these personal circumstances.

JPA:ATO
105-863

cc - Washington Field

RECORDED - 5

INDEXED - 5

EX. - 32

61

ALL INFORMATION CONTAINED
HEREIN IS UNCLASSIFIED

F133
51 JUL 16 1951

TEXT ON THIS PAGE IS ILLEGIBLE
WE HAVE LEFT THE PAGE AS REFERENCE

# FEDERAL BUREAU OF INVESTIGATION

Form No. 1
THIS CASE ORIGINATED AT LOS ANGELES BS FILE NO. 65-1838 ner

| REPORT MADE AT | DATE WHEN MADE | PERIOD FOR WHICH MADE | REPORT MADE BY |
|---|---|---|---|
| BOSTON, MASSACHUSETTS | 7/18/51 | 7/12/51 | [redacted] b7C |

| TITLE | CHARACTER OF CASE |
|---|---|
| THEODORE VON KARMAN, was. | INTERNAL SECURITY - R |

SYNOPSIS OF FACTS: Subject in contact with [redacted] M.I.T., Cambridge, Mass. [redacted] b7C

-RUC-

DETAILS: AT CAMBRIDGE, MASSACHUSETTS:

Confidential Informant [redacted] of known reliability, reported [redacted] Massachusetts Institute of Technology Gas Turbine Laboratory, Cambridge, Massachusetts, had recently communicated with the Subject.

[redacted] M.I.T., informed SA [redacted] that [redacted]

b2
b7C
b7D

ALL INFORMATION CONTAINED HEREIN IS UNCLASSIFIED DATE 6/16/97 BY

COPIES DESTROYED
23 APR 5 1963

APPROVED AND FORWARDED: J E Thornton SPECIAL AGENT IN CHARGE

DO NOT WRITE IN THESE SPACES

RECORDED - 56
INDEXED - 59

JUL 20 1951

b7C

COPIES OF THIS REPORT

5 - BUREAU (100-372386)
3 - LOS ANGELES (105-863)
2 - BOSTON

COPY IN FILE

PROPERTY OF FBI—THIS CONFIDENTIAL REPORT AND ITS CONTENTS ARE LOANED TO YOU BY THE FBI AND ARE NOT TO BE DISTRIBUTED OUTSIDE OF AGENCY TO WHICH LOANED.

ADMINISTRATIVE PAGE

Referenced report requests the Boston Office report results of the interview with [redacted] It is noted this information was previously reported in the Report of SA [redacted] dated at Boston 6/8/51.

It is noted [redacted] was investigated under the Atomic Energy Program in 1948. The Bureau is being advised of this fact by separate letter. The interview with [redacted] was taken from the Report of SA [redacted] dated at Boston, Massachusetts May 10, 1948, entitled [redacted] Information credited to [redacted] own statement was taken from his Personnel Security Questionnaire filed with the Atomic Energy Commission.

b7C
b7D

INFORMANTS

[redacted] - A mail cover on Subject's residence at 1501 South Marengo Avenue, Pasadena, California, as set forth in referenced report.

b2

REFERENCE: Report of SA [redacted] dated at Los Angeles 6/13/51, entitled "CHANGED: THEODORE VON KARMAN, was., INTERNAL SECURITY - R".

b7C

TEXT ON THIS PAGE IS ILLEGIBLE
WE HAVE LEFT THE PAGE AS REFERENCE

[redacted]

FD-72 (1-10-49)

# FEDERAL BUREAU OF INVESTIGATION

354 894
ALL INFORMATION CONTAINED HEREIN IS UNCLASSIFIED

FORM No. 1
THIS CASE ORIGINATED AT LOS ANGELES | NY FILE NO. 65-6747 HCH

| REPORT MADE AT | DATE WHEN MADE | PERIOD FOR WHICH MADE | REPORT MADE BY |
|---|---|---|---|
| NEW YORK | 7/24/51 | 6/4;7/2,10/51 | [redacted] b7C |

| TITLE | CHARACTER OF CASE |
|---|---|
| THEODORE VON KARMAN, was | INTERNAL SECURITY - R |

AGENCY State USAF
REQ. REC'D 1-15-55
REP'T FORW. 1-21-55
BY

b2 b7D

SYNOPSIS OF FACTS:

Confidential Informants [redacted] advise they are not acquainted with subject. B. KLEINMAN apparently identical to ISABELLE KLEINMANN, aka BELLE KLEINMANN. No derogatory information available.

- RUC -

AGENCY [redacted] b2
REQ. REC'D 12/20/54
REP'T FORW. 1/5/55
BY

G.I.R.-5

DETAILS: Confidential Informant [redacted] of known reliability, who is acquainted with the activities of the German Communist Party in Europe during the 1920's, advised he is not acquainted with subject and doubted that subject held a prominent position or was otherwise active in the organization during the above period.

b2 b7D

Confidential Informant [redacted] of known reliability, who was personally acquainted with top functionaries of the BELA KUN regime in Hungary stated he does not know THEODORE VON KARMAN under his true name or known aliases, nor could he identify a photograph of subject. He stated he has a faint recollection of a Professor KARMAN in Budapest, who was an old man thirty years ago and if this individual was in any way connected with subject he must have been subject's father. However, he could give no further information concerning this Professor KARMAN, nor did he know if he had a son or other relative who could have been identical with subject.

This informant said that he had occasion to be well

APPROVED AND FORWARDED: Edward Scheidt SPECIAL AGENT IN CHARGE

DO NOT WRITE IN THESE SPACES

-63 RECORDED - 59
INDEXED - 59

COPIES OF THIS REPORT

6-Bureau (100-372586)
5-Los Angeles (105-863) (2-OSI, District 18, Maywood)
1-Washington Field (Info) (100-22923)
3-New York

JUL 27 1951



SEE REVERSE SIDE FOR CAUTION

acquainted with BELA KUN and his various top level functionaries and, while he does not now recall who held the position of Commissar or Deputy Commissar of Cultural and Educational Affairs, he definitely does not associate subject's name with those offices.

The Los Angeles Office has advised that one B. KLEINMAN, 222 East 202nd Street, New York 58, New York, has recently been in correspondence with subject at his home, 1501 South Marengo Avenue, Pasadena, California. Discreet inquiry at the above address revealed it to be the residence of MORTIMER V. KLEINMANN and his wife ISABELLE KLEINMANN, also known as BELLE KLEINMANN. They are an elderly couple who have resided at this address for several years and bear a good reputation. No identifiable information concerning MORTIMER V. KLEINMANN or ISABELLE KLEINMANN is available in the files of the New York Office.

- REFERRED UPON COMPLETION TO THE OFFICE OF ORIGIN -

ADMINISTRATIVE

INFORMANTS

b7C

The Confidential Informants mentioned in the report of SA [redacted] dated July 24, 1951, at New York are as follows:

b2
b7C
b7D

[redacted] who was contacted by former SA [redacted] on 7/2/51.

[redacted] Contacted by SA [redacted] 6/4/51.

REFERENCES

b7C

Bureau letter to Los Angeles, 5/11/51.
Report of SA [redacted] 5/21/51, New York.
New York letter, 6/7/51.
Report of SA [redacted] 6/13/51, Los Angeles.
Bureau letter, 6/26/51.

STANDARD FORM NO. 64

TEXT ON THIS PAGE IS ILLEGIBLE
WE HAVE LEFT THE PAGE AS REFERENCE

# Office Memorandum • UNITED STATES GOVERNMENT

TO : A. H. BELMONT

FROM : C. E. HENNRICH

SUBJECT: THEODORE VON KARMAN
INTERNAL SECURITY - R

DATE: May 11, 1951

SECRET

CLASSIFIED BY
DECLASSIFY ON: 25X

PURPOSE: INDEXED - 40

To advise you of the status of the above investigation and to recommend that [redacted] be interviewed concerning subject.

b7C
b7D

It is also recommended that no interviews be authorized at this time with [redacted] even though they may be in a position to furnish information concerning subject.

b7C

BACKGROUND:

Personal History

Subject is a world-renowned aerodynamicist, born 1881, Hungary; entered the United States in 1930; naturalized - 1936; employed as Director, Guggenheim Aeronautical Research Laboratory, California Institute of Technology, 1930 to 1942; also employed as full-time Consultant for Air Force, 1942 to date. Subject's present official position is Chairman of Air Force Scientific Advisory Board and maintains offices in the Pentagon. Subject has continual access to highly sensitive air research information. He presently resides at Pasadena, California.

ALL INFORMATION CONTAINED HEREIN IS UNCLASSIFIED EXCEPT WHERE SHOWN OTHERWISE

Basis for Investigation

Investigation of subject was begun March 14, 1951, on the basis of a G-2 report which alleged that subject was Commissar of Culture under the short-lived Bela Kun Communist Government of Hungary in 1919. A further basis was information in Bufiles which reflects subject has associated closely in air research with known Communist Party members and with William Perl, a known

RECORDED - 40 100-372586-
JUL 25 1951

HANDLED BY
STOP
INDEXED - 40

SECRET

:nes
100-372586

AUG 7 1951

FEDERAL BUREAU OF INVESTIGATION

# Part. 2b

## SUBJECT: THEODORE VON KARMAN

## FILE NUMBER: 100-372586 SERIALS 30-END OF FILE

TEXT ON THIS PAGE IS ILLEGIBLE
WE HAVE LEFT THE PAGE AS REFERENCE

SECRET

Soviet agent. He is also closely acquainted with [redacted] b7C

RESULTS OF INVESTIGATION:

1. Because of subject's importance in the Air Force, OSI has conducted the investigation of him in Europe. Two individuals interviewed by OSI there have verified subject's position as Minister of Culture in the Bela Kun Government of Hungary during 1919.

b7C 2. Los Angeles has advised that recently [redacted] b1 (S)

3. [Mail cover on subject reflects he is in contact with one [redacted] of New York who is apparently identical with [redacted] b7C (A)(U)

4. New York Confidential Informant [redacted] has advised that he met subject once in 1945, [redacted] time he was impressed with subject's favorable reaction to Russian Communist domination of Hungary and for that reason, never recontacted subject. New York Confidential Informant [redacted] although he did not know subject personally, stated he had heard that subject and several other assistants of a Hungarian Professor joined the Bela Kun regime in Hungary as a result of the Professor's b2 b7D

SECRET

SECRET

influence over them. Other New York informants, although acquainted with the Bela Kun regime in Hungary, have been unable to identify subject.

[redacted] 5. OSI investigation in Europe identified [redacted] as the original G-2 informant who reported subject's past affiliation with the Bela Kun Government. [redacted] when recently interviewed, denied having furnished such information and stated he met Von Karman about one year ago at the residence of [redacted] which residence he had attended with several other persons at [redacted] invitation for the purpose of [redacted] recalls at that time that subject made the statement, [redacted] believed it to indicate that subject was speaking favorably of the fact that the Hungarian people were presently living under a Communist Government and were apparently voluntarily so doing. [redacted] recalls that one of the other guests remarked, [redacted]

As you are aware, [redacted] recommended that the following persons who were in attendance be interviewed:

[redacted] Baltimore, Maryland

Bufiles reflect CNI memorandum dated April 4, 1949, which lists [redacted] as having been brought to the United States [redacted] because of his excellent background [redacted]

[redacted]

(S) [redacted] 39-1035-56)

b7C
b7D
b1
b7C
Declassified Per CIA letter dated 9-8-99



SECRET

SECRET

[redacted]

b7C

(100-89-54-139)

WFO has also recommended that the following be interviewed concerning subject:

[redacted] Woods Hole, Massachusetts

In a recent letter, Boston advised that [redacted] has been cooperative during several recent interviews. [redacted] however, has a long background of association with Communists and it is noted that he has failed to volunteer information concerning his past associates and has stated that although he desires to cooperate with the Bureau, he will not act as an informant. He has been reliably described as [redacted] and is associated with subject [redacted]

(100-347660)

[redacted]

[redacted] is presently [redacted]

b7D

Our files reflect that he is strongly anti-Soviet although it does not appear that he has ever been used as a source of information.

(105-11669-7;
100-89-158;
100-89-Section 3)

SECRET

SECRET

*RECOMMENDATIONS:*

b1 [redacted] (S)

*Classified per CIA letter 9-8-98

b7D b7C [redacted] 2. That New York be authorized to interview [redacted] concerning subject and that WFO be authorized to interview [redacted] for the same purpose in the event their files do not reflect information unavailable to the Bureau which makes such interviews inadvisable.

If you agree, there is attached an appropriate communication to Los Angeles and auxiliary offices.

Attachment

SECRET

TEXT ON THIS PAGE IS ILLEGIBLE
WE HAVE LEFT THE PAGE AS REFERENCE

FD-
(1-10-49)

# FEDERAL BUREAU OF INVESTIGATION

FORM NO. 1
THIS CASE ORIGINATED AT LOS ANGELES

ALL INFORMATION CONTAINED
HEREIN IS UNCLASSIFIED
DATE 6-5-92 BY

FILE NO. 100-22923

| REPORT MADE AT | DATE WHEN MADE | PERIOD FOR WHICH MADE | REPORT MADE BY |
|---|---|---|---|
| WASHINGTON, D. C. | AUG 2 1951 | 6/22;7/11,20/51 | [redacted] b7C RLS:pb |

| TITLE | CHARACTER OF CASE |
|---|---|
| THEODORE VON KARMAN, was. | INTERNAL SECURITY - R |

**SYNOPSIS OF FACTS:**

[redacted] has met subject only twice, unacquainted with his political activities in Hungary or any Communist sympathies. [redacted] has conversed with subject approximately four times since 1942, considers him strongly pro-Soviet and questionable security risk. Subject has admitted to [redacted] role in Hungary under Kun regime but discounted any sympathies for that government. Visited in Hotel room, D. C., by three Russians shortly after return from Europe, 1945, pertinence of visit not known. No record re [redacted] WFO.

b7C b7D

SEE REVERSE SIDE FOR ADD. DISSEMINATION.

AGENCY [redacted]
REQ. REC'D 12/20/54
REP'T FORW. 1/5/55
BY

AGENCY photo
REQ. REC'D 1-13-5
REP'T FORW. 1-24-5
BY

AGENCY
REQ. REC'D 1-20-56
REP'T FORW. 1-13-56
BY
Re: bro. Nicolas Von Karman

G.I.R.-5

- R U C -

DETAILS: AT WASHINGTON, D. C.

[redacted] who came to the United States from Hungary in the late 1940's, advised that he had heard of subject by reputation generally as a fine mathematician and scientist, but that he knows nothing of his background or political inclinations. [redacted] first met subject at the apartment of [redacted] in Washington around 1949 where, at the latter's invitation, several Hungarian Scientists convened for the purpose of [redacted]

b7C b7D

APPROVED AND FORWARDED: SPECIAL AGENT IN CHARGE

DO NOT WRITE IN THESE SPACES

-65

RECORDED - 111

INDEXED - 111

EX-88

COPIES OF THIS REPORT
6 - Bureau (100-372586)
3 - Los Angeles (105-863)
1 - New York (Info) (65-6747)
2 - Washington Field

COPY IN FILE

PROPERTY OF FBI - This confidential report and its contents are loaned to you by the FBI and are not to be distributed outside of agency to which loaned.

TEXT ON THIS PAGE IS ILLEGIBLE
WE HAVE LEFT THE PAGE AS REFERENCE



Among the individuals present as recalled [redacted] were [redacted] and [redacted] The evening at [redacted] was strictly social in nature, although most of the conversation naturally concerned general scientific matters. [redacted] did not recall any remark by the subject during the evening which had any pro-Communist or Soviet implications.

[redacted] stated that at this time he had been doing some experimental work in his own field and discussed with the subject the possibility of the latter affording him an introduction or recommendation to the Navy Department in order that he might have an entree with this department by which he could possibly gain a contract for experimental work. According to [redacted] subject agreed to write such a letter to the Navy; however, it was not known to [redacted] whether he actually did so. [redacted] had mentioned to KARMAN that he was doing experimentation and study [redacted] and that during the course of his conversation with KARMAN the latter asked [redacted] if there was any possibility to use this method in order to [redacted] Sometime later, [redacted] had occasion to travel to New York City where he visited KARMAN in the latter's Hotel room, the name of the Hotel not being recalled. The visit was of short duration and some general conversation was held between the two men in addition to the somewhat technical discussion of the aforementioned field of experimentation in which [redacted] was engaged. According to [redacted] he has not corresponded with or seen subject since this latter meeting, and that as a result of his slight acquaintance with him, he would be unable to give any opinion as to the latter possessing pro-Communist or pro-Soviet tendencies. During their discussions, he had never observed anything on the part of VON KARMAN which would lead him to believe that the latter was engaged in any subversion or questionable activity.

[redacted] stated that he had never met subject prior to 1942 or 1943, although he had heard of him by his professional reputation, and that it was also generally known in Hungarian circles that VON KARMAN had been involved with the Kun government, and that at its overthrow, he had left Hungary.

b7C b7D

The exact details of this involvement were not known to [redacted] nor could he attribute such information about subject to any particular individual.

In 1942 or 1943, [redacted] who mentioned to [redacted] that as both he and subject were of Hungarian birth and professional men, they would probably enjoy becoming acquainted. Subject at the time was residing in some Hotel in Washington with his sister JOSEPHINE, and they were introduced through [redacted] who is not believed to be particularly friendly nor well acquainted with subject. According to [redacted] he met subject probably two or three times thereafter in the latter's Hotel in Washington, during which time their conversation concerned general world conditions and the "old country, Hungary". The last time that they met was in 1945, shortly after subject had returned from Europe and had evidently visited Russia. At this time, as on the previous occasions, subject called [redacted] at his home and invited him to his Hotel room. On the particular evening, [redacted] went to the Hotel, and as was the custom, went directly to subject's room where he knocked on the door. The door was opened by the subject, who appeared somewhat abashed and chagrined, and rather apologetically stated that he had had visitors who had remained longer than he had expected, but that they were then ready to leave. [redacted] was ushered into the room and introduced to three men, all of whom had Russian names, and either spoke in Russian or in English with a distinct Russian accent. Immediately after the introduction, the men each picked up a briefcase and departed. The names and descriptions of these men are not recalled by [redacted] who further stated that he was certainly not in a position to state that there was anything amiss in the men being in KARMAN's apartment, although at the time, it did appear to him to be extremely suspicious due to the fact that KARMAN had just returned from a trip abroad and was, as known to [redacted] engaged in rather highly important work of a technical nature for this government in this country even though the exact nature of the work was not known to [redacted] Subject never offered any explanation concerning the presence of the men, nor did he thereafter elude to them. Throughout his meetings with subject, the latter had always appeared to be very favorably disposed toward and sympathetic to the Soviet Union, and upon the occasion of their last meeting in the Hotel



/b7C b7D

room, he was profuse in his praising of that nation and apparently could find nothing to criticize concerning Russia.

Subject was not known to be, nor to have ever been, a member of the Communist Party either in Hungary, Germany, or the United States, but it was [redacted] impression that the latter possessed definite pro-Soviet leanings, and as a result thereof, was a very questionable security risk. The subject had mentioned to [redacted] that he had held a position in the educational field during the Kun regime but mentioned that he had never been a Communist Party member nor an actual functionary in the regime, and it was [redacted] opinion that it is quite possible that his reasons for becoming involved with the Kun regime might well have been opportunistic as well as motivated by any ideological considerations.

[redacted] stated that on a number of occasions subject has called him at his home in order to make future appointments to meet with him, but that he, [redacted] has assiduously advoided KARMAN due to the disquieting feeling that KARMAN is pro-Soviet, and that consequently, they have not subsequently met. [redacted] stressed that he would be unable to definitely prove or refer to specific instances wherein KARMAN had appeared to him to be pro-Soviet, and that other than as stated above, this opinion was based on the general feeling which he obtained from his conversations with subject.

Indices of the Washington Field Office reveal no information identifiable with [redacted]

/b7C b7D

- REFERRED UPON COMPLETION TO THE OFFICE OF ORIGIN -

**ADMINISTRATIVE**

REFERENCE: Bureau teletype dated May 12, 1951.
Report of SA [redacted] dated May 3, 1951 at Washington, D. C.
Report of SA [redacted] dated June 13, 1951, at Los Angeles.

b7C

TEXT ON THIS PAGE IS ILLEGIBLE
WE HAVE LEFT THE PAGE AS REFERENCE

RECORDED - 24

100-372586 — 66

CONFIDENTIAL
VIA LIAISON

Date: September 6, 1951

To: Director of Special Investigations
The Inspector General
Department of the Air Force
The Pentagon
Washington, D. C.

354.894 DECLASSIFIED BY 5P5-JC/[illegible]
ON 6-25-99

From: J. Edgar Hoover - Director, Federal Bureau of Investigation

Subject: DR. THEODORE VON KARMAN
[redacted]
MISCELLANEOUS - INFORMATION CONCERNING

[redacted] Holland Hotel, New York City, called at the New York Office of this Bureau on August 6, 1951, and advised that he [redacted] who came to the United States [redacted] to exhibit to the U. S. military authorities an invention which he stated he previously discussed with Dr. Theodore Von Karman, Chairman, Scientific Advisory Committee, U. S. Air Force, in Europe. This invention is [redacted]

b7C

According to [redacted] after his arrival in the United States he contacted Von Karman who sent him to [redacted] Research and Development Branch, Military Planning Division, Army Quartermaster Corps, Washington, D. C. [redacted] referred [redacted] to Reed Research Incorporated, Washington, D. C., but no agreements were consumated by [redacted] with that concern. [redacted] further stated that Von Karman also attempted to have his inventions developed through Aerojet, an organization in which Von Karman has an interest.

Von Karman also introduced [redacted] to [redacted] stated that he believed both Von Karman and [redacted] were Communists but he had no specific data upon which to substantiate this allegation. [redacted] called attention to an

Tolson, Ladd, Clegg, Glavin, Nichols, Rosen, Tracy, Harbo, Belmont, Mohr, Tele. Room, Nease, Gandy

JEM:eal

EX-[illegible]

52 SEP 14 1951

Note: Internal Security - R investigation is being conducted by Bureau on Von Karman. Due to his highly placed position, reports are being disseminated only to OSI and Assistant Attorney General McInerney. The matter referred to in this communication has no connection with the current investigation of Von Karman but should be of definite interest to OSI & G-2. Therefore, information from your file concerning subjects is not being included in instant communication. KACA not being advised inasmuch as [redacted] this organization.

To [illegible] 9/[illegible]

TEXT ON THIS PAGE IS ILLEGIBLE
WE HAVE LEFT THE PAGE AS REFERENCE

article appearing in [redacted] entitled, [redacted] This article reported that data concerning [redacted] was previously furnished to both Von Karman [redacted] but apparently no action was taken for some time leaving the impression that the U. S. military authorities lost many years in this development.

[redacted] attempted to point out the similarity between this article and his experiences by stating that Von Karman [redacted] had discouraged him whereas he believes that his inventions would be of value to the U. S. military authorities.

The information contained herein is being furnished for your confidential use. No further action with respect to [redacted] complaint is contemplated by the Federal Bureau of Investigation.

b7C

cc - Assistant Chief of Staff, G-2
Department of the Army
The Pentagon
Washington, D. C.

Attention: Chief, Security Division

CONFIDENTIAL - VIA LIAISON

[redacted]

b7C

9-11-51

TEXT ON THIS PAGE IS ILLEGIBLE
WE HAVE LEFT THE PAGE AS REFERENCE

STANDARD FORM NO. 64

# Office Memorandum • UNITED STATES GOVERNMENT

TO : Director, FBI

DATE: August 17, 1951

FROM : SAC, New York

SUBJECT: DR. THEODORE VON KARMAN
[redacted]
SECURITY MATTER - C

On August 6, 1951, [redacted] living at the Holland Hotel, 42nd Street, New York City, called at the New York Office with his mother. [redacted] said that he had previously made complaints about the above-named individuals to both the Los Angeles and Washington Field Offices and desired to furnish additional information.

[redacted] is an alien and came to the United States with his mother sometime [redacted] The purpose of his visit to the United States was to exhibit to the American military authorities an invention which he had previously discussed with Dr. VON KARMAN when VON KARMAN was in Europe.

b7C

This invention primarily was [redacted]

[redacted] also invented what he calls [redacted] and he indicated was of much more use to the military authorities than his first invention.

After coming to the United States and meeting VON KARMAN, [redacted] was sent by VON KARMAN to [redacted] Research and Development Branch, Military Planning Division of the Army Quartermaster Corps of Washington, D.C. [redacted] discussed his first invention with [redacted] who attempted to interest [redacted] in having the Reed Research, Inc. of 1048 Potomac Street, Northwest, Washington, D.C. telephone number Decatur 7000, which firm [redacted] indicated could help [redacted] in the manufacture of his invention, look at this invention.

cc: Los Angeles
Washington Field

BDM:MZ
100-0

RECORDED 13
INDEXED 
100-372586-66
AUG 20 1951

HANDLED BY

Letter to Director, FBI
NY #100-0

[redacted] met [redacted] of Reed a [redacted] but [redacted] was dissatisfied and nothing came of the negotiations.

VON KARMAN whose home address is 1501 Marengo Avenue, Pasadena, California, is also the chairman of the Scientific Advisory Committee of the Air Force and has office space in Room 4C, 340 at the Pentagon.

After [redacted] came to the United States and discussed his inventions with VON KARMAN, VON KARMAN tried to get [redacted] to have the inventions developed through Aerojet, a California firm with which VON KARMAN supposedly was affiliated. During the course of [redacted] discussions with VON KARMAN, he had occasion to meet [redacted] believes that both of these individuals are Communists He has no specific information to substantiate this statement that they are Communists although he pointed out an article entitled [redacted] which appears in the [redacted]

This article was written by [redacted] who notes in his article that the information about [redacted] was given to both of the above-mentioned individuals and that apparently no action was taken for sometime, leaving the impression that the United States military authorities lost many years ' time in failing to go ahead with the information which they received from the German Scientist. [redacted] attempts to point out the similarity between the statements made by [redacted] and his own experience, saying that both of these individuals have definitely discouraged him with his two inventions and that he believes both of the inventions would be of material assistance to the United States military authorities and yet no action has been taken to date.

[redacted] noted that both of his inventions had been patented at the United States patent office in Washington, D.C. and that he is represented by the patent law firm of Bacon and Thomas, New York City.

The above is being furnished for the information of the Bureau.

b7C

TEXT ON THIS PAGE IS ILLEGIBLE
WE HAVE LEFT THE PAGE AS REFERENCE

FD-72 (1-10-49)

# FEDERAL BUREAU OF INVESTIGATION

FORM No. 1
THIS CASE ORIGINATED AT LOS ANGELES

FILE NO. 65-1145

| REPORT MADE AT | DATE WHEN MADE | PERIOD FOR WHICH MADE | REPORT MADE BY |
|---|---|---|---|
| CINCINNATI, OHIO | 8-30-51 | 6-20;8-7-51 | [redacted] b7C pkk |

| TITLE | CHARACTER OF CASE |
|---|---|
| THEODORE VON KARMAN, Was. | INTERNAL SECURITY - R |

AGENCY
REQ. REC'D 6-27-56
REP'T FORW. 7-13-56
BY

SYNOPSIS OF FACTS:

AGENCY
REQ. REC'D
REP'T FORW.
BY

b2

AGENCY USIA
REQ. REC'D 1-15-98
REP'T FORW. 1-29-98
BY

b7D

[redacted] advised he knew subject [redacted] subject was Professor at Aachen Technical College, Germany. [redacted] May, 1926, subject made proposal to build up [redacted] and later became [redacted] Subject worked in this capacity at Aachen Technical College and never actually worked at [redacted] Only contact by [redacted] with subject was during [redacted] has had no contact with subject since [redacted] stated it was common knowledge [redacted] subject had been connected with Bela Kun regime Hungary in 1919, where held position of Secretary of Ministry of Education. Source of above information not known to [redacted] never talked with subject concerning experience in Bela Kun regime Hungary [redacted] stated he has no knowledge or way to determine if subject was sympathetic to Bela Kun regime in Hungary, 1919.

- RUC -

ALL INFORMATION CONTAINED HEREIN IS UNCLASSIFIED

HANDLED BY STOP DESK

| APPROVED AND FORWARDED: | SPECIAL AGENT IN CHARGE | DO NOT WRITE IN THESE SPACES | |
|---|---|---|---|
| | | 100 - 67 | RECORDED - 3 |
| COPIES OF THIS REPORT | | | EX-62 |
| 6 - Bureau (100-372586)<br>5 - Los Angeles (1-OSI, District 18, Maywood)(105-863)<br>2 - Cincinnati | | SEP 1 1951<br>13 | |



SEE REVERSE SIDE FOR ADD. DISSEMINATION.

63 SEP 14 1951

U. S. GOVERNMENT PRINTING OFFICE 16—60657-1

Cin. 65-1145

DETAILS: **AT DAYTON, OHIO**

[redacted] stated he knew the subject [redacted] the subject was a Professor at Aachen Technical College, Rhine Province, Germany. During the winters while associated with this College, the subject spent some time in the United States where he was associated with the California Institute of Technology. Sometime during the middle 1920's the subject acted as an advisor to the Japanese, but it is not known whether he acted in this capacity for the Japanese Government or for some private industry in Japan.

In May, 1928, the subject made a proposal to build up [redacted] for the German Government, and he later became the [redacted] the subject never actually worked in Berlin, but carried on his work [redacted] at Aachen Technical College. [redacted] and it was on the occasion [redacted] was in personal contact and associated with the subject.

[redacted] has had no contact with him, in person or by correspondence, since that time.

[redacted] stated it was common knowledge [redacted] that the subject had been associated with the Bela Kun regime in Hungary in 1919. As [redacted] recalls, the subject held the position of Secretary of the Ministry of Education during the Bela Kun regime. [redacted] could not furnish the source of this information, but stated it was common knowledge and everyone [redacted] accepted this fact. The Bela Kun regime in Hungary was considered to be a Communist one, although he, [redacted] stated he could not prove this statement.

[redacted] continued that he never talked with the subject concerning his past experience in Hungary [redacted]

 /b7D

[redacted] advised he has always admired the subject as a man and for his vast knowledge in the scientific field. According to [redacted] he has an excellent character, but whether or not he is a Communist or was in sympathy with the Bela Kun regime in Hungary, he [redacted] has no knowledge or way of determining this fact.

[redacted] stated that during the time he was associated with the subject, there were both "right" and "left" elements [redacted] in Berlin. Neither element questioned the other and in this same manner the subject was accepted [redacted]

/b7D

REFERRED UPON COMPLETION TO THE OFFICE OF ORIGIN

TEXT ON THIS PAGE IS ILLEGIBLE
WE HAVE LEFT THE PAGE AS REFERENCE

Cin. 65-1145

ADMINISTRATIVE PAGE

REFERENCES: b7C Report of SA [redacted] Los Angeles, dated 6-13-51.
Cincinnati letter to Bureau dated 6-28-51.

# Office Memorandum · UNITED STATES GOVERNMENT

TO : D. M. Ladd  
FROM : A. H. Belmont  
DATE: September 12, 1951  
SUBJECT: THEODORE VON KARMAN, was.  
INTERNAL SECURITY - R

## PURPOSE:

To advise that the Bureau is conducting an investigation of captioned subject at the request of the U. S. Air Force and prior to its completion [redacted] Air Force, informed subject that he had been cleared.

To recommend that a letter of protest be sent to the Office of Special Investigations, U. S. Air Force.

## DETAILS:

You will recall that the Bureau is presently conducting an investigation of Theodore Von Karman who is Chairman of the Scientific Advisory Board, U. S. Air Force, and a consultant on the top secret project Vista, sponsored by the California Institute of Technology.

Our investigation was instituted in October, 1950, based upon a G-2 report which stated that in 1919 Von Karman, a professor at Caltech was Deputy Commissar of Cultural and Educational Affairs under the Bela Kun (Communist) Government in Hungary. Investigation revealed that the subject was probably employed by the U. S. Air Force and on January 23, 1951, the U. S. Air Force was furnished available data concerning him and requested to advise of his employment status. The Air Force replied on January 30, 1951, stating that the subject was an Air Force employee.

By memorandum dated February 28, 1951, from Mr. V. P. Keay to Mr. A. H. Belmont, Mr. Keay advised that the Von Karman matter was discussed by SA [redacted] of the Liaison Section, and with [redacted] of OSI headquarters, at which time both [redacted] requested that the Bureau conduct an investigation of Von Karman and that the investigation be of an Internal Security character rather than a Loyalty type because Von Karman was employed under a contractual agreement with the Air Force and, therefore, not subject to the provisions of Executive Order 9835. [redacted] also stated that Von Karman has access to practically all classified data in the Air Force and OSI did not desire that the results of the investigation be disseminated to the Civil Service Commission, which, of course, would be necessary under Loyalty regulations.

100-372586  
Attachment  
JEM:eme

On the basis of the above request from OSI our investigation was reinstituted.

The investigation reflected that Von Karman was an associate of several Communist Party members and an associate of William Perl, a Soviet agent and [redacted] Investigation further reflected that Von Karman was friendly with [redacted] an admitted former Communist Party member [redacted]

b7C

Von Karman was interviewed by Bureau agents in the presence of [redacted] of OSI on May 23, 1951, and on May 29, 1951, in Los Angeles, California. Von Karman admitted that he was connected with the Bela Kun Government in Hungary from March to July, 1919. He denied present or past CP membership and he denied that he had ever furnished classified data to any unauthorized person. He declined to sign a prepared statement but advised that he desired "to think it over." On September 4, 1951, Von Karman appeared at the Los Angeles Office after he was reminded of the statement which he previously stated he would consider signing. At that time he exhibited a letter dated August 22, 1951, from [redacted] U. S. Air Force, Washington, D. C. [redacted] letter reads as follows:

b7C

b7C

"Dr. Theodore Von Karman
1501 South Marengo Avenue
Pasadena, California

Dear Dr. Von Karman:

"I refer to your several inquiries of me concerning the status of the investigation which was recently conducted concerning certain aspects of your past. I am happy to advise you that the case has been concluded and that the matter has been resolved within the Air Force completely in your favor.

"In the light of world conditions and the many complexities of our internal security problems, I am sure you will recognize the imperative need which exists to afford these matters considered attention both in the interest of the country and the individual involved.

"Trusting that we may have the benefit of your continued services for a long time to come, I am

Sincerely,

[redacted] U. S. Air Force b7C

Subject stated that in view of the above letter he assumed the investigation was concluded and he indicated that he had no desire now to sign this statement.

<u>RECOMMENDATION:</u>

Although our investigation is now substantially completed, nevertheless, the Air Force has hampered the proper conduct of the investigation by the action of [redacted] telling Von Karman that the investigation was concluded and resolved in his favor by the Air Force.

b7C

It is recommended that a letter of protest be sent to OSI. If you agree, the letter is attached for your approval.

TEXT ON THIS PAGE IS ILLEGIBLE
WE HAVE LEFT THE PAGE AS REFERENCE

STANDARD FORM NO. 64

# Office Memorandum • UNITED STATES GOVERNMENT

TO : Director, FBI

DATE: Sept. 19, 1951

FROM : SAC, Los Angeles

SUBJECT: THEODORE VON KARMAN, was.
INTERNAL SECURITY - R
(Bufile 100-372586)

Re New York letter to the Bureau dated August 17, 1951 in above captioned matter reporting a complaint made at that office by [redacted] on August 6, 1951 concerning the subject [redacted]

[redacted] also appeared at the Los Angeles Office with his mother on June 18, 1951 giving substantially the same information as indicated in referenced letter, and related a long story of his difficulties in getting sponsorship for his inventions from the subject and others. As a result of these delays and obstacles, he made loose allegations and contended that they are all Communists or Communist sympathizers, without furnishing any substantiating information whatever.

[redacted] lamented and bemoaned getting an alleged "brush off" from the subject [redacted] He felt the same way regarding [redacted] of the International Petroleum Consultants Ltd., Pasadena, California and a [redacted] a lawyer, [redacted] who he also contacted through the subject and was likewise gave him no help, especially in regard to publishing a life story of his father.

[redacted] also remarked that he and his mother had been [redacted] Los Angeles, California, for reasons unknown and feared that they were being followed and requested to know if this office could afford them any protection.

In view of the nature of [redacted] information as reflected above, it has not been considered pertinent in the current investigation of the subject and has not been reported therein. A closing report in this matter is currently being prepared by this office.

OST G-2 advised by letter dated 9-6-51

b7C

JPA:AAD
105-863

RECORDED - 119

100-372586-69

cc: Washington Field (100-22923)
New York (65-4747)

EX. 67

HANDLED BY STOP DESK

ALL INFORMATION CONTAINED HEREIN IS UNCLASSIFIED DATE 6-5-97 BY

TEXT ON THIS PAGE IS ILLEGIBLE
WE HAVE LEFT THE PAGE AS REFERENCE

C.

CONFIDENTIAL

Date: September 12, 1951

To: Director of Special Investigations
The Inspector General
Department of the Air Force
The Pentagon
Washington 25, D. C.

354194
DECLASSIFIED BY SPS JC/102
ON 6-25-97

From: John Edgar Hoover, Director
Federal Bureau of Investigation

RECORDED - 19 100-372586-70

Subject: THEODORE VON KARMAN, was.,
INTERNAL SECURITY - R

X-105

During the course of our investigation of Theodore Von Karman, he was interviewed by representatives of this Bureau in Los Angeles, California, on September 4, 1951. During the interview, he exhibited the below-quoted letter dated August 22, 1951, from [redacted] U. S. Air Force:

b7C

"Dr. Theodore Von Karman
1501 South Marengo Avenue
Pasadena, California

Dear Dr. Von Karman:

"I refer to your several inquiries of me concerning the status of the investigation which was recently conducted concerning certain aspects of your past. I am happy to advise you that the case has been concluded and that the matter has been resolved within the Air Force completely in your favor.

"In the light of world conditions and the many complexities of our internal security problems, I am sure you will recognize the imperative need which

Tolson
Ladd
Clegg
Glavin
Nichols
Rosen
Tracy
Harbo
Belmont
Mohr
Tele. Room
Nease

JEM:me:mes

COMM - FBI
SEP 1 3 1951
MAILED 18

HANDLED BY
STOP DESK

OCT 5 1951

exists to afford these matters considered attention both in the interest of the country and the individual involved.

"Trusting that we may have the benefit of your continued services for a long time to come, I am

Sincerely,

[redacted] U. S. Air Force [redacted]

b7C

As you are aware, our investigation was instituted at your specific request and was not completed on the date of [redacted] letter, August 22, 1951, nor is it complete at the present time. This Bureau considers that the U. S. Air Force has seriously hampered the successful completion of the investigation by furnishing such a letter to the subject.

You are further advised that our investigation in this matter is being brought to an immediate conclusion.

Tolson____
Ladd____
Clegg____
Glavin____
Nichols____
Rosen____
Tracy____
Harbo____
Belmont____
Mohr____
Tele. Room____
Nease____
Gandy____

TEXT ON THIS PAGE IS ILLEGIBLE
WE HAVE LEFT THE PAGE AS REFERENCE

STANDARD FORM NO. 64

# Office Memorandum • UNITED STATES GOVERNMENT

TO : DIRECTOR, FBI

DATE: September 5, 1951

FROM : SAC, LOS ANGELES

SUBJECT: THEODORE VON KARMAN, Was.
INTERNAL SECURITY - R
(Bufile 100-372586)

Re Los Angeles letter dated July 5, 1951.

As noted in referenced letter the subject, after carefully correcting and amending a prepared statement dated May 29, 1951, as to his association with the Communist Bela Kun Government in Hungary in 1919, declined to sign it "at this time" although admitting the facts therein to be true. He indicated that he desired "to think the matter over" and agreed to advise this office later as to his final decision in the matter.

Not having heard from him to date, subject was recently contacted telephonically regarding the possible oversight in this matter, at which time he expressed a desire to come to the Los Angeles FBI Office. Accordingly, subject voluntarily appeared at the local FBI Office on September 4, 1951. He thereupon exhibited the following letter dated August 22, 1951, which he had received from [redacted] U. S. Air Force, Washington, D. C.: b7C

ALL INFORMATION CONTAINED HEREIN IS UNCLASSIFIED DATE 6-5-97 BY [illegible]

"Dr. Theodore Von Karman
1501 South Marengo Avenue
Pasadena, California

Dear Dr. Von Karman:

"I refer to your several inquiries of me concerning the status of the investigation which was recently conducted concerning certain aspects of your past. I am happy to advise you that the case has been concluded and that the matter has been resolved within the Air Force completely in your favor.

"In the light of world conditions and the many complexities of our internal security problems, I am sure you will recognize the imperative need which exists to afford these matters considered attention both in the interest of the country and the individual involved.

JIA:cls/hep
105-563
cc: Washington Field (100-22923)

RECORDED 100-372586-70

EX-105 SEP 1951

[redacted] b7C

"Trusting that we may have the benefit of your continued services for a long time to come, I am

Sincerely,

[redacted] U. S. Air Force b7C

Subject stated that in view of the above letter he, therefore, assumed that the investigation concerning him had been concluded. He indicated that there was apparently no further need and no desire on his part to sign his previously furnished statement. It was again clearly reiterated to the subject that it was purely a voluntary matter on his part and that it was his privilege either to sign or to decline to sign the statement. It was also pointed out to him that he was being recontacted at this time merely to avoid any misunderstanding or oversight on his part in advising this office of his ultimate choice in the matter as he had agreed to do.

Although maintaining a cooperative attitude, it is noted that the subject appeared and also remarked that he was "embittered" somewhat as a result of inquiries having been made about him from former associates and friends in Europe and consequent embarrassment. He contended that he should have originally been contacted and questioned regarding the instant matter when he would and could have explained it in full. Subject was informed that this Bureau did not conduct any active investigation concerning him in Europe; further, that any inquiries made about him in this country were in accordance with the official performance of duties imposed upon this organization and in this instance at the specific request of the United States Air Force.

It is to be noted further that the subject, who still is Chairman of the Scientific Advisory Board, U. S. Air Force, Washington, D. C., stated that he has recently moved his local office from his residence where he has maintained it for some time to the former Arroyo Vista Hotel, Pasadena, California. This new location, he explained, houses the top secret project VISTA sponsored by the California Institute of Technology, Pasadena, California, and for which he is also contacted as a consultant. Subject added that he made this move in order to afford his research papers, documents and materials proper security not available at his residence.

A closing report follows.

TEXT ON THIS PAGE IS ILLEGIBLE
WE HAVE LEFT THE PAGE AS REFERENCE

CONFIDENTIAL
VIA LIAISON

47585

Date: October 16, 1951

To: Director of Special Investigations
The Inspector General
Department of the Air Force
The Pentagon
Washington 25, D. C.

From: John Edgar Hoover - Director
Federal Bureau of Investigation

Subject: THEODORE VON KARMAN, was.,
INTERNAL SECURITY - R

Reference is made to my communication dated September 12, 1951, concerning captioned subject.

b7C Enclosed is one copy of a report by Special Agent [redacted] dated September 27, 1951, at Los Angeles, California.

No further investigation is contemplated concerning this matter.

Attachment

JEM:mes

RECORDED - 102 100-372586 - 7 to

EX. - 15

Delivered OSI 10/17/51

b7C [redacted]

354774

DECLASSIFIED BY 605 JC/lp

ON 6-18-97

Tolson
Ladd
Clegg
Glavin
Nichols
Rosen
Tracy
Harbo
Alden
Belmont
Laughlin
Mohr
Tele. Room
Nease
Gandy

U.S. DEPT. OF JUSTICE
F B I
OCT 18 3 04 PM '51

U.S. DEPT. OF JUSTICE
F B I
RECEIVED-MAIL ROOM

# FEDERAL BUREAU OF INVESTIGATION

Form No. 1
THIS CASE ORIGINATED AT LOS ANGELES

FILE No. 105-863

| REPORT MADE AT | DATE WHEN MADE | PERIOD FOR WHICH MADE | REPORT MADE BY |
|---|---|---|---|
| LOS ANGELES | 9/27/51 | 8/25; 9/4,5,18/51 | [redacted] AAD b7C |
| TITLE | | | CHARACTER OF CASE |
| THEODORE VON KARMAN, was. Todar Von Karman | | | INTERNAL SECURITY - R |

SEE REVERSE SIDE FOR ADD. DISSEMINATION.

SYNOPSIS OF FACTS: Dr. THEODORE VON KARMAN recontacted Los Angeles FBI Office on Sept. 4, 1951 and indicated that he did not desire to sign the statement furnished by him on May 29, 1951 regarding his association with the Communist Bela Kun Regime in Hungary in 1919. VON KARMAN exhibited a letter dated Aug. 22, 1951 from Vice Chief of Staff, U.S.A.F. wherein he was informed that investigation concerning him had been resolved within the Air Force completely in his favor. Former European associates confirm his connection with Bela Kun Govt. though he was not believed to have been a confirmed Communist.

AGENCY 7C-State
REQ. REC'D 6-26-59
REP'T FOR. 7-13-59
BY AEF-9ms

AGENCY 1C [redacted]

b2

- C -

DETAILS:

Dr. THEODORE VON KARMAN voluntarily appeared at the Los Angeles FBI Office on September 4, 1951 in connection with his previous promise to advise this office as to his decision regarding the signing of the amended and corrected statement furnished by him on May 29,1951 concerning his associations with the Communist Bela Kun Government in Hungary in 1919.

Subject thereupon exhibited a letter dated August 22, 1951 addressed to him which he had received from General N. F. [redacted] U. S. Air Force, Washington, D. C.,

b7C

SEE REVERSE SIDE FOR ADD. DISSEMINATION.

| APPROVED AND FORWARDED: | SPECIAL AGENT IN CHARGE | DO NOT WRITE IN THESE SPACES | |
|---|---|---|---|
| COPY IN FILE | | 100-372586-[redacted] | RECORDED - 129 |
| 6 - Bureau (100-372586)<br>2 - Washington Field (100-22923) (Info)<br>1 - New York (65-4747)<br>1 - OSI, District 18 Maywood (Encl)<br>3 - Los Angeles | | OCT 8 1951<br>12 | INDEXED - 129 |

b7C

HANDLED BY STATE DESK

wherein the following portion was noted: "I refer to your several inquiries of me concerning the status of the investigation which was recently conducted concerning certain aspects of your past. I am happy to advise you that this case has been concluded and that the matter has been resolved within the Air Force completely in your favor."

VON KARMAN stated that in view of the above, he, therefore, assumed that the investigation concerning him had been concluded, and he indicated that there was no further need and no desire on his part to sign his previously furnished statement. Subject was again clearly apprised of the voluntary character of this matter and his priviledge to make any choice he preferred.

It is recalled that VON KARMAN, upon originally furnishing his statement, stated that he preferred not to sign it "at this time" and desired instead "to think the matter over." However, in order to bring the matter to a logical conclusion with a definite expression of his choice, he agreed at that time to recontact this office in the immediate future as to his final decision.

VON KARMAN also remarked that he has recently moved his local office as Chairman of the Scientific Advisory Board of the U. S. Air Force, from his residence to new quarters in the former Arroyo Vista Hotel, Pasadena, California, where better security is available. This location, he explained, houses the top secret project VISTA sponsored by the California Institute of Technology at Pasadena and for which he is also now contacted as a consultant.

b2
b7D

[redacted] another Government agency conducting security investigations, advised on May 1, 1951 that [redacted] at Aachen, Germany, had furnished the following information upon interview on April 24, 1951:

[redacted] Subject had served in the Austrian Army during World War I. Immediately upon learning in 1916 that the German Army had requested his services, the Austrian Army employed the subject to develop a helicopter. [redacted] believed that the subject became Minister of Culture in Hungary for a short time.

b7D

According to [redacted] subject accepted the position only because he believed himself to be the most qualified person. Subject was said to be "very difficult to influence" and it was [redacted] opinion that he was never a confirmed Communist.

b2 b7C b7D

[redacted] above advised that [redacted] Aachen, Germany, also furnished the following information upon interview on April 24, 1951:

[redacted] the subject had returned from Hungary in 1919. Subject had been an officer in the Austrian Army where he had been utilized as a scientist in developing a helicopter. Immediately following World War I, subject held the position of Minister of Culture in the Hungarian Government. He was sometimes referred to as a Communist by his enemies, but such statements or accusations, according to [redacted] were made concerning any individual who participated in the Hungarian Government under Bela Kun.

b7C b7D

Subject had two brothers, one of whom had been a bank director and the other a director of a secondary school in Budapest. His father had been a philosopher and died sometime prior to 1919. His mother and sister, the latter being known as "PIPE", both referred to him as "TODOR". "PIPE" was a close friend of [redacted] VON FAKLA, mentioned previously in this investigation.

[redacted] remarked that VON FAKLA was a person of poor character and morals who "utilized" the subject for his personal benefit. It was [redacted] opinion that subject's friendship toward VON FAKLA was activated by the fact that VON FAKLA had aided the subject in escaping from Hungary. VON FAKLA remained in Aachen until 1930, but has not been heard from since.

During the middle 1920's [redacted] stated the subject undertook a private project to produce aircraft fuselages from balsa wood and bakelite. This enterprise proved too costly and he abandoned it. [redacted] further stated that he recently received a letter from [redacted] of the University of Darmstadt at Darmstadt, Germany. [redacted] requested that all [redacted] write a synopsis of their [redacted] enterprises with the subject and forward it to [redacted]

Detailed accounts of the above were to arrive in the United States not later than "October, 1951". These narratives are to be presented to the subject at the National Congress For Applied Mechanics in Chicago, Illinois on "June 14, 1951".

[redacted] also reported that [redacted] had also furnished the following information upon interview on April 25, 1951:

Subject served as Minister of Culture in the Hungarian Government for a brief period shortly after World War I. [redacted] stated that he was convinced that the subject is not a Communist and never adhered to Communist ideals. Subject returned to Germany in August, 1945 accompanied by [redacted] of the Joy Manufacturing Company, Pittsburgh, Pennsylvania; [redacted] now residing in Pasadena, California; [redacted] all of whom were [redacted]

[redacted] above also advised that [redacted] at Goettingen, Germany, had been interviewed on April 26, 1951, at which time he stated that he had first met the subject in [redacted] During their ensuing acquaintance politics were never discussed and he had no knowledge of the subject's activities in the Bela Kun Regime in Hungary. In 1933, during a meeting in Akron, Ohio, subject confided to [redacted] that as a result of excellent resources and equipment afforded him in this country, he would remain in the United States.

[redacted] stated that [redacted] Darmstadt, Germany, was interviewed on April 27, 1951, at which time he stated that [redacted] He was not aware of subject's participation in the Bela Kun Regime. He stated that the subject had been a First Lieutenant in the Austrian Army during World War I and served at an experimental institute in Fischament, near Vienna, Austria. [redacted] related also that the subject, at the time of this interview, was then in Europe and that he had received a letter on the previous day from [redacted] U. S. Air Attache, Paris, France, which stated that the subject had requested to see [redacted] in Paris on May 4, 1951.



b2 b7C b7D

b7C
b7D

According to this letter, subject would return from Italy on April 26, 1951 and would depart for the United States on May 6, 1951. [redacted] was aware that the subject is currently a chief scientific advisor of the U. S. Air Force.

b2
b7D

[redacted] a former young officer in the Hungarian Army during the Bela Kun Regime in 1919, advised on June 14, 1951 that he did not recall anyone by the name of VON KARMAN connected with that regime in an official capacity. It is [redacted] contention that if the subject had been an important personality in Hungary during that period, he would certainly remember him.

The Los Angeles Daily News of June 27, 1951 carried an item announcing a farewell reception to be held in honor of forty-six Israeli air students on June 30, 1951 at the Institute of Aeronautical Science, 7660 Beverly Boulevard, Los Angeles, California, where the main speaker would be Dr. THEODORE VON KARMAN. The students were described as having completed one year's training in aeronautics, having been sent to Cal-Aero Institute in Glendale, California to learn American techniques in airplane mechanics in order to be able to maintain the civil and military aircraft of Israeli. [redacted]

b7C

The Los Angeles Times of July 3, 1951 reported the death of subject's sister, Dr. JOSEPHINE de KARMAN on July 2, 1951 as a result of a heart attack suffered at their home, 1501 South Marengo Avenue, Pasadena, California. The article related that she had been noted for her work in the field of International Scientific Relations. She had been a research specialist at the University of Southern California from 1937 to 1940 and had been decorated by the French Government for her work in promoting European goodwill by the organization of Scientific Congresses during the past five years. She was 57 years old and had been born in Budapest, Hungary where she obtained her doctorate and came to this country 21 years ago. She worked in close cooperation with her brother, Dr. THEODORE VON KARMAN, Chief Scientific Advisor to the U. S. Air Force, who, prior to his acceptance of this position in 1949, had been Director of the Guggenheim Laboratory at the California Institute of Technology.

LA 105-863

ENCLOSURES: TO OSI, DISTRICT 18, MAYWOOD:

Report of SA [redacted] dated May 31, 1951, at Washington, D.C.

Report of SA [redacted] dated August 2, 1951, at Washington, D.C.

b7C

- CLOSED -

ADMINISTRATIVE PAGE

INFORMANTS:

b7C

[redacted] OSI report by SA [redacted] dated 5/1/51, OSI file #33-49.

b2

b7D

[redacted] [redacted] Paris, France, who was interviewed by the Legal Attache of the American Embassy, Paris, France on 6/14/51. It is observed that on this occasion [redacted] described himself merely as a young officer in the Hungarian Army in the Bela Kun Regime in 1919, whereas during the course of a previous interview in January, 1951, he had indicated that he had worked [redacted] in the Bela Kun Regime.

b7D

REFERENCE:

Los Angeles letter to Bureau and Washington Field Office dated 9/5/51.
Report of SA [redacted] dated 6/13/51 at Los Angeles.

b7C

TEXT ON THIS PAGE IS ILLEGIBLE
WE HAVE LEFT THE PAGE AS REFERENCE

Assistant Attorney General
James M. McInerney

October 18, 1951
47582

Director, FBI

CONFIDENTIAL

THEODORE VON KARMAN, was.,
INTERNAL SECURITY - R

N

Enclosed is one copy of a report by Special Agent [redacted] dated September 27, 1951, at Los Angeles, California.

b7C

No further investigation is contemplated concerning this matter.

Attachment

DECLASSIFIED BY SPS JC/[illegible]
ON 6.17.97

G.I.R.-5

JEM:mes
100-372586

EX.-6

RECORDED-14 | 100-372586-77
OCT 20 1951
80

RECEIVED ... U.S. DEPT. OF JUSTICE

Tolson
Ladd
Clegg
Glavin
Nichols
Rosen
Tracy
Harbo
Alden
Belmont
Laughlin
Mohr
Tele. Room
Nease
Gandy

61 OCT 29 1951

BANNED BY
STOP DESK
10/29/51

TEXT ON THIS PAGE IS ILLEGIBLE
WE HAVE LEFT THE PAGE AS REFERENCE

C

SECRET

This Case Originated at Los Angeles (105-863) File No.

ROL:AM

| Report Made at | Date when Made | Period for which Made | Report Made by |
|---|---|---|---|
| Paris, France | 12-17-51 | 6-14;12-4-51 | [redacted] b7C |

| Title | Character of Case |
|---|---|
| THEODORE VON KARMAN, was, Theodor Karman, Theodore Von Szoelloestcictak | INTERNAL SECURITY - R |

Synopsis of Facts :

[redacted] (S)

b1

- RUC -

no dissemination warranted. 12/29/51

ALL INFORMATION CONTAINED HERE IS UNCLASSIFIED EXCEPT WHERE SHOWN OTHERWISE

G.I.R.

1cc - Los Angeles by R/S 12-29-51

Case closed LA origin. 12/29/51

CLASSIFIED BY SP5JC/pap
DECLASSIFY ON: 25X 6

Reference :

[redacted] b7C

| Approved and Forwarded | Legal Attache | Do Not Write in These Spaces |
|---|---|---|
| **Made Available to** | **Copies of This Report** | 100-372586 - 73 |
| Embassy<br>M. A.<br>N. A.<br>Others | 7-Bureau (100-372586)<br>1-Paris (100-252) | RECORDED - 16<br>INDEXED - 16<br>EX. - 103<br>HANDED BY ... DESK 12/26/51 |

COPY IN FILE

COPIES DESTROYED
APR 5 1963

61 JAN 9 1952

SECRET

TEXT ON THIS PAGE IS ILLEGIBLE
WE HAVE LEFT THE PAGE AS REFERENCE

THEODORE VON KARMAN, was.

b2 b7D

By memorandum dated December 4, 1951, Confidential Informant [redacted] (S)

[redacted] (S)

b1

[redacted] (S)

[redacted] (S)

[redacted] (S)

SECRET

ADMINISTRATIVE PAGE

SOURCE OF INFORMATION b2 b7D [redacted] (S) b1

DISSEMINATION

No copies are being distributed in Paris since the information in this report is of no particular interest to other agencies here.

Sufficient copies of this report are being furnished to the Bureau for transmittal to Los Angeles, the office of origin.

REFERENCE:

b7C Bulet May 9, 1951 and report of SA [redacted] Los Angeles dated April 27, 1951.

TEXT ON THIS PAGE IS ILLEGIBLE
WE HAVE LEFT THE PAGE AS REFERENCE

April 2, 1952

359,894
DECLASSIFIED BY SP5 JC/
ON 6-17-97

THEODORE VON KARMAN
Born 5-11-81
Budapest, Hungary

SECURITY INFORMATION - CONFIDENTIAL

This Bureau, in October, [illegible] instituted a security type investigation of Theodore Von Karman, Chairman of the Scientific Advisory Board, U. S. Air Force, and a consultant on the top secret project, Vista, sponsored by the California Institute of Technology. This investigation was based upon a report from another governmental agency which stated that in 1919, Von Karman, a professor at Cal Tech, was Deputy Commissar of Cultural and Educational Affairs under the Bela Kun (Communist) Communist Government in Hungary. The investigation revealed that he was probably employed by the U. S. Air Force. The Air Force indicated on January 30, 1951, that he was an Air Force employee. Thereafter, the Air Force requested this Bureau to continue its investigation of Von Karman, but not under Executive Order 9835, as he was not subject to the provisions thereof. The Air Force advised that Von Karman had access to practically all classified data. The investigation was reinstituted and reflected that Von Karman was an associate of several Communist Party members [redacted] a Soviet Agent, and [redacted] of Mikhail Gorin. Gorin was convicted of Soviet espionage in 1939. Investigation further reflected that Von Karman was friendly with [redacted] an admitted former Communist Party member. [redacted]

Von Karman was interviewed by agents of this Bureau on May 23, 1951 and May 29, 1951, in Los Angeles, California.

b7C

(100-372586-71)

Attachment (1)

RECORDED - 66 100-372586-74

Original to Secretary of Defense

APR 7 1952

EX-99

[redacted] jar

b7C

6 APR 19 1952

SECURITY INFORMATION - CONFIDENTIAL

He admitted that he was connected with the Bela Kun Government in Hungary from March to July, 1919. He denied present or past Communist Party membership and he denied that he had ever furnished classified data to any unauthorized person. He declined to sign a prepared statement, but advised that he desired "to think it over." On September 4, 1951, Von Karman appeared at the Local Office of the FBI in Los Angeles and indicated there was no further need and no desire on his part to sign his previously furnished statement. X For your consideration in this connection, there is transmitted herewith a copy of the report of Special Agent [redacted] dated 9-27-51, at Los Angeles in the case entitled, "Theodore Von Karman, was; Internal Security - R". b7C

The above information is furnished for your confidential use only and is not to be distributed outside your agency. This is the result of a request for an FBI file check only and is not to be considered as a clearance or nonclearance of the individual involved.

Belmont_____
Clegg_____
Glavin_____
Harbo_____
Rosen_____
Tracy_____
Mohr_____
Tele. Rm._____
Nease_____
Gandy_____

TEXT ON THIS PAGE IS ILLEGIBLE
WE HAVE LEFT THE PAGE AS REFERENCE

STANDARD FORM NO. 64

# Office Memorandum • UNITED STATES GOVERNMENT

SECRET

TO : Director, FBI

FROM : SAC, Buffalo (100-0)

DATE: May 19, 1952

SUBJECT: Professor VON KARMAN, aka
Professor Karman [redacted]
INTERNAL SECURITY - C

b7C

ALL INFORMATION CONTAINED
HEREIN IS UNCLASSIFIED
EXCEPT WHERE SHOWN
OTHERWISE

THEODORE VON KARMAN

11-1
5-1

[redacted]

(S) b1

b1 (S) [redacted]

[redacted]

(S)

b1

already in Bufile

The above is transmitted for information purposes.

100-372586-75

CLASSIFIED BY SP2CLJ/MS
DECLASSIFY ON: 25X

LJK:MAH

Classified by CIA Letter dated 4-29-98

RECORDED

EX-32

59 JUN 23 1952

SECRET

RECEIVED

MAY 23 1952

[redacted]

b7C

b7C

UNRECORDED COPY FILED IN 65-5475

TEXT ON THIS PAGE IS ILLEGIBLE
WE HAVE LEFT THE PAGE AS REFERENCE

354894
DECLASSIFIED BY SP5 JC/ORN
ON 6-17-97

July 1, 1952

THEODORE VON KARMAN
B. 5-11-81
Hungary

SECURITY INFORMATION - CONFIDENTIAL

It appears from a review of the records of this Bureau that the Attorney General is already in possession of all the pertinent data on file concerning the above named individual.

It is presumed that that information is available to you. It also appears that the Local Office of INS in New York City is already in possession of the pertinent data on file concerning Theodore Von Karman. It is likewise presumed that this information is available to you. However for your convenience the following information is set forth. (100-372586)

This Bureau, in October, 1950, ~~instituted a security~~ Summary type investigation of ~~Theodore Von Karman~~, Chairman of the Scientific Advisory Board, U. S. Air Force, and a consultant on the top secret project, Vista, sponsored by the California Institute of Technology. This investigation was based upon a report from another governmental agency which stated that in 1919, Von Karman, a professor at Cal Tech, was Deputy Commissar of Cultural and Educational Affairs under the Bela Kun (Communist) Communist Government in Hungary. The investigation revealed that he was probably employed by the U.S. Air Force. The Air Force indicated on January 30, 1951, that he was an Air Force employee. Thereafter, the Air Force requested this Bureau to continue its investigation of Von Karman, but not under Executive Order 9835, as he was not subject to the provisions thereof. The Air Force advised that Von Karman had access to practically all classified data. The investigation was reinstituted and reflected that Von Karman was an associate of several Communist Party members and an associate of William Perl, a Soviet Agent, and [redacted] b7C

(100-372586-74)

100-372586-76

RECORDED-29
INDEXED-29 13 JUL 31 1952

Original to: [redacted]
Assistant Commissioner
Immigration and Naturalization Service

b7C

[redacted]:men

SECURITY INFORMATION - CONFIDENTIAL

58 AUG 5 1952

[redacted] Mikhail Gorin. Gorin was convicted of Soviet espionage in 1939. Investigation further reflected that Von Karman was friendly with [redacted] an admitted former Communist Party member, [redacted] Von Karman was interviewed by agents of this Bureau on May 23, 1951 and May 29, 1951, in Los Angeles, California. He admitted that he was connected with the Bela Kun Government in Hungary from March to July, 1919. He denied present or past Communist Party membership and he denied that he had ever furnished classified data to any unauthorized person. He declined to sign a prepared statement, but advised that he desired "to think it over." On September 4, 1951, Von Karman appeared at the Local Office of the FBI in Los Angeles and indicated there was no further need and no desire on his part to sign his previously furnished statement.

b7C

The above information is furnished for your confidential use only and is not to be distributed outside of your agency. This is the result of a request for an FBI file check only and is not to be considered as a clearance or nonclearance of the individual involved.

Tolson ____
Ladd ____
Nichols ____
Belmont ____
Clegg ____
Glavin ____
Harbo ____
Rosen ____
Tracy ____
Laughlin ____
Mohr ____
Tele. Rm. ____
Holloman ____
Gandy ____

SAC, Los Angeles (105-863) July 31, 1952

Director, FBI (100-372586)-77

THEODORE VON KARMAN, was.
INTERNAL SECURITY - R

RECORDED-137
EX. - 106

Reference is made to the closing report of Special Agent [redacted] dated September 27, 1951, at Los Angeles, California, concerning captioned subject. b7C

[redacted] Office of Special Investigations, U. S. Air Force, informed that Von Karman recently traveled to Europe where he was introduced to [redacted] Von Karman casually mentioned to [redacted] that he had a brother in Hungary who, for some time, has been attempting to gain entrance into Chile. [redacted] allegedly stated to Von Karman, "Maybe we can do something for you." b7C

According to [redacted] Von Karman has now returned to the United States but he has heard nothing more from [redacted] Von Karman has stated that he will inform the FBI if he receives any further word from [redacted]

Los Angeles is requested to interview Von Karman and to secure complete details concerning his meeting with [redacted] any additional pertinent remarks by [redacted] and further identifying data concerning Von Karman's brother, including his full name. Von Karman should be requested to immediately contact the Bureau if he receives word from [redacted] b7C

This matter should be afforded expeditious attention and the results furnished to the Bureau in report form.

cc - 2 - Washington Field (For Information) (100-22923)

JEM:mes:brg

U.S. DEPT OF JUSTICE
F B I
RECEIVED MAIL ROOM

AUG 7 10 PM '52

COMM — FBI
AUG 1 1952
MAILED 28

363
67 AUG 12 1952

354894
ALL INFORMATION CONTAINED
HEREIN IS UNCLASSIFIED
DATE 6-5-97 BY SP5 [illegible]

TEXT ON THIS PAGE IS ILLEGIBLE
WE HAVE LEFT THE PAGE AS REFERENCE

Director
Mr. Tolson
Mr. Ladd
Mr. Belmont
Mr. Laughlin

Mr. Baumgardner
Mr. Branigan
Mr. Callan
Mr. H. L. Edwards
Mr. Hennrich
Mr. Scatterday
Mr. Stanley

Miss
Room
[redacted]

Ident. Div.
[redacted]
Rm. 7229
Mail Room
Rm. 5533
Reading Room
Rm. 5531

Records Section
Routing Unit
Send file
up-to-date
Send reference
Place on record
and return

See Me
Phone Me
Please [redacted]

Mr. Keay
[redacted]
Room 3708
[redacted]
Mr. Bates
[redacted]
Mr. Conroy
[redacted]
Mr. Daunt
[redacted]
Mr. Roach
[redacted]
Mr. D. J. Sullivan
[redacted]
Mr. W. C. Sullivan
[redacted]

ALL INFORMATION CONTAINED
HEREIN IS UNCLASSIFIED
DATE 6-5-92 BY

b7C

file
b7C

9/29/52 [redacted] advised that Von Karman called on him personally upon his return from Europe & gave him the info. — N. W. PHILCOX NWP
(over)

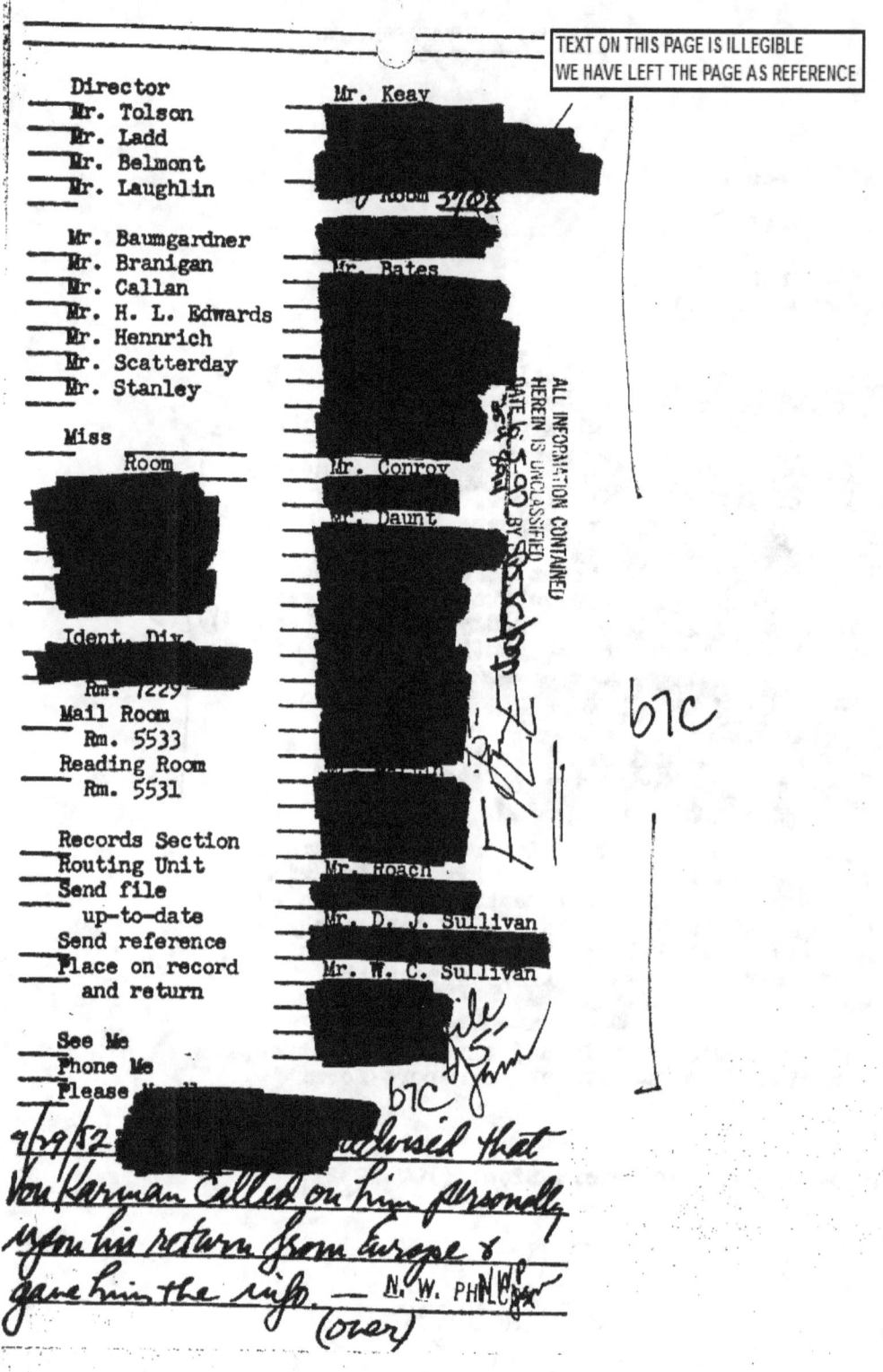

TEXT ON THIS PAGE IS ILLEGIBLE
WE HAVE LEFT THE PAGE AS REFERENCE

b7C

Von Karman is connected with
the Fulbright Foundation &
as such spends a considerable
amount of time in
Europe. His meeting &
conversation with [redacted]
[redacted] was a very casual
one & conversation lasted
only a few minutes —
[redacted] tried to
get further details from
Von Karman at time but
apparently none available.
[redacted] has no
objection to Von K. being
interviewed.

OSI had no coverage
on Von K. in Europe

TEXT ON THIS PAGE IS ILLEGIBLE
WE HAVE LEFT THE PAGE AS REFERENCE

STANDARD FORM NO. 64

# Office Memorandum • UNITED STATES GOVERNMENT

TO : MR. V. P. KEAY  DATE: July 17, 1952

FROM : [redacted] b7C

SUBJECT: DR. THEODORE VON KARMAN,
CHAIRMAN, SCIENTIFIC ADVISORY BOARD,
U.S. AIR FORCE;
ATOMIC ENERGY ACT

[redacted] received from [redacted] Office of Special Investigations (OSI).

He advised that he had received information via [illegible] Air Force channels that Dr. Von Karman, one of the outstanding scientists of the United States, had recently made a trip to [redacted] Europe. During his visit there, he had been introduced to [redacted] Von Karman stated that he had casually mentioned that he has a brother in Hungary who has been trying for some time to gain entrance to Chile. According to Von Karman, [redacted] stated, "Maybe we can do something for you." According t[redacted] did not enlarge upon this situation t[redacted] Von Karman and Von Karman has heard nothing further from [redacted] Von Karman is presently back in the United States and has advised that he will immediately contact the FBI if he receives any further word or advances from [redacted]

b7C

RECOMMENDATION:

It is recommended that this memorandum be forwarded to Supervisor [redacted] of the Espionage Section.

b7C

ALL INFORMATION CONTAINED
HEREIN IS UNCLASSIFIED
DATE 6-5-97

NWP:hke

RECORDED-137

-77

file
100-372586

re-open case

TEXT ON THIS PAGE IS ILLEGIBLE
WE HAVE LEFT THE PAGE AS REFERENCE

STANDARD FORM NO. 64

# Office Memorandum • UNITED STATES GOVERNMENT

TO : A. H. Belmont

FROM : W. A. Branigan

DATE: July 31, 1952

Tolson
Ladd
Clegg
Glavin
Nichols
Rosen
Tracy
Harbo
Belmont
Mohr
Tele. Room
Nease
Gandy

SUBJECT: THEODORE VON KARMAN, was., INTERNAL SECURITY - R

PURPOSE:

[redacted] OSI reported that Theodore Von Karman recently met [redacted] in Europe and Von Karman informed [redacted] that his brother was attempting to leave Hungary for Chile. [redacted] allegedly replied, "Maybe we can do something for you."

It is recommended that Von Karman be interviewed for complete details concerning this incident.

DETAILS:

b7C

Reference is made to the memorandum from [redacted] to Mr. Keay dated July 17, 1952, informing that [redacted] OSI, stated that Theodore Von Karman recently visited Europe. While abroad, Von Karman was introduced to [redacted] Von Karman casually mentioned to [redacted] that his brother in Hungary was attempting to go to Chile. [redacted] allegedly stated, "Maybe we can do something for you."

According to [redacted] Von Karman has heard nothing further from [redacted] Von Karman has now returned to the United States and has stated that he would immediately contact the FBI if he received any further word from [redacted]

[redacted] stated he has no objection to Von Karman being interviewed by the Bureau.

[redacted] As you are aware [redacted] publicly admitted member of the Communist Party.

Von Karman is a well-known aerodynamicist of Hungarian birth, presently employed by the U. S. Air Force as Chairman of the Scientific Advisory Board. He was investigated by the Bureau in 1951, because of reported

ALL INFORMATION CONTAINED HEREIN IS UNCLASSIFIED

100-372586
Attachment
JEM:mes:dmd

100-372586-78

INDEXED-137

AUG 5 1952

RECORDED-137

66 AUG 12 1952

b7C

*past CP membership in Hungary. Investigation reflected he associated with several CP members and with William Perl, a known Soviet agent. During the investigation, Von Karman admitted to Bureau Agents that he was an official in the Bela Kun Government (Communist) in Hungary in 1919. He denied present or past CP membership and he denied that he had ever furnished classified data to unauthorized persons. He has been interviewed on several occasions concerning William Perl and other matters and he has been cooperative.*

***RECOMMENDATION:***

*It is recommended that Von Karman be interviewed for complete details concerning his recent contact with* [redacted] b7C

*If you agree, there are attached for your approval appropriate instructions to the field.*

TEXT ON THIS PAGE IS ILLEGIBLE
WE HAVE LEFT THE PAGE AS REFERENCE

[redacted]

# FEDERAL BUREAU OF INVESTIGATION

Form No. 1
THIS CASE ORIGINATED AT LOS ANGELES

**SECURITY INFORMATION - CONFIDENTIAL**

| REPORT MADE AT | DATE WHEN MADE | PERIOD FOR WHICH MADE | REPORT MADE BY |
|---|---|---|---|
| LOS ANGELES | 8/28/52 | 8/15/52 | [redacted] pam b7C |

| TITLE | CHARACTER OF CASE |
|---|---|
| THEODORE VON KARMAN, was | INTERNAL SECURITY - R |

AGENCY ICC [redacted]
REQ. REC'D 12/ /54
REP'T FORW. 1/5/55
BY

SEE REVERSE SIDE FOR ADD. DISSEMINATION.

AGENCY State 1151/
REQ. REC'D 1-15-58
REP'T FORW. 1-24-58
BY

SYNOPSIS OF FACTS: Dr. THEODORE VON KARMAN had occasion to meet [redacted] [redacted] in May, 1952, at a meeting of the French Academy of Sciences in Paris, France. Upon learning of VON KARMAN's brother and latter's wife, MIKLOS (NICHOLAUS) and MARGIT KARMAN, living in Hungary and unable to get exit passports to leave that country, [redacted] remarked, "Maybe we can do something for you." No other explanation made. In compliance with [redacted] suggestion, VON KARMAN, on June 6, 1952, furnished him their names and personal data and also advised United States Air Force authorities at the same time. No further word received from [redacted] to date. b7C

ICC.CSI
-RAB
EM-9-19-52

\- C -

AGENCY State
REQ. REC'D 6-26-56
REP'T FORW. 7-13-56
BY
Re: b7c. Nicolas Von Karman bro

DETAILS:

b2 [redacted], another Government agency which conducts intelligence investigations, advised that Dr. THEODORE VON KARMAN was recently in Europe where he met [redacted] [redacted]. VON KARMAN casually mentioned to [redacted] that he had a brother in Hungary, who for some time had been attempting to gain entrance into Chile, whereupon [redacted] allegedly stated to VON KARMAN, "Maybe we can do something for you." b7C

SEE REVERSE SIDE FOR ADD. DISSEMINATION.

Dr. THEODORE VON KARMAN, who recently returned from Paris, France, and is temporarily at his residence, 1501 South Marengo Avenue, Pasadena, California, was interviewed

APPROVED AND FORWARDED:

DO NOT WRITE IN THESE SPACES

COPY IN FILE

100-372586-79

SE-32

COPIES OF THIS REPORT

SEP 3 1952

6 - Bureau (100-372586) (Reg.)
1 - Washington Field (100-22923) (Info) (Reg.)
3 - Los Angeles (105-863)

RECORDED - 35
INDEXED - 35
EX. - 28



SECURITY INFORMATION - CONFIDENTIAL

on August 15, 1952, in connection with the above matter, at which time he furnished substantially the following information:

During the course of a meeting of the French Academy of Sciences at Paris this past May, VON KARMAN again had occasion to meet [redacted] whom he had known from previous scientific gatherings, including the 1945 Moscow Meeting of the 220th Anniversary of the Academy of Sciences of the Union of Soviet Socialist Republics.

After expressing his regrets to VON KARMAN on the death of his sister, JOSEPHINE DE KARMAN, last summer and his failure to contact him earlier, [redacted] inquired if he had any other relatives. VON KARMAN responded that he had a brother and the latter's wife in Budapest and that he had been unable to get them passports to leave Hungary and enter Chile. [redacted] then remarked, "Maybe we can do something for you," and he suggested that VON KARMAN put on paper the name, address and personal data about his brother and his wife. No other discussion whatever took place regarding this incident. No promises, threats, bribes or inducements were made by [redacted]

Thereafter, on June 6, 1952, in compliance with [redacted] previous suggestion and prompted by the possibility of some assistance, he wrote to [redacted] A substantial translation of VON KARMAN's copy of this letter, written in French and made available to the writer, is as follows:

"June 6, 1952

[redacted]
Antony/Seine

"Cher [redacted]

"In accordance with the recent conversations which we had on the occasion of our meeting at the Academy of Sciences, you were kind enough to tell me that you would give me aid in helping my brother and his wife in obtaining permission to leave Hungary.

"As I told you, He and his wife are my only relatives since the death of my sister, whom you knew very well.



b7C

TEXT ON THIS PAGE IS ILLEGIBLE
WE HAVE LEFT THE PAGE AS REFERENCE



"In accordance with your suggestion, I am furnishing you the address and other information.

"Dr. MIKLOS KARMAN; born in Budapest in 1884; address, 3 Molotov Ter, Budapest; employment, retired bank employee, incapable of working.

"MARGIT KARMAN, nee DUKESZ, his wife; born in 1895; without profession.

"It is useless for me to say I would be very happy if the Hungarian Government would allow a passport to be issued to him and his wife. I may depart from Paris in a few days and will not return until September. Will you please address any communication in my absence to [redacted] Paris 13e.

"With my most sincere thanks to you for granting me this favor, my dear [redacted] I am

"Your friend,

"THEODORE v. KARMAN"

On the same date that the above letter was written, VON KARMAN also wrote to [redacted] Department of the Air Force, Office of the Chief of Staff, Pentagon, Washington, D. C., setting forth in detail his above-described meeting with [redacted] and the action taken by him. In view of [redacted] VON KARMAN expressed a desire that [redacted] be apprised of the circumstances "just in case some special service discovers that I was in contact with [redacted]

Dr. VON KARMAN explained to the writer that this contact with [redacted] was the only one made with him during his stay in Paris since early last fall.

It is recalled that VON KARMAN during the past year had been in Paris where he has been lecturing at the Sarbonne. He also has recently been made chairman of a newly organized Research and Development Board of NATO with headquarters in Paris and also continues to be chairman of the Scientific Advisory Board of the United States Air Force.



b7C

TEXT ON THIS PAGE IS ILLEGIBLE
WE HAVE LEFT THE PAGE AS REFERENCE



VON KARMAN stated that he has not received any acknowledgment from [redacted] of the above-mentioned letter and has not otherwise heard from him since that time.

VON KARMAN described [redacted] as a Communist [redacted]

VON KARMAN explained too that for approximately a year he has endeavored to get his brother, Dr. MIKLOS (NICHOLAUS) KARMAN, and his wife, MARGIT KARMAN, out of Hungary. He arranged to get two visas for them to enter Chile in view of the quota restrictions on entering the United States. The Hungarian Government has, however, consistently refused their application for an exit permit to leave that country. VON KARMAN stated that he is at a loss to understand their refusal to grant them an exit passport. He added, however, that the Hungarian Government would definitely have a financial interest in a citizen of that country who was an heir to an estate. Upon his sister's death in Pasadena, California, in July, 1951, his brother became one of the heirs, and a representative for the Hungarian Government made an appearance in Los Angeles in connection with a probate of his sister's estate in November, 1951. VON KARMAN is unable to determine whether his brother's inability to leave Hungary is connected with this estate settlement or whether it is because of other unknown reasons.

VON KARMAN stated that his brother is approximately sixty-eight years old and was formerly a director of a bank in Budapest until it was nationalized by the Hungarian Government about three years ago. He was then forced to retire on a small pension.

VON KARMAN theorized that if the estate settlement has any bearing on Hungary's action, then it must balance [redacted] influence, if any, in allowing an exit permit to be issued as against the monetary gain which would accrue to Hungary from one of its citizens being an heir to an estate. In the meanwhile, final estate settlement is purposely being held up locally in order not to jeopardize his brother's chances of leaving the country if that has not yet entered the picture.

VON KARMAN advised that he will depart from Pasadena at the end of August to attend a symposium at the Massachusetts Institute of Technology at Boston, Massachusetts, during the first



b7C

week of September. He will thereafter be in Washington, D. C., for about a week to attend Scientific Advisory Board Meetings prior to his return to Paris.

- C -

TEXT ON THIS PAGE IS ILLEGIBLE
WE HAVE LEFT THE PAGE AS REFERENCE

LA 105-863

ADMINISTRATIVE PAGE

INFORMANTS

b2 b7C

SOURCE: [redacted] OSI, United States Air Force, Washington, D. C., as reflected in Bulet dated July 31, 1952.

1. Upon his return from Paris in early June, 1952, VON KARMAN also advised [redacted] as indicated above.

2. VON KARMAN's copy of his letter to [redacted] dated June 6, 1952, made available to the writer is as follows:

"June 6th 1952

"14, rue de la Cure
Paris, 16e, France

[redacted]
Department of the Air Force
Office of the Chief Air Staff
Pentagon
Washington, D. C.

b7C

"Dear [redacted]

"You will remember that about a year ago you kindly helped me to get into contact with the Ambassador of Chile in order to obtain a visa for my brother and his wife. Later [redacted] was also kind enough to write a letter of recommendation to the Ambassador of the Chilean Government and the Government of Chile granted the two visas.

"However, a new difficulty has arisen because the Communist Government in Hungary consistently refused my brother's application for an exit passport.

"Last month, in the French Academy of Sciences, I ran into [redacted] (we both are members of the Academie, as well as General EISENHOWER, for that matter). You will remember [redacted] when he came to

TEXT ON THIS PAGE IS ILLEGIBLE
WE HAVE LEFT THE PAGE AS REFERENCE



ADMINISTRATIVE PAGE

lunch with us at the Ritz. It was the first time that I saw him since my sister died. He inquired if I had other relations and I told him that I have a brother in Budapest and that I was unable to get a passport for him to leave Hungary. He told me that possibly something could be done about this and asked me to put on paper the name, address and personal data about my brother and his wife.

"Now I should like to ask you a personal favor, provided it is not disagreeable to you. I understand that [redacted] is seriously ill and that [redacted] is the Acting Chief. I wonder if you would be kind enough to see [redacted] and tell him how [redacted] helped me to obtain a visa for my brother, tell him about the difficulties of my brother to obtain the visa and tell him about my meeting [redacted] as I have written above. I do not want any kind of permission or any official cognizance of this matter. However, I prefer if [redacted] knows about it just in case some special service discovers that I was in contact with [redacted] He was certainly mean in the matter of biological warfare and also not very intelligent. However, I believe that he is under command of the party and cannot do as he pleases.

"I am in indirect contact with my brother and what I know of him comes to me by way of letters to my New York attorney by some underground way from Austria. I thought it was better for me not to write him direct.

"Now, dear [redacted] I tell you this story and if you think it is all right to tellthis to [redacted] please go to him and give him this informa-tion for me. If you do not like the idea, I shall wait and talk with the General myself after my return to the States.

"I have not heard from you for a long time and of your plans for the future. Be sure to drop me a line to the following address:



b7C

ADMINISTRATIVE PAGE

"Advisory Group for Aeronautical Research and Development
Palais de Chaillot
Paris, France

"Room 332

"In old friendship,

"Very cordially yours,

"THEODORE v. KARMAN"

3. Identity of the subject's brother was previously set forth in writer's report dated June 13, 1951, Page 9.

4. VON KARMAN advised that in the event he is recontacted by [redacted] he will immediately advise the Federal Bureau of Investigation. b7C

REFERENCE: Bureau letter to Los Angeles dated July 31, 1952.

TEXT ON THIS PAGE IS ILLEGIBLE
WE HAVE LEFT THE PAGE AS REFERENCE

ORDED-65
100-372586-80

Date: November 6, 1953

EX-110 To: [redacted] b7C

Director, Security Division
Office of the Secretary
Department of Defense
The Pentagon
Washington 25, D. C.

354,894
DECLASSIFIED BY SP5JC/DGM
ON 6-3-97

From: John Edgar Hoover, Director
Federal Bureau of Investigation

Subject: THEODORE VON KARMAN, with aliases
Theodor Karman
Theodore Von Szoelloestcictak

Reference is made to your communication dated October 20, 1953, furnishing information concerning captioned subject. Your communication stated that the data contained therein had not been furnished to any member of the North Atlantic Treaty Organization Standing Group pending a decision as to what action will be taken by this Bureau.

You are advised that an investigation of the subject was previously conducted by this Bureau in 1951-52, and copies of investigative reports were furnished to the Director of Special Investigations, The Inspector General, Department of the Air Force, The Pentagon, Washington 25, D. C., and to the Criminal Division of the Department of Justice inasmuch as the subject was Chairman of the Scientific Advisory Board of the U. S. Air Force.

No additional investigation concerning this matter is contemplated by the Federal Bureau of Investigation inasmuch as the data appearing in referenced communication was disclosed in our investigation.

cc - 2 - Los Angeles (with cc of incoming) (105-863)

JEM:elc

COMM - FBI
NOV 6 - 1953
MAILED 28

69 718402
NOV 10 1953

SECURITY INFORMATION - SECRET

TEXT ON THIS PAGE IS ILLEGIBLE
WE HAVE LEFT THE PAGE AS REFERENCE

CAUTION ... TION MUST
NOT BE DISSEMINATED ...
. MR. LADD.

b7C
b7D

*MEMORANDUM TO* [redacted] Derived from Conf. Source [redacted] 10/27/53

*I spoke to my informant this morning about Theodore von Karman, who is now Chief of the Scientific Advisory Board, Office of the Chief of the Air Force. This informant advised that Theodore von Karman is a scientist of world-wide fame, and and expert on "aviation balance" (he works on the balance apparatus for the various aircraft that are designed and produced.)*

*During the Communist regime of Bela Kun in Hungary in 1919, the man was very badly compromised, and as a result after the overthrow of that regime, he had to leave the country because he was a Communist. During the last war he was held in high esteem, and worked in high technical positions for the Government.*

*The informant further states that van Karman's political record in the past has been distinctly bad and objectionable, but since von Karman has been over here informant has heard nothing whatsoever of his activities. This, informant adds, might be either great precaution on his (von Karman's) part, or it might be a change of heart.*

*With regard to his not being an American citizen, informant thinks that might be an indication that perhaps there has been a change of heart with regard to Communism on his part, for, as informant says, if he were doing a job for the Communists in his present position or over here in any position, he would camouflage his intents and purposes by becoming a citizen.*

354-894
ALL INFOR...
HEREIN
DATE 6-5-97 SP5JC/lagm

I. R. -3

CAUTION ... ON MUST
NOT BE DISSEMI...
. MR. LADD.

RECORDED-14
EX-102 25 OCT 29 1953

68 NOV 10 1953

TEXT ON THIS PAGE IS ILLEGIBLE
WE HAVE LEFT THE PAGE AS REFERENCE

SECRET

American Embassy
Paris 8, France

47579

Date: December 28, 1953

To: Director, FBI (105-23010)

From: Legal Attache, Paris (105-376)

Subject: [redacted] b7C
INTERNAL SECURITY - R & FR

6-5-97
CLASSIFIED BY
DECLASSIFY ON: 25X

ReBulet November 30, 1953.

The indices of the Paris office reveal that a Bureau representative was in personal contact with the captioned subject in Paris in November 1951, and on several occasions thereafter, in connection with arrangements for personal interview with Dr. THEODORE VON KARMAN, subject of Bufile 100-372586. The Bureau was informed of this contact with subject as set forth on the administrative page of the report of SA [redacted] dated March 10, 1952, at Paris, France and entitled "Unknown subject, was. [redacted] Espionage - R", Bufile 65-59543. b7C b1

ALL INFORMATION CONTAINED HEREIN IS UNCLASSIFIED EXCEPT WHERE SHOWN OTHERWISE

In calling upon the Paris office on November 16, 1951, this subject revealed himself to be [redacted] At that time, subject indicated that he had been associated with VON KARMAN casually for the previous four years, explaining that he (subject) [redacted] As the Bureau is aware, VON KARMAN is presently Chairman of the NATO Advisory Group for Aeronautical Research and Development, having been so designated in March 1952.

b7C
b7D

On December 17, 1953 [redacted] VON KARMAN was using him mostly as a [redacted]

HPW:AM

100-372586-

NOT RECORDED
199 JAN 5 1954

SECRET

TEXT ON THIS PAGE IS ILLEGIBLE
WE HAVE LEFT THE PAGE AS REFERENCE

Director, FBI                SECRET                47590

Re: [redacted]
IS-R & FR

and that the professional aspects of his contact with VON KARMAN had turned out to be nil. Since [redacted] had accepted the position in the hope of deriving professional advantages from the contact, he left the position upon learning that it had no possibilities for him. [redacted]

- 2 -

b7C b7D

SECRET

TEXT ON THIS PAGE IS ILLEGIBLE
WE HAVE LEFT THE PAGE AS REFERENCE

SECRET

ALL INFORMATION CONTAINED
HERE IS UNCLASSIFIED EXCEPT
WHERE SHOWN OTHERWISE

100-372586 — 82

RECORDED - 23

SECRET VIA LIAISON

ALL INFORMATION CONTAINED
HEREIN IS UNCLASSIFIED EXCEPT
WHERE SHOWN OTHERWISE.

[redacted] b7C

Date: July 16, 1954

To: Director
Central Intelligence Agency
2430 E Street, N. W.
Washington, D. C.

Attention: Deputy Director, Plans

CLASSIFIED BY SP5JC/pqv
DECLASSIFY ON: 25X 1

From: John Edgar Hoover, Director
Federal Bureau of Investigation

Subject: DR. THEODORE VON KARMAN, with aliases
Theodor Karman,
Theodore Von Szoelloestotatak
INTERNAL SECURITY - R

Class. & Ext. By
Reason-FCIM II, 1-2.4.2
Date of Review

[redacted] b1 (S)

For your information and assistance, there is attached a memorandum containing a summary of pertinent information concerning Theodore Von Karman from our files.

Attachment

cc - 2 - Los Angeles (105-863) (Attached is copy of memo referred to above; [redacted] (S)

ATTENTION: SAC, Los Angeles should immediately submit a report (7 copies for Bureau) suitable for dissemination containing pertinent information [redacted] b1

JEM:fjm

MAILED 3
CC ONLY
JUL 16 1954
COMM-FBI

Tolson
Boardman
Nichols
Belmont
Harbo
Mohr
Parsons
Rosen
Tamm
Sizoo
Winterrowd
Tele. Room
Holloman
Gandy

68 JUL 21 1954

SECRET

TEXT ON THIS PAGE IS ILLEGIBLE
WE HAVE LEFT THE PAGE AS REFERENCE

SECRET

100-372586 - 82 SECRET July 16, 1954 SECRET

RECORDED - 23

EX-129

Re: DR. THEODORE VON KARMAN, with aliases
Theodor Karman,
Theodore Von Szeelloestotetak

The Federal Bureau of Investigation, in October, 1950, instituted a security type investigation of Theodore Von Karman, Chairman of the Scientific Advisory Board, U. S. Air Force, and a consultant on the top secret project, Vista, sponsored by the California Institute of Technology. This investigation was based upon report from another governmental agency which stated that in 1919, Von Karman, a professor at Cal Tech, was Deputy Commissar of Cultural and Educational Affairs under the Bela Kun (Communist) Communist G[illegible] in Hungary. The investigation revealed that he was probably employed by the U. S. Air Force. The Air Force indicated on January 30, 1951, that he was an Air Force employee. Thereafter, the Air Force requested this Bureau to continue its investigation of Von Karman, but not under Executive Order 9835, as he was not subject to the provisions thereof. The Air Force advised that Von Karman had access to practically all classified data. The investigation was reinstituted and reflected that Von Karman was an associate of several Communist Party members and an associate of William Perl, a Soviet Agent, and [redacted] Mikhail Gorin. Gorin was convicted of Soviet espionage in 1939. Investigation further reflected that Von Karman was friendly with [redacted] an admitted former Communist Party member. [redacted]

Von Karman was interviewed by agents of this Bureau on May 23, 1951, and May 29, 1951, in Los Angeles, California. He admitted that he was connected with

Tolson ____
Boardman ____
Nichols ____
Belmont ____
Harbo ____
Mohr ____
Parsons ____
Rosen ____
Tamm ____
Sizoo ____
Winterrowd ____
Tele. Room ____
Holloman ____
Gandy ____

This Blank Memo is being prepared

[redacted] fjm

b7C

b7C

SECRET SECRET

-2-

TEXT ON THIS PAGE IS ILLEGIBLE
WE HAVE LEFT THE PAGE AS REFERENCE

SECRET SECRET

Bela Kun Government in Hungary from March to July, 1919. He denied present or past Communist Party membership and he denied that he had ever furnished classified data to any unauthorized person. He declined to sign a prepared statement, but advised that he desired "to think it over." On September 4, 1951, Von Karman appeared at the Los Angeles office of this Bureau and indicated there was no further need and no desire on his part to sign his previously furnished statement. (X) u

- 3 -
SECRET

SECRET

TEXT ON THIS PAGE IS ILLEGIBLE
WE HAVE LEFT THE PAGE AS REFERENCE

~~CONFIDENTIAL~~

~~SECRET~~

# FEDERAL BUREAU OF INVESTIGATION

(354-899) 5-1398
CLASSIFIED BY SP5 JC/pgm
DECLASSIFY ON: 25X 1

SEE REVERSE SIDE FOR ADD. DISSEMINATION

Form No. 1
THIS CASE ORIGINATED AT Los Angeles

| REPORT MADE AT | DATE WHEN MADE | PERIOD FOR WHICH MADE | REPORT MADE BY |
|---|---|---|---|
| Los Angeles | 8/27/54 | 8/26/54 | [redacted] HWP b7C |

| TITLE | CHARACTER OF CASE |
|---|---|
| THEODORE VON KARMAN, was. b2 | INTERNAL SECURITY - R |

AGENCY ICC [redacted]
REQ. REC'D
REP'T FORW. 11/5/55
BY

Re: bro. Nicolas Von Karman

AGENCY ICC-State
REQ. REC'D 6-26-58
REP'T FORW. 7-13-58
BY

SYNOPSIS OF FACTS:

b1

[redacted]

AGENCY
REQ. REC'D 8-12-59
REP'T FORW. 8-19-59
BY

(S)

Re: associate Lee Arnold Spec. reg.

b2

[redacted] another Government agency conducting intelligence investigations advised on [redacted]

b1

(S)

[redacted]

(S)

AGENCY ICC OSI (0-14)
REQ. REC'D
DATE FORW.
HOW FORW.
BY

AGENCY Photo USIA
REQ. REC'D 1-15-58
REP'T FORW. 1-24-58
BY

b7C [redacted]

ALL INFORMATION CONTAINED

| APPROVED AND FORWARDED: | SPECIAL AGENT IN CHARGE | DO NOT WRITE IN THESE SPACES |
|---|---|---|
| | | 83 RECORDED-62 |

COPIES OF THIS REPORT

7 - Bureau (100-372586) REGISTERED
1 - WFO (Info.)(100-22923) REGISTERED
3 - Los Angeles (105-863)

INDEXED-62

EX-121

SEP 10 1954

COPY IN FILE

PROPERTY OF FBI—THIS REPORT IS LOANED TO YOU BY THE FBI, AND NEITHER IT NOR ITS CONTENTS ARE TO BE DISTRIBUTED OUTSIDE THE AGENCY TO WHICH LOANED.

U. S. GOVERNMENT PRINTING OFFICE

LA 105-863

ADMINISTRATIVE PAGE

INFORMANTS

[redacted] (S) b1

REFERENCE: Bureau letter [redacted] (S)

TEXT ON THIS PAGE IS ILLEGIBLE
WE HAVE LEFT THE PAGE AS REFERENCE

HOTEL EL CORTEZ
GEARY ST. NEAR TAYLOR
SAN FRANCISCO, CALIF.

OTHER FRITZ HOTELS IN SAN FRANCISCO
HUNTINGTON HOTEL
HOTEL SUTTER
PARK LANE APARTMENTS
BROCKLEBANK APARTMENTS



Dear Mr. Hoover —

The enclosure is self-explanatory.

Sincerely yours

[redacted]

Aug 16, 1954
Mr. J. Edgar Hoover
Director, FBI
Washington, DC

b7C

RECO[redacted]D - 77 memo Belmont 8-26-54
Ltr to ... re SF 8/26/54
9-1
AUG 19 1954
EX-
J.E.M. 84

Acknowledged letter from ... 8/24/54
J.E.M.

August 16,1954

Professor Theodor von Karman
Pasadena Calif.

Dear Sir:

Your name, mentioned in the New York Times of August 2nd in a dispatch from Innsbruck, Austria, about rockets, interests me.

Some time ago I was informed in New York that a professor von Karman, in California, had been a member of the abortive Communist regime of Bela Kuhn in Hungary in the early twenties.

I should like to know if you are this person; and, if so, were you at the time a member of the Communist organization in Hungary?

Since I am asking these questions -- making no statement or implication of fact, of coursd -- due to my active interest as a citizen in national security for the United States, I am sending a copy of this letter to J.Edgar Hoover, director of the F.B.I.

Needless to say, I hope it proves to be the case that you are not the same person -- that you were never a member of the Communist conspiracy; and, until the facts are proven one way or the other, I'll reserve judgment.

Your reply will reach me at my address in New York City -- [redacted]

b7C

[redacted]

354-894
ALL INFORMATION CONTAINED
HEREIN IS UNCLASSIFIED
DATE 6-5-92 BY

TEXT ON THIS PAGE IS ILLEGIBLE
WE HAVE LEFT THE PAGE AS REFERENCE

# Office Memorandum • UNITED STATES GOVERNMENT

TO : A. H. Belmont

FROM : W. A. Branigan

DATE: August 26, 1954

Tolson
Boardman
Nichols
Belmont
Harbo
Mohr
Parsons
Rosen
Tamm
Sizoo
Winterrowd
Tele. Room
Holloman
Gandy

SUBJECT: DR. THEODOR VON KARMAN
INTERNAL SECURITY - R
(100-372586)

b7C [redacted]
MISCELLANEOUS - INFORMATION CONCERNING
(100-355122)

b7C

By letter dated August 16, 1954, [redacted] furnished a copy of a letter, same date, which he wrote to Theodor Von Karman asking Von Karman if he was formerly a member of the Bela Kun Communist regime in Hungary in the early 1920's. Set forth below is pertinent information concerning [redacted] and Theodor Von Karman:

[redacted]

b7C

[redacted] He [redacted] been anti-Administration, anti-Selective Service and anti-Communist. He has corresponded with the Bureau since 1948 and he allegedly criticized the Bureau in a speech before [redacted] in Detroit, Michigan, in 1948. Since 1948 he has praised the Bureau and the Director. On June 26, 1954, he inquired by letter if the FBI requested the presidents of Temple and Denver Universities to retain on their faculties individuals considered to be security risks. We informed [redacted] that our policy precludes furnishing such information. [redacted]mer president of Denver University was interviewed and stated no such request had been made by the FBI. President of Temple University stated it was his impression that such a request may have been made of an official of the University. Additional inquiries failed to substantiate this allegation.

<u>Theodor Von Karman</u>

Investigation of Von Karman was conducted in 1951 at specific request of Air Force. Von Karman is naturalized U. S. citizen, world's leading aerodynamicist and Chairman of Air Force Scientific Advisory Board. No derogatory data developed during investigation. Upon interview, Von Karman admitted on

RECORDED - 77

Attachment

JEM:elc

ALL INFORMATION CONTAINED
HEREIN IS UNCLASSIFIED
DATE 6-3-97 BY SPS

SEP 14 1954

ESP. SEC.

May 29, 1951, he had been Deputy Commissar of Cultural and Educational Affairs in Bela Kun's Government in Hungary in 1919 for a short period of time. He denied past or present CP membership. Pertinent information furnished to interested Government agencies.

RECOMMENDATION:

b7C [redacted] It is recommended that New York interview [redacted] for any information he may have concerning possible communist activities by Theodor Von Karman, and at the same time his communication to the Bureau can be orally acknowledged. If you agree, a letter to New York is attached.

SAC, New York

August 26, 1954

RECORDED

Director, FBI

DR. THEODOR VON KARMAN
INTERNAL SECURITY - R
(Bufile 100-372586)

[redacted]
MISCELLANEOUS - INFORMATION CONCERNING
(Bufile 100-355122)

By letter dated August 16, 1954, on the letterhead of Hotel El Cortez, San Francisco, California, [redacted] New York City, furnished a copy of a letter he wrote under date of August 16, 1954, to Theodor Von Karman. [redacted] asked Von Karman concerning his past Communist affiliations. A copy of the letter from Long to Von Karman is attached.

b7C

You should contact [redacted] at his New York City address at the earliest possible time, orally acknowledge his letter to the Director dated August 16, 1954, and ask him concerning any available information in his possession concerning the past Communist activities of Theodor Von Karman. You should inform the Bureau of the results of the interview with [redacted] at the earliest possible time.

A copy of this communication with attachment is being designated for San Francisco. In the event New York is unable to locate [redacted] at his New York residence, San Francisco should be requested by teletype to handle the matter.

Attachment

cc - 2 - San Francisco (Attachment)

JEM:elc

RECEIVED AUG 27 ... AM '54 ... ROOM

Tolson
Boardman
Nichols
Belmont
Harbo
Mohr
Parsons
Rosen
Tamm
Sizoo
Winterrowd
Tele. Room
Holloman
Gandy

MAILED 8
AUG 27 1954
COMM - FBI

354-894
ALL INFORMATION CONTAINED
HEREIN IS UNCLASSIFIED
DATE 6-3-97 BY SPS JC/ogm

TEXT ON THIS PAGE IS ILLEGIBLE
WE HAVE LEFT THE PAGE AS REFERENCE

Mr. Tolson
Mr. Boardman
Mr. Nichols
Mr. Belmont
Mr. Harbo
Mr. Mohr
Mr. Parsons
Mr. Rosen
Mr. Tamm
Mr. Sizoo
Mr. Winterrowd
Tele. Room
Mr. Holloman
Miss Gandy

FEDERAL BUREAU OF INVESTIGATION

UNITED STATES DEPARTMENT OF JUSTICE

AIR-TEL

8/31/54, NEW YORK

Transmit the following Teletype message to: BUREAU

DR. THEODORE VON KARMAN; IS-R (BUFILE 100-372586); [redacted] MISCELLANEOUS-INFORMATION CONCERNING (BUFILE 100-355122). RE BULET, 8/26/54. INQUIRY AT COLUMBIA UNIVERSITY CLUB, NYC, REFLECTS THAT [redacted] IS NOW LIVING AT THE LOS ANGELES ATHLETIC CLUB, LOS ANGELES, CALIFORNIA AND IS NOT EXPECTED TO RETURN TO NY FOR AT LEAST A MONTH. A COPY OF BULET DATED 8/26/54 AND COPY OF LETTER OF [redacted] TO PROFESSOR THEODORE VON KARMAN DATED 8/16/54 ARE BEING FORWARDED AS ATTACHMENTS HERETO TO LOS ANGELES. LOS ANGELES WILL CONTACT [redacted] AT THE LOS ANGELES ATHLETIC CLUB, ORALLY ACKNOWLEDGE HIS LETTER TO THE DIRECTOR DATED 8/16/54 AND QUESTION HIM

b7C

RECORDED - 162

4 - BUREAU (100-372586)
(1 - BUFILE 100-355122)
2 - LOS ANGELES (105-863) (Encs. 2) (REGISTERED AM)
2 - SAN FRANCISCO (REGISTERED AM)
1 - NY 100-90576

RECORDED
27 SEP 1 1954

EX-124

JAH:EAM (# 6)
65-6747

ALL INFORMATION CONTAINED
HEREIN IS UNCLASSIFIED
DATE 6-3-97 BY SPSJC

Mr. Belmont

Approved: ____________ Sent ______M Per ______
Special Agent in Charge

FD-36

FEDERAL BUREAU OF INVESTIGATION

UNITED STATES DEPARTMENT OF JUSTICE



Transmit the following Teletype message to:

ABOUT ANY INFO HE MAY POSSESS CONCERNING THE PAST COMMUNIST ACTIVITIES OF VON KARMAN. LOS ANGELES SHOULD IMMEDIATELY INFORM THE BUREAU OF THE RESULTS OF THE INTERVIEW WITH [redacted] FOR THE FURTHER INFO OF LOS ANGELES, NY HAS BEEN ADVISED BY THE BUREAU THAT [redacted] HE HAS BEEN ANTI-ADMINISTRATION AND HAS OPPOSED THE SELECTIVE SERVICE PROGRAM. IN A SPEECH BEFORE A [redacted] IN DETROIT IN 1948 HE REPORTEDLY CRITICIZED THE BUREAU. THE BUREAU HAS HAD CORDIAL CORRESPONDENCE SINCE THAT TIME AND ON OCCASION [redacted] HAS SUBMITTED SEVERAL ARTICLES AND BOOKLETS [redacted] TO THE BUREAU.

b7C

[redacted]

b7C

Approved: ______________________ Sent ________M Per ____________
Special Agent in Charge

FD-36

FEDERAL BUREAU OF INVESTIGATION

UNITED STATES DEPARTMENT OF JUSTICE

AIRTEL

Transmit the following teletype message to:

FBI, LOS ANGELES (105-863) 9/9/54 9:30 A.M.

DIRECTOR, FBI (100-372586; 100-355122)

DR. THEODORE VON KARMAN; IS-R (BUFILE 100-372586); [redacted] MISCELLANEOUS-INFORMATION CONCERNING (BUFILE 100-355122). RE NEW YORK AIRTEL 8/31/54 AND ATTACHED ENCLOSURES. INQUIRY AT LOS ANGELES ATHLETIC CLUB, LOS ANGELES, REFLECTS [redacted] CHECKED OUT ON 9/4/54 INDICATING HE WAS RETURNING TO NEW YORK CITY. RUC.

b7C

MALONE

2CC: NEW YORK (100-90876; 65-6747) REGISTERED-AIR MAIL
2CC: SAN FRANCISCO (REGISTERED-AIR MAIL)

REGISTERED
AIR MAIL

JPA:HWP

354-894

6-3-97 SP5JC/pgm

EX-125

[redacted]

b7C

UNRECORDED COPY FILED IN

Approved: ________________ Sent ________ M Per ______
Special Agent in Charge

100-372586-87

TEXT ON THIS PAGE IS ILLEGIBLE
WE HAVE LEFT THE PAGE AS REFERENCE

AIR-TEL

SEPTEMBER 21, 1954

SAC, NEW YORK

47578

DR. THEODORE VON KARMAN, INTERNAL SECURITY - R, BUFILE 100-372586; [redacted] MISCELLANEOUS - INFORMATION CONCERNING, BUFILE 100-355122. BULET AUGUST 26, LAST, REQUESTED THAT [redacted] BE INTERVIEWED. LOS ANGELES AIR-TEL SEPTEMBER 9, LAST, INFORMED [redacted] LEFT LOS ANGELES FOR NEW YORK. EXPEDITE INTERVIEW AND SUREP RESULTS.

HOOVER

JEM:jla

b7C

354-894
ALL INFORMATION CONTAINED
HEREIN IS UNCLASSIFIED
DATE 6-3-97 BY SP5 JC/dgh

RECORDED-20

MAILED 11
SEP 21 1954
COMM - FBI

EX-110

100-372586-8
SEP 22 1954
113

Tolson
Boardman
Nichols
Belmont
Harbo
Mohr
Parsons
Rosen
Tamm
Sizoo
Winterrowd
Tele. Room
Holloman
Gandy

58 SEP 27 1954

TEXT ON THIS PAGE IS ILLEGIBLE
WE HAVE LEFT THE PAGE AS REFERENCE

SAC, New York October 4, 19[illegible]

Director, FBI

DR. THEODORE VON KARMAN
INTERNAL SECURITY - R
(Bufile 100-372586) — 89

RECORDED - 84
EX-103 [redacted]
MISCELLANEOUS - INFORMATION CONCERNING
(Bufile 100-355122)

Reurmemo dated September 27, 1954, replying to Bureau memorandum dated August 26, 1954.

Bureau memo dated August 26, 1954, instructed that [redacted] be contacted and asked regarding his knowledge of past Communist activities of Theodore Von Karman.

b7C

Your reply dated September 27, 1954, does not reflect that you inquired of [redacted] as instructed.

Advise immediately what [redacted] related concerning the past activities of Von Karman. If [redacted] was not asked concerning this matter, recontact him and advise by memorandum no later than October 10, 1954.

JEM:sjr

354-894
ALL INFORMATION CONTAINED
HEREIN IS UNCLASSIFIED
DATE 6-3-97 BY [illegible]

Tolson
Boardman
Nichols
Belmont
Harbo
Mohr
Parsons
Rosen
Tamm
Sizoo
Winterrowd
Tele. Room
Holloman
Gandy

F-387

MAILED 3
OCT - 4 1954
COMM - FBI

OCT 12 1954

U.S. DEPT. OF JUSTICE
F.B.I.
RECEIVED - MAIL ROOM

TEXT ON THIS PAGE IS ILLEGIBLE
WE HAVE LEFT THE PAGE AS REFERENCE

STANDARD FORM NO. 64

# Office Memorandum • UNITED STATES GOVERNMENT

TO : Director, FBI (100-372586) DATE: 9/27/54

FROM : SAC, New York (65-6747)

SUBJECT: DR. THEODORE VON KARMAN
IS - R
[redacted]
MISCELLANEOUS - INFORMATION
CONCERNING

ReBulet 8/26/54 and Los Angeles air-tel 9/9/54.

On 9/20/54 [redacted] was contacted at his residence, [redacted] NYC. He was advised of the receipt by the Director of his letter of 8/16/54 and he was asked whether he had received any reply from Dr. VON KARMAN. He advised he had not received any communication from Dr. VON KARMAN and believed he would not receive any reply to his inquiry. He advised that he had been in Los Angeles during the latter part of August but that he did not call Dr. VON KARMAN at his residence in Pasadena. He stated, "I suppose he is still in Austria." He advised that in the event he did receive any reply from Dr. VON KARMAN he would notify this office.

For the information of the Bureau, a representative of OSI contacted this office on 9/22/54 for information concerning [redacted] The OSI representative advised that an urgent request had come in from the Chief of Staff of the Air Force in Washington, D. C., for available information in various agencies concerning [redacted]

In the event that [redacted] contacts this office in the future the Bureau will be promptly advised. C

1 - Bureau (100-355122)

Reg. Mail

1 - NY (100-90576)

RECORDED-42 89

11 SEP 28 1954

EX-124

JAH:DC

354-894
ALL INFORMATION CONTAINED
HEREIN IS UNCLASSIFIED
DATE 6-3-92 BY

Substance to OSI 11/2/54 by [redacted] at OSI request

b7C

TEXT ON THIS PAGE IS ILLEGIBLE
WE HAVE LEFT THE PAGE AS REFERENCE

SAC, New York

September 28, 19[illegible]

Director, FBI

DR. THEODOR VON KARMAN
INTERNAL SECURITY - R
(Bureau file 100-372586)

47577

[redacted]
MISCELLANEOUS - INFORMATION CONCERNING
(Bureau file 100-355122)

b7C

ReBumemo dated August 26, 1954, and Bu teletype dated September 21, 1954, requesting New York to interview [redacted] concerning his knowledge of Theodor VonKarman.

Attached is a Photostat (two pages and envelope) of a communication dated August 20, 1954, addressed to [redacted] the State Department from [redacted] which concerns Dr. VonKarman. The Photostat was received from the State Department.

Attachment

cc - 2 - San Francisco (Attachment)

RECORDED-41

100-372586-90

13 SEP 29 1954

EX. - 107

ALL INFORMATION CONTAINED
HEREIN IS UNCLASSIFIED
DATE 6-3-97 BY [illegible]

Tolson
Boardman
Nichols
Belmont
Harbo
Mohr
Parsons
Rosen
Tamm
Sizoo
Winterrowd
Tele. Room
Holloman

JEM:plv

55 OCT 4 1954

COMM - FBI
SEP 28 1954
MAILED 30

TEXT ON THIS PAGE IS ILLEGIBLE
WE HAVE LEFT THE PAGE AS REFERENCE

STANDARD FORM NO. 64

# Office Memorandum • UNITED STATES GOVERNMENT

TO : Director, FBI (100-372586)

DATE: 10/8/54

FROM : SAC, New York (65-6747)

SUBJECT: DR. THEODORE VON KARMAN
IS - R

47576

[redacted]

MISCELLANEOUS - INFORMATION CONCERNING

Rebulet 10/4/54.

b7C

When [redacted] was contacted on 9/20/54 he was asked whether he had any information concerning the past Communist activities of DR. VON KARMAN. He advised that he did not have any information concerning VON KARMAN or any of his Communist activities. He stated the only information he had concerning VON KARMAN was the fact that his name was mentioned in the "New York Times" of 8/2/54. This office has not received any further information from [redacted]

1 - BU 100-355122
1 - NY 100-90576

Substance to OST by letter 11/1/54, by request of OST

ALL INFORMATION CONTAINED HEREIN IS UNCLASSIFIED DATE 6-3-92 BY SP5JC

RECORDED - 43

RECORDED
8 OCT 11 1954

ESP SEC

55 OCT 14 1954

61 NOV 2 1954

# Office Memorandum • UNITED STATES GOVERNMENT

TO : MR. R. R. ROACH

FROM : MR. C. W. BATES

DATE: January 19, 1955

SUBJECT: THEODORE VON KARMAN, wa.
INTERNAL SECURITY - R
ATOMIC ENERGY ACT - APPLICANT
100-372586

Tolson
Boardman
Nichols
Belmont
Harbo
Mohr
Parsons
Rosen
Tamm
Sizoo
Winterrowd
Tele. Room
Holloman
Gandy

354894

ALL INFORMATION CONTAINED
HEREIN IS UNCLASSIFIED
DATE 6-3-97 BY [redacted]

b7C

The Atomic Energy Commission (AEC) requested an applicant-type investigation of Von Karman in February, 1954, in view of his position with the Scientific Advisory Board of the Air Force. The Bureau conducted an Internal Security - R investigation of the subject in 1951 and 1952 based on an allegation that Von Karman was once an official of a Communist government in Hungary. Investigation reflected that he associated with several Communist Party members and with William Perl, known Soviet agent. He admitted to Bureau Agents during the investigation that he was an official in the Bela Kun Government (Communist) in Hungary in 1919. He denied present or past Communist Party membership. Copies of all the Bureau's reports in the Atomic Energy Act - Applicant and Internal Security investigations have been furnished to the Air Force and to the Atomic Energy Commission.

b7C

[redacted] Washington Area Security Office, AEC, advised Liaison Agent Bates on January 18, 1955, that in accordance with the AEC clearance procedures, the Air Force was asked by the AEC to obtain certain information from Von Karman so that the AEC could make a clearance determination since the Air Force had originally requested the atomic energy clearance. On December 20, 1954, Von Karman wrote a letter to [redacted] of the AEC. He referred to the AEC letter to the Air Force in which the AEC had requested a statement from Von Karman concerning certain derogatory information. Von Karman referred specifically to the request for a statement from him concerning "Alexander Goetz with whom Von Karman's deceased sister is reported to have been friendly and whose political ideology is allegedly strongly pro-Nazi."

RECORDED - 92

In Von Karman's letter to [redacted] he stated that he considered the above quote an inexcusable insult against the memory of his "beloved sister." He stated he could not see what such a statement had to do with his access to atomic information.

254

He requested that (1) those responsible for this incident be seriously reprimanded and that (2) he be given a formal and official apology.

[redacted]

CWB:fjb
(4) 1 - [redacted] 1 - Section tickler 1 - Mr. Bates
Attachments (3) ENCL.

b7C

Memo to Mr. Roach
from Mr. Bates

[redacted] pointed out that [redacted]tended to reply to Von Karman's letter and to "placate him." [redacted] contacted [redacted] and stated that such a reply would be inadvisable and that he should certainly not apologize to Von Karman.

b7C

Later, [redacted] received instructions to take no further action on Von Karman's clearance. [redacted] felt that the Bureau should have this information and furnished the attached copy of the letter from AEC to the Air Force, copy of Von Karman's letter to [redacted] and a copy of [redacted] memorandum concerning the matter.

<u>ACTION:</u>

This is submitted for your information.

TEXT ON THIS PAGE IS ILLEGIBLE
WE HAVE LEFT THE PAGE AS REFERENCE

Tickle [redacted] b7C

SAC, Los Angeles (105-863) (Original & 1) April 14, 1955

Director, FBI (100-372586) SECRET

THEODORE VON KARMAN, wa
INTERNAL SECURITY - R

b1 [redacted] (S)

Los Angeles is requested to interview Von Karman and ask him if he has ever been approached either directly or indirectly for classified information. Von Karman should be requested to immediately report to the Bureau any contacts that might be considered a possible approach for classified information. He should also be asked the identities of [redacted] and the extent of his association with them. b7C

The results of the interview with Von Karman should be submitted in report form suitable for dissemination.

Enclosure (1)
cc - Washington Field (100-22923) (For Information)

CLASSIFIED BY
DECLASSIFY ON: 25X 1

A cover memo from Belmont to Boardman was prepared by JEM:jca on April 11, 1955 in connection with this outgoing mail.

EX-110

RECORDED - 97 100-372586-
INDEXED - 97
EX-116

COMM - FBI
APR 14 1955
MAILED 19

Tolson
Boardman
Nichols
Belmont
Harbo
Mohr
Parsons
Rosen
Tamm
Sizoo
Winterrowd
Tele. Room
Holloman
Gandy

JEM:jaa
(5)

APR 21 1955

SECRET

TEXT ON THIS PAGE IS ILLEGIBLE
WE HAVE LEFT THE PAGE AS REFERENCE

SECRET

SECRET

G.I.R.-7

esa 100-372586-94

BY COURIER SERVICE

Date: April 14, 1955

To: Director (Original and one)
Central Intelligence Agency
2430 E Street, N. W.
Washington, D. C.

Attention: Deputy Director, Plans

From: John Edgar Hoover, Director
Federal Bureau of Investigation

EX-124

Subject: THEODORE VON KARMAN
INTERNAL SECURITY - R
FBI File 100-372586

b7C

[redacted]
SECURITY MATTER - C
FBI File 117-2713

CLASSIFIED BY SP5JC/pgm 5-13-98
DECLASSIFY ON: 25X1

[redacted]

b1

(S)

Professor Theodore Karman is undoubtedly identical with Theodore Von Karman, a naturalized United States citizen, who is Chairman of the Scientific Advisory Board of the United States

NOTE: A cover memorandum from Belmont to Boardman was prepared by JEM:jaa on 4-11-55 in connection with this outgoing mail.

SECRET

BY COURIER SERVICE
9 0 APR 1 5
COMM - FBI

APR 25 1955

JEM:jaa
(5)

SECRET

Tolson
Boardman
Nichols

116-2713

 ET

SECRET

Air Force. He has access to practically all classified information, according to the United States Air Force. A summary memorandum dated July 16, 1954, concerning Von Karman was furnished to you by letter also dated July 16, 1954. [redacted] is undoubtedly identical with the individual of the same name who is a naturalized United States citizen [redacted] also has access to considerable classified data. [redacted] are not identifiable in our files.

b7C

[redacted]

b1

(S)

b7C [redacted] It is our intention to interview Von Karman and the results will be furnished to you.

Your early attention to this matter will be appreciated.

SECRET



X

# Office Memorandum • UNITED STATES GOVERNMENT

TO : L. V. BOARDMAN  DATE: 4-11-55

FROM : A. H. BELMONT

ALL INFORMATION CONTAINED HEREIN IS UNCLASSIFIED EXCEPT WHERE SHOWN OTHERWISE

SUBJECT: THEODORE VON KARMAN, wa.
INTERNAL SECURITY - R
(Bufile 100-372586)
(WFO file 100-22923)
(LA file 105-865 - Origin)

[redacted]
SECURITY MATTER - C
(Bufile ~~117-2712~~ 116-2713)
(WFO file 100-22422)
(SF file 116-4183 - Origin)

Tolson, Boardman, Nichols, Belmont, Harbo, Mohr, Parsons, Rosen, Tamm, Sizoo, Winterrowd, Tele. Room, Holloman, Gandy

b7C

b1

[redacted] (S)

[redacted] (S)

Theodore Von Karman is the subject of a closed security investigation. He is a naturalized US citizen, and he is Chairman of the Scientific Advisory Board, United States Air Force. In 1919 he was an official of the Bela Kun (Communist) Government of Hungary. He is not known to have engaged in any Communist activities. He has been interviewed on a number of occasions and has been co-operative.

[redacted] has been the subject of an extensive security investigation by this Bureau. [redacted] He has associated with individuals who are known to have pro-Communist beliefs. [redacted]

b7C b7D

Enclosure re
Sicklers - [redacted] b7C
Mr. Boardman
Mr. Belmont

JEW:jac
(5)

RECORDED - 113
INDEXED - 113
100-372586-9
APR 19 1955
EX-107

UNRECORDED COPY FILED IN 116-2713

354 894 5-13-98
CLASSIFIED BY SPSJC
DECLASSIFY ON: 25X 1
Classified per CIA letter dated 10/28/98

[redacted] b7C

SECRET

b7C

[redacted] *No evidence which would verify this is available and he has denied the allegation.* [redacted] *He has been interviewed in the past and has been co-operative.*

*There is no identifiable information in Bufiles concerning* [redacted] (S) b1

*RECOMMENDATIONS:*

b7C

*1. It is recommended that Von Karman* [redacted] *be interviewed and asked if any approaches have ever been made to them either directly or indirectly for classified information. During the interviews it should be impressed upon them that they immediately contact the Bureau in the event such approaches are made in the future. If you agree, letters to the field are attached.*

b1

2. [redacted] (S)

- 2 -

TEXT ON THIS PAGE IS ILLEGIBLE
WE HAVE LEFT THE PAGE AS REFERENCE

Mr. Tolson
Mr. Boardman
Mr. Nichols
Mr. Belmont
Mr. Harbo
Mr. Mohr
Mr. Parsons
Mr. Rosen
Mr. Tamm
Mr. Sizoo
Mr. Winterrowd
Tele. Room
Mr. Holloman
Miss Gandy

FEDERAL BUREAU OF INVESTIGATION

UNITED STATES DEPARTMENT OF JUSTICE

-----------

AIRTEL

Transmit the following message to:

FBI, LOS ANGELES 5/12/55

DIRECTOR, FBI (100-372586)

THEODORE VON KARMAN, wa.
IS - R

Reurlet 4/14/55.

b7C b7D [redacted] VON KARMAN, 1501 So. Marengo Ave., Pasadena, Calif., advised on instant date that VON KARMAN is currently in Europe and is not expected to return to the U. S. until approximately June 18. He is presumed to be in Paris now but information regarding his exact current whereabouts in Europe can be obtained at his NATO office of the Advisory Group for Aeronautical Research and Development (AGARD), Palais de Chaillot, Paris.

MALONE

Mr. Belmont

JPA:CEA
(4)
LA 105-863

RECORDED - 67

-96

354-894
ALL INFORMATION CONTAINED
HEREIN IS UNCLASSIFIED
DATE 6-3-97 BY

EX-113

MAY 14 1955

REGISTERED - AIR MAIL

cc Branigan MAY 24 1955

Approved: ________ Special Agent in Charge

Sent ________ M Per ________

TEXT ON THIS PAGE IS ILLEGIBLE
WE HAVE LEFT THE PAGE AS REFERENCE

STANDARD FORM NO. 64

# Office Memorandum • UNITED STATES GOVERNMENT

TO : Mr. Tolson

DATE: 6/8/55

FROM : L. B. Nichols

SUBJECT: Dr Theodore Von Karman
Internal Security - R

Tolson
Boardman
Nichols
Belmont
Harbo
Mohr
Parsons
Rosen
Tamm
Sizoo
Winterrowd
Tele. Room
Holloman
Gandy

[redacted] had been to see him. He related that Dr. Theodore A. Von Karnan, a German aircraft industrialist, who operated a factory near Moscow, is now connected with the NATO Aeronautical Research; that Von Karnan at one time was in the Bella Kuhn government and is known to have been a Communist. [redacted] thought that this might be of interest to us.

b7C
b7D

cc - Mr. Boardman
Mr. Belmont

LBN:fc
(4)

RECORDED - 94

SE 5

[redacted]

b7C

EX-122

354-894
ALL INFORMATION CONTAINED
HEREIN IS UNCLASSIFIED
DATE 6-3-97 BY SPS JC/bpm

TEXT ON THIS PAGE IS ILLEGIBLE
WE HAVE LEFT THE PAGE AS REFERENCE

Mr. Tolson
Mr. Boardman
Mr. Nichols
Mr. Belmont
Mr. Harbo
Mr. Mohr
Mr. Parsons
Mr. Rosen
Mr. Tamm
Mr. Sizoo
Mr. Winterrowd
Tele. Room
Mr. Holloman
Miss Gandy

FEDERAL BUREAU OF INVESTIGATION

UNITED STATES DEPARTMENT OF JUSTICE

-----------

AIRTEL

Transmit the following ~~XXXXXXX~~ message to:

FBI, LOS ANGELES 6/30/55 5:00 P.M. [redacted]

DIRECTOR, FBI (100-372586)

THEODORE VON KARMAN, IS-R.

0-1 to LA 11-1-55

Reply dated 11-7-55 see 65-63432-23

Your attention is called to the fact that during the course of an authorized interview with VON KARMAN, on 6/28/55, re another matter, VON KARMAN casually exhibited a copy of a 2 page AEC letter concerning him, dated 10/13/54, which had been directed to the District Commander, 4th OSI District Office, Washington, D.C. and signed by [redacted] Washington Area, Security Operations.

This letter opened with the paragraph, "Transmitted herewith are copies of reports of investigation concerning subject which have been prepared by the FBI pursuant to the AEC Act of 1946. These reports are forwarded for your review and determination as to whether your department desires this office to further consider your request for clearance of the subject for access to restricted data".

At the bottom as enclosures was the notation, "FBI reports (31)".

This letter set forth an itemized bill of particulars re VON KARMAN which were presumably considered to be derogatory. These charges were subsequently answered in detail by VON KARMAN on 12/20/54, with copies being allegedly furnished to the Air Force, AEC, and the Bureau. VON KARMAN also personally saw AEC [redacted] re these allegations.

VON KARMAN was obviously irritated by these open allegations. He was especially bitter concerning an allegation that his deceased sister had been "friendly" with Professor ALEXANDER GOETZ of the Calif. Institute of Technology, and "whose political ideologies were strongly

ALL INFORMATION CONTAINED HEREIN IS UNCLASSIFIED DATE 6-3-97 BY [illegible]

354-894

JPA:kkh
(4)
105-863

RECORDED - 83 Mr. Belmont

100-372586-

AIR MAIL REGISTERED

24 JUL 1955

memo Boardman to Belmont 7-6-55

[redacted] b7C

Approved: [signature] Special Agent in Charge

Sent ______ M Per ______

Pro-Nazi". VON KARMAN interpreted the latter comment re his sister as meaning that she was GOETZ' mistress, a [illegible] point which he vehemently denied. He felt that it obviously had no bearing whatsoever on a matter of clearance re him; was an "indecent" insult to the memory of his sister; and was a matter which he w[illegible]d [illegible] avenge. Although VON KARMAN was not specifically critical or bitter toward the FBI or its observations, he naturally assumed that the allegations itemized were contained in the indicated FBI reports, and the resentment created by the open revelations contained in the above AEC letter was clear.

The interview, however, terminated on an amiable note, and VON KARMAN indicated that he was now relieved, and that this was simply a matter that he had to get off his chest.

For the further info of the Bureau, VON KARMAN is currently Chairman of the NATO Advisory Group for Aeronautical Research and Development, with headquarters in Paris, and is also Chairman Emeritus of the Scientific Advisory Board of the USAF. He plans to remain in this Country until September, at which time he will return to Paris.

MALONE

cc: MR. BELMONT
~~AND SUPERVISOR~~
DOM. INTEL. DIVISION

TEXT ON THIS PAGE IS ILLEGIBLE
WE HAVE LEFT THE PAGE AS REFERENCE

# Office Memorandum • UNITED STATES GOVERNMENT

TO : L. V. Boardman

DATE: July 6, 1955

FROM : A. H. Belmont

ALL INFORMATION CONTAINED
HEREIN IS UNCLASSIFIED
DATE 6-17-97 BY

SUBJECT: THEODORE VON KARMAN, with aliases
INTERNAL SECURITY - R

Tolson, Boardman, Nichols, Belmont, Harbo, Parsons, Rosen, Tamm, Sizoo, Winterrowd, Tele. Room, Holloman, Gandy

Von Karman is a world-renowned aerodynamicist, born 1881, Hungary; entered the United States in 1930; naturalized in 1936. He is currently Chairman of the North Atlantic Treaty Organization Advisory Group for Aeronautical Research and Development, with headquarters in Paris, and is also Chairman Emeritus of the Scientific Advisory Board of the United States Air Force.

Von Karman was investigated by Bureau in 1950 under character of Internal Security - R and in 1954 as applicant matter at request of Atomic Energy Commission (AEC) (Reports to AEC and OSI). Investigation reflected Von Karman associated with several Communist Party (CP) members and with William Perl, known Soviet agent. He admitted to Bureau agents during the investigation that he was an official in the Bela Kun Government (Communist) in Hungary in 1919. He denied present or past CP membership.

Los Angeles air-tel dated 6-30-55 reflects that during an interview with Von Karman on 6-28-55 he casually exhibited a copy of a 2-page AEC letter concerning him dated 10-13-54, which had been directed to the District Commander, 4th OSI District Office, Washington, D. C., and signed by [redacted] Washington Area, Security Operations. This was a letter of transmittal to OSI of 31 Bureau reports and contained a bill of particulars of adverse information developed concerning Von Karman. Von Karman said he assumed the bill of particulars was based on FBI reports. He stated he had answered bill of particulars with copies going to AEC, Air Force and Bureau. Von Karman expressed his irritation over charges re his sister's association with Alexander Goetz, who was allegedly pro-Nazi. Bufiles fail to reflect Von Karman's sister was friendly with Goetz, but do reflect Von Karman was alleged to be friendly with Goetz and that Von Karman's sister was alleged to have declared herself to be a Nazi sympathizer. Investigation, however, disproved both allegations.

b7C

ARJ:ss
(5) CC: LVBoardman
AHBelmont
CWBates

RECORDED - 83

100-372586-

2 JUL 20 1955

UNRECORDED COPY FILED IN

64 JUL 100-372586 [redacted] b7C

*Memorandum for Mr. Boardman*

*There is no indication Von Karman received FBI reports, contrariwise, as reflected in Los Angeles airtel, Von Karman stated he naturally "assumed" that the allegations itemized in AEC letter were contained in FBI reports. Inasmuch as AEC letter to OSI referred to FBI reports, the inference arises that this info re Von Karman's sister came from FBI reports.*

*Bureau has been furnished previously with copy of AEC letter to OSI dated 10-13-54 and with Von Karman's reply thereto dated 12-20-54. These were received from* [redacted] *AEC, 1-18-55, who advised that in accordance with AEC clearance procedures the Air Force was requested to obtain certain information from Von Karman so that AEC could make a clearance determination.*

*In this reply 12-20-54 to AEC* [redacted] *Von Karman made reference to the AEC letter to the Air Force dated 10-13-54 in which AEC had requested a statement from Von Karman concerning certain derogatory information. Von Karman referred specifically to a request for a statement from him concerning "Alexander Goetz with whom Von Karman's deceased sister is reported to have been friendly and whose political ideology is allegedly strongly pro-Nazi." In Von Karman's letter of reply he stated he considered the above quote an inexcusable insult against the memory of his "beloved sister." He stated he could not see what such a statement had to do with his access to atomic information.*

b7C

*A notation by* [redacted] *appeared on Von Karman's letter reflecting that* [redacted] *would not reply in writing to Von Karman. One Photostat each of AEC letter to OSI dated 10-13-54 and Von Karman's letter to* [redacted] *dated 12-20-54 is attached.*

**RECOMMENDATION:**

*Liaison should discuss this matter with AEC and point out FBI files do not contain the allegation re Von Karman's sister. AEC should be advised context of its letter to OSI referring only to FBI reports and summarizing charges led Von Karman to the assumption that alleged erroneous charges came from FBI reports and resulted in his protests and threats to avenge the "indecent" insult to the memory of his sister.*

*AEC should be asked to advise us of any action they take to straighten out this matter.*

STANDARD FORM NO. 64

# Office Memorandum • UNITED STATES GOVERNMENT

TO : MR. L. V. BOARDMAN

DATE: July 12, 1955

FROM : MR. A. H. BELMONT

SUBJECT: THEODORE VON KARMAN, with aliases
INTERNAL SECURITY - R

Tolson
Boardman
Nichols
Belmont
Harbo
Mohr
Parsons
Rosen
Tamm
Sizoo
Winterrowd
Tele. Room
Holloman
Gandy

354894
ALL INFORMATION CONTAINED
HEREIN IS UNCLASSIFIED
DATE 6-7-99 BY

Reference is made to my memorandum dated July 6, 1955, pointing out that Von Karman was investigated by the Bureau in 1950 under character of Internal Security - R and in 1954 as an applicant at the request of the Atomic Energy Commission (AEC). Investigation reflected Von Karman associated with several Communist Party members and with William Perl, known Soviet agent. He admitted to Bureau Agents that he was an official in the Bela Kun Government (Communist) in Hungary in 1919. He denied present or past Communist Party membership. By airtel dated June 30, 1955, from Los Angeles it was pointed out that during an interview with Von Karman on June 28, 1955, he casually exhibited a copy of a two-page AEC letter concerning him which had been sent by the AEC to the 4th OSI District Office, Washington. The letter transmitted Bureau reports to OSI and contained a number of questions which the AEC desired OSI to ask Von Karman. One of the questions concerned Alexander Goetz and the AEC letter stated "Goetz - with whom his deceased sister is reported to have been friendly and whose political ideology is allegedly strongly pro-Nazi." Bureau files failed to reflect Von Karman's sister was friendly with Goetz. They do reflect that he (Von Karman) was allegedly friendly with Goetz and that his sister was alleged to have declared herself to be a Nazi sympathizer. Investigation, however, disproved both allegations.

It was recommended that Liaison discuss this matter with AEC and point out that Bureau files do not contain the allegation regarding Von Karman's sister's association with Goetz and that the AEC letter led Von Karman to the assumption that erroneous charges came from FBI reports which resulted in his protest.

[redacted] This matter was discussed by Liaison with [redacted] of the AEC on July 11, 1955. [redacted] stated that the wording of the AEC letter to OSI concerning Von Karman's sister was in error. b7C

UNRECORDED COPY FILED IN 62-...

CWB:fjb
(7)
1 - Mr. Boardman
1- Mr. Belmont
1 - Mr. Branigan
1 - [redacted] b7C
1 - Liaison Section
1 - Mr. Bates

RECORDED - 83 100-372586-

2 JUL 20 1955

EX-/SEQ

JUL 26 1955

TEXT ON THIS PAGE IS ILLEGIBLE
WE HAVE LEFT THE PAGE AS REFERENCE

Memo to Mr. Boardman
from Mr. Belmont

[redacted] stated he had taken action to insure that the persons responsible for this would not again make such a mistake. He advised that the only information that the AEC had on Von Karman was from the Bureau's reports. [redacted] was informed that the manner in which this was handled made it appear that the FBI was responsible for these erroneous charges. [redacted] stated he was extremely sorry for this and could assure that it would not happen again. He stated that he was lodging a strong protest with [redacted] of OSI regarding the fact that OSI had given Von Karman a copy of the AEC letter which was classified "Confidential." [redacted] further advised that Von Karman had protested strongly to the AEC and that [redacted] had talked to Von Karman to try to calm him down.

b7C

[redacted] again expressed his regrets that the AEC letter was in error. He stated he would let the Bureau know the results of his protest to [redacted] It was reiterated to [redacted] that extreme care should be exercised in the handling of FBI information so that no unjust criticism could be reflected upon the Bureau.

**ACTION:**

This is submitted for your information.

- 2 -

TEXT ON THIS PAGE IS ILLEGIBLE
WE HAVE LEFT THE PAGE AS REFERENCE

SECRET

SECRET

100-372586 - 10
354-894

RECORDED - 70

BY COURIER SERVICE

Date: August 9, 1955

To: Director (Original & 1)
Central Intelligence Agency
2430 E Street, N. W.
Washington, D. C.

Attention: Deputy Director, Plans

From: John Edgar Hoover, Director
Federal Bureau of Investigation

Subject: THEODORE VON KARMAN

CLASSIFIED BY SP5JC/pm
DECLASSIFY ON: 25X

ALL INFORMATION CONTAINED HEREIN IS UNCLASSIFIED EXCEPT WHERE SHOWN OTHERWISE

[redacted] b1

A review of Bureau files reflects that the subject's name as Szeelloestciotak was furnished to us by the Office of Special Investigations. You may wish to communicate with the Office of Special Investigations in this matter.

cc - 2 - Director of Special Investigations BY COURIER SERVICE
The Inspector General
Department of the Air Force
Building Tempo E
4th and Adams Drive, S. W.
Washington, D. C.

BY COURIER SVC.
54 AUG 10
COMM - FBI

NOTE: Info received from OSI in report dated 3-20-51 (100-372586-20).

WTW:ss
(5)

SECRET

SECRET

FBI - DISLANCE RECORD SECTION

AUG 12 1955

TEXT ON THIS PAGE IS ILLEGIBLE
WE HAVE LEFT THE PAGE AS REFERENCE

cc - Liaison

SECRET

[redacted] b7C

RECORDED - 70

100-372586 - 103

SECRET

354894 5-8-98
CLASSIFIED BY SP5JC/

DECLASSIFY ON: 25X 1

Class. per CIA letter dated 9-8-98

ALL INFORMATION CONTAINED HEREIN IS UNCLASSIFIED EXCEPT WHERE SHOWN OTHERWISE

Date: September 19, 1955

BY COURIER SERVICE

To: Director (orig. & 1)
Central Intelligence Agency
2430 E Street, N. W.
Washington, D. C.

Attention: Deputy Director, ~~Plans~~

From: John Edgar Hoover, Director
Federal Bureau of Investigation

Subject: THEODORE VON KARMAN [redacted] (S)

[redacted] (S)

b1
b3

You have been previously furnished reports of our investigation of Theodore Von Karman [redacted] (S)

ARJ:mk:eb
(5)

NOTE ON YELLOW: Subject is a world-renowned Aerodynamicist. A naturalized citizen, he is currently chairman of the NATO advisory group for aeronautical research and development and is chairman emeritus of the Scientist Advisory Board of the USAF. [redacted]

b1
b3

Tolson
Boardman
Nichols
Belmont
Harbo
Mohr
Parsons
Rosen
Tamm
Sizoo
Winterrowd
Tele. Room
Holloman
Gandy

BY COURIER SVC.
11 SEP 20
COMM - FBI

58 SEP 22 1955

SECRET

SECRET

TEXT ON THIS PAGE IS ILLEGIBLE
WE HAVE LEFT THE PAGE AS REFERENCE

STANDARD FORM NO. 64

# Office Memorandum • UNITED STATES GOVERNMENT

TO : DIRECTOR, FBI (100-372586) DATE: 9/15/55

FROM : SAC, LOS ANGELES (105-863)

SUBJECT: DR. THEODORE VON KARMAN, was.
IS - R

354-f04
ALL INFORMATION CONTAINED
HEREIN IS UNCLASSIFIED
DATE 6-25-82 BY SP5 JK/ajm

[redacted] Dr. THEODORE VON KARMAN, 1501 So. Marengo Ave., Pasadena, Calif. (Chairman, NATO Advisory Group for Aeronautical Research and Development with headquarters in Paris, and Chairman Emeritus, Scientific Advisory Board, U. S. Air Force, Washington, D. C.), telephonically advised this office on 9/7/55 that she has become increasingly upset in recent months concerning the "attitude" taken by [redacted] where VON KARMAN is primarily engaged. [redacted] related that [redacted] a divorcee about 50, had written her a letter on 8/30/55 wherein she stated that [redacted] while he visits in the States." [redacted] took particular exception to the word "visits" used by [redacted] whom she described as a U. S. citizen, and pointed out that VON KARMAN was not "visiting" in the United States when he returns to this country since the United States is his home.

[redacted] inferred that this attitude by [redacted] might reflect her feeling toward this country, but she could furnish nothing else of a specific nature that would reflect on her loyalty to this Government.

[redacted] explained that [redacted] who was born and raised in Dayton, Ohio, had formerly worked in [redacted] during World War II, and that through her own assistance while formerly employed at the [redacted] had returned to the United States about 1948 or 1949 and also was employed [redacted] She thereafter replaced [redacted] when the latter came to [redacted] and subsequently joined [redacted]

It is noted that [redacted] also about 50, has acted in the capacity of [redacted]

b7C

JPA:CEA
(3)
REGISTERED MAIL

RECORDED-29

INDEXED-29

SEP 16 1955

-109

[redacted]

It is of course unknown by this office what the real purpose of [redacted] call may have been, but it is speculated that it may well have been motivated by possible jealousy rather than any well founded concern for the national security. Although [redacted] has been cooperative with this office in the past and has been considered reliable, it is recalled that she has on occasions previously called this office on nonspecific matters at irregular hours under circumstances indicating her to be under the possible influence of intoxicants. The above complaint, though given by her in a rational manner at about 5:40 PM, was followed on the same date by a telegram to this office at 10:04 PM. It read as follows:

> "Please give message to [redacted] concerning her letter [redacted] while he visits - repeat visits in the States.' For [redacted] information, VON KARMAN doest not 'visit in the United States.' The United States is him home and when he is here he is not visiting when he returns.
>
> [redacted]

The indices of the Los Angeles Office contain no information regarding [redacted] Her former husband's first name was unknown to [redacted]

The above is furnished to the Bureau for information only, and no further action is being taken by this office.

b7c

TEXT ON THIS PAGE IS ILLEGIBLE
WE HAVE LEFT THE PAGE AS REFERENCE

ice - Liaison [redacted] b7C

SECRET

100-372586 - 105

RECORDED - 64

EX - 113

BY COURIER SERVICE

(35+394) 5-8-98
CLASSIFIED BY SP5JC/00m
DECLASSIFY ON: 25X1
Classified per CIA Letter date 9-8-98

ALL INFORMATION CONTAINED HEREIN IS UNCLASSIFIED EXCEPT WHERE SHOWN OTHERWISE

Date: October 26, 1955

To: Director (orig. & 1)
Central Intelligence Agency
2430 E Street, N. W.
Washington, D. C.

Attention: Deputy Director, Plans

From: John Edgar Hoover, Director
Federal Bureau of Investigation

Subject: THEODORE VON KARMAN
[redacted] (S) b1 b3

[redacted] (S)

[redacted] Therefore, we are leaving to your discretion the decision as to what dissemination you desire to make in this matter. (S)

b1
b3

cc - 1 - Director of Special Investigations
The Inspector General
Department of the Air Force
Building Tempo E
4th and Adams Drive, S. W.
Washington, D. C.

BY COURIER SER

Tolson
Boardman
Nichols
Belmont
Harbo
Mohr
Parsons
Rosen
Tamm
Sizoo
Winterrowd
Tele. Room
Holloman
Gandy

FLJ:hpl
(6)

SEE NOTE PAGE 2

BY COURIER SVC.
OCT 27 1955
COMM - FBI

60 OCT 31 1955

SECRET

OCT 5

SECRET

Letter to Director
Central Intelligence Agency

NOTE: Subject is a world-renowned Aerodynamicist and a naturalized citizen. He is currently Chairman of the NATO Advisory Group for Aeronautical Research and Development and is Chairman Emeritus of the Scientists Advisory Board of the USAF. [redacted] (S)

[redacted] (S)

b1
b3

SECRET

T [redacted] b7C

(Orig. & 1)

SAC, Los Angeles(100-95266)

June 27, 1956

Director, FBI (100-164610)

[redacted] wa. b7C
FRAUD AGAINST THE GOVERNMENT
ESPIONAGE - CZ & R

Enclosed is a copy of a letter from the Legal Attache, Paris, dated 6-14-56 requesting that Dr. Theodore Von Karman be interviewed concerning his relationship with the subject.

You should arrange to interview Von Karman to determine his knowledge of and relationship with b7C [redacted] The result of this contact should be set forth in memorandum form suitable for dissemination.

W

cc - 1 - Paris (105-259) (info)
cc - 1 - 100-372586 (Von Karman)
cc - 1 - Foreign Liaison Unit
Enclosure

RES:dmn
(7)

100-372586-
NOT RECORDED
176 JUN 29 1956

354895 col
ALL INFORMATION CONTAINED
HEREIN IS UNCLASSIFIED
DATE 4/22/02 BY SP-5 BCE/HG
354-894/SPS JC/DQM 6-25-97

ORIGINAL FILED IN 100-164610

YELLOW
DUPLICATE
JUN 27 1956
MAILED

8 JUL 5 1956

TEXT ON THIS PAGE IS ILLEGIBLE
WE HAVE LEFT THE PAGE AS REFERENCE

MR. L. V. BOARDMAN

7-13-56

A. H. BELMONT

cc-s - Mr. Boardman
Mr. Belmont
Liaison
[redacted]

[redacted]

INTERNAL SECURITY - ITALY

[redacted]00-372586 (Theodore Von Karman)

[redacted] Bufiles reflect subject used as reference Dr. Theodore Von Karman, who personally recommended subject for present consultant position [redacted] Von Karman, aged 75, naturalized US 1936. Von Karman is one of founders of Aerojet-General Corp. Per Bufiles, as of October, 1955, Von Karman was currently Chairman of the NATO Advisory Group for Aeronautical Research and Development and Chairman Emeritus of the Scientists Advisory Board of the USAF. Internal Security investigation of Von Karman by Bureau in 1950 and AEC Applicant investigation in 1954 reflected he was associated with several CP members and with William Perl, known Soviet agent. No subversive or espionage activity developed and, on interview, Von Karman admitted in 1919 he was briefly a member of communist regime of Bela Kun in Hungary but denied past or present CP membership. [redacted]

Attention was called to Von Karman's personally recommending subject for current employment [redacted] as consultant. Re Von Karman, OCNO advises G-2 investigations of him in 1941 and 1948 were favorable. Subsequently in 1948, G-2 received allegation Von Karman had been CP member in Hungary in 1918. Additional inquiry by G-2 failed to prove or disprove this allegation and Von Karman was recommended for position of trust and confidence. [redacted] he had been recommended for employment by Von Karman. [redacted]

b7C

ORIGINAL COPY FILED

Enclosure
ETB:kfc
(6)

354-894
ALL INFORMATION CONTAINED
HEREIN IS UNCLASSIFIED
DATE 6-25-97 BY SP5 [illegible]

NOT RECORDED
191 JUL 20 1956

TEXT ON THIS PAGE IS ILLEGIBLE
WE HAVE LEFT THE PAGE AS REFERENCE

L. V. Boardman

September 7, 1956

A. H. Belmont

cc - Mr. Boardman
Mr. Belmont

[redacted]

INTERNAL SECURITY - ITALY

ALL INFORMATION CONTAINED HEREIN IS UNCLASSIFIED DATE 6-25-97

[redacted]

(d) Subject was personally recommended for employment by Dr. Theodore Von Karman. Concerning Von Karman, OCNO advised he was investigated by G-2 in 1941 and 1948 with favorable results. Later in 1948 G-2 received allegation Von Karman had been CP member in Hungary in 1918. Additional inquiry by G-2 failed to prove or disprove this allegation and Von Karman was recommended for position of trust and confidence. [redacted] he had

100-372586 (Theodore Von Karman)
Enclosure
(5)

NOT RECORDED
117 9-11-1956

SEP 12 1956
105-50728

b7C

Memorandum for Mr. Boardman

been recommended for employment by Von Karman.) [redacted] Bufiles reflect only that he has used Von Karman as a reference. Concerning Von Karman Bufiles reflect he is one of founders of Aerojet-General Corporation and as of October, 1955, was currently chairman of NATO Advisory Group for Aeronautical Research and Development and Chairman Emeritus of the Scientists Advisory Board of the USAF. Internal Security investigation by Bureau in 1950 and AEC applicant investigation in 1954 reflected Von Karman associated with several CP members and with William Perl, known Soviet agent. No subversive espionage activity developed and, on interview, Von Karman admitted that in 1919 he was briefly a member of communist government regime of Bela Kun in Hungary, but denied past or present CP membership. [redacted]

**OBSERVATION:**

[redacted]

**RECOMMENDATION:**

[redacted]



b7C

TEXT ON THIS PAGE IS ILLEGIBLE
WE HAVE LEFT THE PAGE AS REFERENCE

OPTIONAL FORM NO. 10
MAY 1962 EDITION
GSA FPMR (41 CFR) 101-11.6

UNITED STATES GOVERNMENT

# Memorandum

SECRET

TO : ACTING DIRECTOR, FBI DATE: NOV 15 1972

FROM : SAC, NEW YORK (105-new) (P)

SUBJECT: THEODORE VON KARMAN
IS-R
(OO:LA)

ALL INFORMATION CONTAINED HEREIN IS UNCLASSIFIED EXCEPT WHERE SHOWN OTHERWISE

[redacted] (S)

[redacted] (S)

[redacted] (S)

The NCPD advised on [redacted] The NYO does not know the significance of this information: (u)

CLASSIFIED BY: SP5 JC/cqm 354.844 6-30-97
REASON: 1.5 (c,d)
DECLASSIFY ON: X 1,6

THEODORE VON KARMAN (Ed.)
California Institute of Technology
Guggenheim Aeronautical Laboratory

Recipient offices are requested to identify subject and to handle the investigation in accordance with Section 10 Manual of Instructions. In any investigation no reference should be made to the original source of this information.

[redacted] (S)

b1

3 - Bureau (RM) REC-48 MCT-14 [redacted]
[redacted] (S)
2 - Los Angeles (RM) 100-372586-109X
1 - New York [redacted] NOV 20 1972
1 - New York [redacted] (S)

DDO:kap
(7)

70 DEC 7 1972 SECRET ESPIONAGE b7C



5010-108

SECRET

NY 105-

Subject may be identical to Bufile 100-372586 and LAfile 105-863.



SECRET

TEXT ON THIS PAGE IS ILLEGIBLE
WE HAVE LEFT THE PAGE AS REFERENCE

2 (Rev. 1-22-60)

Federal Bureau of Investigation
Records Branch

SECRET 11-27, 1972

- [ ] Name Searching Unit - [redacted]
- [ ] Service Unit [redacted] 652 [redacted]
- [ ] Forward [redacted]
- [X] Attention [redacted] Ext [redacted] b7C
- [X] Return to [redacted]

Supervisor Room Ext.

Type of References Requested:
- [ ] Regular Request (Analytical Search)
- [X] All References (Subversive & Nonsubversive)
- [ ] Subversive References Only
- [ ] Nonsubversive References Only
- [ ] Main ________ References Only

Type of Search Requested:
- [ ] Restricted to Locality of ________
- [ ] Exact Name Only (On the Nose)
- [ ] Buildup
- [ ] Variations

Subject Theodore Von Karman
Birthdate & Place
Address California Institute of Technology
Localities Los Angeles
R# ______ Date 11-27 Searcher Initials [illegible]
Prod.

| | FILE NUMBER | SERIAL |
|---|---|---|
| | 100-378586 | |
| | 100-397668 | |
| | [redacted] (S) b1 | |
| | 40-13556 | |
| | 40-18867 | |

approx 250 Serial
left not listed.

CLASSIFIED BY: SPS JC/pgm
REASON: 1.5 (C)
DECLASSIFY ON: X-1

ALL INFORMATION CONTAINED
HEREIN IS UNCLASSIFIED EXCEPT
WHERE SHOWN OTHERWISE

SECRET

OPTIONAL FORM NO. 10
MAY 1962 EDITION
GSA FPMR (41 CFR) 101-11.6

UNITED STATES GOVERNMENT

# *Memorandum*

SECRET

TO : ACTING DIRECTOR, FBI (100-372586) DATE: 1/12/73

FROM : SAC, LOS ANGELES (105-863)(C)

SUBJECT: THEODORE VON KARMAN
IS - R

OO: LA

ReNYlet to Director dated 11/15/72. b7C b7D

[redacted] Jet Propulsion Laboratories, Pasadena, California, advised on 1/9/73 that Dr. THEODORE VON KARMAN has been deceased since 1963.

In view of the above no further investigation being conducted.

2- Bureau (RM)
1- New York [redacted] (RM) b1
1- Los Angeles
WLM:fet
(4)

EX-105

REC-49

CLASSIFIED BY [illegible]
(C)
DECLASSIFY ON: X

[redacted] b7C

SECRET

MAY 8 1973

*Buy U.S. Savings Bonds Regularly on the Payroll Savings Plan*

www.ingramcontent.com/pod-product-compliance
Lightning Source LLC
Chambersburg PA
CBHW080923020526
44114CB00043B/2454
*9781955087193*